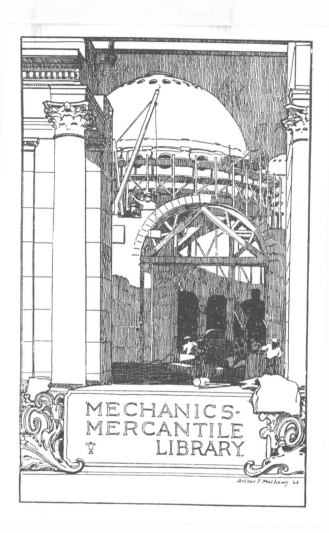

MECHANICS-
MERCANTILE
LIBRARY.

THE MAN ON WHOM
NOTHING WAS LOST

MOLLY WORTHEN

THE MAN ON WHOM
NOTHING WAS LOST

*The Grand Strategy of
Charles Hill*

HOUGHTON MIFFLIN COMPANY

BOSTON · NEW YORK

2005

For information about permission to reproduce selections
from this book, write to Permissions, Houghton Mifflin Company,
215 Park Avenue South, New York, New York 10003.

Visit our Web site: www.houghtonmifflinbooks.com.

Library of Congress Cataloging-in-Publication Data
Worthen, Molly.
The man on whom nothing was lost : the grand strategy of
Charles Hill / Molly Worthen.
p. cm.
Includes index.
ISBN-13: 978-0-618-57467-4
ISBN-10: 0-618-57467-0
1. Hill, Charles, 1936– 2. Diplomats — United States — Biography.
3. Political consultants — United States — Biography. 4. United
States — Foreign relations — 1945–1989. 5. United States — Foreign
relations — 1989– 6. Hoover Institution on War, Revolution, and Peace —
Biography. 7. College teachers — Connecticut — New Haven — Biography.
8. Yale University — Biography. 9. Worthen, Molly. I. Title.

E840.8.H535W67 2005
327.73'0092—dc22   2005013233

Book design by Melissa Lotfy

A NOTE ABOUT THE TYPE

This book is typeset in FF Scala, the award-winning typeface designed
by Martin Majoor in 1990. The form principle of FF Scala finds its roots
in the first vertically-stressed typefaces of the mid-eighteenth century
French typographer Pierre Simon Fournier, with influences from the
humanist model as found in the first printing types.

PRINTED IN THE UNITED STATES OF AMERICA

QUM 10 9 8 7 6 5 4 3 2 1

For my family
John, Julie, and Danny Worthen

ACKNOWLEDGMENTS

This book would never have happened without the help of many people. Foremost are Charlie Hill and his family, whose cooperation, patience, and trust allowed the biography to be the intimate and accurate portrait that I hope it is. I am also grateful to International Security Studies at Yale University for providing me a home for the eighteen months that I needed to research and write.

Kate Epstein and her parents, Tony and Karen, always had a spare bed waiting for me when interviews and archival work took me to Washington, D.C. They lent me their car and — when I needed a place to interview the former ambassador to Israel — their living room, where their cat, Prancer, was a charming host as well, climbing into the ambassador's lap and nuzzling him all through his account of the Lebanon War.

I spent several weeks working through Charles Hill's papers at the Hoover Institution at Stanford University, a task made substantially easier by the help of the archivists there, particularly Grace Hawes, Carol Leadenham, and Linda Bernard. I cannot say enough to thank George and Michelle Caughey, who housed me, fed me, lent me their car, and humored me at their dinner table every night while I rambled on about my latest findings. The only person more generous with his patience was their son Devin, who was at my side from the origins of this project during our junior year at Yale through the very end.

Several friends and teachers were of critical assistance, either by reading the manuscript or by listening to me talk about it so much that they might as well have read it. Justin Zaremby read the entire manuscript in its earliest incarnation and was the first one to convince me that I may have pulled off something worthwhile. Michael Morgan spent long, brow-furrowing evenings with pen in hand, patiently weaning me off my addiction to semicolons. Andrew Horowitz treated me to weekly lunches of wise advice and Tater Tots in our old college dining hall, without which I would have been much hungrier and far crankier. Kevin Sladek spent hours deliberating over potential titles with me, even though I was too fearful to let him read the manuscript. Deborah Friedell had more confidence in me than I had in myself. Aaron Lemon-Strauss treated me like a celebrity whenever I was in a bad mood. Aaron O'Connell was a priceless problematizer and strategist on matters on and off the page. Becca Baneman, Sandra Chwialkowska, David Goa, and Jeff Miller were all great listeners and even better cheerleaders, each in his or her own way, and they are only a few of the countless friends and classmates who helped me on the endless slog of writing a biography. Additionally, the students and staff of Jonathan Edwards College provided fellowship, humor, and encouragement throughout my time at Yale and beyond.

David Brooks was an enthusiastic supporter of my work from my junior year, when I was his student in a Yale seminar, through the end of the project, when he read the manuscript and wrote a column about it in the *New York Times*. Without his help, no literary agent or publisher would have taken the book seriously. Without his ability to make a college undergraduate feel like a respected peer, I don't know whether I would have been able to take myself very seriously, either. My thanks, as well, to my agent, Andrew Wylie, and to my editor at Houghton Mifflin, Amanda Cook, who was instrumental in guiding the book into its final form.

This book began as a term paper in John Gaddis's seminar class, The Art of Biography. John oversaw the project from its beginnings — when I was too nervous even to ask Charlie to let me write about him — through the end of my undergraduate career, when he advised my senior thesis on Charlie's role in the Iran-Contra affair and convinced me that I was writing a book whether I realized it or not. John made this book happen, in body and in spirit: he read every draft of every chapter and secured the office space and funding that allowed me to commit myself full-time and turn an idea into reality. I learned what it meant to be a biographer in John's classroom, but I actually became one during those hours after class, in his office, at his dinner table, or in front of the fireplace in his living room, where he was my advocate, critic, and guide. He is the finest mentor a student could hope to have.

He is the reason that my college career ended with a true education, not just a Yale diploma.

Finally, a word on the dedication. My family is my ballast, and they have made everything possible. Their influence may be found on every page of this book, as in everything that I have done and will do.

PREFACE

Professor Hill found my first paper lacking. "At times, you almost begin to analyze the text," he wrote, "only to invariably wander off into pretentious displays of pseudopsychological erudition. C–." It was my first grade at Yale, and I deserved it. The assignment was to write about Herodotus, and I guessed from the faces of my classmates in Hill's History and Politics freshman seminar that I had not been alone in mangling the father of history with nervous overreaching. Something about Professor Hill made us wildly anxious to prove ourselves, evidently to the point of self-ruin. I could not pinpoint what we found so intimidating. As yet, we didn't know enough about him to be awed by his résumé. We had no idea that he had been a Foreign Service officer for most of his life, not an academic; that he had been one of the most influential "advisers to the prince" in recent diplomatic history, counseling Henry Kissinger, George Shultz, and Boutros Boutros-Ghali. But I later learned that even worldly-wise graduate students who took the celebrated Grand Strategy seminar co-taught by Hill still felt, in his unsmiling presence, as tense as we freshmen did.

The Yale landscape has a way of humbling the most bushy-bearded and aristocratic professor, for no matter the cold line of his spectacles and the imposing length of his bibliography, he cannot help the fact that he is surrounded by gargoyles and Gothic turrets. The lecture hall shrinks him to the manageable size of an average human being. Somehow Professor Hill was immune to these laws of scale. He was like the unblinking moon.

Professor Hill was a mystery begging to be cracked. An opportunity arose when I enrolled in a history seminar, John Gaddis's "The Art of Biography." I was too terrified to approach Hill myself and ask him to be the subject of my thirty-page biographical essay. Gaddis offered to mention the idea to him on my behalf. He posed the question over dinner one evening, and to everyone's surprise—including that of Hill's wife, who arched her eyebrows and squinted at her husband incredulously — he did not hesitate. Or so Gaddis told me when he relayed the news a few days later. I will never understand why Hill agreed to cooperate. He must have forgotten my pretentious, pseudopsychological displays.

I first attempted to cram Hill's entire life into one semester of research and writing. After a dreadful fortnight during which I tramped up the hill to his office for a two-hour interview every day, seven days a week, and spent every night beating on my computer keyboard, I accepted the impossibility of covering it all. I limited myself to writing about his youth, ending the story when he was about twenty, my age at the time. The Charlie Hill that I had written about—in many ways a quite ordinary child—fascinated me because he was the rootstock of the Professor Hill that I knew, the aloof campus personality and diplomat of intrigue and influence. I could not put the story away until I had followed those roots to their conclusions, both logical and unforeseen.

I applied to transfer my major to the History Department so that I might continue to work on Hill's biography and funnel the labor into applicable term papers where I could. Hill never challenged my purposes or my bouts of prying questions. At some point late in the spring of my senior year, when the ivy on the dormitory walls was beginning to sprout small green fingers, I screwed up my courage and said to him, "I'm planning to make this into a book. I want to publish it. Is that all right with you?" He nodded and waited for the next question. I felt silly. He had known it all along, long before I myself thought I was writing anything more than an ambitious term paper.

His biography became my occupation. I spent my days reading history volumes, poring over back issues of newspapers and political journals, trying to teach myself in a few months everything I had forgotten or failed to learn in college that I needed to know to tell his story. Hill gave me permission to paw through his personal papers. I began to seek out dozens of people who knew, or had once known, my subject. I continued to drop by his office and interrogate him, politely, about his life. With permission, I started to call him Charlie.

Charles Hill's biography is a story about growing up in small-town New Jersey in the middle of the last century. It is an insider's experience of foreign policy crises at points around the world as well as within the highest ranks of our own government. It is a chronicle of choices made between life's incompatibilities—cultural and intellectual, personal and professional. Finally, it is the test of a grand strategy. Hill teaches his students that the virtuous, the wise, and the brave among them must take note of life's details but always reside in the realm of ideas. Each should aspire to be a person on whom nothing is lost, without ever getting lost himself or herself. Such a philosophy is bewitching in the classroom, but the real test of grand strategy is not the final exam at the end of the semester. The test is what happens when that grand strategy is lived.

Charles Hill's story is the ultimate lesson a teacher can give, for he permitted a student to write it. He knew that he could answer my questions, allow me to read his papers, and find me the names of old friends and colleagues in his address book, but in the end he would have to leave his life bare for me to judge on my own. The biography that began in his classroom was, sooner or later, bound to leave it.

In this way, the book became more than a chronicle of Charlie's life. From the beginning, I took notes on my conversations with Hill and people who have known him, but soon I began to take notes on myself as well. I had read plenty of biographies (in class and for pleasure—I was an addict) and saw similarities between their authors and myself, but I also began to realize that there was something profoundly different about my enterprise. The dynamic between teacher and student is complex to begin with, and as I continued my work, I sensed that my relationship with my professor was changing in ways I had not expected and could not control. When interviews about Hill's own education and the mentors who guided him made me reconsider his teaching style today at Yale, I wrote it down. When I faced a difficult conversation with Hill's ex-wife, or the strange fortune of interviewing one of his former classmates in prison, I made sure to record my feelings and reactions. The task of writing the life story of my professor—of slogging through not only his great achievements, but also his moments of banality, and even his mistakes—sometimes grew so exasperating that I wanted to throw down my pen and abandon the project. I wrote about those moments, too. I found myself telling the story from the inside out.

In the end, the story is a personal one, a hybrid of a biography and a memoir. This is a book about a grand strategy, a grand man, and a student who is forever changed.

THE MAN ON WHOM
NOTHING WAS LOST

1

THE GENIUS OF CHARLES HILL IS HIS SILENCE. IN BOOKS and in school we had encountered the far-off places and the Great Men whom he served: Hong Kong, Vietnam, and Israel; Ellsworth Bunker and Henry Kissinger, George Shultz and Boutros Boutros-Ghali. But he never mentioned them in class, and as artless freshmen we had yet to pick up on the gossip that the upperclassmen traded after his lectures. Most of us were too young to remember the Iran-Contra affair, at the time preferring Saturday morning cartoons to Oliver North. We did not know that our professor's notebooks helped to break open the investigation. Our ignorance was for the best. His presence, his hold on the class, was enough to make us freeze in our seats. Filled at first with the happy murmur of weekend gossip, the room snapped silent at nine o'clock when Professor Hill walked in. He wore a stone-colored suit, and he did not speak or look at us until he had taken his seat at the head of the table and pulled his yellow legal pad from his backpack. The backpack, please note, was made of dignified brown leather and detracted only slightly from the overall gravity of his image.

He sat leaning close to the table, his back straight and motionless as a marble figure tipping imperceptibly from its column. During the week we spent studying the Romans, Professor Hill passed around a picture of the bust of Emperor Vespasian. He called it "The Roman Face." There was a resemblance between my instructor and the emperor's ancient countenance, rough-hewn and furrowed, with wide, sad eyes that laid bare a life of hard decisions. Vespasian, too, had a strong mouth that rarely looked to speak, and then only to rapt attention. The emperor even had the same ears—medium-sized, protruding just a bit. Professor Hill claimed to have never thought of the likeness.

He always began class with a quiet voice, his elbows resting upon

1

the table in perfect forty-five-degree angles. He held this position for the entire hour, save an infrequent nod or a reach for the notepad. There was never a pen or paper clip in his hand. Professor Hill did not fiddle. He called on us by our last names — I had never been called Ms. Worthen before — and whenever any of us spoke, he made a tiny mark on his notepad, as if he were an Olympic figure-skating judge. None of us ever knew whether those marks portended good or ill. Within minutes we did not trust ourselves to think or speak. We had to, however, for Professor Hill assigned one of us to lead the discussion each day. Over the course of the semester some of my classmates came to class unprepared. When they turned red and stuttered that they had forgotten it was their turn to lead, Professor Hill stared at them, silent, waiting to see what they would do. Most composed themselves and found something to say, eventually. The rest of the class took the lesson to heart. Some of us learned to stay up late, crafting the following day's "spontaneous" insights in our notebooks, to be referenced subversively whenever we raised our hands.

Our other teachers were not like this. They were prone to wearing blue jeans to class and were lenient with those who wanted to chew on a granola bar or show up in sweatpants, but the discussions they led were often fraught with droning and self-importance. No one brought snacks to Professor Hill's class — especially after one girl, a well-meaning Californian named Ellen, accidentally tipped her orange juice into Professor Hill's lap. He stood, brushed the excess from his trousers, shook off his notebook, and picked up where he had left off. He said nothing — he did not even warn her never to bring a beverage to class again. But Ellen was never the same, always shy and jittery after that, like a beaten cat. If the rest of us ever forgot to grab breakfast beforehand, we chose to go hungry.

Almost no one in Professor Hill's class talked too much or wandered off the subject. This was a result of the self-discipline that comes when your instructor is stiff and serious-voiced, when every clearing of his throat sounds like the strike of the hour. A classmate named Sky Schouten remembered that "Every class with him felt like a political summit meeting. You had to come prepared — every seminar I knew I'd see him, I tucked in my shirt and shaved. That was how he made you feel, that this was a serious enterprise . . . and you owed it to the founding fathers who wrote these books."

Professor Hill has always taught like a diplomat, not an academic.

He is not loquacious. On a university campus noisy with undergraduate chatter and self-important faculty pontification, he is different. He is a magpie of words and forms, relentlessly clipping newspaper articles, photocopying the legends of seventeenth-century maps, van Gogh sketches, or passages of Nathaniel Hawthorne to demonstrate an instance of symbol, word craft, or precise expression. His students never write long-winded seminar papers. He assigns Herculean tasks of distillation, essay prompts that require them to sweep and analyze Virgil or Machiavelli in a paper the length of an office memo. He is known for striding over to the chalkboard to scratch out three words and a triangle and pronounce, "That is Thomas Hobbes," or reduce *The Peloponnesian War* to a six-part logic chain. Everything to its category, teaches Professor Hill, and in due course the world and its history are bound according to War, Empire, Culture, Language, Revolution, and other hopelessly broad slices of human experience. The view is captivating. Students slide forward in their seats and trace the diagrams in their notebooks. For many in that freshman seminar, these were the only notebooks we did not throw out at semester's end.

Other Yale professors are more famous than Hill, have longer bibliographies, and receive more requests to appear in PBS documentaries. A half dozen command enthusiastic fan clubs among undergraduates. Even in such company, Hill has been unusual from the start. While his colleagues prefer to teach packed lecture halls and graduate seminars, when he began teaching at Yale full-time in 1997 Hill found a place in the Directed Studies first-year humanities program, among roomsful of impressionable freshmen. The freshmen are the core of his following. They are awed by Yale, intimidated by their professors, and thrilled that one would take an interest in them. A student named Al Jiwa recalled that after finishing his final Directed Studies exam, he staggered up to Hill to turn in his essays, haggard from having pulled an all-nighter. "He shook my hand, and it was firm—but not too firm," Al said. "I went home and told my suitemates, 'I just shook Charles Hill's hand.' I will spend the rest of my life trying to re-create that handshake." Upperclassmen too are susceptible to the influence of charismatic authority, but nothing compares to the guileless wonder of an eighteen-year-old still finding his way around Yale's Gothic spires and windowless secret society tombs.

By the time the term is over, many of his freshmen are composing tentative e-mails to ask Hill to be their academic adviser. When he writes back saying "it would be an honor to work with you"—for he never turns anyone down—they are giddy. Over the next three years they trade elaborate theories about how he signs his e-mails—always "==CH" directly after his last sentence, without hitting the space bar or enter key to separate his message from the body of the letter and the trail of earlier correspondence below. Some are convinced that this must be a CIA practice (for rumors are always floating around that Hill is an undercover agent). Others suggest that the appearance of his cursory sign-off is part of his studied plan to appear as a highflier with barely time to squeeze in correspondence between all of his secret meetings with diplomats and heads of state. Finally, with the benefit of several years' distance from my own freshman year, I asked Hill about it myself. "I never really thought about it," he answered. "It just seemed good to do something a little distinctive." He had succumbed to electronic communication only two years earlier, when the university library insisted that he have an e-mail account to check out books. Hill is a relic of a lost age. His conservatism is less easily caricatured than the liberals on campus would like to believe.

To break through their professor's stone-faced mystery, even for only a moment, is always a great victory for students. It becomes a game—one that begins in the classroom, where "if Hill said something to you, or said your name in class, you'll tell ten of your friends," said a student named Bryan Cory. "He's so studied, he weighs his words so carefully, that it's difficult not to analyze every move he makes. If you get a smile, that's huge." The game continues when students spot him striding gruffly down the street and try to embarrass him into saying hello. Bryan recalled an afternoon when he was walking with his girlfriend, also Hill's student. As they approached Hill, he lowered his head and covered his face with his hat. "Only after I said a big hi and smiled did he shyly smile and say hello." That smile is uncommon and coveted. "All you get when you walk into his office is one quarter of a smile," said Eliana Johnson. "Then he stops—as if he's thinking, 'wait, I don't do that.'" It took me four years to get Hill to laugh, and even then it was only by accident, by way of an anecdote I told about my father's peewee football team. He emitted a sound somewhere between a cough and a sneeze—it disappeared too quickly for me to tell for sure. I felt as if I had seen a store-window mannequin move.

Sometime after I turned in my final exam in the winter of freshman year, and I knew that I would not see Professor Hill in the classroom for several months, I worked up the nerve to go to his office hours a few times. The third-floor hallway of 31 Hillhouse Avenue was narrow, gray, and uninviting. At most hours of the day, I would trip over a classmate leaning against the table at the end of the corridor, backpack sagging off one shoulder, paging through the reading material offered in that cramped and perilous waiting corner. A few feet away, a slit of light spilled onto the carpet from the cracked door to Professor Hill's office. Voices spoke quietly inside. I shifted my backpack to the other shoulder and waited my turn.

The selection of magazines spread across the table was bewildering: a thick *Wall Street Journal;* the latest *Harley-Davidson Magazine;* a monthly newsletter published by the National Rifle Association; a robin's-egg blue copy of *Foreign Affairs.* The mess of periodicals was a collage of the Professor Hill myth. To his students, he is a renegade in a well-tailored suit, a man of wild travels and wise opinions who has been known to clomp into class in motorcycle boots. Like the others who waited their turn next to the table, I ran my hand across the incongruous assortment of magazines and wondered about the man who subscribes to them all and leaves them outside for the speculation of his visitors.

When I opened his office door, I always found him in the same position — leaning over a pile of papers, his chair pulled close to his desk. He glanced up, and there was a flicker of a smile, but it burned out quickly. His eyes were expectant, and never surprised.

Bookshelves lined the walls of his small office, packed with volumes ranging from classical literature and Emerson to Chinese-American diplomacy. A ponderous English dictionary, its unabridged pages trimmed in red gilt, lay open at his elbow next to a legal pad and fountain pen. The rest of the books overflowed onto the tops of his filing cabinets and onto the floor in piles below the window, like refugees flocking for shelter, without any bibliographic order. On the far side of the room beneath the dormer window was an armchair, a floor lamp, and a stack of essay booklets waiting to be graded. A few feet away sat a black Windsor chair, uncomfortable-looking and probably the sort that Puritan colonists used, its backrest embellished with the seal of the U.S. Department of State. The office walls were bare but for a framed black-and-white photograph of the Parthenon, which leaned on one of the filing cabinets. Next to it, for a reason I could not imagine, lay a weather-beaten baseball glove and a scuffed ball.

The office reflected the man who worked there: unadorned, serious, and never wholly explained. My classmates and I trudged up the three flights of stairs to his office for more than an opinion on our rough drafts. We wanted life advice, and for once we found a professor who would tell us what we ought to do. After a few conversations with Professor Hill, a student named Ewan MacDougall was convinced to join the Marines: "I saw [the Marine representative] in the rotunda one day and called Hill for advice on it, and he made a series of predictions about the Marine training that summer, and they all came true." Hill told Ewan that the Marines would push him until he thought he would break. He would learn to be a leader, and he would learn how to yell— when he got home in the fall, his father wouldn't recognize him. "I laughed at the time," Ewan said. "But he was right on, in every regard."

There are no waffling questions or doting effusions—never a "What feels right to you?" or "Perhaps you should take some time for self-discovery." Professor Hill tires of the usual answers, the short-term jobs and stints in the Peace Corps that college students turn to by default, to stall life's decisions. Melissa Wisner thought she was all set to work in investment banking, but her plans changed with an e-mail from her professor: "I did a lot of interviewing at I-banks, and he hates I-banks," she said. When an opportunity arose to work for Halliburton in Kuwait, she mentioned it to Hill. But her parents were horrified by the idea, so instead Melissa accepted an offer from Morgan Stanley in New York. "Hill got wind of this—this was a moment when a professor interceded and changed my life—and he sent me a one-line e-mail that said, 'Come to my office. We need to reexamine your decision.' I went and he said, 'I understand your parents' concern, but think about it, and do it because you want to.' So I'm going to Kuwait. My parents hate him now."

Any professor who encourages his students to join the military and work for Halliburton will not find many allies among the liberal Yale faculty. Professor Hill has few. Most of his colleagues respect his intellect, but they are uneasy about his influence here. That influence has grown in recent years. Increasing numbers of students flock to his office hoping for unambiguous counsel, a foolproof grand strategy. For it does seem that he has mapped out a life plan for each of them. Somewhere, whether amid the pages of Professor Hill's countless notepads or in the back of his mind, there are records and predictions begun with the first eviscerations penned in red ink on his students' papers freshman year, continued all the way through the job interviews and senior essays.

During office hours, the time when professors are supposed to put their feet up on their desks and students are supposed to strike up casual conversation, the Charles Hill myth persists. He does not invite banter or personal confidences. He rarely engages in small talk, and then only with reluctance and artlessness. When the phone rings while Hill is meeting with a student, he never suggests that they continue the conversation another day. But he will pick up the phone and talk or, more commonly, listen and scribble for five or ten minutes, while the student pretends to read the titles of the books on the shelves, stares at her watch, and wonders whether she missed some cue to leave. If she packs up her books and rises for the door, he will often wave her back to her seat. In part Hill does this because it is efficient; few of his phone calls are long. And in part, although he would never admit this, allowing a student to eavesdrop on his conversations with George Shultz or people from the vice president's office is not bad for his reputation around campus. Aaron O'Connell, a skeptical graduate student, related one rumor he'd heard: "Someone once said—and this story is emblematic even if it's false—that he heard Hill has a secure phone in his office so he can call Washington. He said that Hill picked up the phone and said, 'Hill here, go ahead.' It evokes the image of Batman picking up the Batphone. That's part of the seduction."

For more than thirty years, Professor Hill worked in the back corridors of the State Department, a silent yet tirelessly effective officer whose name made few newspaper headlines but remains attached to many of the watersheds in twentieth-century American diplomatic history. The rumors his students whisper during lecture are, for the most part, true. And although by now he is mostly retired from active duty, Washington is often on the other end of those clipped telephone conversations we are permitted to overhear in his office. The same force of mind and power of expression that propelled him through the ranks of the Foreign Service have made Professor Hill one of the most effective and provocative instructors at Yale University. He is also one of the least understood. His students are either awed or repelled. In either case, they do not get far beyond the jumble of periodicals on the table outside his office.

There is always discussion in Professor Hill's seminars. But at the end of the hour, most of the notebooks that flap closed and slide into backpacks are filled with the thought trees and idea charts that he drew on the board at the start of class. He teaches by verdict, not by question, and the lessons are difficult to dispute. Carolyne Davidson is a graduate student who argued with him regularly. "He rarely frames an idea as his opinion—always as the given truth," she said. "This is his diplomatic style. After all, if you were presenting a memo to Kissinger, you wouldn't want him to have to think about it. You'd want him to take it as truth. But it's hard to launch into a debate after that."

Hill does not hesitate. He always knows. He considers it his duty to redeem those misguided minds that disagree with him, and the cold simplicity of his arguments seduces us. Professor Hill is a teacher, a role model, and a counselor for many of my classmates. But to others, he is a sermonizer and an influence to be avoided. Students like Dan Kurtz-Phelan, who enrolled in Hill's yearlong international studies lecture course but dropped it after a semester, worry that his teaching style prevents them from figuring things out on their own. "Many of his students are willing to be spoon-fed, and that terrifies me a little. He passes off his unique interpretations of events as standard beliefs, his conservative political views as 'methodological differences,'" Dan observed. "He has a stronger agenda than he lets on . . . and if you disagree, his answer is, 'But this is the way things work in the real world.' You can't really argue with that."

I worry that once upon a time, I was one of those willing students. Toward the end of that first semester freshman year, I wrote on the inside cover of my notebook, "Charles Hill is God." The evidence is still there, in red marker, all capital letters. I am embarrassed by it now, but I can't bring myself to rip off the cover or cross out the words. That would be like tearing up my third-grade school photograph, that awful picture featuring the floppy unicorn sweater and buckteeth—a mortifying moment in my personal history, but a necessary one.

It was of some comfort to learn that I wasn't alone. Charlie's teaching style dazzles and offends in the same way that religious indoctrination does. Other professors have a powerful presence at the lectern, but "with Hill it's different," said Lindsay Hayden, who studied Literature with him. "Some people can't stand him and his views. Others won't hear a word against him. It's scary. It's like a religion." A classmate of Lindsay named Amia Srinivasan said that her boyfriend "worships Professor Hill," although her own opinion was ambivalent. "It's like I'm an atheist and he's a believer," she said. She told me they tried not to talk about Hill's class too much because they ended up only fighting. Weeks later, at the semester's end, I ran into Amia on the street and she grabbed me by the arm. "I've converted! I believe!" she cried. Her boyfriend stood beside her like a proud godfather.

Hill's students sense that they must work to earn admission into the small circle that has his respect: the few who "get it." His pedagogy is Puritan, fashioned around an enlightened elect. Outsiders are damned to the darkness of ignorance. There is no middle ground. And there is nothing more powerful—or more dangerous—than true belief.

There is another class that Professor Hill teaches. This one I never took. I had not seen it listed in the course catalog but later learned that the course was indexed in the graduate school bulletin. At first I heard about it only through a couple of more vigilant friends who were not intimidated by the class's listing as History 985a. This was in the days before word of the course got out—before the course was advertised all over campus with color posters featuring Churchill and Roosevelt at Yalta; before each year's applications soared into triple digits; before observers began to whisper words like "elitist," "conservative," and "cult"—words considered synonyms by many at Yale.

The Grand Strategy seminar, only a few years old, has become one of the marquee classes at Yale. Every year over a hundred students apply for some twenty slots. For the lucky few who are admitted, Hill and his colleagues John Gaddis and Paul Kennedy collaborate on a year-long curriculum that combines study of the classic texts of strategic thought with real-world practice. Students spend the spring semester reading everything from Sun Tzu and Thucydides to Winston Churchill and Henry Kissinger. After a summer internship spent learning about grand strategy abroad, in business, or elsewhere outside the classroom, they return for the fall to plan complex "policy briefs" on vast subjects like Culture, Technology, or the Environment. In the interest of producing graduates with enough mettle to brief the White House someday, the professors and students do their best to tear apart their peers' presentations. Interwoven among these lessons are extracurricular lectures and dinners with ambassadors, policy analysts, and other "grand strategists" (many are famous friends of Hill) who talk to the class about applying their lessons in real life. Grand Strategy invades like the Blob, seeping into mealtimes, summer activities, friendships, career plans, and every facet of its students' lives. Other courses begin and end at the classroom door, but not this one.

The course is intended to train generalists who can grasp the broad picture without glossing over details and who are brave enough to tackle uncomfortable questions of power, war, and human life. The syllabus is predicated upon the belief that there are foundational ideas by which the world's great leaders have governed states and led armies to battle, and that these ideas remain relevant today. It is an ambitious goal, perhaps overreaching. It runs against almost everything else that Yale students learn in their narrowly focused history courses and political science programs based upon neat statistics and rational choice theory's forecasts of logical human behavior. Whether or not the students agree with the claims of Grand Strategy, they are forced to consider what they believe about right and wrong, and the way history operates.

Grand Strategy, like Professor Hill, has its own myth. The liberals on campus call the class Grand Fascism. They are kidding, but only in part. Many Yale students and faculty are suspicious of the program. Some revile it openly. Graduate students who take the class—particularly those in the History and American Studies Departments, where politics tend toward Ralph Nader territory—find that GS leaves them "tainted" in the eyes of their peers. They spend a lot of time defending their professors to students who have never heard a lecture by Gaddis, Kennedy, or Hill, fending off accusations of brainwashing and Machiavellian amorality. The connections between Grand Strategy professors and people in George W. Bush's administration are known, and liberals on campus are eager to spin conspiracy theories. Many accuse GS of operating from the same principles that supposedly moved the Bush administration to place the intelligence of experts subservient to the policies of ideologues, to distrust hard science, to suspect hidden agendas in outside analysts, and to lend no ear to human compassion. They accuse the Grand Strategy program of packing its curriculum with Dead White Males, teaching students how to lust for power, and encouraging them to trade in humane sensitivities for realpolitik—or even more frightening, for a sense of mission.

By the time the Grand Strategy phenomenon had burst forth on campus, I was a second-semester junior unable to fit the course into my few remaining months at Yale. But I could sit in occasionally, attend some of the extracurricular activities, and talk to the people involved. There were numerous ways to find a place on the margin and observe.

Students awed or repelled by the Grand Strategy course are the same ones who are awed or repelled by Professor Hill, and for the same reasons: the aura of power, the whiff of elitism, the promise of an answer to life's messiest questions. Hill embodies the course's philosophy. In the end, though, Grand Strategy is only a class, and its tenets mean nothing without some sense of what happens when they are put to work in the course of a human life. The ultimate lesson, therefore, must begin where Charles Hill began: in southern New Jersey, in a place and time two hundred miles and seven decades distant from the seminar table in New Haven.

Charles Hill was fifteen when he first kissed a girl. This feat was more momentous than any speech he would write for Henry Kissinger or any back-channel diplomacy he would ever conduct for George Shultz.

For all the lecturing, moralizing, and peer pressure that pervaded the average American boyhood, no authority had anything useful to say about girls. Charlie recalled his adolescent puzzlement: "I was a slow developer. I was attracted to girls but I didn't know what they were. I couldn't imagine what their anatomy could be like—we had no media to tell you these things. I was in a state of fascination, but always at a great distance . . . kind of like Don Quixote and Dulcinea."

Only a singularly brazen girl could rescue him. Mary Anne Gbur was unconventionally attractive. Her poise and charisma made her beautiful and earned her a spot at the center of the high school's in-crowd. She played tennis and directed class plays; she was a leader. She sat in front of Charlie in their eleventh-grade American history class. Charlie knew who Mary Anne was—everyone did—but he had never spoken to her. One day in the spring, she turned around in the middle of class and asked Charlie what he thought of her outfit.

She was wearing a pleated skirt. Charlie thought it was nice.

From that day forward, Mary Anne spent a good portion of each class twisted around in her seat, quizzing Charlie on the fashion triumphs and gaffes committed by girls in the class. They gossiped until the teacher reproached them. One Saturday morning, Mary Anne telephoned Charlie at home. She was directing the class play and suggested that he come with her to the high school and help rearrange the set.

This was the first time Charlie had received a phone call from a girl. He agreed unhesitatingly.

He met Mary Anne outside her house and they walked together to the high school auditorium, where Charlie moved the furniture that

Mary Anne had assigned him, then sat down to lounge on the couch. She finished her work and came over to join him, sitting fairly close, Charlie recalled. They chatted a while. The conversation ended in a kiss, half accidental and half inevitable, in the manner of most romances.

When Charlie first touched on the subject of Mary Anne—fleetingly, in the same monotone that he used at the lecture-hall podium—I was filled with a mixture of glee and horror. The story of Professor Hill's first kiss—what fun! What disarming humanity! What priceless gossip at the dining-hall table! But as I sat across from Charlie's desk, I avoided his stare. There was something radically improper in my professor's confession of having once been a hopeless adolescent.

Charlie sensed it too. He had never dodged a question before, but now there was a hesitation when I asked him, during our second meeting, about Mary Anne. He mentioned her only in passing, as if his first girlfriend were in the same tedious but necessary category as first birthdays and high school graduations. He would prefer to talk instead about the stuffed Cooper's Hawk mounted on his bureau when he was young, or his favorite boyhood adventure stories.

But I wanted to know more about Mary Anne, so I asked the most innocuous question I could think of. Where did he take her on dates—to the movies? to share a soda? What did teenagers do back then?

My question met with a brief but ponderous silence. Charlie cleared his throat solemnly (Charlie often prefers to put the punctuation marks at the beginnings of sentences). "Well . . . ," he said, "as a general principle, I think the question of people's careers and what they do and what is being written about in biographies, and then the side that is love and romance and sex is an interesting question . . . It's a biographer's dilemma to try to sort this out and it's never been done quite right."

I groaned inwardly. For the next five minutes, he lectured me on the blunders of every biography ever written and its author's mistaken ideas of private life. Some biographers could not resist the voyeuristic interlude. Others, by excluding matters of the heart, did not realize that men spend more time thinking about sex than about anything else. I kept my eyes focused on my notebook. There was nothing outlandish about his statement, but coming from the same mouth that I knew as a font of wisdom on Herodotus, it was a scandal.

I thought that would be our first and last conversation about Charlie's private life. It was not. He went on, with minimal prodding, to spend an hour telling me about that first kiss, during which his voice and facial expression never deviated from the imperturbable mask. Over the course of my research I would ask him personal questions only as a last resort. But even on the most sensitive matters he answered with thoroughness and patience, never stiffening at my prying. His openness was a troublesome blessing, for it would force me to decide, as our conversations progressed, how far I would push. His childhood would remain shrouded in the mists of teleological boyhood play and purity of heart, but muddier waters were to come.

I'm not sure what my goals were in the beginning. I think I only wanted to hear a few more of my professor's stories. I did not set out to write a hagiography, but I didn't begin with the express aim of cutting him down to size either. I realized early on, however, that my work would be more complicated than regular installments of Story Time with Professor Hill. I not only had the task of handling the most delicate details of a man's life but the mandate to judge that life. It was a presumptuous enterprise. I could have no foreknowledge of the outcome back then — no historian or biographer ever does. As Herodotus, the greatest storyteller of all (and the one who introduced Charlie and me), might have said: stories have a way of telling themselves. The teller might learn a bit about herself by letting them speak.

During the first part of the last century, Bridgeton, New Jersey, was a small truck-gardening and manufacturing town of about sixteen thousand, surrounded mostly by farmland. It was an isolated place. Photographs from the time reflect a classic mid-Atlantic town: soda jerks standing in their white jackets and slicked hair in front of Cut-Rate Drugs, and Bailey's Hometown Store, hosting a sale on LeStourgeon's Kew-Bee bread, where Merle Bailey himself stands out front in his ill-fitting jacket. In another picture, uniformed members of the Onized Club Band, the official employee band of the local Cumberland Glass Works plant, sit solemnly holding their instruments, like infantry in a Civil War daguerreotype. It was a place where white houseboats festooned with flags floated down the Cohansey River on Labor Day, and at the end of the growing season in September, when the trucks lined up for two miles to deliver tomatoes to Ritter's Catsup factory, the whole town smelled like tomato paste. Women managed their own gardens, men went to work, everyone went to church, and nobody thought much beyond growing up to be just like his parents. By all obvious measures, Bridgeton was Yale University's perfect antipode. Charles Hill* was born there on April 28, 1936. His parents, Morton and Alvenia, brought him home to 30 Institute Place, a simple white clapboard house overlooking the Cohansey and miles of woodland beyond.

Charlie was both a logical creature of his parents and a stranger to them. At the heart of the ideas and attitudes that Yale liberals have come to loathe in Charlie Hill is the imprint of Morton, a frank, squarish man with ears like a terrier. Morton Hill was the son of a stonemason who died young and a lonely, wearied mother who raised him and his four siblings in a small house in Dividing Creek, a scruffy town on the edge of the pine barrens in rural South Jersey. After high school he enrolled in dental school and ran his own practice in town for the next thirty years. He worked out of duty, never passion. His happiness came from making things with his hands. He bought the dilapidated shells of old Packards and Pierce Arrows and spent hours every night restoring them in a garage he had built behind the house. He carved duck decoys for friends and often spent three or four hours a night caning chairs with cane he had pulled himself from a nearby marsh.

Morton was conservative by instinct and ethos. He pulled himself out of a poor childhood and saw no reason why other men couldn't do the same. He was the sort of man who taught his son to swim by tossing him out of a rowboat and paddling away until the thrashing, gasping boy figured out how to keep afloat by himself. He soon did. Charlie was a fast learner.

One of his grandmothers used to tell a story about baby Charlie. One afternoon he was playing with a beach ball in his playpen in the front yard. An older neighborhood boy came along, picked up the ball, and bounced it off Charlie's head. His grandmother ran out of the house screeching, but Charlie just laughed. He was unflappable, even as an infant.

Charlie grew into an average-looking boy, skinny with banister legs and a fuzzy sand-brown crewcut that rose in a cowlick at the crown, like a patch of grass neglected by the lawnmower. His ears stuck out

---

* Charlie's given name is Morton Charles Hill. From the start and always, he has gone by Charlie. The name Morton would have confused him with his father.

just a little and made him seem perpetually alert. From the earliest he had a sense of his world and what he wanted from it. His mother once asked whether he would like to have brothers and sisters. He said no. It seemed like a bad idea. No child, when allowed to ponder the consequences of siblings, would wish to divide his parents' attention and impair his own authority. Charlie already had plenty of friends in the neighborhood. He would remain an only child, quite capable of taking responsibility for his own amusement.

Perhaps he was too capable. No one learns the limits of grand strategy as quickly as a child with a sibling or two—a fellow little person who absorbs an equal amount of his parents' attention, hope, and frustration, whose inconvenient presence forces the alteration of every childhood calculus. An only child, on the other hand, is always master of his domain. In a world where friends came and went but ideas were eternal playmates, it might have been easy to get carried away by their power. But Charlie's students would find themselves lucky for this. Imaginative and lonely boys grow up to be men of ideas.

Charlie's childhood revolved around World War II and ball games, the two realities that dominated the lives of most boys at the time. He made his mother sew sergeant's stripes on the sleeves of his T-shirts. His father carved model fighter planes for him, complete with spinning propellers and tiny swastikas stamped on the nose to signify enemy aircraft shot to pieces. After the bombing of Hiroshima, Morton carved his son an enormous model B-29, which perched magnificently on the bookshelf next to a disarmed hand grenade given to him by his hero, a soldier neighbor come home from the war. Charlie lounged on the floor of his bedroom for hours beneath these brave artifacts, meticulously assembling the cardboard Spitfires and German Messerschmitts that were printed on the backs of cereal boxes. Once a week, while his grandmothers looked on and hooted, Charlie whizzed them gleefully into the burning trash barrel and watched them blacken and curl in the backyard antiaircraft fire. Then he trotted inside to read or listen to the radio. Despite afternoons spent with scissors and paste, he had no attachment to the planes. He thrilled in the moment of their climactic combustion and moved on.

In place of baseball cards, he and his friends collected trading cards of military heroes, each pack complete with a crumbly stick of bubble gum. Charlie belonged to the generation of boys that chose for their role models not sports stars, as their successors would, but four-star generals, fighter pilots, and men who gave their lives for their country. Charlie kept his heroes as he would later keep his classroom: pious to the old gods, classical in aesthetic.

In a family that had for generations lived and died without venturing out of southern New Jersey, Aunt Elsie, Morton's older sister, was the sophisticated one. She went north to college and had a career as principal at a nearby school. She was interested in the world and always had the itch to travel. Bridgetoners, to her, were "dull normals." When Charlie was about seven, she hooked him on books of escape: stories about world travelers, old copies of *National Geographic,* and *Terry and the Pirates* comics, an exciting series for boys based on the Flying Tiger pilots in China. Elsie bribed her nephew to climb up to the attic and set mousetraps for her by allowing him to choose one book from the dusty stacks he found while he was up there. For all his love of running around with neighborhood pals when the weather was nice, during rainy days, when all children reveal their true characters, Charlie read books in his room instead of playing Monopoly or making messes with his friends. He began taking notes — thoughts and scribbles that popped up as he read, doodles sparked by dazzling heroes and vicarious triumphs in worlds far more compelling than Bridgeton. The pages he filled were not profound, but they contained the germ of habit.

Charlie began school a year earlier than his classmates. He was an unremarkable student, bored by most of his classes. There was, during one fall term in high school, an English teacher who led an absorbing study of Boswell, Johnson, and their London circle. But when Charlie returned after the winter holidays he found that new state guidelines had replaced his favorite class with a more sensible telephone-etiquette training program. As to his classmates, he had no more interest in their parties and cruising for girls than he did in phone manners. He became a marginal character. He told himself that he had decided to be so.

At the seashore, however, Charlie was always at the center. On the sand at Ocean City, where his father built a cottage and his family vacationed every summer, the other boys — who had never met Bridgeton Charlie — listened to him and relied on him. In their endless games of beach football, he played quarterback. As the years went by, the Ocean City boys too fell prey to fruitless cruising for girls, and Charlie's father began to insist that he spend his days in back-searing construction work. He built bulkheads and worked as a gondola kicker, scrambling inside railroad cars loaded with coal to kick loose chunks of coal jammed in the chute. He joined the International Hod Carriers and Common Laborers Union and came home every day gritty and tired, but never too exhausted to join his friends playing in the surf. Fundamentally, "there was something democratic about the beach," said his Ocean City friend Joe Evans. "We created it from scratch." The beach was the first place where Charlie learned that power lies in the proper balance of self-invention and self-extirpation. It was a lesson he would live and teach without even knowing it.

Charlie was not long for South Jersey. In the years to come, he would nurse a special pride for the place, and all of his stories would lead back home. But those sentiments came only after he left. At the time he felt nothing but the urge to sever his moorings. As his senior year rounded to a close, the notion of college became his preoccupation. His bedroom walls were pinned with the standards of Army, Navy, Brown, Princeton, and Yale—a representation of the selection available in the hardware store display window, rather than an affinity for any particular school. In the garage behind his house was an ancient phonograph discarded by an anonymous relative, nearly five feet tall, built to play records an inch thick. College life romanced him with its music. Charlie spent hours in the garage listening to debonair pop singers like Rudy Vallee and Fred Waring and the Pennsylvanians croon about the bliss of fellowship, beer drinking, and football. He had no idea what college actually meant—does any eighteen-year-old, then or now?—but it promised an escape. It would be a suit jacket and tie reincarnation of the Ocean City boys' club, filled with the vigorous male camaraderie in which Charlie felt most comfortable. Yet it would also be a place where he could hole up, consume great books, and hone his seriousness of character. To most who knew the skinny young man, that seriousness was a benign pox that had marked Charlie since birth (perhaps a recessive gene inherited from Aunt Elsie). For the majority of Bridgetoners, to leave home for a university, for another life, would be unbearable self-exile, the last resort of the sick man who must leave for the health of the tribe. But for Charlie, there could be no other way.

His mother saw no reason why her boy had to go so far away to school. His father had always harbored the desire—expressed in Charlie's earshot only once or twice—for his son to attend the Naval Academy at Annapolis, but Charlie didn't have the grades to get in and would have flunked the physical by being nearsighted. A neighbor named William Doherty, a veterinarian who held a University of Pennsylvania degree, stocked his bookshelves with impressive volumes like *God and Man at Yale* and never let anyone forget that he was not a Bridgeton native (thereby earning Charlie's awe). He continually reminded Charlie that no one from Bridgeton could succeed at a "real" college.

Of the small, unplanned assortment of colleges to which Charlie applied, Brown and Duke sent acceptance letters. He chose Brown because it was in New England and (so he reasoned) it was a more serious place. For the first time, a boy who had always been timid at parties and middling in class finally stood out from his classmates. "To go to a New England, Ivy League school from Bridgeton was a real rarity," said Bob Woodruff, who went to high school with Charlie. "Charlie was maybe one in ten thousand."

That final summer before college was not much different from the summers before. Charlie spent the days working on a road gang, returning home dirty and sore. But come evening, he was never too tired to head out with his friends and throw spirals down the beach. At first glance it seems strange — a shame, perhaps — that he didn't absorb the social skills and confidence he learned at the shore and bring his summer persona home with him. The truth is that Charlie was, from boyhood, both an adroit team player capable of taking the lead when conditions so demanded and a slightly awkward loner, often happier in the company of no one save his books and his thoughts. This observation will come as no surprise to the anxious, slightly mystified students who line up outside his office door each afternoon, rehearsing opening lines in their heads. What is less obvious is that their Professor Hill — commanding at the lectern, yet shy on the street; elusive diplomat with important phone calls to make, yet accessible adviser always free in his office — was never a person of contradiction. He was, rather, an individual who learned to make choices as to what he would be. This is not grand strategy, but it is a beginning.

2

ONE DARK AFTERNOON IN DECEMBER, I PULLED OPEN THE heavy wooden doors of the Hall of Graduate Studies and followed a trail of voices down the corridor of the nearly vacant building. Room 211 was wood-paneled and upholstered in burgundy leather. The walls were hung with enormous oil portraits of deans and professors emeritus tipping their Meerschaum pipes and staring into the room with expressions of grave significance. The radiators against the walls were ancient, and the room was too hot.

I found a seat in the back and watched the students milling around, too dressed up for a Friday afternoon at semester's end—boys in button-downs and khaki trousers, some even wearing belts, girls in skirts and nice sweaters. There was a predictable assortment of chips, veggies, and dip on a table in the corner of the room. It was mostly untouched, because of nerves, I think. John Gaddis, wearing his characteristic tweed jacket and wire-rim aviator glasses, sat at a table in the front of the room and fidgeted imperceptibly. Paul Kennedy was away from campus that afternoon and could not attend. Charlie Hill arrived a few minutes late and took a seat at the other end of the table. He was dressed in a neat gray sweater and tie. His hands were clasped, hiding his mouth.

The students, like small animals that sense an earthquake before the rest of us, found their seats and quit their chatter without any prompting. Gaddis stood and surveyed the room with a smirk. Then, the prefabricated opening line:

"Welcome to Grand Strategy. You may not know what you're going in for."

This year there were 110 applications for 15–20 seminar slots, he told them. He and Professors Kennedy and Hill were pleased. A word on the origins of the course—it went back five years, "when several of us started looking around in our classes, calculating how many future presidents, cabinet members, and CEOs we had, or how many bums and taxi drivers. We found the percentage of the first was higher." Polite chuckles, thinking of all those who applied to get in and failed. We are the elite, we are the survivors; already an esprit de corps is taking root. Gaddis went on. "We started thinking, are we putting the right things into your heads? Because we're concerned that, twenty or thirty years from now, when you're running things and we're upset about it, and we call you up to tell you so, you won't take our calls. So while we have your attention now, there are certain things you ought to know."

No other institution teaches a course like this, he continued. There is the Strategy and Policy course at the Naval War College in Newport, where Gaddis taught for two years and picked up the bug. He told the audience about Stansfield Turner, the great admiral who took charge of the Naval War College, fired the faculty, and brought in a new crew to teach the "Thucydides curriculum"—whereby unsuspecting midshipmen at sea would receive brown paper packages from the admiral and a note scrawled with their orders: "Read this." Inside, a copy of *The Peloponnesian War*. Welcome, Gaddis thinks. Welcome, young men and women, to your plebe year, when you will learn to man the ship of state.

Charlie stood. "I'm sorry I was late. I was delayed with a matter of grand strategy." More polite chuckles, delighted, getting into the mood. "This program tries to recall and re-create, in an elaborate way, the education that was available informally to those in the late nineteenth century and the first half of the twentieth century in Britain and the U.S that enabled them to rise to cope with, and understand, the grandest designs of international affairs." He spoke calmly, hands at his sides. "Our philosophical basis goes back to Hegel—" Ah, Hegel! Already such scholarly altitude, and only five minutes in! "—who saw high politics and international affairs as the most challenging, indispensable realm of human endeavor. The most important decisions and acts are played out in the realm above that of the state." This was the education that Winston Churchill had, Charlie continued. The study of the classics, interaction with the great and powerful. (There were rumors that last year's class got a private lecture from Henry Kissinger. The rumors were true.)

He spoke next of his career, in the briefest of sentences, ending with the point that he had seen firsthand the deterioration of statecraft as an art. He mentioned the frustrated graduate students and their tiny social science studies, the encroachment of social science upon the virtuous humanities, and, for the undergraduates, the "graduate schoolization of college." Grand Strategy would be everything that the rest of Yale was not. So not only are they elite, they are rebels. They have a cause—and a standard-bearer, a curious one, soft-spoken and grayhaired. I sat quietly, taking notes.

The striking thing was how much the scene in the Hall of Graduate Studies shared with Charlie's portrait of his own undergraduate years. The faces of tradition framed along the walls glowered down upon students dressed in ties and skirts, leaning forward in their chairs, committed to an enterprise that they did not yet understand. In the professors' speeches and the students' faces, there was a communal sense that they had been elected for a mission, and it was now time to grow up. Grand Strategy was not to be another class in a fun but impractical liberal arts education. The air in the room, the gravity in the professors' voices, were meant to convince the initiates that the year to come would be the ultimate vocational training. No matter what these kids did in their free time outside of class, in Grand Strategy they were transformed into well-behaved, serious-minded students intent on fulfilling their own promise—young elites who would not have looked out of place on the campus of Brown University, circa 1953.

Brown, in those days, was a place of classical texts and natty blazers, the clatter and chatter of silverware and boyish voices in the refectory, the boom of the president's voice at mandatory Friday afternoon chapel. Charlie registered for classes in the great works of literature. He went out for the crew team, that quintessential and most Emersonian of East Coast college sports. He was the smallest of the freshman oarsmen, but the coach set him to rowing bow and discovered that the skinny teenager pulled the blade through the water instinctively. He made first boat within the week. At the alphabetically arranged freshman orientation events, Charlie succeeded in making a few friends (mostly young men whose last names began with H). He had an immediate gift for playing the model Brown man. Still, Charlie was ill at ease, convinced that his peers were smarter and worldlier than he was. But he relished the common thirst to flee the practical world, the classmates who recoiled at the idea of going home to man their fathers' businesses, pined to be editors of *The Atlantic,* devoured books by American émigrés, and fantasized about Paris cafés and cold-water flats. For Charlie, learning to keep up was the most obvious means of avoiding the fate of a nameless member of Elsie's dull normals.

Fraternities were the center of campus life at Brown during the 1950s. More than two thirds of all undergraduates lived, ate, and socialized in the elegant colonial frat houses around the perimeter of the Wriston Quad. Charlie played the part expected of him. He endured the requisite four days of smokers, shuffling from house to house with his pack of freshman buddies, nursing cans of beer and making awkward conversation. Toward the end of the bid process, he received a last-minute invitation from Alpha Delta Phi, the elite intellectual fraternity. The fraternity "totally transformed my life," Charlie recalled. "I was now in a structured social environment where everybody assumed you would be a certain way . . . you couldn't be a bum, you had to wear certain clothes, eat properly, discuss literature with them . . . I'd never had to conduct myself or be mannerly in the way they were requiring me to be, or to have to perform in literary conversation . . . as I got further along, I realized I was being turned into a totally different kind of person. I was being turned into a respectable, presentable Ivy League product you could take places and not be embarrassed by."

After a quiet three years, Charlie's name would come up as the dark horse candidate for fraternity president. The brothers recognized something in the unassuming boy who never missed a chapter meeting or a Saturday night party, even if he mostly stood by the record player sipping a beer. They saw the same qualities that the boys at the Jersey seashore had recognized. During his senior year, Charlie felt ridiculous presiding over meetings from the paneled throne. By his own account, he was a lousy president. Leadership was not a role that Charlie consciously assumed — nor was it a fact of his personality. He had come to Brown intent on making himself into a college man, and by senior year he had done such a thorough job that those around him got the feeling he ought to be in charge. He had firmness of mind. That is not the same as leadership, but it can be a good proxy.

In the classroom, Charlie was an average student. But the American Civilization major was a good fit for him. Still in its academic infancy, the discipline had begun to blossom throughout the Ivy League just as Charlie arrived at college. American Studies, as the program was called elsewhere, evolved from programs established at a handful of universities in the final years of World War II to train American soldiers in the export of American culture. The discipline began in earnest at Yale University, emerging from the Far Eastern Civil Affairs Training School, where funders had "sought to construct American Studies as something beyond the study of American literature and history," wrote one historian. They intended the program to become "an enterprise that would be, among other things, an instrument for ideological struggle in what some among them termed the American crusade in the cold war." American Studies was strident about the superiority of Western civilization. It was proudly interdisciplinary, not yet Balkanized and debased by the political agendas of the 1960s (when the discipline would come to embody everything that its former student grew to despise in academia). Charlie was a shy undergraduate who, for all his love of reading, made average marks and still spent his summers working construction jobs at the Jersey shore. But he wanted badly to be a man of ideas.

On a warm evening in late April at the end of junior year, students at Brown and sister school Pembroke came home from an afternoon spent picnicking on the banks of the Seekonk and watching the crew races to wash and dress for the Spring Weekend festivities. AΔΦ was hosting a party in the Pine Room, a paneled, tavernlike chamber in the basement of the fraternity house. Darkness fell, the band took a break, and couples began to wander downstairs, lured by the sophisticated Manhattan piano bar music wafting from the record player. Charlie leaned against the bar near the hallway, talking to no one. Suddenly, a woman in a purple velveteen dress stepped out of nowhere, kissed him hard on the lips, turned, and ran upstairs.

Martha Mitchell was the most beautiful girl at Pembroke. With wide, intelligent eyes, high cheekbones, and velvet brown hair styled in a pageboy, she had a classic grace that may no longer exist. She was a girl who could have had any boy she wanted. Most thought she was the last girl on earth who would go for retiring Charlie Hill. But at a recent party she overheard Charlie's friend Frank Hills chattering to someone about how he and Charlie had gone mountain climbing while they were backpacking in Europe the previous summer. One day, mid-climb on a peak in the Alps, it began to snow. Frank wanted to head back down, but Charlie — "Chaahlie," in Frank's East Coast prep accent — wanted to continue the ascent. So they parted ways, and Charlie went up alone, dressed in sneakers and shorts. Martha was intrigued. "I was thinking, Wow, that guy who went up the mountain must be something," she said later. "Then I encountered Charlie in the hallway at Brown, and I remember thinking, 'those are the saddest blue eyes I've ever seen.' Then I kissed him, and walked away."

After she dashed off, Charlie was stunned. Bystanders were shocked too, elbowing him to follow her upstairs, but he didn't. "I was too stupid," he explained. "It was so improbable that she would have ever done that, I just could not summon thoughts. Others wanted to talk to me about it, but I didn't, so they eventually left me alone. This went on [after summer] into the next term, people pleading with me to ask her out, telling me I was stupid . . . I did see her a couple times in the library, but I was shy and nervous." Nevertheless, not long after classes resumed the following September, the two began dating. Charlie was smitten. He discovered Martha was as gifted as she was beautiful. She was an art major and a painter, and "her ideal was to be a genius, a great artist." But she was also down-to-earth. She had left Indiana University for Pembroke because she'd felt suffocated there by her classmates' planning out their lives in predictable ways. Charlie found he could be himself around her. They spent their first date sitting on the steps of a Pembroke dormitory and talking for hours, from the time when the other boys came to collect their dates, through the evening, until the same couples wandered home to make curfew.

Like Mary Anne Gbur, Martha was a girl that, as Charlie put it, "decided she would be in charge of him." Whether he was afraid, unsure, or simply had no such compulsion, Charlie never instigated a relationship. So far the two girls that had managed to draw him out did not fit the 1950s mold of femininity. They behaved like men. They grabbed him by the collar and gave him little choice in the matter.

It was decided, naturally, that Charlie Hill and Martha Mitchell would be married at the end of August 1957. They were in love. And marriage was what the proper college graduate ought to do.

Charlie and Martha fled her hometown of Oak Park, Illinois, immediately after the wedding for Philadelphia, where Charlie would attend law school at the University of Pennsylvania. Faced with the doubts that come when one's undergraduate years end too soon and the certainty of a father loath to pay for anything but a real professional education, Hill had chosen law school as the least of all evils. He had no notion of what it meant to be a practicing lawyer. The idea of going to school to become "a legal mind" probably caught Hill's attention, if less because of the legal component and more for his ambition to be any sort of "mind" at all. But law school has never been a place for romantics. Charlie would have no choice but to struggle through and become, decades later, a crypto-J.D. known for warning Yale seniors seeking his advice that there was no greater mistake—if they had any yen for the life of the mind at all—than to go to law school.

In September 1957 Charlie and Martha moved into a West Philadelphia clapboard duplex on 48th Street, in an agreeable lower-middle-class Irish neighborhood. Charlie's first year of classes was full of history and ideas, in general a happy continuation of his undergraduate work. His interest in legal history began at Brown, with Professor Edmund Morgan's course on colonial American thought, and he continued to read books about the Puritans long after the semester ended. This particular interest would absorb him through his graduate studies and beyond. The Puritans were not unlike the World War II heroes he had admired as a boy. They were idealistic soldiers of God with an immediate, Calvinist sense of evil. For all their supposed fatalism, they met the hardships of colonial life head-on. The "Christian life was indeed strenuous, but the more desperate the situation, the more action it evoked," wrote one scholar. Hill's coursework and reading also tugged at something deeper: his own genealogy reached past the Civil War heroes and Revolutionary War generals of whom the family was so proud, all the way to the Puritan founders. More important, something in the Puritans' story echoed the independent, obstinate spirit of South Jersey and his father's sense of duty.

But in subsequent years, he found himself buried in an uninspiring selection of Sales, Evidence, and Land Transactions. Hill labored toward his degree while taking a minimum of required courses and hiding out as much as possible in legal history and philosophy. Despite his waning interest, he never ceased to take too many notes. He recorded every word of every lecture because he was intimidated by the sons of attorneys and accountants in the seats next to him. He thought there was no other way to possess the knowledge his peers already seemed to have, other than to trap it in his notebook, like a dutiful monk inscribing leaves of parchment with the writings of the church fathers. His classmates dressed in tweed accessorized by briefcases heavy with casebooks, for they knew how a young attorney should look, and they answered professors' interrogations with effortless strings of commercial code and contract vocabulary. Hill decided that his place was, and would always be, on the margin. "Law school wrestled him to the ground," Martha observed. He kept to his studies and the couple of friends he made by virtue of alphabetical seat arrangements. "We chose — or had chosen for us — the paths of loners," said Hill's close friend in law school, Rodney Henry.

Hill's notes in class were frantic. Often he was "taking notes rather than thinking," he said later. "You have to think and sort out while you're taking notes, but it also requires you to shut off the instantaneous reflective quality of writing. Intellectually you have to be extremely alert to nuances and central points, but at the same time you can't pause to reflect, say 'I disagree,' or raise a question. You're intellectually active but also self-obstructed." His penchant for the pen would turn out to be a lucky predilection, but he would have to learn to master it. Long after he had done with school, he would continue — in the words of the eminent Augustinian monk Martin Luther — in "the toil of scribbling."*

Hill would be forever a note taker.

As the end of law school approached, Hill flailed briefly in numerous professional directions. All the evidence that remains of careers that might have been is a handful of polite letters from headmasters of private schools with vague offers of interviews, expressing puzzlement as to why a law graduate would want to teach high school (the eternal prospect for graduates who don't know what to do with themselves). Hill's papers contain at least one yellowed note from a real working Philadelphia law firm, but the suggestion that Hill call for an interview came to nothing. He did pass the bar exam on his second attempt — more a testament to his fear of disappointing his father than a desire

---

* The Puritans whom Hill found so appealing are credited with popularizing, if not inventing, the habit of meticulous note taking during lecture. In their efforts to move the English faith's focus of devotion from the Mass to the sermon, Puritan worshipers took to bringing notebooks to church and recording every word. To point at this curious echo in Hill's academic habits is not to suggest that he consciously modeled himself after Puritan churchgoers, but it was not a meaningless coincidence. Hill, like the Puritans, took notes because he believed it was his duty to improve himself. He was becoming more serious-minded. In the university lecture hall, that feeling was probably encouraged more by nervous compulsion than historical consciousness. But Hill, in true Puritan form, never doubted that what he was doing was important and correct, and ought to be recorded.

to practice the profession. Hill's law school career was not preparation for a respectable vocation but a step in a course that led, he knew not where, but up and out.

Charlie fell out of touch with his friends from law school when they ceased to have anything of interest to say to him. This happened almost immediately after graduation, discounting the occasional Christmas greeting card. When I looked up the whereabouts of those classmates and began retracing his life in Philadelphia, I found myself in the unexpected role of Charlie's ambassador to his own past. Upon locating two of his close law school friends, Rodney Henry and Beatty Chadwick, I went to meet them prepared with my own questions, only to spend the first hour of our conversation trying to satisfy them with an adequate summary of Charlie's life since the early 1960s. They missed him.

For the biographer, old friends are sometimes most useful as reminders that people's lives can follow unthinkable paths from the same starting point. They diverge wildly from sensible predictions, and half a century later old classmates may inhabit worlds so different that it is hard to believe they ever had anything in common.

I visited Beatty Chadwick on a bright November morning in Delaware County Prison in Thornton, Pennsylvania. Rodney, who had not seen his friend in years, accompanied me. Rodney had spent his life as a lawyer in Quakertown, an hour northwest of Philadelphia. He was tight-lipped when I first contacted him—in the way that good lawyers are trained to be—but once satisfied that Charlie approved of my project, he was thrilled to oblige. He sent me stream-of-nostalgia e-mails packed with the curious but useless details that always enjoy preeminence in the human memory: the time a pedestrian shouted to Charlie that he was driving the wrong way on a one-way street, and Charlie sneered back, "No shit!"; the time they contemplated joining the local National Guard unit to avoid the draft but decided against it upon learning they would have to march in the Memorial Day parade; the favorite study carrels, the favorite books, the half-forgotten classmates. When I called Rodney to tell him that I was driving down to Philadelphia to explore Charlie's old haunts, he offered to put me up so that we could visit Beatty together. I spent the night in a small white guest room, all traces of the now-grown offspring who once inhabited it desiccated or packed away. We left for the prison early in the morning, my throat still sour with the aftertaste of unsweetened muesli from the oversized plastic cereal bin in the Henrys' kitchen.

After sitting in an idling car for forty-five minutes, occasionally inching forward in the line of cars toward the guard booth at the prison entrance, I rolled down the window and gave the guard our names and the identification number of the inmate we had come to see. "Oh, Beatty Chadwick," the guard smiled. "We know Beatty. Go on ahead."*

I had never been inside a prison before, apart from a childhood trip to Alcatraz during a family vacation. The visiting room, which probably functioned as a cafeteria during other hours, was now noisy and crowded. Inmates and visitors sat across from one another at undersized plastic tables, like those found in a preschool classroom. Beatty saw us before we saw him. He was standing, grinning. His appearance was raw-boned and too thin—his only physical activity, he told us, was the thirty minutes per day during which he was allowed to walk around in circles. His face had the drained look of a father who has stayed up all night waiting on a teenager out past curfew. Beatty had already spoken to me over the telephone in the prison library (he had earned as many inmate privileges as could be hoped). The interview had fished every hole I thought of value. This visit was for the sake of seeing his face, and to visit a man in prison, who had nothing except one weekly phone call from his son.

Our conversation was pleasant and predictable—the men talked of study sessions at the Hills' house in West Philadelphia and the embarrassments inflicted upon them by pitiless professors. They tried to jog each other's memories for the names of old lunchtime dives, or which

---

* Beatty was unlike most of the other inmates in Delaware County Prison. He had earned Phi Beta Kappa at the University of Pennsylvania and spent his free time volunteering in Presbyterian Church organizations. He had been a successful lawyer and community citizen. At the time of our interview he had been in prison for eight years on an order of civil contempt of court. After a failed second marriage to a woman twenty years his junior, he was charged with concealing $2.5 million in potential alimony assets before his ex-wife's lawyers could pursue equitable distribution, according to *New York Times* reports. Her lawyers had spent much time and money tracing Beatty's stash and had tracked it through several Swiss and Panamanian accounts, only to lose the scent. Beatty claimed he lost all the money in an overseas investment that went sour. When he failed to turn himself in, the police staked out his dentist's office and nabbed him when he came in for a routine cleaning. He had been in jail ever since—in one of the longest civil imprisonments in American history—without conviction or much hope for appeal.

library reading room Charlie once liked to study in. They usually failed. They asked me repeatedly about Charlie's politics. Rodney had seen him speak on a foreign affairs television program and was shocked that his old friend's views sounded so conservative and hawkish. Back then, Charlie was the finest example of a liberal mind, they told me. It gradually emerged that the three of them had never really discussed politics much, and that their evidence of their friend's political leanings lay in the observation that Charlie read a tremendous number of books, which meant he was interested in all kinds of ideas. This was, to them, the sign of a "good liberal."

The following week I received a lengthy letter from Beatty. After two pages of musing on the discipline of law, he turned to questions he had about atrocities in the Vietnam War. "I hope that your work will be able to explore, in the context of Charlie's role, the process of foreign policy decision making which, at certain critical times, seems to produce such disastrous results," he wrote. He wondered too about later aggressions against countries out of U.S. favor. "I am sure there are voices raised in official meetings, but would like to know Charlie's reasons for why such voices have not had more effect." His thought finished with an unwritten question: Was my friend part of those things?

Beatty, like Rodney, sounded confounded by his former classmate. If I had asked, I know they would have told me that he must still be the same old Charlie, but it sounded as if they didn't quite recognize him. As I pieced together his law and graduate school years, I saw not a different person but one whose character and proclivities hadn't yet the chance to unfold. It is hard, in biography, to track changes of character, to ask a living subject about his youth and separate his current voice from the young man he describes.

The encounter with Beatty and Rodney made me wonder whether my own college friends and I would recognize one another in forty years. We think of ourselves as well-formed individuals, already two decades on the earth and — as I saw in the new batch of Grand Strategy initiates sitting in the lecture hall on that December day — susceptible to delusions of grandeur. But many of us have barely begun to figure out who we will be in our adult lives. Most of the students who gathered in the Hall of Graduate Studies on that winter afternoon were gearing up to learn about the generalship of history without the slightest idea of their own grand strategies. If we return to our fiftieth reunion transformed and strange to one another, does that mean the friendships we formed as students—which, perhaps, would never have happened if we had met one another later in life—were somehow less real or valuable? When is an individual in his most authentic form—when he is young and fresh to the world, or when he is gray, paunchy, and armed with reminiscences, probably spoiled for good, but by most accounts much wiser?

The question to ask is not whether it was the shy law school student or the aloof professor who is the real Charlie. I wondered instead where that young man is now, and how he fits into the character of the Professor Hill that his students know. What happens when Professor Hill encounters him, however reluctantly? I know that he prefers to avoid any such meeting. I have never been to a high school or college reunion, and I can only speculate about what happens to people when they attend. But I am certain that Charlie has never been, for such events are horribly boring for people like him, who are repulsed by the memory wallowing that such affairs require. Charlie's high school acquaintances told me no one was surprised when he didn't show up at the fiftieth reunion not long ago, and those few who had been his close friends knew better than to try to track him down. Takao Yoshida,* one of Charlie's few friends from Bridgeton, told me that he and another classmate named Gary Brandt wondered often about how their old friend was doing. But they were reluctant to call up Charlie to reminisce. "Gary's afraid," Yoshida said. "We were probably his closest friends in Bridgeton, but even we have apprehensions about jumping on a train and seeing Charlie. I think he wanted to erase Bridgeton from his mind."

---

* Yoshida's family was one of a large Japanese-American community that came from the World War II internment camps to Charles Franklin Seabrook's South Jersey frozen foods company and lived in Seabrook's mass employee housing along the highway northwest of Bridgeton. Soon an influx of Estonian immigrants joined them, refugees from the westward advance of the Soviet army during the last months of the war, as well as a few scattered Italians, Poles, Germans, and Jamaicans, all holdovers from previous waves of immigrant labor. This sudden influx of new faces into classrooms of working-class New Jersey natives happened just about the time that Charlie entered high school. None of the local residents seemed to pay much attention, at least not the Bridgeton students. It is significant that Charlie spent an indifferent youth in the company of kids of diverse colors and backgrounds. A series of sociological coincidences—Philadelphia Catholics' fondness for his family's narrow strip of the Jersey seashore, the immigrant workers on his summer construction jobs, and a labor shortage at the local frozen foods plant—created a backdrop for Charlie's childhood more vibrant than one might have expected in a small Jersey town in the middle of the twentieth century.

History is written by the victors, as all good grand strategists know. When one looks back over the story of a life, it is easy to see only the elements of personal character that won out in the end—in Charlie's case, the single-mindedness that dictated his goals, the obstinacy and sense of duty that achieved them. Subtler sensitivities faded away or lay dormant. The Charlie Hill that Beatty and Rodney knew was a far cry from the man who would stalk the halls of the State Department and captivate classes at Yale. Yet I don't think the two are all that different. Charlie himself admits that in countless ways he is the same as he was at age seven, lounging with a book in the sunroom, knobby knees hooked over the arm of his chair. The crux is to find the young within the old, the life within the education and experience. The aim of biography is not an essence, but balance.

3

CHARLES HILL'S LAW DEGREE WAS SENT HOME TO KINDLE parental pride and collect dust. Of sole significance for his future was the acceptance letter from the University of Pennsylvania's graduate program in American Civilization. There Hill would encounter professors and peers who, like him, preferred history, literature, and cultural meditations to the more remunerative occupations intended to follow the bar exam. He had not thought deeply about becoming a professor himself. His aims were those of a novice wandering about the agora in search of knowledge and sophistication. If Martha and his parents were beginning to lose patience with their beloved boy's never-ending pursuit of wisdom, they did not show it.

In the fall of 1960 Charlie enrolled in the American Civilization program to study material culture, the things that ordinary human beings made—artifacts in which scholars of more orthodox disciplines took little interest. The doyen of material culture at the University of Pennsylvania was Anthony Nicholas Brady Garvan, a Yale man who had made his career in the anthropology of industrial societies. His peers considered him an intellectual pioneer, the first chairman of American Civilization at UPenn. Garvan was like many men at the crest of successful careers who, in their generous hopes for the world they must eventually depart, begin to see their own reflection everywhere they look. He grew fond of his bright protégé. He adopted Hill, involved him in his academic projects, and eventually asked Charlie and Martha to move in.

Garvan's home in rural Spring House, Pennsylvania, was a nineteenth-century gentleman scholar's estate, with drafty halls and a long paneled library with tall windows and globes and antique astrolabes on oak tables. The estate's inherited name was Llan Gwydden, or "Church We Knew." Garvan preferred to translate the Welsh as "Height of Ecstasy." He told Charlie and Martha that their new home, the Tuscan-style three-story stone tower that stood behind the cottage amid horse and sheep pastures, had once been the rendezvous of J. P. Morgan and a certain Frances Markoe, the lady of the house and his mistress. Regardless of the tower's romantic past, there was no central heat and the toilet barely worked. Critters of some kind were always around — Priscilla, Mrs. Garvan's spoiled and diarrhea-prone Persian cat, whom the Hills had to baby-sit when she was sick, or the impudent horses that stuck their noses through the kitchen window at breakfast.

When I set out to find Llan Gwydden in the fall of 2003, Charlie thought I was embarking on a wild-goose chase. The estate had surely been subdivided and sold off to developers by now, he said. He was wrong. After some meandering, Rodney and I found a narrow dirt drive snaking through ancient oaks and maples from the nearest road, Penllyn Pike. Exhausted from his day as my tour guide, Rodney made one last check to be sure I had some idea how to get back, then climbed into his car and left me to explore on my own. The main house looked untouched since Charlie's time — photographs I brought back to show him confirmed that. The house was designed in the classic New England–Maine style, with a long, steep roof, dormer windows, and walls faced with wood shingle and stone. No one answered my knock, so I wandered around. A few yards away stood a cottage of similar style but more modest lines and, beside it, a long stone carriage house. Beyond those buildings were the barnyards and, a bit farther, Charlie's Tuscan tower.

In the cottage I found Beatrice, Anthony Garvan's second wife. She was dressed in jeans and wore her gray hair like a college girl. She couldn't have been much older than Charlie and had come to the estate long after Charlie and Martha departed, but she was quick to invite me in, dismiss some myths, and fill in others. "That J. P. Morgan story about the tower is garbage," she began. She had been through the archives herself. But the tales of beagling across the surrounding acres of forest and open fields were true. For a year Hill had earned his keep on the estate as the dog boy, for Garvan loved the hunt. As Beatrice explained, her husband kept thirty-five hunting beagles, and each Sunday Garvan, Charlie, and hunting friends invited along donned green jackets and black hunting caps and rode off at sunrise, whipping the beagles over the countryside in pursuit of an ill-starred jackrabbit. The prey were not native to Spring House. Garvan sent away to Kansas for them and they arrived each weekend in the mail, compressed in a cardboard box punched with breathing holes, held paralyzed but with enough life to rocket into the forest when Hill opened the box on Sunday morning.*

When I asked whether I could walk around and take pictures, Beatrice shrugged and left me on my own to imagine the hunts and the horses. I marveled at this time capsule that I had found, hidden away in a corner of suburban Philadelphia among odd Welsh street signs, scraggly remnants of woodland, and creeping strip malls. Beatrice later told me that the water table was too close to the surface of her property to allow digging, protecting it from developers. Before I left I shot a roll of film, black and white. To use color would have been off-key, poisoning what I was so delighted to capture, like setting a lost medieval chant to rock music.

Hill reveled in the lifestyle of Llan Gwydden. He had always wanted to be an aristocrat, even if he had suffered the misfortune to be born in small-town New Jersey. He was earning the straight As he had never received in law school and was beginning to find life in academia agreeable. But Garvan hired Hill with the idea that he would do all the work required to maintain the estate and still have time to finish his graduate research while joining in the weekend hunts and emulating his professor as much as possible. The task was too much. Hill could hardly be a full-time student when he had to paint and repaint ancient barns, muck out the stables, exercise the dogs and clean their kennel, among other, more morbid chores. "I had to bury a horse," he recalled. "It takes all day long. Try moving a dead horse. You can't be a grad student and do all these things."

There was also the problem of the United States Selective Service. After President John Kennedy's call to begin limited mobilization in August 1961 (in response to growing tensions with the Soviets over the status of Berlin), the pace of the national draft accelerated. Hill's acceptance into college and law school had earned him several years of exemption, but now that he had finished his second advanced degree, the draft board grew skeptical of his continuing academic pursuits. He

---

* The rabbits proved unsuitable to the mid-Atlantic climate, and soon foxes became the prey of choice.

suspected that his days as a farmhand intellectual were at an end, whether he liked it or not. The previous winter, well before he read about President Kennedy's announcement in the newspapers, Hill had taken—and passed—the Foreign Service exam. At the time enrollment in the Foreign Service released a young man from the predations of the draft board, but the appeal ran deeper for Hill.

He was a creature of his time. For those too young to remember the early cold war, it is impossible to comprehend the anxieties of those years: both the physical insecurity of the nuclear age and the intellectual peril that Western thinkers saw in the rise of Communism. As Whittaker Chambers wrote in *Witness,* his memoir of his time as a Soviet spy and testimony in the Alger Hiss espionage trial, "Few men are so dull that they do not know that the crisis exists and that it threatens their lives at every point. It is popular to call it a social crisis. It is in fact a total crisis—religious, moral, intellectual, social, political, economic. It is popular to call it a crisis of the Western world. It is in fact a crisis of the whole world." For Americans in the late 1950s and early 1960s —even sheltered university students—the anxiety was pervasive. Only a few years earlier, Secretary of State John Foster Dulles had stood at Philadelphia's Independence Square, not far from where Hill now lived and studied, and proclaimed that "freedom was at stake." Hill was drawn to government service just as a young man of faith might be drawn to serve his church as a missionary abroad.

Ever since Hill entered college he had read, and believed, the steady drift of journal articles and scholarly books decrying the crumbling of modern man and the philosophical and moral threats hatching on the other side of the Iron Curtain. From boyhood onward, he had been among that quiet breed of thinkers for whom books are the thing. As a university student, his most vivid intellectual moments were less often midnight dormitory debates with roommates than solitary encounters with ideas in print. He read John Buchan novels and books like Richard Weaver's *Ideas Have Consequences* (1948), all of which left him with a profound sense that the civilization he had been taught to worship and feed on was tenuous at best. If he did not grasp and defend its essentials, it might slip away. He heard a call to duty that he could not answer in a cloistered position in academia. And although he had yearned since his teen years to emulate American émigré writers in Paris, his first role models were those on his boyhood trading cards: the World War II heroes, men of patriotism and duty to a cause larger than themselves. A child's first hero often proves his most lasting one.

In less cerebral terms, Hill was bound by his parents' ideal of a responsible, professional son. He and his fellow students might be considered the last American generation that self-identified not as "youth"—self-appointed rebels fundamentally distinct from their parents—but as merely younger, though no less serious, versions of their mothers and fathers, their hometown doctors and attorneys. He was one of many like-minded young men at the University of Pennsylvania. But he was perhaps exceptional, among the scions of old Philadelphia families, for his South Jersey background, the sweltering days spent digging ditches next to black and immigrant workers, and the father who required him to take those summer jobs. Hill was always "anxious to please his father, and his father was not about to be pleased," recalled childhood friend Joe Evans. Charlie had been unable to fulfill his father's dream of a son in uniform at Annapolis. But the Foreign Service sounded a higher call that resonated with a familiar craving—that childhood appetite for adventure abroad, heretofore quenched only in storybooks found in Aunt Elsie's attic. The Foreign Service would take him as far from South Jersey as any Bridgetoner had yet gone.

However, to end the explanation there would be to dismiss what Hill claims was the greatest immediate motivation for his decision to join the Foreign Service: his mother-in-law.

Charles Hill had never encountered a personality like Florence Mitchell's. "She was always civil, always polite, but the genius of her was that she could convey volumes of emotion, feeling and censoriousness—or approval—through simply the nuances of tone in her language," Hill said. "She was a Grande Dame kind of woman who dominated any room she was in." Mrs. Mitchell did not want her daughter to marry Charlie. She herself had been offered a scholarship to Smith College but gave up her education to learn shorthand and support her mother. She was determined that Martha would not sacrifice herself in the same way. On Brown's graduation weekend, long after the other guests of Providence's Biltmore Hotel had retired for the evening (including Martha's father, whom Mrs. Mitchell had cudgeled into obedience years earlier), Florence argued with her daughter well into the night. She probably did not disapprove of Hill personally. A quiet, unassuming young man who appeared to fear women instinctively, Hill was among the least objectionable fiancés her daughter could have chosen. Mrs. Mitchell objected to the idea of Charlie—of anyone who would hinder her daughter's independence. "When I wanted to get married, she wasn't happy," Martha recalled. "I had the feeling that she would have loved to go to college, and she looked at me and thought, 'you went to college, and look what you did—just what I did.'"

The argument stormed on for more than five hours. Hill did not witness his fiancée's battle for independence. He stood uncomfortably in the corridor while Martha shuttled between him and her mother's bedroom all night. Mrs. Mitchell's chief concern was for her daughter to have a career in art. Every time Martha reappeared and summarized the most recent version of this demand, Hill tried to say something to convince Mrs. Mitchell that a married woman could have a career too. Martha trudged back to her mother to relay the message. In recalling the scene much later, Hill likened the scurrying back and forth to proximity talks during diplomatic negotiations in the Middle East—where Hill, as the diplomat, would prove skilled at concealing uncomfortable truths and allowing the negotiating parties to interpret ambiguities as they liked.

The wedding in August 1957 was pleasant in an awful sort of way, because Mrs. Mitchell would not stand to be defeated twice. Having lost control of her daughter, she seized command of the reception and managed every aspect of the event until it was impossible for anyone to enjoy it. "Everything was exactly right," Hill recalled. "The church was right, the dress was right, the bridesmaids were right, the guests were right. Everything was perfect. But her mother, maneuvering in and around the rooms and the church, just made—sheerly by her presence, not by any words she said—everybody know she was in a state of unimaginable fury about all of this, and that we would pay in one way or another."

Ever since the wedding, they had paid dearly. Martha's mother made the weekends miserable with Sunday phone calls that stretched for hours. From his safe position in the other room, Hill saw that his wife would hold the receiver to her ear without speaking, listening to her mother's harangue. The "conversations" often left Martha in tears. It's not clear that Hill knew how to comfort her. They usually spent what was left of the day occupied with the weekend chores. This cycle of domestic agony probably contributed more to Hill's decision to join the Foreign Service than the threat of the draft or the intellectual ferment of the 1950s. Many married people feel cursed by their in-laws, but Hill's recollections portray Florence Mitchell as a breed unto herself. "My mother and Charlie both had strong personalities, and that was never a wonderful relationship," Martha tactfully explained. Hill did not know how to achieve a truce with Mrs. Mitchell and bring the family to some kind of equilibrium. For all his later skill as a diplomatic negotiator, in his own home Hill saw no option but to flee. The Foreign Service was an ideal escape. It was a flight from family quarrels and a possible stint in the military, an evasion of his father's critical eye, and a response to an inner call to service. It was, more than all of these, an absolute break with the dull normals in his hometown, with whom he knew he did not belong.

Halfway through the Foreign Service Institute's tedious training program for new officers, Hill's instructors passed out note cards on which they asked the officers to write down their top choices for assignment abroad. They were also told to note the highest position in the Foreign Service to which they aspired. Hill wrote that he would like to go anywhere but Europe and that he aspired to become a member of the Policy Planning Staff. At the course's conclusion, the instructors announced that everyone in the class but Hill had listed Europe as first choice. Everyone except Hill yearned to become an ambassador.

In the tradition of bureaucracy's indifference to its smallest, youngest cogs, the initial assignments announced at the end of training had nothing to do with the new officers' wish lists. In the end Hill did not go abroad at all. He was assigned to Washington, D.C., to the Bureau of European Affairs, in the office that coordinated relations with the United Nations. A month after Hill's arrival, in October 1962 U-2 surveillance photographs revealed Soviet missile launch pads under construction in Cuba. The discovery plunged the world into the two-week brush with nuclear war known as the Cuban Missile Crisis.

Hill worked in Washington and cabled the paperwork to the U.S. Mission to the United Nations in New York, but the crisis meant more staff were needed on-site, so Hill was sent north. The day before the U.N. Security Council convened for what promised to be a protracted debate, he ducked into the men's room and found himself standing at a urinal next to Adlai Stevenson, the American ambassador to the United Nations. Stevenson looked over at Hill and asked, "Son, are you a diplomat?" Hill said that he was. Stevenson nodded and said, "Well, the first rule of diplomacy is: never pass up a chance to take a leak."

At the behest of his supervisor, in the days after Khrushchev's retreat and the end of the crisis Hill wrote a memorandum arguing that the time was ripe for a nuclear test-ban treaty. His was one of many memos suggesting the same thing, and although he never heard from his supervisor about the fate of his memo, he remains convinced that it was critical in prompting the round of negotiations that resulted in a treaty less than a year later. To credit the inspiration for renewed American-Soviet negotiations to a twenty-six-year-old junior officer fresh from his training seminar is a little preposterous, but Hill has never thought so. The lesson he learned from the incident—that he could personally affect policy decisions—had little to do with whether anyone important ever read his draft. It did not matter that no one noticed it. It was enough for Hill to believe he had made an impact. "It was all perfectly normal. This was what I had read about historian and diplomat George Kennan and others doing, and I was just doing it too," he told me. "This was what my education had prepared me to do. Here came a crisis, and this was the natural thing to ask, and I was the person to do the writing . . . I didn't see any reason why I shouldn't have been on the Policy Planning Staff right then."

This story is one of Hill's perennial favorites, one of the rare anecdotes from his Foreign Service career that he divulges in class. When I first heard the tale of the memo that inspired the first nuclear test-ban treaty, he was in the middle of a lecture on environmental issues in international relations. After recounting the anecdote, he smiled—an event like a total solar eclipse—and said, "I only say this in order to brag." The class slavered. I dutifully took down the story in my notebook and always wanted to know more. When my interviews with Charlie reached his early Foreign Service years, I asked after the now-famous memorandum. He told me the story again in all its theatric detail, the hours spent pacing his office and pulling books off the shelf, scratching out paragraphs in which he drew on his work in American Studies and anthropology, right down to his boss's enthusiasm when he read the draft. I dutifully took it all down once more.

Then I did a little homework. I pawed through the holdings in the Digital National Security Archive and at the National Archives in College Park, Maryland, squinting at endless rolls of State Department microfiche. I never found Charlie's memo—all that survives is a dog-eared routing slip—but I did find dozens of others that proposed essentially the same ideas. I began to wonder why Charlie's draft would have garnered more attention than other memoranda from senior officials that also proposed a thaw in the stalled test-ban treaty negotiations. A closer look at the one piece of evidence I had, the routing slip, did reveal an enthusiastic exhortation from Charlie's boss: "Take a look at this cosmic stuff!" But it also indicated that the memo was not sent straight to the top of the State Department, as Charlie had implied, but to Soviet Affairs, where it probably got stuck in a middle-tier bureaucrat's in box.

As my research continued, every other claim that Charlie made about his achievements would bear out when I checked it against other sources, and in the end it was surprising that the story of the test-ban treaty memo was the only tale that a proud old man embellished. Well, perhaps it wasn't the only one. Toward the end of my interview with Charlie's Ocean City friend Joe Evans, I asked about those football games on the beach. Was Charlie really the star quarterback, as he loved to claim? He was OK, Evans said, but certainly no better than anyone else. Charlie's claim that the other boys always deferred to him was hogwash. Really it was just a lot of smart-asses kicking up sand and tripping over one another, and who could make strategy out of that? Any man's memory can grow a bit rosy over the years. The moral is that reality often has little to do with the tactics of the mind.

In the Bureau of European Affairs, where Charlie finally left the university behind and began his work in the Foreign Service, his fantasies of a career in the realm of ideas — at least from the biographer's vantage point — were falling flat. It is hard to believe that a junior officer could find many intellectual challenges in the day-to-day paper pushing of a sprawling bureaucracy. Yet Charlie didn't see it that way. Other officers in his position probably resented the requests for memoranda, seeing them as busywork that no superior would actually read, but to Charlie there was no more meaningful act than putting his ideas to paper and feeding them to the great foreign policy machine. Was he optimistic or delusional? A timid cubicle dweller who was most comfortable writing alone, or a thinker with unusual confidence?

He was probably all these things. One of the great challenges that college graduates face is how to survive the revelation that the real world does not conform to the world of ideas. When he compared his generation to my own, Charlie would always point at my peers' desire to remain adolescents forever, to stay in school, join the Peace Corps, put off marriage, and do anything else to postpone adulthood. Perhaps his eager acceptance of the grown-up mantle, and the role model of a father who worked for decades at a job he never liked, eased Charlie's acceptance of the banalities of working life. But as I delved into his correspondence from those early years, I grew convinced that he was not bothered by the mundane parts of life for a more profound reason: he was instinctively able to transcend them, or at least convince himself that he had done so. These early years would have their tiresome moments, but Charlie would move on to loftier enterprises so quickly that he never entirely realized what he was leaving behind.

Charlie and Martha had barely settled into their quiet, shady neighborhood in Arlington when he learned that he was assigned to go to the U.S. consulate in Zurich, Switzerland, in early 1963. In the diary entry written after he got the news, Hill wrote one word: "depressed."

Martha was both excited and dismayed at the prospect of living abroad. In cheerier moments she saw her husband's new career as he did—an opportunity for adventure and service. Her attitude toward service sprang, like Hill's, from her upbringing. Since her childhood in the Congregational Church, Martha had been taught to embrace duty to one's fellow man: "it was easy for me to transfer that thinking to the Foreign Service," she explained. Nevertheless, she was scared for all the reasons a young wife would be scared of leaving home for a strange country. Martha's story—compelling to me at first only as a window onto the sliver of Charlie's life spent away from his work—would later force me to radically revise my understanding of my subject, and of myself. Here, a quiet young woman devoted to her husband entered the story on kitten's feet. But decades later, she would not exit the way she came.

To be a Foreign Service wife in the 1960s was a full-time occupation. The protocol and ceremony of the diplomatic social world was grueling, and if a woman performed her duties with anything less than complete social grace and cheerful spirit, she risked being "a hindrance to her husband's career and detrimental to the best interests of our country." Every new Foreign Service wife was warned that her husband would be judged not only on his own professional ability but on the merits of his spouse as well. The role of the Foreign Service wife had long been acknowledged—at least informally—as a challenging job that could benefit from a bit of education in the intricacies of social calls, diplomatic entertaining, and culture shock. By 1962, training took the form of a two-week course called General Orientation for Wives and Dependents, taught by Foreign Service officer Mary Vance Trent, one of the few women then in the service. By this time the course had evolved from an emphasis on social form to focus on subjects ranging from "problems of emerging nations; the function of the American Mission . . . how to answer questions about the United States" to suggestions on packing. Martha found the course pleasant. She received her graduation certificate in early December 1962 from Lady Bird Johnson. She also read through "that silly book," the Foreign Service Institute's official protocol handbook, *Social Usage Abroad,* complete with its helpful twelve-page appendix on the art of calling cards.

Martha's attitude toward her new life seemed buoyant to her husband. Although in one evaluation report Charlie's superior officers would argue over whether Martha was too "quiet and retiring" to be "an effective and pleasant hostess," the consensus seemed to be that "Mrs. Hill is a charming person, supporting [her husband] completely in his career plans, and is an excellent partner for representation purposes."* But it is difficult to reconcile the memory of the dynamic Pembroke undergraduate who had enchanted Hill not long ago — a blossoming artist who won her husband by strutting up to him unintroduced and kissing him on the mouth — with the deferential, status-seeking Foreign Service wife. Martha was not "the typical Foreign Service wife, by any means," said William Widenor, who served with Hill in Zurich. "She was much more intellectual — less interested in socializing, more interested in the arts. She was a very private person." Miss Trent assured her students that "the American wife in her role abroad does not have to try to make herself over into a different person when she goes to an overseas post, but rather . . . she needs mainly to recognize and learn to use the talents she has and pursue the interests she already possesses." If she heard those words, Martha must have had her doubts.

---

* Department of State Efficiency Report, July 13, 1964. Although the State Department's 1972 "Policy on Wives" would ostensibly release Foreign Service spouses from government service, the social obligations of women in Martha's position would for the most part remain. Feminine disgruntlement continued. Many Foreign Service wives still resented their "duties" and believed the policy statement was actually a setback, because at least in earlier years State Department efficiency reports (which evaluated the performance of both officer and spouse) had recognized their services. After 1972, although wives were still obligated to fulfill prescribed diplomatic social functions, they were invisible in the eyes of the government.

There was a simple explanation for why Martha made the sacrifices she did: she was very much in love with her husband. Notes and cards written to Charlie from Martha in the first years of the Hills' marriage are childlike in their affection. From the Hills' time in Philadelphia, there is a "get well soon" note, replete with tearful stick figures, scribbled in red pencil on the back of a University of Pennsylvania Library circulation slip. In a card presumably from Christmas 1957, Martha wrote a poem that leaves little doubt about her feelings for Charlie, although the lines are puzzlingly wistful for a newlywed celebrating her first holidays with her husband:

> The first Christmas
> Sparkles as the spiraling glitter of tinsel . . .
> The soft sadness
> Of past Christmases murmurs a whisper . . .
> I wrapped my package
> With love for you, and hid within the folded paper
> A special kiss which asks to be remembered
> Throughout the year.
> As we count our Christmases
> And the sad and happy times enrich the fugal tune
> Our love as solitary as the star
> Will create melody of our song.

The verse, printed carefully in swirling letters, is signed "Marty." The script is that of an artist, lovingly tooled. These cards are the handiwork of a young woman in love who thinks about her husband during odd moments at work and grabs the nearest scrap of paper to express her feelings, who is somberly romantic or heedless in her silliness when the mood strikes her. They are evidence of tender and committed love that—more than any sense of traditional feminine duty—was foremost in making a woman like Martha content to give up her own ambitions to support her husband. And it is worth noting that her husband—who would later speak with boastful frankness of losing touch with old friends and moving through life without a pang of nostalgia—saved even that penciled library slip for so many years.

The Hills arrived in Zurich in late February after nearly two weeks at sea (they landed at Genoa and rented a car to drive the rest of the way), checked into a hotel, and Charlie reported for work. The job quickly fell short of the romantic call to duty that had entranced him in Philadelphia. He spent his first day trying to arrange airplane transportation back to New York for an American woman who had suffered a nervous breakdown at a Swiss mountain resort and was now bound in a straitjacket and only partly pacified after three days of heavy sedation. The next day he had a contract dispute on his hands; on his third morning, he found himself drawing on his knowledge of criminal law. Hill, as the only consular employee with legal training, shortly became the consulate's de facto legal consultant, daily applying the segment of his education that satisfied him the least. The American consulate was tiny—staffed by only a half dozen at its busiest—and despite Hill's inexperience, his abilities did not go unnoticed. An early evaluation includes an observation that would, over the years, prove increasingly astute: "Mr. Hill has a keen and well-trained mind. His background in history, anthropology, and law give[s] him the advantage of several frames of reference. He is able to see several solutions to a problem and to evaluate their various effects. He is logical always, and if he were any sounder in his judgments he would lose the originality which he possesses in abundance."

Hill wrote his parents that his job was "interesting and not dull, but I am not pleased with it. Too much of it seems unnecessary and not too important. I have the feeling that if the Consulate closed, the business that it does would just cease to exist . . . the problems wouldn't have to be taken elsewhere; they would just die a natural death. It's like when you have a physician for a neighbor, you constantly talk to him about medical problems but if he left town you wouldn't go elsewhere, you'd just stop talking about it."

He escaped the office as often as he could. To Hill, Switzerland was, as Lord Byron once described it, a "curst, selfish, swinish country of brutes placed in the most romantic region in the world." The couple took day hikes with friends, learned how to ski, and made the occasional excursion to find a prehistoric Alpine cave Hill had discovered in a book. Hill's job took him into the countryside as well, for among the duties of consular employees was carrying out the last will and testament of any U.S. citizen who died on Swiss soil. The Swiss landscape attracted Americans of a whimsical sort; many requested that after cremation their ashes be scattered over some Swiss natural wonder prominent in their rosiest memories. This task fell upon Hill. He waited until four or five urns collected on his office shelf, then took a couple of days' leave to fulfill his countrymen's last wishes—which brought him to the Jungfrau, the north face of the Eiger, and other dramatic sites of eternal rest. These weren't summit-bound quests equipped with crampons and ice picks, but one can ascend surprisingly high in an ordinary, unassisted fashion, even in the Alps.

Hill reveled in the days he spent by himself, but Martha's letters home, filled with blithe accounts of parties and ski vacations, betray loneliness.* She kept busy with the apartment and consular social functions, and she also studied German and volunteered long hours visiting Americans in area hospitals. When the Hills finally found an apartment after months of a hotel-room existence, most of their belongings shipped from home were still lost in transit. But this inconvenience didn't exempt Martha from her social duties, so she served dinner on packing crates draped with a tablecloth. Her inventiveness paid off, and she came to know a few people she could call on as friends. But now and then, she admitted it outright: "Sometimes the days can get very lonely," Martha wrote to Bridgeton on August 27, 1963. "If I didn't go to the hospitals there would be many days when I would never speak to a soul with the exception of perhaps the butcher."

Zurich felt strangest and loneliest on the cold day in late November when the Hills learned that President Kennedy had been shot. Martha later recalled that she and Charlie had been out late that evening. As they parked the car and walked up the front steps, a neighbor leaned out her window and shouted, "Turn on the radio. Something's hap-

---

* Besides Charlie, the character that figures most prominently in Martha's letters is their cat, Molly. Rare is the letter that ends without reference to Molly's latest mischief in the garden, her feline opinions of the Swiss people, or Martha's concerns over the cat's emotional state. The cat's importance in these letters is endearing and curious. Particularly touching is Martha's account of a summer night on which Molly escaped the apartment to roam the neighborhood: "Charlie and I also roamed all night and didn't get a wink of sleep. Can you see us in the dead quiet of a Swiss neighborhood down on hands and knees, climbing over fences whispering 'Molly.' I was sure she was killed of course but he was worried too. About 5am we were exhausted and went to bed with our clothes on. About 6:30 C. got up to look again and there she was crouched at the door. We could have killed her." A reader who did not know better would assume Molly was a lost toddler, rather than a pet cat notorious for eating Martha's bean plants and then vomiting them onto her kitchen floor, not to mention the occasional act of strategic defecation upon Charlie's pillow. How could the phlegmatic Charles Hill be so distressed about a cat? Perhaps he was only humoring Martha. Or perhaps a cat, no matter how unfriendly and finicky about her canned food, wins a special place in a childless family still new in a strange country.

pened to your president." They rushed in, switched on the news, and sat cross-legged on the floor, crying. Martha was called to pull together notes of sympathy to send back to the States. When she interrupted a party for this purpose, the hostess was shocked and offended. "We seemed to be on a different wavelength than everyone we talked to and never felt more out of touch with America than that Friday night and the following day," Martha wrote to Bridgeton. In their first tour abroad, both Charlie and Martha had grown frustrated squinting homeward with only the aid of press reports, memoranda, and belated letters. Kennedy's assassination was a harbinger of the mounting upheaval in the country they had left. But it gave no sign of the country they would find when they returned.

The Hills were not long for Zurich. One weekend that winter, high in the mountains at Stoos, while skiing by himself on wooden skis with ancient bindings that scarcely worked, Hill slammed into a hidden log and broke his left ankle. He managed to get down to the base of the mountain, by which time he appeared to bystanders to be in a state of shock. There followed something of a hero's welcome. Afterward he was cemented into a cast and told not to move for several weeks. "That was when I decided this is no way to live in this lousy European place," he said.

Hill applied for hard language training.* The Foreign Service offered him the choice of Chinese or Farsi; he chose the former, thinking it would qualify him for more posts. After little more than a year at the Zurich consulate, a place of small problems, unmemorable human tragedies, and the first cadences of patterns that would continue in later years on other continents, the Hills departed Switzerland. They spent an unremarkable year back in Washington while Hill studied Mandarin at the Foreign Service Institute in the first year of a two-year language program. The following year he would continue his studies on Taiwan. Then he assumed his post as a China watcher at the U.S. consulate in Hong Kong, analyzing from afar the obscure giant to the north, where American diplomats were not permitted to set foot. He wanted responsibilities more exciting than his job in humdrum Zurich, and he would find them. Work in Hong Kong would begin in summer 1966: the early months of China's Great Proletarian Cultural Revolution.

---

* Foreign Service jargon for training in non-European languages.

4

CHARLIE AND MARTHA CONCLUDED WHILE LIVING IN SWIT-
zerland that they would not be able to have children of their own. The
medical reasons were never clear, but Hill reasoned that creosote, a
brownish-black oily liquid used as a wood preservative, which he had
handled during summer construction jobs as a young man, had seeped
through his skin and damaged his reproductive organs. Not long after
their arrival in Taiwan, Martha had immersed herself in the adoption
process. She first mentioned the idea of adopting a Chinese baby in a
letter to Bridgeton in the late fall of 1965. She assured Charlie's parents, Morton and Alvenia, that adoption was "a very natural thing to
do," even when the baby was separated from South Jersey blood by
thousands of miles and the eyes, skin, and hair of another race.

A month later there came another letter. After Martha wrote about
the fat little cedar she had decorated for Christmas in their living room
and the carols issuing from the record player, she told of two twin boys.
Martha wanted to bring them home, but after she and Charlie visited
the orthopedic surgeon in Changhua, the babies were diagnosed with
congenital hip dysplasia. The Chinese doctor, to be precise, told them
the boys had "hip displeasure" and noted that the condition was thoroughly treatable, even in the more seriously afflicted twin, as long as
that little boy spent his first six months lying on his back in a brace.
Martha was attached to the twins but knew it would be smartest to wait
and take a healthy baby. Charlie said they would have no boys at all —
not in China, where the only boys left in the orphanages were sickly or
retarded. But they had spent long days with the twins, taking them
from doctor to doctor and watching the babies cry and laugh. "I just
can't get the poor little things out of my mind," Martha wrote to
Bridgeton at Christmastime.

The first baby Martha brought home was a three-week-old girl named Sara Elizabeth. The doctor assured the Hills that she was one of the healthiest orphans he had seen. With this approval, Charlie went to Taipei to handle the paperwork and Martha began shopping madly, she told Morton and Alvenia in a letter dated March 26, 1966. Adoption day was a profusion of misplaced passports and contrary Chinese officials. By the time Martha found a moment to sit down with pen and paper, Sara was peaceful in her crib, sleeping on her tummy for the first time, "beautifully," Martha wrote — as any new mother would write of her child, particularly a mother for whom the child was not a biological miracle but a hard-earned one.

If the doctors had had the proper instruments to listen, they would have detected in Sara's tiny chest an irregular echo hardly discernible beyond the healthy heartbeat. But they did not hear it, and the first sign of the hole in the baby's heart came when her mother noticed a bluish tinge to her lips. Charlie was away on a business trip in Hong Kong. A medic drove Martha from their home in Taichung to the hospital in Taipei where she stayed with Sara, sleeping a few hours each night at a friend's house and keeping vigil over her baby, who had already learned to smile and laugh when Martha peered over her crib. Charlie drove up to the hospital on weekends, although Sara was still a stranger to him.

The little girl died after three weeks in the hospital. They buried her in an old missionary cemetery at Tan Shui, west of Taipei, alongside the churchmen and clipper-ship sailors who had found rest there too, long ago.

Not long afterward, Martha's friend Sue Fowler came racing up the road on her bicycle. Sue had been watching her friend's agonizing attempts to adopt a child, and she had told Martha, as Martha probably knew herself, that they must have a baby before she and Charlie departed for his post in Hong Kong. Now Sue had news of one, a beautiful baby, a real screamer. Martha hopped on her bicycle and the two hustled to the orphanage.

Flushed and out of breath, Martha fell instantly in love. This baby was fierce and loud. Her size and sturdiness — more impressive than that of the other babies in the Taiwan Provincial Orphanage — hinted that her parents were from the north, but no one could know for certain. She had tawny skin and bright almond eyes the color of ink. Her fuzzy black hair stood up straight. Most of all, Martha loved how the baby yelled from the depths of her swaddling clothes, because it was a loud, determined, healthy sound and the child kept at it with no sign of stopping.

However, it was not easy for an American couple to adopt a Chinese child, particularly parents due to leave the island so soon. They had adopted Sara with the help of Western missionaries, but the Taiwan Provincial Orphanage was run by Chinese who had never dealt with couples—let alone Americans—who wanted to adopt. Adoption for them was an odd and unnatural thing. The children in orphanages, they believed, were castaways and derelicts.

Several tense weeks of negotiation ensued over the fate of the little girl, who would be named Catharine Lynne (Katie). Mrs. Li, the stern, square woman who ran the orphanage, came over for tea. Happily, she was impressed by the Hills' Brown class yearbook, which happened to be lying around. She took the fact that the Hills had been classmates as an "auspicious sign" and proof that they were educated, responsible, and as adequate as could be hoped for foreigners. "The next day she handed me Katie and said, 'You can have her,'" said Martha. "There was no paperwork, not a scrap."

It was delicately suggested that the Hills might make a donation to the orphanage and hold a traditional baby shower for all local "friends," Chinese and American. The Hills purchased a noodle machine to trade to the orphanage for their baby and held the party—for which Martha and Sue had to prepare seventy red eggs, one for each guest, to represent their dismay at having a girl, and hopes for good luck with having a baby boy next time. The boiling and the dyeing took nearly all night, and the eggs required immediate distribution because of the hot weather and cheap pigment in the dye, purchased at the local market. It stained the women's fingers a blotchy scarlet.

The party's first order of business was a group photograph, for which no one smiled except Sue. Mrs. Li stood in the center and cradled Katie solemnly, like a wary grandmother about to entrust a breakable to neighbor children of probable recklessness. Then the group trundled over to the language school, rang a celebratory note on the building's large bell, and set Katie in her plastic rocker in the middle of a table inside. Everyone peered at her. "The Chinese in our language school were dubious about this. They thought we were getting a throwaway child," said Martha. "But we dressed Katie up, and she was very well behaved, and they were all impressed." Martha and Sue passed around the eggs. The dye was sticky in the sweltering heat, and within minutes everyone's fingers were red.

Repulse Bay, on the Pacific side of Hong Kong Island, was green and shaped like a yawning mouth. Charlie and Martha took an apartment in a building not a hundred yards from the gracious Repulse Bay Hotel, a sprawling Victorian structure built over the foothills bordering the beach. It was a quiet place for a baby. Martha found it agreeable. Cloud-topped inland hills lay between her family and the beaming electric signs for Rolex and Hitachi, the swarming streets, shantytowns, and glass and metal high-rises vaulting above Victoria Harbor. There would be rumors, during more disturbed times, of pale bodies floating from the mainland down the Pearl River, but these were always less terrible for their demands on her imagination.

Hill's life would be in the city, at the American consulate. The consulate, like every other manmade structure, was nearly swallowed by Hong Kong's spectacles of wealth and entanglements of horrible poverty. From the air, roofs of squatter huts appeared as one contiguous tiled surface, and downtown the rickshaws, taxis, and narrow stairstep "ladder streets" wound their way through the din of market stalls, steaming food, electric signs, flapping laundry, and hawkers of every conceivable good. The crowds spilled over onto the water, where one hundred thousand people lived on thirteen thousand junks and sampans, some connected by wooden planks to form floating villages with their own restaurants, tailors, and markets, and water taxis for trips to school, work, or the red-light districts in Wan Chai and Kowloon, perpetually ablaze with neon light.

Although the gleaming skyscrapers were the first image a visitor saw when approaching the harbor from the north, one of every twelve Hong Kong residents lived in a self-made wooden shack, morbidly perishable structures piled on top of one another's rotting pilings and tin roofs. In recent years, after a fire in 1953 destroyed many of the settlements, the British authorities had moved the homeless into mass resettlement estates. There were hundreds of these airless, dismal apartment complexes in the colony by the time the Hills arrived. The dingy cement blocks were ringed by green, red, or yellow balconies fluttering with laundry, like huge dormant serpents shedding their scales, all within striking distance from the luxurious high-rise apartments just above the city. In nearby Causeway Bay, a floating village of hundreds of houseboats lay packed together behind the typhoon shelter, only yards from the glistening white sailing rigs of the Hong Kong Yacht Club.

The city was engorged with life, growing, consuming, and dying, like an anthill at the foot of a looming mountain. The presence of mainland China was eternally palpable in the stony faces of People's Liberation Army border guards on the other side of the barbed wire beyond the New Territories on the mainland (the farthest reaches of British colonial control), and in the cheaply printed Communist leaflets that fluttered about the streets with the rest of the city's rubbish, warning of Red power and grinning with Chairman Mao's round face. The Communists acquired nearly half their annual hard currency — some $500 million — through foreign exchange and commerce in the colony, most of which was controlled from the Bank of China building downtown. Whatever its imperialist affront to Chinese pride, Hong Kong was safe from serious interference because, for those on the mainland, it remained more profitable than embarrassing.

Hill was a China watcher. The United States had no diplomatic relations with the People's Republic of China,* so he and his colleagues could not visit the country themselves, seek meetings in Beijing, or use any of the tools normally available to diplomats charged with bridging the distance between their country and another. In July 1966, when Hill began the job, Mao Zedong's Great Proletarian Cultural Revolution was near its apogee. The corpses in the Pearl River and streams of refugees testified to the brutality of the upheaval but told China watchers little else. They had to rely on what the Chinese told themselves in their daily newspapers.

Chairman Mao's first call for renewed criticism against "reactionary bourgeois ideology" came the year before Hill's arrival in Hong Kong. In the fall of 1965, Mao, his radical wife, Jiang Qing, and other ideo-

---

* The United States continued to recognize the Guomindang, the Nationalist government that had taken up residence on Taiwan since its defeat on the mainland in 1949, as the legitimate government of China. Americans were not permitted entry to the People's Republic of China until détente with Beijing following President Nixon's 1972 visit, which allowed for controlled cultural exchanges and tourism. Relations between the United States and China were not formalized until 1979.

logues in his inner circle launched an attack on a playwright named Wu Han, whose allegorical work was construed as criticism of the chairman. Mao used the playwright as a scapegoat from whose disgrace he could launch a renewed push to purge China of those who were impeding total revolution by "taking the capitalist road" or otherwise weakening Mao's grip on the country. Although driven in part by Mao's personal insecurities and the ambitions of his wife and People's Liberation Army commander Lin Biao, the Cultural Revolution would prove much murkier than simply an evolving conflict between those who vied for control of China. It became a wild effort to refocus the energy of China's younger generation to re-create the revolutionary spirit Mao remembered from his days on the Long March. As is true with most social movements that inspire the young and the opportunistic, it became impossible for the old leadership to control. Life in China was incomprehensible to most living in the midst of it. One can only imagine the task of the men hunched over desks somewhere on the tiny island to the south.

By the summer of 1966, Mao declared that the Communist Party had failed to purge itself of "revisionist elements" or fully mobilize the masses. He disbanded the team of high Party officials that had been in charge of the Cultural Revolution and effectively turned over power to the Red Guards, newly assembled squads of students who were to become the vanguard of the proletarian revolution. Mao called on them to "bombard Party headquarters." The Red Guards instituted a reign of terror on China's intellectual community, beating their professors and dragging "bourgeois intellectuals" out of their homes to march in the street, wearing dunce caps and placards around their necks. They took captive old cadres and subjected them to "airplane flight," hanging their victims in the air and swinging them by ropes tied to each limb — one of the milder punishments in the Red Guard repertoire. Younger children were caught up in the fury, which made for even more shocking scenes. A correspondent for the West German magazine *Kristall* recorded a procession of fifty eight- and ten-year-olds carrying sticks, pieces of iron, and leather straps who seized an old woman who had fallen nearby and beat her until she bled. The police did not intervene.

In Hong Kong, struggling to keep his head above the constant inflow of information, Hill had no time to assess thoughtfully the leftist extremism among pockets of youth on the mainland, the radical groups that broke away from Mao's commandments and tried to wrest power for themselves. But a couple of years later the Foreign Service would send him home for a brief time to reflect. Then he would see China's radical youth in the context of student demonstrators on American campuses and at universities around the world. While watching China, Hill first glimpsed youth as a force, as mystic believers, as defiers of reason who were puritanical in their self-righteousness and absolutism, cavalier in destroying the record of their own history and culture. Mao, in selecting the youth of China as the primary engine for his Cultural Revolution, perhaps underestimated these qualities. For Hill, whose true encounter with what the 1960s had wrought upon his own country would come only after he returned there in person, the story of the American decade began here, in the view from Hong Kong.

Out of this violent ferment, foreign observers tried to decipher who held real power in China and in what direction that power was headed. The China watchers were also under orders from Washington to look for any indication that China might interfere in the conflict in Vietnam, where the United States was increasingly mired in its attempt to buttress the government of South Vietnam against aggression by the Communists in Hanoi. Additionally, Hill and his colleagues were to watch for who in the Communist Party's top ranks might be "moderates" capable of encouraging policies less hostile to the West—pragmatic officials who might prove to be more flexible, especially after Mao's death. But fieldwork in Communist China was impossible for American officers and would remain so for the foreseeable future. Dispatches written by non-American journalists and political officers who were permitted entry into the country were of limited usefulness because Beijing kept close control over what foreign observers could see and with whom they were permitted to speak. Interviews with refugees from the mainland had their place in the consulate's intelligence, but it was a restricted one, as most of the refugees were from nearby Canton and could hardly provide a full, unbiased account of a country the size of a continent.

For the China watchers in Hong Kong, these limitations left only the surfeit of material published by the Communist Party. China watching had been more straightforward in the years before the Cultural Revolution, when the Chinese model of command publication still resembled that of other totalitarian states. As Lenin had written in his 1902 treatise, *What Is to Be Done?*, the functions of every official newspaper after the revolution were amplified to become the primary expression of Party will. Newspapers were the central link between the Party and the masses. They contained signals of policy changes, requests for practical implementation, and notice—although encoded in puzzling propaganda and catch phrases—of sea changes in political power and personal favor. Every word was deliberately selected and consistently employed. Language, in the Party's view, was not so much for expressing information as for controlling it.

By the summer of 1966, however, this framework had changed. Beijing no longer controlled the country's mass media. The explosion of Red Guard factions and other opportunist rebel groups, many of whom seized control of existing publications or created their own, made it much more difficult for China watchers to determine the source or motive of the information they received. Hoaxes and falsified reports were a constant concern. There were endless lines of "refugees" with questionable personal histories and great scoops to sell. At one point in Hill's Hong Kong tenure, a secret radio broadcast that claimed to be "the voice of the liberation army" urging rebellion against Mao was eventually traced to a group of Nationalists on Taiwan. After the Cultural Revolution began, China watchers were flooded with "much less reliable material," said Hill's colleague in Hong Kong Nicholas Platt. "But much more interesting. All of it represented a truth of some kind."

Hill's job, therefore, was to be a person on whom nothing was lost. He could miss no subtle change in vocabulary or allusion in propaganda editorials, no unannounced reordering of officials in a Party photograph. He had to see everything. He became "a one man information retrieval center," wrote his supervisor, "promptly producing either from memory or orderly files the raw material [used] by other officers for analytical reports." He came to work early to read the day's newswires, papers, and radio broadcasts (translated both in-house and by a helpful Jesuit priest who translated Chinese radio from his basement apartment). There followed a late-morning meeting with the other officers in his section, with whom he discussed what he'd read. Once a week, the more serious-minded China watchers and journalists posted in and around Hong Kong met for lunch at a Wan Chai restaurant to trade hunches and talk about Chinese politics. Hill spent each afternoon researching and writing cables and sometimes in the evenings attended parties where the guests stood around debating what in the world it all meant. Martha went too and found these gatherings more tolerable than the parties in Zurich. "We weren't talking about nothing," she said. "You had the feeling that history was happening while you were living there."

Hill became an expert on the political personalities of the Chinese Communist Party. Preserved in his papers are innumerable index cards of names, ranks, and dates of each figure's most recent public appearance. He maintained thick dossiers on every Party official, major and minor, complete with grainy mug shots. He drew most of his information from propaganda, the stories that different factions were telling themselves for their own purposes. One is reminded of the opening to Book I in Herodotus's *History*, in which Herodotus grants space to the Persian chroniclers' self-serving account of the Trojan War. Herodotus clearly sympathizes with the Greeks, but for him it is important to grant "how the Persians say it happened." There is often some truth in even the most outrageous lie—if that is how one party explains reality to itself—which always merits recording.

As months passed and Hill continued to watch, record, and work through the available material, it became clear that he lacked the sympathy many of his colleagues felt for Communist China. His training in American Studies predisposed him to react strongly to what he saw happening on the mainland, where those obliged to safeguard cultural artifacts were destroying them. Hill was a student of every civilization he encountered in the same manner as he had studied his own at graduate school. In what little free time he had left in the evenings, he stayed up late reading any book he could get his hands on about life in imperial Beijing, regional Buddhist practices, turn-of-the-century missionary accounts, or classical Chinese poetry. He came to adore Confucius, and he read voraciously of the ancient ethicist and would-be imperial counselor. In the seventeenth century John Milton, another of Hill's intellectual heroes, wrote that Confucius deserved all credit for preserving China from the throes of revolution—his wise lawgiving sustained the Chinese people, nourished their religion, and braced their monarchs. Now China was insane, willfully destroying its internal coherence, the accountability that came with respect for antique virtues. This, for Charles Hill, was the gravest of crimes.

To Hill, the Cultural Revolution was also proof of a disturbing fact: not twenty years after the Communist revolution, China's leaders had produced a generation of youth capable of tearing down thousands of years of tradition and social structures, and eager to do so. The great

English keeper of institutions, Edmund Burke, had warned of this when Hill read his *Reflections on the Revolution in France* (1790) as an undergraduate. If Hill had not seized on that conservative creed then, he did now. The Cultural Revolution proved the fragility of culture, no matter how old and formerly esteemed. It showed up the total breakdown that happens when adults fail—or refuse—to pass down cultural inheritance to their children. And perhaps the dark-haired child playing quietly with Martha on the calm green side of the island was a living reminder of youth's blank slate and restless energy. She may have done her part, when she greeted her father upon his arrival home every night, to make him ponder the force of the young and the guidance owed them.

All at once, the chaos on the mainland was not so remote.

The Hills had never known Hong Kong as a peaceful place. There had been times when the consulate warned Foreign Service families to avoid going downtown. Martha had heard stories of homemade pipe bombs left in paper bags on park benches or hidden inside children's playthings. Once while she was walking downtown by herself, a middle-aged Chinese man walked up to her and shouted at her in Chinese. She shouted back in Chinese, which ended the confrontation. But violence was the exception rather than the rule, until the spring of 1967.

It was in May that the Communists in Hong Kong decided to organize. Possibly they were encouraged by the Portuguese capitulation on Macao the previous winter and the recent Maoist political victory in Canton, just up the Pearl River. Whatever the impetus, in May Communist agitators chose to exploit a strike at Hong Kong Artificial Flower Works and a dispute in a local cement factory, touching off the worst riots the colony had yet seen. The fighting spread in waves through Kowloon's slums, then spilled through the banyan trees on Nathan Road, where British police struck back at the Communist demonstrators with clubs and guns that fired wooden bullets. As spring turned to brutally hot summer, the riots lost momentum, but local strikes and unrest continued. The colony's water supply, which came from reservoirs on the mainland, grew tenuous—turned on only briefly every few days. When they could, residents stockpiled buckets of water in their apartments. The shortage affected those on the island's quieter eastern coast as much as it did those in the city, including Martha, who had a tiny girl to bathe and feed.

The photographs of the riots published by the Communist press in Hong Kong were graphic: helmeted British police in smart khaki shorts and shiny boots beating back protesters with billy clubs and tear-gas cannons; lines of Chinese clutching Little Red Books despite broken noses and bloodied shirts, standing at mass rallies shaking their fists in the air before an enormous portrait of Mao. Hill recalled standing on the roof of the consulate as endless lines of Red Guards marched around the building and on down Garden Hill Road—so many that the procession lasted six or seven hours. In the aftermath, corner shops were reduced to burnt-out husks and Communist-run "patriotic" schools lay ransacked by the British. Factory loudspeakers were silent, shot through with bullet holes when the police had tried to silence their blaring Maoist anthems. The sidewalk was scorched, in some places, from gunfire.

Hill later maintained that he was not scared that summer. "I've never been perturbed by things like that," he said. "It's just a sense that that's the way the world is. I think it's how my father brought me up—to be courageous, intrepid, to know that this is what you do. I don't think it through and say, 'now I've got to be brave.' I've just been phlegmatic about these things." There is, of course, a difference between unqualified guts and the deft camouflaging of fear, perhaps even from oneself. Hill had one or the other, and for all practical purposes, it did not matter which.

Newsweek claimed that the riots were subdued by classic Brit tenacity and the Hong Kong silent majority's distaste for violence. A more substantial reason may have been Premier Zhou Enlai's successful expulsion of the Party's ultra-radicals in late 1967, which coincided with the abrupt end of the Hong Kong uprisings. The China watchers tried to determine how closely, if at all, Beijing had directed the riots. Despite the striking timing of Zhou Enlai's ouster of the radicals, most observers quoted by American newsmen believed that the Hong Kong Communists, removed from the mainland's convulsions in the Cultural Revolution but anxious to prove their loyalty to Chairman Mao, were agitating without guidance from Beijing. Nick Platt, recalling one afternoon he spent on the consulate roof watching Hong Kong cadres drive up to the governor's mansion in their Mercedes-Benzes and wave their Little Red Books in the air, suggested that the Hong Kong Communists, eager to pretend they weren't completely bourgeois, saw the riots as a chance to cover themselves. Platt wasn't so sure that Beijing had no control, but many of his colleagues concluded that Beijing's leaders were too overwhelmed by the domestic crisis to have the time or the energy to control or incite their minions abroad. "The chaos in China is so great," said an American observer to *Newsweek*, that Communist rioting outside the country "might as well be carried out by the Rotary Club of Dubuque for all the meaning it has for Peking."

Hill was convinced that Beijing directed the riots that summer. Perhaps Mao's inner circle did not monitor every union strike or demonstration, but the unrest would not have happened if they had not wished it to. Otherwise the Cultural Revolution, which had begun on the mainland almost two years earlier, would have long ago spilled over into Hong Kong. By the time of the Hong Kong riots, the Chinese army had already begun to rein in the chaos on the mainland. "The prairie fire was out at the center," said Platt. "But, as in prairie fires, the edges were still hot." He and Hill believed Beijing had kept the chaos in check, only now allowing its operatives in the colony to instigate riots serious enough to demonstrate to the British, the Americans, and the rest of the world that China could have Hong Kong if it so desired. It was part of the Communists' grand Maoist strategy. The Cultural Revolution had begun, after all, with a plan to restructure society, to reengineer the lives and the minds of billions of individuals. Nothing could be grander than that. But Mao made graver mistakes than failing to read his Edmund Burke. A leader who tries to ignore the will and imagination of his citizens may get far, but inevitably the leviathan begins to move to its own rhythms, with or without him.

Hong Kong, despite its precarious status, had more to offer Martha than any other post to which the duties of a Foreign Service spouse had yet taken her. There is nothing like a new baby to occupy a woman's mind and heart, and Katie took up most of Martha's time and energy while her husband was at work in the city. Charlie loved his new daughter, but he was, like many professional men of his time, a father of medical emergencies, athletics, and mandatory-attendance academic ceremonies. Until Katie grew old enough to begin having some of those, his involvement in her life was limited. He later admitted that he did not make enough time for his family in Hong Kong, "and that's not an admirable characteristic," he said. "But I was wrapped up in my work. I thought that was the most important thing." When he did come home, he never left his work at the office. "At dinner, we talked about The World," recalled Martha. "Maybe we should have talked more about ourselves." The daily stuff of diapers, skinned knees, and favorite storybooks was mostly up to Martha and the Hills' amah, Ah Wong, who made herself more indispensable every day.

In the final months of 1968, when Katie was two years old and the Hills had lived in Hong Kong long enough to feel partly at home, they decided to adopt a second child. Hill ran across a tiny advertisement in one of the colony's Chinese newspapers that read, "A leaf has fallen from the tree of Hua," announcing that a new baby had been abandoned in a doorway on Mindin Road and taken to the colony orphanage. The orphanage was a bleak concrete building located in a scrubby part of the New Territories. The façade was in ill repair and there was a sad metal swing set in the inner courtyard. In the places where the hard dirt had not been rubbed naked, there were mean brown patches of grass. There were never any children on the playground.

A Miss Yang was the Hills' caseworker. She hardly compared to Mrs. Li, but she was formidable in her own right. She did not permit the Hills to enter the building; Martha later said that she was grateful they had not been allowed to see the state of affairs inside. A staff member met the Hills in the reception center with the tiny girl, swaddled in the traditional manner of orphanages that were barely equipped to handle their charges at all, let alone permit babies to roll over, crawl about, or put things in their mouths.

The baby, whom the Hills would name Emily, was quieter than Katie but seemed to them just as beautiful. Half a year passed before they were able to finish all the paperwork and bring her home. Because Emily had been abandoned, the British orphanage allowed the natural parents a six-month grace period to reclaim her. One day at the end of December, Miss Yang called at eleven in the morning to inform them that the final release paper had arrived and they could pick up Emily that day if they could get there by the 12:30 P.M. closing time. They raced across the island by car, caught a ferry, and made it to the orphanage at 12:15. By then, Emily had spent her critical first six months unable to move her arms or legs in her swaddling clothes or do much of anything except stare at the ceiling and "play with her fingers in a complicated fashion, as if they were 'toys,'" recalled Martha. Emily had been deprived of almost all sensory stimulation and hardly responded to anyone or anything until the ferry ride on the *Twinkling Star* across Victoria Harbor to Hong Kong Island, when she began to wake up. In a letter to Bridgeton, Martha described Emily's state after a week in her new home, when she finally began to smile and show interest in toys: "She is a bubble blower and a real gurgler and seems to be highly amused at all activity around her . . . Emily is very alert and sparkly eyed although like mush physically. She has never been put on her tummy so the back of her head is awful looking — all bald from where it has been rubbed so much and slightly scarred from the boils she has had from lying on it so much (she doesn't have them now). She has never been outside either so a lot of things will have to come slowly."

The first week was hard. Emily, like any baby, was distressed as she began to realize her life had changed, and her older sister was not sure what to make of this new creature in the house that was suddenly receiving all her parents' attention. Martha held Emily all through her first night home, while Charlie lay with Katie, who clung to him and kept waking up and crying about horrible nightmares. Over the next few days, the baby found her struggles to sit up or turn over enhanced by a constant stream of neighborhood admirers, who peered at her and raved loudly at Emily, who was oblivious, in front of Katie, who was not. "Charlie was just wonderful and when Kate did get over her head with all the excitement and newness, he would just take her out and get her away from it for a while," Martha wrote to Morton and Alvenia. Charlie did his part to help because what was needed of him was obvious. Small children are much more rational than their teenage and adult counterparts. But he could not remain home for long and neglect his work at the consulate, which had grown more demanding than ever in the past few months. Happily Ah Wong, their amah, was still available to run errands and help Martha manage the house. She was so taken by her employers' adopted girls that she asked the Hills to intercede with their contacts at the British orphanage to help her adopt a baby of her own when the Hills' tour in Hong Kong was due to end in a few months' time. No one could blame her. The Hill family was outwardly an attractive model, like a fine piece of china whose glaze's tiny cracks seemed more likely to be natural crazing, an unavoidable result of the kiln and part of the look of the piece, rather than real fissures that would crumble with time.

In late 1968, Hill's focus at work shifted from China's internal politics to growing trouble along its 4,300-mile border with the Soviet Union, where clashes with the Soviets over desolate borderlands had caught the attention of Washington. Tension with the Russians in China's northwestern border region dated back centuries. As American politicians often forgot, the brief period of strategically expedient goodwill between Beijing and Moscow from 1949 to the late 1950s was an anomaly amid centuries of mutual suspicion and conflict. Border incidents between the Soviets and the Chinese had reignited in 1959. In early 1966, the Soviets began shifting well-trained troops equipped with the latest weaponry from posts in Eastern Europe to the Far East. There followed the abrupt appearance of nuclear-tipped surface-to-surface missiles in the Siberian border regions and overtures toward the Mongolians, who suddenly found themselves the beneficiaries of Soviet-led modernization. Beijing boiled at reports of Soviet attempts to provoke insurrection among ethnic minorities in China's border regions. Unnerved in August 1968 by the Soviets' brutal suppression of the Prague Spring democratizing movement in Czechoslovakia, the Chinese began publicly to denounce Soviet troop movements and violation of Chinese airspace. After all, Moscow's criticisms of the Chinese had been far more vociferous than its complaints against the Czechs. Soviet opinion of the Cultural Revolution was made clear in the journal *Kommunist:* "Events in China are not exclusively an internal affair . . . The policies of the Mao Zedong group are harming the cause of socialism throughout the world."

As their hostility toward Moscow increased, the Chinese also accused Washington of joining the Soviets in a "ring of encirclement" around China and dividing up the world. Despite such icy signals, when the first steps toward détente with Communist China began, Hill and his colleagues were not as surprised as most. To those in Hong Kong, the shift was first observable in the form of little-publicized encounters, or even non-encounters, between persons on each side. Hill recalled a reception he attended in Kowloon in the fall of 1968. It was an otherwise ordinary social event, its impetus now forgotten. Local Communists normally attended gatherings like these, but the American officers and the Communists sedulously avoided one another. On this occasion, however, a Chinese man working as a translator for the American consulate approached Hill and gestured to a few men hovering several yards away. "The Communists are across the room," he told Hill, "and they're willing to talk to you." "I went over and it was a 'hello, how are you, how's the weather' exchange," Hill recalled. "But it signaled a monumental change." His supervisor, in an evaluation of Hill's performance not long afterward, affirmed that "to him goes the credit for bringing off the first meaningful conversation between a Consulate General Officer (himself) and a local Chinese Communist official. These officials had previously fended off attempts to establish such contacts . . . and while they may now be more receptive, it was Mr. Hill's adroit handling of the encounter that turned it into a substantively interesting conversation." Evidence of a thaw continued. In an undated letter probably from early 1969, a colleague of Hill's stationed in Ottawa related a recent conversation he'd had with the local New China News Agency bureau chief. It had been a mild exchange, and the newsman had offered only perfunctory criticism of President Nixon. Notably, he did not use the phrase "American imperialism" even once. Hill scrawled in the margin: "the frost is off the oarlock."

The fact remained that Beijing did not promulgate policy changes through individual conversations with journalists. The Party press, once more under Beijing's control as the chaos of the Cultural Revolution continued to subside, remained the official mouthpiece of new foreign and domestic strategy. Official newspapers gave no sign of compromise on Beijing's traditional hobbyhorses. In early 1969 the Communist press published continuous tirades against the United States, including *People's Daily* editorials purportedly authored by "the masses," a technique normally reserved for major propaganda campaigns. The items asserted that American peace proposals in Vietnam were a fraud: "[how] can we believe Nixon will suddenly become a Buddha and desire peace?" one article demanded. Hill described the tone of the press as "cocksure sarcasm." It remained unclear whether Beijing was simply using the Soviet border threat to galvanize internal party unity, or whether genuine geopolitical realignment was in the making.

The answer came in the spring of 1969, on a tiny, uninhabited fragment of land about 250 miles down the Ussuri River from the Soviet city of Vladivostok. Called Damansky by the Russians and Zhen Bao by the Chinese, the island appeared to be of only symbolic worth. Little over a mile in length and a half mile in breadth, Zhen Bao and its environs were mostly swampland and under water for much of the year. The island is closer to the Chinese side of the river, but both countries had long claimed it. According to Soviet press reports from March 2, 1969, that morning 300 Chinese troops on the island opened machine-gun fire on a Soviet patrol of frontier guards, killing 31 and wounding 14. The Soviets sent reinforcements, but these too were ambushed. Chinese accounts of the encounter, predictably, blamed the aggression on the Soviets (counting 70 Soviet dead), and although at first most Western observers jumped at a chance to blame the Chinese, the reality of that cold morning remained foggy. Both sides had withdrawn from the island by the afternoon, but Zhen Bao marked only the beginning of the conflict. As spring turned to summer, violence erupted again on Zhen Bao as well as thousands of miles to the southwest, on the border between Soviet Kazakhstan and China's Xinjiang province, and along the Amur River. These skirmishes were more prolonged and bloody than the first brief encounter in March. Both sides issued conflicting accounts of the hostilities, but the geography of the battle sites in Xinjiang—easily accessible from nearby Soviet installations, and hundreds of miles from the nearest Chinese railhead at Ürümqi—suggested that the Soviets started the trouble there.

It was Hill's job to report on the border conflicts in daily cables to Washington. His commentary was circumscribed by lack of trustworthy eyewitness accounts, and as always he relied heavily on careful reading of the rhetoric coming out of Beijing and Moscow. But by 1969, these had become well-worn limitations for Hill. He was used to sorting through fighting versions of the same story and extracting some shadow of the truth. The responsibility was thrilling. The cables required him to draw on all his experience as a China watcher and to write cogently under extreme pressure—a skill that is learned only by necessity.

Once Nixon and his staff had time to reflect on Hill's anonymous cables, the significance of intensifying conflict between the world's two Communist giants was clear. As then national security adviser Henry Kissinger reflected in his memoirs, a Soviet invasion of China would capsize "not only the geopolitical but also the psychological equilibrium of the world; it would create a momentum of irresistible ruthlessness." Moscow's periodic threats to attack Chinese nuclear installations or employ nuclear weapons to push People's Liberation Army forces back from the border were particularly disturbing to Washington. On the other hand, an opportunity suddenly existed to soften China's raving isolation and cultivate a triangular balance among the world's three great powers. The situation was delicate. Beijing's propaganda still accused America of colluding with the Soviets in a renewed attempt at "imperialist encirclement."

In the months that followed, Kissinger became a prime mover behind a series of symbolic gestures and guarded diplomatic advances toward China. On a late summer world tour, Nixon remarked cautiously about opening channels with the Chinese to intermediaries in Romania and Pakistan, who, it was assumed, would relay the message to Beijing. As the Soviets grew increasingly nervous that autumn, Kissinger authorized the end of the U.S. destroyer patrol in the Taiwan Strait—a signal whose military significance was dwarfed by its symbolic value. What followed, Kissinger wrote, was "an intricate minuet between us and the Chinese so delicately arranged that both sides could always maintain that they were not in contact, so stylized that neither side needed to bear the onus of an initiative, so elliptical that existing relationships on both sides were not jeopardized."

Those brief clashes in the desolate reaches of southeastern Siberia set off a geopolitical chain reaction that would culminate in President Nixon's much-vaunted trip to China in 1972. His visit, to those who had been watching most vigilantly, was less a diplomatic coup than an inescapable executive act confirming several years of geopolitical transformation. The shift in the balance among the Soviet Union, China, and the United States was, for those who knew what to look for, well marked along the way—in official editorials' compromised turns of phrase, in remote clashes over an inhospitable bit of land, and, sometimes, in what was not said at all.

Hill was never bothered that Kissinger, for whom he would be a top speechwriter in a scant few years, had no idea who had written the cables he read with such interest. Although no reasonable junior officer expected to see his name attached to most of his work, Hill was distinct in his attitude. "Others said, 'We're working like dogs, but the time will come when we'll be ambassadors and we'll cash in,'" he recalled. "I didn't. I thought this was great—way beyond anything I'd been asked to do before." Hill's self-confidence was more valuable for its noiselessness. It was unusual in a profession that attracted ambitious men and women intent on achieving power and making names for themselves. That breed of officer was often frustrated in the Foreign Service—a highly constrained job, bounded by meddlesome supervisors and a lethargic bureaucracy that shuttled its officers around the globe, granting them little notice or say in their futures. Hill was better suited to it than most. Although every telegram he drafted was revised and chewed up by his superiors, his ideas still confined by a system that offered no guarantee that those on high would listen, he felt that the months spent covering the Sino-Soviet border dispute were the apex of his career thus far. He loved the chance to shape information, to tell the story of the border clashes as he saw it. His was a silent ego, not a meek one.

In our conversations about Charlie's years in Hong Kong, his tone of voice recalled those sunny afternoons pitching a football across Ocean City sand. He was in his element. Thirty years later at Yale, he still taught class like a China watcher. He drew oblique meanings from tiny articles in the back pages of the *New York Times,* as if our break-fast-table newspaper were the *People's Daily.* Every cultural artifact was somehow relevant to foreign policy. He once devoted a lecture on state-craft to exegesis of Shakespeare's *King Lear.* Another day, he convinced us that the architecture of Yale's campus—a nucleus of Gothic towers framed on the outer edges by rigid brick colonial lines—was a sym-bol of America's historical novelty. Over the course of the year, the boundaries of distinct cultural territories became permeable. Art, Reli-gion, Literature, and Politics all informed one another, and it suddenly seemed that to consider them separately would be to live with tunnel vision, like intellectual moles.

China made sense of Charlie in the classroom, but it confused my view of him as a teacher because it marked the beginning of his story as a father, an ordinary man with a family. There were no embarrassing (or even normal) displays of emotion as he described his daughters. His voice remained in the same impassive monotone that he used to discuss Chinese Communist politics. In fact, he hardly talked about the girls at all, dwelling mostly on the amusing procedures of their adoptions. With the arrival of children—the event that can heave a cou-ple from a universe of self-absorption into true adulthood—Martha, who had not possessed an identity of her own since she graduated from college, became a mother with her entire being. But the babies did not alter her husband's sense of self so much as broaden his notion of duty, and even that did not bring him home from the office any earlier. The Hills were in large part an ordinary Foreign Service family whose lives revolved around the grueling hours and transcontinental assign-ments of a hard-working man. That man supported his family, compli-mented his wife's paintings, and insured that his daughters' natural-ization papers were in order. I still was not sure, however, whether he could bear to call himself a "family man," a role that smelled of Bridgeton's dull normals. Nor was I sure how much I wanted to know about my professor's life as a father and husband. It would turn out that my apprehension was well founded. Private lives are never as neat and easy as a diagram on the chalkboard.

Later, in rooting through his archives, I read letters from Martha that described family outings, and I paged through photographs of Charlie, young, tan, and in blue jeans, with his daughters on his lap. He could no longer be the sexless don who reigned over my seminar table, whose office light glowed well after dark (who is to say it was ever extinguished?), whose entire being was occupied with scholarship. That is the image most of us have of our teachers, from kindergarten through the university. It is a proprietary emotion, one that exists to some extent in all our personal relationships. This is why it is alarming to run into your teachers buying coffee at Starbucks or punching their PIN number into the same ATM that you use. How could their lives continue apart from your contact with them in the classroom? How could they engage in anything ordinary or mundane?

To my shock, I began to find myself more interested in the "ordinary and mundane" parts of my subject's life than I was in the historic moments of his career. No one could blame me for preferring Martha's vibrant, personal letters to Charlie's dry Communist Party dossiers, memoranda, and maps of the Soviet border clashes, but still I felt guilty. Every time I found my narrative winding in Martha's direction, I tried to pull back. Somehow writing about Charlie's personal life felt cheap, voyeuristic, and "unscholarly." Too bad it was so compelling.

I began to have imaginary fights with Charlie in my head. We argued savagely over which parts of his life story mattered the most. The problem of personal ego, of desire to control the story rather than allow it to unfold, lies at the heart of writing any kind of history. The pull is particularly strong in biography, where creating a narrative that departs from how the subject would tell the story himself is at the heart of the biographer's raison d'être. At the outset of our first conversation Charlie stated that he would answer only the questions I asked, so as to leave the direction of the discussion up to me. He would never read my drafts, even if I wanted him to. He would give me total access to his personal papers: no box in his archive was closed to me, even those containing personal diaries and correspondence. So from the start I was better off than many other biographers faced with subjects more domineering or evasive in interviews and possessive of their intellectual property.

Yet the terms of our agreement could not alter the power dynamic between professor and student. Nor could they change the fact that no matter what Charlie suggested about my controlling the conversation, the truth was that he had thought quite a bit about his own life, and he had opinions about the most important elements and the proper value judgments. My interviews with him were always fruitful; he possessed a remarkable memory, and he offered more personal information than I had ever expected. But each time I packed up my notebook and left his office, I could not help feeling a bit brainwashed. As months passed I increasingly sensed that he was consciously trying to rein himself in and let me control the dialogue—because he knew that in the end there would be no intellectual integrity, and even less historical value, in a monologue dutifully recorded by a scribe. But Charlie is a grand strategist by nature and by experience, and the cardinal rule of grand strategy is the control of information. He could not obviate his instinct, and neither could I.

To a certain extent, there is no one more qualified to judge a life, and no one more likely to be right, than the person who lived it. It is not incorrect or lazy scholarship, per se, for a biographer to agree with her subject. But candid interviews with other sources and weeks spent prowling through Charlie's little-censored papers made it easier to counter his interpretations with ideas of my own. I became more critical. His permission to call him by his first name hastened, if not his fall from the pedestal, then at least a clearer view of his cracks and imperfections. But gradually I developed a predicament opposite from Charlie's indoctrination: I found myself less and less eager to approach my primary resource, sitting in his office at 31 Hillhouse Avenue. I wanted the story to be mine. Somehow, even if I reached certain conclusions on my own, if in a later interview Charlie independently brought up similar inferences before I had the chance to share them with him, it was as if he had stolen the ideas from me. I felt robbed of my agency as a thinker and a writer. Early on in our conversations, I hit upon the motif of his football games on the beach. I had ideas about how the barefoot, sandy-haired quarterback foreshadowed his older counterpart. Sometime later Charlie started referring to the patterns visible at Ocean City. As he plundered my literary symbols by announcing them out loud, I felt my throat constrict. Months later, when he told me that he considered himself an "Edmund Burke conservative," I wanted to scream at him, Don't you realize that I figured that out long ago?! Can't I have just a bit of credit?

I was no psychoanalytic genius. Objectively, I realized that it was a good thing for my subject to confirm independently ideas that I had about him. If I was honest with myself, I had to acknowledge the possibility that those thoughts had occurred to me because he had put them there. It was the same problem I'd had while writing papers for his classes — trying to apply what I had learned, yet also to shake my mind free from his lecture catch phrases and blackboard diagrams and develop my own ideas. And the truth was that for every idea of mine that he ratified, there were ten that he relegated to the waste bin of junk theory. But the emotional course of the biography was irreversible. As I grew wiser in examining the trajectory of Charlie's life, as I began to read his letters, talk with his friends and family, second-guess his memory, and see him from vantage points other than his own, so too did I become possessive of his story. I felt freer to write about what I believed was most interesting, no matter what Charlie thought. But I knew that the first principle of historical scholarship is never to allow one's early hypotheses to shape one's research. I could not let myself see only the facts convenient to my theories about his life. Biography, like all history, requires of the author confidence and creativity, but also discipline and a healthy amount of self-denial. In the end, as in all relationships of ego, it was a question of balance. I worked, and wrote, like a cat on a fence.

5

HILL HAD BEEN STATIONED IN HONG KONG FOR FOUR years—two complete tours of duty—when the call to return home finally came. Neither he nor Martha was unhappy to leave. The State Department assigned Hill to serve as diplomat-in-residence at Harvard University for the fall 1969 and spring 1970 terms, but the political section chief in Hong Kong protested that the China scene was too hot to release Hill in the late summer of 1969. The Harvard assignment was canceled. However, a Professor Ezra Vogel at Harvard's East Asian Research Center knew of Hill's work in Hong Kong and was fixed on the idea of bringing him to Cambridge. Hill had no role in the bargaining—as he never seemed to have in matters that would determine the logistics of his life—but when Harvard finally offered to pay Hill's salary (under the terms of the Diplomat-in-Residence program, the State Department would normally foot the bill), those in Washington relented. He was freed for the year to introduce his daughters to their adopted country, tarry in classrooms, eat lunch with faculty, and read for hours on end—all as he had not had the chance to do since joining the Foreign Service in 1962.

The Hills found an apartment in a residential neighborhood not two miles from Harvard Yard. The modest building at 95 Lexington Avenue was built in the shape of a U around a cheerful center courtyard. The Hills lived on the ground floor of the three-story building. A German couple lived on the top floor, and below them lived a professor and his wife, Peter and Ellen Castle. By pleasant coincidence the Castles had two adopted children, a Thai and an American, roughly playmate-age for Katie and Emily. Ellen and Martha ran "a sort of commune," Martha remembered, the neighborhood mothers alternating baby-sitting and the children sharing all toys.

No matter how perfect Cambridge was for a young family, no matter how welcoming the Harvard community, the Hills' transition into the stream of life in the country they had not known for eight years — save short visits on leave — was not easy. Martha in particular was in for a traumatic adjustment. Of all the American decades to miss, the 1960s was possibly the most critical, especially for a young woman. Foreign Service wives did not exist in a vacuum, isolated from the changing attitudes toward women's place in society. Martha recalled vividly the senior diplomatic wife in Hong Kong who invited the officers' wives to tea, then stormed around the room filling their teacups, "going on about how this was a ridiculous way to live, and she was only doing it because she had to, and she didn't like it." But the reawakening of American feminism, marked by the 1963 release of Betty Friedan's *The Feminine Mystique,* was in a state of arrested development among wives abroad. If much of the demeaning and tedious protocol had diminished, there was still less self-awareness among Martha's peers abroad and little means for nurturing a strong female community. Grumbling, as the Hong Kong senior wife did, was not the same as discussing and organizing.

While her husband was posted abroad, each Foreign Service wife had to navigate a strange place to obtain her family's basic needs, help her children adjust to new schools and new friends every couple of years, and somehow find time to restart her own life. There was little time to put down roots or overcome the unfamiliarity of a place. Moreover, the American feminists of the 1960s, like their abolitionist forerunners in petticoats who met at Seneca Falls in 1848, drew their strength of purpose and their organizing know-how from their civil rights activism. Foreign Service wives were physically removed from the ferment of the American 1960s and had no access to that social momentum. The result was that women like Martha could not truly understand what was happening back home. As Martha settled into Cambridge and got to know other women in the neighborhood, she realized that in her absence, American women's view of themselves had transformed.

In Cambridge, Martha soon befriended her upstairs neighbor. Ellen was a progressive-minded woman studying for a Ph.D. The obvious contrast to Martha's last sojourn in the academic world — her quiet, dusty days as a librarian in the University of Pennsylvania library while her husband heard lectures and studied — could not have escaped her.

Martha had read *The Feminine Mystique*, but only upon coming to Cambridge did she begin to talk over Friedan's ideas with Ellen and other women. Martha found herself thinking that "marriage was a one-sided affair. It takes from you, and at the end you feel like you've given all there is to give. I was like a chameleon, being this way in one country, that way in another, always adjusting to a new place. Who am I? What am I doing? Those questions would bob up periodically, but I bought the idea of service to my country. I convinced myself that this is what it meant. But still, I was not doing anything I worked for in college."

Friedan's explanation for the discontent and silent frustration of so many housewives and mothers—the generation of women who had "gone back to the home" after the war and believed that "career woman" was a dirty word forty years after their grandmothers won the right to vote—was that today's women were suffering from a crisis of identity. Most had not envisioned their lives beyond age twenty-one. They had loved college but lost the opportunity for intellectual growth when they married and confined themselves to the kitchen and the carpool, and limited their identity to—in Martha's case—"Charlie's wife" and "Katie and Emily's mother." The dream of Martha Mitchell, the artist and independent thinker who could keep up with her husband's intellectual pace, was boxed away and hidden out of sight. The rhythms of her life, the suppertimes, the toddler feedings, the household errands, all revolved entirely around her husband and daughters.

Many of the women whom Friedan interviewed during her research had expressed a terror of turning out like their mothers. "Almost all our mothers were housewives, though many had started or yearned for or regretted giving up careers," Friedan wrote. "Whatever they told us, we, having eyes and ears and mind and heart, knew that their lives were empty. We did not want to be like them, and yet what other model did we have?" Florence Mitchell, it now seemed, was ahead of her time. She saw too clearly her own crippled ambitions. She knew the source of her unhappiness, and she feared a similar fate for her daughter. Martha saw it as well now. In 1957, like so many other college graduates her age, she had seen only that marrying the man she loved must be the simplest route to a fulfilled life. It is possible that part of her desired to defy her mother, and perhaps she thought there would be some chance of an independent career after she became Mrs. Hill. Perhaps, like so many college seniors, she was just terrified at the idea of leaving her friends and family and trying to figure out her life on her own.

Martha and her mother reached a delicate equilibrium in which Mrs. Mitchell stopped her lecturing as long as Martha was attentive and wrote her often. It was Martha's impression that her mother was pleased at her son-in-law's impressive-sounding jobs and placated by the arrival of grandchildren. Charlie did not detect the same mellowing in his mother-in-law's spirit. He thought "she did not care about my job or the grandchildren in the slightest. She was utterly fixated on Martha . . . Martha loved her mother with an enormous power beyond description. I guess it's love; maybe it's fear, constantly watching your mother's face and body language for the slightest expression of disapproval, then leaping to overcome that."

He perceived no independent intellectual passions on the part of Mrs. Mitchell. To him, she was focused only on living vicariously through her daughter. While Martha saw her mother as a whole being with sympathies and interests, Charlie perceived her mainly as a dissident element in his wife's consciousness. Charlie saw his wife as he saw himself—as an essentially consistent being that was becoming more and more true to himself and his capabilities as time passed. It followed, then, that Martha's frustrations were an inevitable part of an unavoidable process, and he could not be expected to do anything to help. Whereas Mrs. Mitchell's lectures were once "an underlying, subversive thing in her background, now the women's revolution pulled her away like a powerful tide," he said. "She thought her mother had been right all along. I stayed away from home more and more."

Reflecting on that era decades later, Hill said that at the time he genuinely believed the institution of marriage was dead. He took feminists at their word when they deemed it one of the gravest evils of male chauvinism, an act of physical and social despotism. The Radcliffe coeds he encountered were the most aggressive, echoing the rhetoric of radical feminists like Shulamith Firestone, for whom the goal of women's liberation was not just an end to the dominance of heterosexual males, but the elimination of sexual distinction altogether—the rise of a kind of "pan-sexuality," Susan Sontag's "depolarization of the sexes." "Every encounter with every woman was a confrontation," Hill remembered, no matter what their age. Middle-aged housewives continued their age-old cultural habits, hosting dinner parties and directing their households, but Hill recalled that nearly every dinner party he attended was ruined when the hostess launched into feminist grievances in the middle of the meal she had slaved to prepare.

Hill's descriptions of his own reaction to the emotions and rhetoric of the women's movement were not unlike his recollections of China's Cultural Revolution — even though the present upheaval occurred not in a strange country but in his own classrooms and home. "I was a bystander," he said. "I took it totally seriously. I thought what women were saying was what they meant, and that it would revolutionize gender relations thereafter." He accepted the manifestos, the irate housewives, and the defiant Radcliffe students with the detachment of an anthropologist or a bewildered infantryman patrolling a strange front. He wasn't interested in reading the feminist literature Martha occasionally brought home. "I wasn't deep about it," he explained. "I just thought, 'This is a revolution, this is the way it's going to be. Now we'll have a world of passing affairs between men and women, open sex, and that will be that. We'll live through our lives with the opposite sex as if we were sixteen-year-olds.' There was no sense in discussing it because it was everywhere, and it never ceased."

Martha joined a women's book club at her church, and at one meeting each member was assigned a chapter of Simone de Beauvoir's *The Second Sex* (1949) to paraphrase for the benefit of the group. When it was her turn, Martha stood up and explained de Beauvoir's notion of the asymmetry of gender relations and the subjugation of women as "the Other." "When I finished, I got a round of applause — I really had my heart in it totally," Martha recalled. "I thought, 'I'm going to try this at home!' But it didn't work. Charlie argued that it [de Beauvoir's argument] was a crazy idea. The implication was that it wasn't worth talking about."

She never exploded in diatribes against male oppression, like the Radcliffe women Charlie encountered on campus. But Charlie overheard her talking about the radical things she read and saw with Ellen and other women friends. In her offhand comments and dinnertime remarks "there was an edge to her — not towards me, but towards the unfairness she saw around her," Hill said. Still, Martha and her peers had already abandoned their college degrees to the attic trunk, married early and birthed their broods, joined PTA committees, and focused their energies on shopping for quieter, more efficient vacuum cleaners. It was impossible to rescind those life choices. And while Cambridge was a strident, progressive community, it was also a rewarding place to raise a family, abounding with suburban mothers wheeling their toddlers down the street, preschool arts and crafts projects, and active church congregations. The pleasant life there perhaps made it easy for Martha to think on those feminist arguments, yet suppress them and do her best to believe she was content.

Her husband chose to exist in the world he understood best. If Martha considered herself part of "a generation in transition," advancing painfully forward and leaving behind an obsolete notion of womanhood, Charlie was also in some sense a man in motion. But he was moving alone and backward in time. Since college—since boyhood, really—his ideal had resided in the past: the old model of the self-possessed aristocrat well versed in all ways of the world, the educated elite that his neighbor Dr. Doherty had told him so long ago he could never be. While his wife was wrestling with the future, he continued to aim behind him, toward an age that, by 1970, appeared all but extinct. If there was any place left in the world to seek out that existence, it was Harvard University, the nation's bastion of reason, tradition, and enlightenment for its own sake.

Hill was classified as a fellow in the East Asian Research Center, with no official teaching responsibilities, and he studied as much as a full-time student. Freed from State Department limitations on his course selection, he took classes in subjects ranging from John Milton to Buddhism. He took the enterprise seriously and earned all As or A-minuses. He ate lunch with other faculty members in the East Asian Research Center, and although there was a moment of insecurity reminiscent of his freshman anxieties at Brown, he discovered that the Harvard faculty were eager to include him in their conversation and listen to what he had to say. He was considered an equal. Hill co-taught a small graduate seminar with Professor Vogel on Chinese politics and the Cultural Revolution, and he loved his first taste of classroom life on the other side of the podium. Vogel took care of the structure of the course and the lesson plans. Hill's primary job was to sit in the room and be an authoritative resource. "Ezra wanted him there as sounding board, to provide some dose of on-the-ground realism, because we were foggy-headed grad students," said former student Jay Mathews. "We were all fascinated with him."

In the early months of 1970, the Harvard community was still catching its breath from the student revolts of the previous spring. On April 9, 1969, radical students opposed to the Vietnam War, led by the Harvard chapter of Students for a Democratic Society (SDS), had chosen University Hall as a surrogate target for Washington. They seized

Harvard's administrative building and ordered the deans and staff out. Administrators who tried to continue with their jobs were violently hustled out of their offices. Student leaders issued a statement declaring that they were holding University Hall to force the Harvard Corporation to yield to "nonnegotiable" demands, including elimination of the military training programs, replacement of Reserve Officers Training Corps scholarships with regular scholarships, a rollback of rents, and a halt to slum teardowns in Harvard-owned neighborhoods (a futile attempt by SDS to ally with Cambridge's blue-collar workers). As the occupation of University Hall continued, some of the students crowded outside began to taunt the occupiers — most bystanders sympathized with the cause, but not the violent methods. Faculty reaction was mixed.

Harvard President Nathan Pusey, known as a stubborn aristocrat who enjoyed little affection from either students or faculty and had previously dismissed student unrest as "belligerent nonsense" of students "who feel they have a special calling to redeem society," decided to call in the riot police. When most occupiers refused to vacate the building, the police — cops from Cambridge, Somerville, Belmont, and Boston who had little sympathy for rich Harvard brats — swarmed University Hall with billy clubs, beating and dragging the students. Predictably, the violence swung many moderate students into support for the occupiers. At a meeting that night, fifteen hundred students voted for a three-day boycott of classes. Even after the 1969 episode ended and classes at Harvard let out for the summer, SDS and other activists did not cease their antiwar, antibureaucracy drumbeat.

On April 30, 1970, President Nixon announced on national television that the United States would send combat troops into Cambodia to wipe out North Vietnamese and Viet Cong sanctuaries along the border with South Vietnam. The campaign would fail utterly, cause great destruction in Cambodia, and provide endless ammunition for the administration's critics. A few days after the news broke, when students at Kent State University staged a massive protest, Ohio Governor James Rhodes called in the National Guard. In the subsequent confrontation nine students were wounded and four killed. National reaction was immediate and fierce. Even observers who thought the protesters were draft-dodging bums were horrified by the image of the state gunning down its own children. Demonstrations erupted on campuses across the country, Harvard included.

Although he had not been in Cambridge to witness the unrest of the previous year, Hill believed that in some ways the upheaval of 1970 was worse. "The whole campus had been transformed, rather than most students just watching a small radical group," he said. "In 1970, it was the entirety of the university. And it became clear to me that the issue was international." The student protesters were entranced by the revolutionary aesthetic. They wanted to be Red Guards, to transform their institution into one that would "serve the people." To the more radical protestors, Harvard was a tool of bourgeois capitalist oppressors, a hireling of "the system" deliberately perpetuating an unwinnable, unjust war in Vietnam for the benefit of Wall Street and the "military-industrial complex." Hill was fascinated. He attended the rallies and watched from the back. "In Memorial Hall filled with hundreds of people, someone would start to speak, and someone would push them away from the microphone. It was a matter of who was the biggest political bully," he recalled. "Some people just had that political ability." The student rallies were not devoted to denouncing the Harvard administration alone. Faculty too were "struggled," to use the Maoist term. Student leaders demanded that John Fairbank, Harvard's legendary Asian studies scholar, stand up before them and listen while they denounced him and his work, "his insufficient attention and care for the Chinese people and the Communist movement," according to Hill. Fairbank patiently heard them out and tried to defend himself; he was a noble, down-to-earth man who reminded Hill of an elder judge of the county seat, or a revered small-town minister. But Fairbank was invariably drowned out by the hisses and boos of a crowd too young to remember when this same professor had been branded a Communist sympathizer by Wisconsin Senator Joseph McCarthy and his henchmen.

Hill's reaction to the student movement was complex. There was an academic veneer: he retreated to his office and contemplated the student movement in terms of Rousseau's General Will, the combination of all individual wills in a society. However, Hill must have been struck —as more than a dispassionate analyst—by the look and the sound of the young Harvard men of 1970. They were loud, long-haired, and rudely dressed. They bore little resemblance to that old Brown alumni magazine cover, printed with a photo of a young Charlie Hill striding across the Brown campus in jacket and tie. These young men dressed in jeans and ratty T-shirts (when they wore shirts at all). Everything about their speech and their appearance screamed to adults and faculty, "We do not look like you. Don't try to understand us or stop us." They were the "now generation," a horde of unkempt bums. Their "demands" were nearly always lists of immediate, simple-minded reforms that showed no knowledge of the lessons of history that Hill took so seriously. Their behavior was anti-intellectual—worse, it was unaccountable, the kind of phony individualism that surrenders all responsibilities to the emotions of the mob. They were a mass of overeager youngsters who had grown up within the sanctuary of well-ordered, democratic society untouched by the hideous violence of the early twentieth century. Sheltered by the protective rulings of Chief Justice Earl Warren's liberal Supreme Court, this generation took for granted the essential means of free expression and had no idea of the rightist persecutions many of their teachers and parents had endured only twenty years earlier. A *New York Times* editorial, written during the first week of the 1969 protest, fumed: "Several hundred lawless students at Harvard have accomplished what the virulently antiliberal forces of the late Senator Joseph McCarthy failed to achieve. They have disrupted the historic rule of reason and academic freedom . . . The time has clearly come to stop pretending that the disruptions are adolescent pranks or justifiable excesses of young idealists. What is at stake now is nothing less than the perpetuation of universities as centers of reason in a free society."

The essential lubricant of intellectual discourse at the university—and of life in general, as Hill had always known it—was civility. This meant, in part, deference to social hierarchy: his generation had instinctive respect for those in positions of authority. The college students of 1970 thought nothing of manhandling their deans and shouting down distinguished professors. Hill's generation had entered the university dressed like their parents and eager to be grownups; the student rallies he watched from the back of the hall must have appeared, to some extent, like the temper tantrums of children.

The students had not experienced the world wars, the Holocaust, or the McCarthy hearings, but they knew Vietnam. The Vietnam War was the horror that drove them, a summons that resonated across generations. The undergraduate body was the font of protest, but Hill found that his colleagues on the faculty, too, were persuaded by the same intellectual mentality. "No one defended the war," recalled Professor Merle Goldman, a regular at the Research Center lunches. There was no debate on the subject. Everyone whom Hill talked with assumed that he was appalled by the war too, and he was. There was no other possible reaction to the media reports coming out of Vietnam, Hill said later. Every television broadcast was a horror story, every newspaper editorial a scathing critique of Washington's mismanaged strategy and intentional deception. If an individual had any trust in what he read and saw, he had to believe that the war was a heinous crime.

"I really did become a dove with the activist doves, the hard-line doves," he said. Hill was not a Foreign Service bureaucrat on vacation at a cushy university. He was a young man, worried about his world, eager to act, and vulnerable to the fervor around him. "I remember he was quite conflicted [about the war]," recalled Deborah Davis, then a graduate student who knew Hill. "He was 'the good Foreign Service officer,' doing his job, loyal to his government, but that didn't mean he stopped thinking." In his informal report to the State Department official overseeing his term at Harvard, Hill wrote that even more interesting than the classes he was taking was a duty that "came about as a result of the May 1970 university strike to protest the Cambodian incursion. Strike headquarters was located in the office directly opposite mine. The strike steering committee . . . invited me to take the role of 'devil's advocate' in a series of debates which lasted until mid-summer and which I found to be an exhilirating [sic] exercise in student-government interaction."

"Devil's advocate" may have been a politic way of describing his role to the federal government, but the truth was that he often found himself agreeing with the students. Hill attended meetings of the pro-Maoist Committee of Concerned Asian Scholars and wrote antiwar articles in the campus newspaper and scholarly publications. A book published by the committee, *The Indochina Story,* was organized by leftist political icon Noam Chomsky—a self-described libertarian socialist who would seem, to the students Hill would teach decades later, a shocking bedfellow for their conservative professor. The book purported to help end the war by explaining to the American people "what they have often seen only through the fragmenting and distorting eyes of their television sets and local newspapers." This was a war whose "essential features" were "massive bombardment, destruction, and population removal to concentration camps; the disdain of the American soldiers for the dinks [Vietnamese] whose villes [villages] they are forced to burn . . . and the unquestioned acceptance by most soldiers, and by the majority of the American reading public, that this is perfectly all right."

The introduction to *The Indochina Story* goes on to liken the Viet Cong to the American revolutionaries of 1776. What follows is a 350-page account of various facets of the war, from counterinsurgency tactics and air war to war crimes and the "brainwashing" of the American people by their government. The individual articles bear no bylines. Hill said later that he and other contributors were given lists of questions to respond to, and their answers were cobbled together by the book's editors. It is likely that Hill's responses were not so incendiary in tone as the articles they were used to produce, but there is no mistaking his sympathies at the time for the publication's message. In the front pages, Hill is listed as a contributor under the pseudonym "Sidney Beech." He chose the pen name after Sylvia Beach, the famous proprietress of the Shakespeare and Company bookstore on Paris's Left Bank. Beach had once lived in Bridgeton, the hometown that Hill had never quite left behind. He was one of the few Bridgetoners who knew of the role she later played in the life of literature. The pseudonym had more practical purposes than indulgence of birthplace whimsy; Hill knew that State Department officials would be furious if they learned that one of their own was publishing arguments against the U.S. government. It was a risky thing to do. His colleagues swore that if Washington found out, they would close ranks around him.

In the fall of 1970, as the end of Hill's sabbatical to academia approached, he received his next assignment. The thin envelope contained a single page, a brisk personnel memorandum. Hill was to go to South Vietnam.

In 1932, public intellectual Walter Lippmann wrote of an engraved headstone in St. Michael's churchyard in Charleston, South Carolina. Charlie keeps the clipping in his files, although he rarely finds a place for it in his lectures. The headstone marks the resting place of a James Louis Petigru, a Unionist who died there during the Civil War. The inscription reads as follows:

> Unawed by Opinion
> Unseduced by Flattery
> Undismayed by Disaster
> He confronted Life with antique Courage
> And Death with Christian Hope

It goes on:

> In the great Civil War
> He withstood his People for his Country
> But his People did homage to the Man
> Who held his conscience higher than their praise
> And his Country
> Heaped her honours on the grave of
> the Patriot
> To whom living
> His own righteous self-respect sufficed
> Alike for Motive and Reward

For all of Charlie's sympathy with the antiwar movement and the Harvard protesters, to him they failed the Petigru test of virtue. The atmosphere on campus was one of mob rule, not individual integrity. Among the Harvard students Charlie no longer recognized the Petigru brand of "righteous self-respect," the South Jersey warrior's code.

Those years witnessed a cultural upheaval, a reinvention of the American character akin to a civil war. In our conversations about the 1960s and early 1970s, Charlie agreed with the general wisdom regarding the good things that came out of those years. But he was quick to point out the corruption of the civil rights movement after the death of Martin Luther King Jr., the mutual confusion between the sexes as to how to relate to each other, and women's struggle to acclimate to their new authority. He lingered on the general infantilization of American men: "What we were acculturated to think of as what an honorable adult man should be was torn down, and in its place came nothing but adolescent posturings, a beer-commercial way of thinking of oneself . . . the antithesis of an honorable gentleman, which is what's necessary for a marriage to succeed."

Charlie grew up in the old culture. He has cleaved as best he can to the old values, the notion of a gentleman, not because he is valiant but because he was programmed that way by his parents, his community, and his heritage. He was brought up to believe that manners are morals writ small. The student rampages on University Hall and the mob's abuse of Professor Fairbank abetted Charlie's general conclusion: society was no longer attentive to the fact that everything matters. The students' lack of manners in dealing with their opponents implied to him an absence of essential morals, no matter how humanitarian their rhetoric. The old morality, the conservative reverence for history and individual honor espoused by the Founding Fathers, which to Charlie defined what it meant to be American, appeared moribund. He felt like a loyalist trapped, like James Petigru, in a country overrun by the enemy.

The university has always been a schizophrenic institution, with dual allegiances to tradition and to progress. It is civilization's safest vault of secrets. It is also a cultural testing ground where young people routinely delight in iconoclasm—sometimes just to work a bit of rebellion out of their systems, but with the occasional consequence of shocking social change. Charlie, having arrived at Harvard straight from the upheaval of the Cultural Revolution, had an unusually sober perspective on the student upheavals he witnessed in Cambridge. He could not help but see the university as the fulcrum on which civilization balanced. He had always been acutely aware of that delicate equipoise—partly because of the ferment of the early cold war years, which he had absorbed as a young man, but mostly for the strange and not entirely clear reason of his South Jersey birthright. He still carried the imprint of that stubborn old place, a swath of fens and pine barrens that insisted upon remaining a self-contained frontier, where the belching factories and creeping highways could not entirely overrun the call of the reed birds fluttering through the cattails in the Cohansey marsh.

For all his sensitivity to the frailties of modern man, Charlie's conservatism has never been dour. His creed is marked, like Petigru's, with antique courage and hope. Charlie, I came to realize, believes that intrepidity is the essence of optimism, and that emotions are tools not only of the heart, but also of the mind. A good grand strategist can always "dial up the exact mood that he must project," whether at a press conference or a seminar table, Charlie says. He is not a religious person in the churchgoing sense, but there is a redemptive quality in his political philosophy. His dark, Calvinist appraisal of humankind's current state is balanced by a confidence in free will and the power of personal ability to change, the earmarks of his childhood Baptist faith (despite his boyhood preference for the church basketball league over the pew). To Charlie, perhaps the real horror of the scenes in Memorial Hall was the perverted self-righteousness, the vandalism of Reason's sacraments: the irreligiosity of it all.

Charlie came to Yale at the best of times, for him and for his students. My generation looks nothing like the unwashed throngs that greeted him thirty years ago at Harvard. We are, as journalist David

Brooks wrote, "the organization kids," almost Edwardian in our faithful trot down established paths of success, our idealistic commitments, our placid disposal toward moral threats and our belief that the world is basically just and good. Despite a reluctance to return to the Brooks Brothers wear of Charlie's college days, we are eager to cooperate with the system and achieve by its rules. We are enthusiastic to listen to people like Charles Hill—a paragon of achieving by the rules, of working hard and reaping his due reward. But there is something else too—a sense that Charlie knows unswervingly what he stands for. He is like dry land to sailors too long at sea.

Each generation reacts to the one that came before, whether by will or by instinct. Many of the professors who teach at Yale are products of the 1960s, but their students are sometimes of a different mold. We are not particularly valiant or courageous; we are just kids, and we are often self-absorbed and think we know more than we do. But Charlie sees in us "antique virtues," an awareness of context broader than one's personal interests and the current moment in time, a yearning for loyalties higher than patriotism.

If you call this a conservative backlash, the American media agrees. Gallup polls and the *New York Times* have reported, with no small degree of alarm, that my generation is more conservative than our parents. Growing numbers of conservative undergraduate activists "describe themselves as defenders of 'individuality' and 'freedom' against a campus, and a world, overrun by groupthink liberalism and pious political correctness," observed a lengthy piece in the *New York Times Magazine*. "They also share a belief that despite the common perception of youth being synonymous with progressive, liberal ideals, the true spirit of their generation is solidly, if quietly, conservative." They long to be modern-day James Petigrus in blue jeans.

It is hard to determine the truth of this alleged ideological shift. Only a wishful-thinking Republican recluse who never set foot beyond the bounds of bow-tied Tory Party debates could believe that Yale is no longer a liberal place. Most of us have been steeped since birth in the culture of tolerance born in our parents' youth. Open-mindedness and refusal to pass judgment on others seem to be the only hard and fast imperatives that we bring with us to college. Fewer and fewer come with strong religious convictions or even concrete political worldviews, aside from those that have accreted around pet issues like the Environment or Sweatshops, in which we invested ourselves during high school—sometimes out of genuine zeal, sometimes in the interest of gussying up college applications. We began college without our grand-parents' faith, or even our parents' fiery feelings about Vietnam and civil rights. "In previous times, students came assured of certain things, and college was supposed to shake you up," said a classmate of mine named Jeff Morris. "Today students don't have anything to shake up."

A young William F. Buckley wrote in *God and Man at Yale* that he was troubled by a university education that transformed creative, God-fearing, capitalist-minded young men into barren, Godless socialists. But even Buckley would have been obliged to admit that no matter who was winning or losing the battle for Yale men's souls, ideas were the primary weaponry of both sides. The foundationalist in him had to cherish that. Today's students are starved for foundations. Many of us start to realize it only when we get to college. The few of us lucky enough to know what we believe have no underlying framework, no good reason for why we believe what we do. One of Charlie's col-leagues, Greek historian Donald Kagan, pointed out some students' semiconscious drift toward courses on the Western canon and big ideas, the sort that Charlie teaches: "When they have no one around to teach it, they don't even know they feel it—they're just vaguely un-happy," he said. "They seek out anybody who has that interest."

I came to Yale from an average public high school in Illinois, where I spent my weekends dressed up in JC Penney polyester suits and mak-ing speeches at debate tournaments. I occupied the weekdays with physics study groups and illicit lunchtime expeditions to get Slurpees from the nearby 7-Eleven. Come senior year, college admissions offices were concerned mainly with my SAT scores and the number of speech medals dangling from my bulletin board. They were in no way inter-ested in what I thought about the world. This was a lucky thing for me, because I had no idea what I thought.

When I arrived at Yale, I discovered that people expected me to have opinions. If I'd had any budding political inclinations during high school in staid, Republican Glen Ellyn, they were of the liberal streak. These were formed only in opposition to my little brother, my first po-litical adversary. He was in junior high at the time and in a phase of pretending to read the *Wall Street Journal* at breakfast with my father every morning and making crass proclamations about his disdain for public welfare. I argued with him mainly out of intellectual pride, drag-ging the both of us into maelstroms of boorish outbursts and ad hom-inem interludes, the sum of which my mother christened the Battle of the Nincompoops.

At Yale I discovered dining halls and common rooms populated by socially conscious eighteen-year-olds who were experts on everything and spoke in interchangeable catch phrases. Many of them were "liberal" because it was trendy, like Birkenstocks and Nalgene water bottles, not because they had thought carefully about the issues. The Yalie mainstream infuriated me—not because it leaned to the left, but because it was a bandwagon that enabled and encouraged my classmates to make loud, mindless declarations at the dinner table. I could not bear to sit in the dining hall every evening surrounded by older, bearded (or at least fuzzy) versions of my little brother. I fought back in the only way I knew how. I became, once again, a consummate contrarian, arguing often from the conservative point of view just to keep my classmates from getting off so easily.

But contrarianism is not a political philosophy. Perhaps the reason that Charlie never provoked this childhood reaction in me was because my first encounter with him was in my freshman History and Politics seminar, where the subjects were Herodotus, Thucydides, and Tacitus, not hot-button political issues. The genius of Charlie is that he wins converts through the elegance of his thinking on ancient texts whose age has made them politically neutral, at least to the unenlightened. Only later, after you have marveled at his lectures on the Roman character and traced his chalkboard diagrams into your notebook, does he begin to talk about current affairs. By that time you are sold, and to apply his philosophies there, too, is the only logical thing to do. After all, his main lesson is that everything is connected—that liberals' most serious crime is to ignore what Thucydides has to say about the Vietnam War, or what Herodotus teaches us about the clash of civilizations.

Charlie is, for better and for worse, an antidote to the stultifying PC language and moral equivocation that students encounter elsewhere at Yale. The accusation that he is a brainwasher has a shade of truth, for it is the Hill cast of mind that Charlie tries to cultivate in his students. But what Charlie calls "antique virtues" are really the oldest of human intellectual and moral aches. The feeling is like a veteran's ghost pain in his phantom leg long after the real limb has been amputated— a persisting sense that something ought to be there, holding everything up.

If we don't crave God, then at the very least we crave Grand Strategy.

6

HILL DECIDED TO REFUSE THE ASSIGNMENT. THE PAPER that he held in his hand required him to go to South Vietnam as an officer of Civil Operations and Rural Development Support (CORDS), the American program to help secure and strengthen Vietnamese villages in the hopes that they would soon be able to fend off Viet Cong infiltration for themselves. CORDS was under the jurisdiction of Military Assistance Command, Vietnam (MACV), but it was largely staffed by Foreign Service officers like Hill. He traveled to Washington to speak with the State Department personnel officers in person. In a meeting on June 30, he laid out his rationale: the CORDS assignment would place him under military command, and he had not joined the Foreign Service to serve in the military (quite the opposite). "I think he just didn't want to go to Vietnam," said Fred Brown, a CORDS recruiter and colleague of Hill's posted in Danang.

At the time, Hill was not aware that large numbers of officers throughout the Foreign Service had been ducking out of Vietnam assignments. Because of chronic CORDS dodging, the State Department officers informed him, President Nixon had recently issued a directive declaring that any officer who refused the assignment would be required to resign his commission. Hill was not deterred: "I said, 'Well, that's it, then. I'm not accepting it.'" He left Washington on July 1 with the assumption that he would soon be asked to resign, and headed north to Ocean City before proceeding home to Cambridge. He said later that the decision had not been difficult. "There was no agonizing, no holding my head in my hands. I'd drawn my conclusion. There was no long debate." Martha was relieved that her husband was no longer off to a war zone. Hill's colleagues assured him that they would take care of him. Professor Fairbank had already begun making calls to get him an appointment to the prestigious Social Science Research Council. It looked as if Hill would become an academic, after all.

But the State Department had not closed his case. Not long after he began preparations to continue university life indefinitely, a phone call came from Washington. Hill was informed that he was the first Foreign Service officer to refuse a Vietnam post since Nixon's order had gone into effect. As such, his case had gone before a legal review board. Lawyers from the White House had read his argument and concluded that he was right; they could not require a Foreign Service officer to serve under the military. The CORDS assignment was withdrawn.

In November, another thin envelope arrived. Hill was assigned to a traditional embassy post — in Saigon, South Vietnam.

He had three months to pack up and prepare to leave Cambridge and his family behind (the Saigon post prohibited officers from bringing dependents without special clearance). "I said, 'Well, those are the terms I made, and I'll stick with it,'" Hill recalled. "I was never trying to 'get out of Vietnam.' I was making a political point. This was the job I was in, and this is what we did. There was no recrimination, resentment, or wailing — this is what you do, and you go off and do it."

On February 14, 1971, Hill departed on an overnight flight bound for Tokyo. From there he continued on to Hong Kong, where he paused during his layover to watch an evening soccer match between Hong Kong and South Vietnam at Happy Valley Stadium. "I was really affected by that," he said. "I had never thought, from what I'd heard in the United States, that there would be any such thing as a soccer team coming from Vietnam. It didn't make any sense to me because Vietnam was supposed to be in flames. I found it very puzzling." From there Hill flew southwest across the South China Sea. The shamrock-print upholstery around him was strangely cheerful — Hill deduced that Air Saigon had leased the plane from the Irish airline Aer Lingus. As the plane approached Saigon, it flew high over the city at a peaceful cruising altitude, then plummeted downward at a nauseating angle to land at Ton Son Nhut airbase on the city's edge. This approach was best for eluding antiaircraft fire. It was the standard descent in a place besieged by war.

The American presence in Vietnam dated back to 1961, when President Kennedy sent three thousand military advisers and support personnel to aid the South Vietnamese government in its war against the Viet Cong, insurgents allied with the Communist regime in North Vietnam. Vietnam was the primary Pacific front of the cold war. To permit the country to fall to the Soviet-backed regime in Hanoi, it was believed, would incite a "domino effect" whereby all of Southeast Asia would topple to Communism. In the spring of 1964, prompted by a North Vietnamese offensive in neighboring Laos, President Lyndon Johnson moved to dramatically increase American air and naval power in Southeast Asia. In August Congress passed the Gulf of Tonkin Resolution, providing Johnson with the freedom to take whatever action he felt necessary to defend Southeast Asia from the Communist threat.* The first American ground forces arrived early the following year. General William Westmoreland led the American ground troops in a strategy of attrition and search-and-destroy missions, with continual hope for head-on clashes where his men could wipe out large swaths of the enemy. But Vietnam was a new breed of war for the Americans. The Viet Cong guerrillas preferred to dictate the place and time of engagement, descending on American troops with sniper fire and then retreating into the jungle.

On January 30, 1968, only months after Westmoreland said he had never been more encouraged by events in Vietnam and that the end was in sight, the Communists launched a wave of attacks on more than one hundred cities and towns in the South. The surprise attack, which came over the Tet holiday celebrating the new lunar year, resulted in catastrophic losses for the Viet Cong and North Vietnamese Army. But the Tet Offensive is best remembered for its disastrous psychological blow to American public support for the war. Americans, despite repeated assurances that the war was nearly at an end, now saw that the contest was far from over. Enemy buildup in the South had continued throughout Westmoreland's tenure, despite Johnson's willingness to grant most of the general's persistent requests for more American troops (the number would peak at 543,400 in 1969). Westmoreland neglected pacification efforts in the countryside and had little interest

---

* The details of the incident that prompted the resolution, an alleged North Vietnamese attack on the U.S. destroyer *Maddox*, are still unclear. Later evidence suggested that no North Vietnamese forces were present during the second "battle," as the captain of the USS *Maddox* initially claimed. Critics charge that the Johnson administration sensationalized the incident to create an excuse to escalate its military involvement in Vietnam.

in advising and training the Army of the Republic of Vietnam (ARVN, the South Vietnamese forces). After Tet, Washington was finally convinced that Westmoreland's strategies were wrongheaded. He was replaced in April by Creighton Abrams, a gruff, courageous general renowned as a tank commander in World War II. The previous spring, Ellsworth Bunker had replaced Henry Cabot Lodge as ambassador in Saigon, and not long afterward, a career CIA officer named William Colby (earlier the chief of station at Saigon) arrived to take over American support of the pacification program. With the arrival of this new guard, the war would change radically.

Abrams immediately abandoned Westmoreland's approach to the war. He cemented the fragmented American strategy into "one war" with the central objective of securing South Vietnamese villages and hamlets from infiltration by the Viet Cong. By this time the withdrawal of American troops had begun, and Abrams was faced with recasting the conduct of the war under the constraints of limited financial and human resources. His troops were finally authorized to take actions they ought to have taken years earlier—such as a limited raid into Cambodia to strike at Viet Cong sanctuaries and cripple the Ho Chi Minh Trail—but by this point American popular opinion forced President Nixon to severely hem in such efforts, nullifying their ultimate success. Nevertheless, by late 1970, as Charlie Hill received his notice to pack up for Saigon, the war could have been considered "won," at least by the standards Washington had set for itself. The Vietnam War —an internal struggle of national liberation fundamentally misunderstood by the U.S. government in terms of cold war objectives—could never end in a true victory for the United States, but by this point rural South Vietnam was widely pacified; that is, American and South Vietnamese forces had greatly reduced Viet Cong "taxes," thefts, and impressment of villagers, and surrounding ARVN units were freed from stationary security tasks. The People's Self-Defense Force was well established, and ARVN expanded to become more capable of repelling aggression without the help of American ground forces—if (an important "if") American logistical, financial, air, and naval support was available in case Hanoi violated a cease-fire agreement.

But Hill had read nothing of these developments. After the Tet Offensive, the American press had largely lost interest in the war on the ground and was fixated on the antiwar scene in the United States. The Pentagon Papers—the study of the conduct of the war commissioned by a disillusioned Robert McNamara in his final months as secretary of defense—were published the month of Hill's arrival. The thousands of pages detailing the escalation and wrong turns of American involvement in Vietnam ended their story in 1968, just before Abrams's new strategies and the pacification program had begun to show results. As Hill would understand soon after his arrival, the achievements of recent years were totally obscured. They would remain so for decades.

Saigon in 1971 was a frothing Asian city. It was hot, overcrowded, and undersanitized, its boulevards lined by the husks of a French provincial past and brimming now with little blue-and-yellow Renault taxis, pedicabs, bicycles, and snarling motorbikes that left throngs of pedestrians coughing in clouds of blue smoke. The marketplaces smelled of rotting fish delicacies and overripe fruit and clamored with beggars, often limbless, diseased, and many no older than the war itself, who tailed their prey for blocks with fingers outspread for a few piasters. Propaganda posters for the Republic of Vietnam regime, that of Nguyen Van Thieu, covered most bare wall surfaces.

The sense of precariousness was pervasive even in the quieter neighborhoods where the foreigners lived. After a dinner party, it was typical for the host to offer his guests a handgun for safety on the walk home, like the courtesy of a loaned umbrella on a rainy night. Nor did personal leisure time go unaffected. During the rare afternoons when Hill could afford to take a quiet row down the Saigon River in one of the local rowing club's antique French shells, the Vietnamese man hired as the coxswain wore a steel helmet in case of sniper fire from the shore. At night, Hill sometimes sat on the roof of the embassy and watched the firefights across the Saigon River, like a perverted Fourth of July.

The original American embassy in South Vietnam had been bombed beyond repair in the early 1960s. The new building, gleaming a half mile away, was surrounded on all sides by a reinforced concrete rocket screen. When Hill first arrived, he was driven to the Italian embassy on Rue Pasteur, where the Americans had rented an apartment suite to accommodate new personnel. The building was inside a walled compound on a busy street just beyond the center of the city, next to the Military Assistance Command/Special Operations Group, the center of American paramilitary operations. Hill was assigned as deputy to the Mission Coordinator, the office responsible for coordinating the civilian branches of the mission and liaison between the embassy and MACV. He sat across the room from his army counterpart, a lieutenant colonel named Arthur Cates. Cates was a handsome southerner who wore a crewcut and the black-framed glasses popular in those days. He was a wheeler-dealer always trying to work an angle on merchandise at the Post Exchange, or a housing upgrade, or a backdoor way to get the proper paperwork to take his Vietnamese wife and their son to the United States, "all with a wonderful happy tricky expression" on his face, Hill said. If you wanted something, you went to Art Cates.

Cates and Hill hit it off, sharing the same adventurous attitude toward their jobs. In their spare time they served as ad hoc air-traffic controllers for the helipad on the embassy roof, waving in Cates's friends from the 1st Division of the 9th Air Cavalry. The Air Cav were buccaneer types who wore black cowboy hats and brought Hill along as an observer on some of their missions. "It was exciting. This was a helicopter war, and it was terrific fun," he remembered. "The helicopters would go at treetop level, just roaring over rice paddies, skinning the tops of the vegetation to avoid getting hit. That was a lot of fun."

Hill soon learned that in addition to his job as DMC, he was assigned as personal aide to Ambassador Ellsworth Bunker, the grand old man of American diplomacy. Bunker had graduated from Yale in 1916 and worked for decades in his family's sugar-refining business in Latin America before turning to public service, where he would serve seven presidents over a twenty-seven-year diplomatic career. He was a master negotiator, a veteran of Latin America, India, and the Middle East, who won the respect of arrogant dictators and understood the diplomatic value of oral argument and ambiguous language. He had devoted his career to protecting American interests in the midst of European decolonization and the cold war. Since coming to Saigon in 1967, he had shrewdly brought the reluctant South Vietnamese into peace negotiations at Paris.

Bunker was ancient, by the standards of most American personnel in Saigon, but he showed no sign of slowing down. He regularly hiked about the countryside on tours with CORDS officers and field commanders. His tennis shot, Hill noted, was unerring. Bunker was an austere, slender figure of total dignity. He wore his gray hair neatly combed off his high forehead. He had small, foxlike eyes and the kind of pursed mouth that is always thinking. No one could bear to tell a lie to his face. For all his gravity, Bunker was also a witty, relaxed man who shared Hill's ironic sense of humor. They broke the ice by betting on the Yale-Brown football game, the first of the season.*

Hill loved his job immediately. His office was next to the ambassador's suite, at the nerve center of American operations. From the start he kept long hours, working into the night, then walking back to the Italian embassy to collapse for a few hours' dead sleep. During the day he was immersed in supervising incoming reports on the pacification efforts of ARVN and American forces. Reports on the security of "strategic hamlets," the fortified villages where Americans corraled South Vietnamese peasants, were notoriously inaccurate, especially during the first half of the conflict. Hill and his coworkers often headed into the field to check the reports against reality. The American military had never encountered a war like Vietnam, and no one was sure how to take stock of a conflict in which the enemy had such irregular forces and techniques of engagement. General Abrams had long ago realized that it was futile to estimate enemy casualties or count square mileage of embattled territory as "cleared" of Communist forces. There was no good indicator of the amount of land and people that friendly forces actually controlled. "It was almost a philosophical question of how you count things," said Hill.

Hill began drafting correspondence and speeches for Bunker — not important orations, but the brief remarks and addresses necessary for the endless minor public events that filled the ambassador's calendar. His superiors were impressed: "[Hill] is a superb craftsman who, I feel certain, will become one of the top drafters in the Foreign Service . . . He thinks on his feet, organizes his points so logically and quickly, and is able to persuade others so tactfully they hardly realize their opinions have been changed," lauded one supervisor in Hill's evaluation report. Hill did his work quietly and competently. "Charlie doesn't talk too much. He keeps his words to himself," said Fred Brown, then posted in Danang. "That's part of why great men like him." He quietly

---

* Nor was Bunker without compassion or, as busy as he was, time in his schedule for the very young. After Easter 1973, he addressed a note on embassy stationery to "Miss Catharine Hill": "Dear Kate," he wrote to Hill's oldest daughter, "Thank you very much for the picture of the big Easter bunny who is very handsome and all the little bunnies. I am especially glad to have the golden Easter egg which ought to bring me a great deal of luck. This made my Easter very happy and I hope you had a happy Easter also. With love from, [signed] Ellsworth Bunker.

won admittance to meetings of the Mission Council—where Bunker, Abrams, Colby, and other senior officials met to discuss the course of the war—by offering to take notes. His notes were not particularly thoughtful or meticulous. They were functional documents used to task the action items that emerged from each meeting. But the chore "gave him cover." Those who might have otherwise questioned the junior officer's presence at a high-level meeting didn't think twice about it when he presented himself as "the note taker" and kept his mouth shut.

As spring turned to summer, Hill was struck by the gap between the Vietnam War he had understood back in Cambridge and the results of General Abrams's new strategy combined with the civilian administration led by Bunker and Colby. Despite the continuing drawdown (Nixon had ordered troop strength cut by an additional sixty-nine thousand by May 1) and the negative assessments of an ARVN campaign in Laos, stability in South Vietnam was increasing. Hill later recalled driving in a Jeep from Saigon to the old French resort town of Dalat in the Highlands—he and a colleague were the only ones in the deserted hotel in a skeleton town that hadn't seen a tourist dollar since the French left. But they drove there like ordinary tourists, with no weapons beneath their seats, in a straight line from the city into the once-contested Highlands. Abrams's "one war" strategy "was creating a stable, relatively safe Vietnam," said Hill.

His opinion of the war also changed upon his encounter, in the streets of Saigon, with real South Vietnamese people. "They really didn't want to be Communist," he realized. "I was stunned by the fact that mailmen, policemen, shopkeepers, and people with families were all trying to make everything work as best they could—it really was a country." He'd had no sense of this from the antiwar polemics at Harvard or what he'd read in the American media. The American press—as well as the self-righteous intellectuals he had encountered in academia—were not, as a more naive Hill was tempted to believe, unfailing keepers of the record. They were storytellers, with their own agendas.

The relationship between the press corps in Vietnam and the American embassy was the polar opposite of the cooperation and mutual respect that Hill had enjoyed with reporters in Hong Kong. Now there was nothing but suspicion, derision, and animosity. The press operated as if their prime job—and career opportunity—was to expose disaster wrought by the hands of the American government. In a reminder of more congenial days, Hill had lunch once a week with *Time* magazine's Saigon bureau chief H.D.S. Greenway, whom he trusted as a responsible reporter. But on his way to Greenway's office each week, he had to slink out of the embassy when no one was looking and hurry down the street, occasionally lurking behind trees. If someone at the embassy saw him consorting with a member of the press, he would be blamed for the next inevitable information leak. "It was as if I were a spy in Vienna before World War I," he said.

As the spring of 1972 approached and Hill was up for reassignment, he expressed some desire to be transferred out of Saigon to a post in Chinese affairs; over the course of the year he had continued to study Mandarin in the evenings. But Bunker preferred to retain his principal aide, and in a short time Hill was induced to volunteer for another year of duty in Vietnam. The executive mission coordinator had left, and Hill was promoted to replace him. But as American withdrawal continued and personnel numbers dwindled, there was no one to take his place as deputy. Under the title executive secretary of the mission, Hill took on both jobs himself. He was "the principal aide to the Ambassador and a one-man Secretariat," read one performance evaluation.

Soon he would have the added responsibility of a family. Hill wrote Martha that the ambassador had asked him to extend his tour, but he had refused to do so unless she, Katie, and Emily were permitted to join him. To persuade Hill to stay, the ambassador had granted him an exception to the post's rule against dependents.

Martha read that letter with ambivalence. "I didn't want to go, but he convinced me," she explained. "This was me being the Foreign Service wife." Over the past year, Martha had made do with life alone in Cambridge. She wrote to Charlie nearly every night, clipping newspaper articles about the war and including a packet of them in each envelope, as he had requested. Hill had been home for a few brief days of leave. Once, in one of the less-expected duties of the Foreign Service, he was given sole charge of eleven Korean babies on a flight from Seoul to New York. He spent the plane ride walking up and down the aisle trying to quiet one after another and sheepishly pleading with the flight attendants to change them. But the faces of their adoptive American parents when the plane door opened at JFK airport was a rich reward.

At least one photograph survives of Hill cradling an anonymous bundle—it portrays a rare side of him, one that, perhaps, found in the baby a reminder of what was waiting for him at home. Despite the political ferment of Cambridge, those visits had been pleasant, filled with the relief that comes with a reunited family. For all her misgivings, Martha was probably glad that they would be together again in Saigon.

She took the girls to visit her family in Oak Park for the Easter holiday, and they prepared to depart on April 6, 1972. Charlie flew home to get them. In a photograph taken in the Mitchells' home that morning, Martha is kneeling in a white dress next to Katie and Emily, both outfitted in patriotic red-and-white-striped jumpers and tights. They look as little girls often do before the camera—shyly clinging to their mother's shoulder or the arm of the couch. Martha's hands are not around her daughters but clasped tightly on her knees. She is not smiling. Her expression is resigned, as if posing for the camera were just one in a long line of unpleasant duties, and not half so bad as most.

When Hill flew back to the United States to collect his family, he assured them that Vietnam had quieted down. He believed it had. The first months of 1972 had witnessed the lowest level of fighting yet. Then, on Sunday, March 30, while the Hills went to church and enjoyed an Easter ham with Martha's parents, the Communists launched their Easter Offensive.

To chew up as many ARVN units as possible, prove that President Nixon's "Vietnamization" strategy wasn't working, and increase their leverage at the negotiating table, the Communists had launched a traditional World War II–style assault. The North Vietnamese Army (NVA) assembled by the thousands along definable front lines, raining Soviet shells and flattening the countryside with Soviet-made tanks. With the northern part of South Vietnam in chaos, Hanoi launched an effort to take the provincial capital, An Loc, and surrounding areas, and would bring the fighting within thirty miles of Saigon during the Hills' first week together in the city. The noise of artillery fire was constant. By mid-May, the situation turned around and, in the end, just as after the Tet Offensive in 1968, the enemy crawled away into the jungle, devastated. But like Tet, the Easter Offensive threatened similar psychological damage to Americans' support of a war effort that was supposed to be winding down. From the start, news coverage of the clashes portrayed the Nixon administration and the Pentagon as misguided bumblers who should have seen the warning signs of the coming attack and, once again, underestimated Hanoi's resolve.

Hill's assurances to his wife that the war was practically over must have seemed less than credible. As they departed from Chicago and flew west to arrive in Saigon on April 9, the Communist offensive continued to rage, and no matter its eventual conclusion, it would set the tone for Martha's feelings about the war. "I read that 'Peace at Hand' crap and then saw the bomb craters as we flew over Saigon," she recalled.

47 Phan Thanh Gian—the French villa that Art Cates had finagled for himself and Hill and that, as Cates was now moving out, would be the Hill family home—was originally built for the concubine of Emperor Bao Dai, a woman named Mong Diep. The guard at the gate still remembered when the emperor regularly sent one of his cars along the gravel drive to pick up his mistress. No one knew what happened to his lovely Diep, but in the years since, her villa had become notorious as the bachelor pad for young hotshots making their careers off the war. Located on the edge of the city, number forty-seven was not a particularly grand villa, surrounded by noisy streets pungent with motorbike fumes, but a tall fence encircled the grounds and provided some sense of privacy. It was a comfortably large house with white stucco walls, a tile roof, and a screened porch overlooking the neat front yard. A sprawling plane tree stood in the middle of the grass, perpetually festooned with dangling Vietnamese children.

The ground level hosted a built-in bar and a large sitting area that could be cleared of chairs to create a makeshift dance floor. It was "one of the best known villas in Saigon for bright young things," according to the *New York Times*. Three or four American men had lived there at a time with a small staff and occupied much of their time throwing boisterous parties, including famous New Year's Eve soirees. The invitation to the fourth annual party, poking fun at a common slogan of Vietnam War optimism, had beckoned, "The Flower People of Saigon invite you to see 'the light at the end of the tunnel.' Act Four. New Year's Eve 1970." Luckily for Martha and her little girls, as the United States inched backward out of Vietnam over the past year, the bachelors had cleared out of the villa. Art Cates was the last to leave.

When Hill arrived at the villa with his wife and daughters, the Vietnamese family that staffed the house was waiting out front. They broke into enormous grins when they saw the American couple arrive with two little Chinese girls in tow—"this family that doesn't go together," in Martha's words. Hill invited his embassy coworkers to the villa for drinks. "They said, 'Hi, how are you,' and then all talk was about the war for the rest of the night," she remembered. "It was mostly men at the post, and the women who were there were going crazy." "Home" felt like an army base camp. Her first night in her new house, Martha found a homemade assault weapon called a "grease gun" in the upstairs bedroom—"my bedroom, in the house where my little girls were going to live."

Hill's impression was that Martha "was excited to be there." He thought she agreed with him about the difference between American press accounts of the war and realities on the ground. As best he remembered, "she fully agreed with me that this was very different from what we'd heard, and it was significant to be there, to be seeing and understanding this, supporting [the American effort] because it had been so derided and besieged." He also believed she was glad to escape her mother once more. "Everything is fine here," Hill wrote his parents on April 20.

> Fifty percent of what you read is exaggerated . . . Our main problem is that the PX [U.S. Army Post Exchange] is out of vodka. Katie's main problem is that the dog barber who promised to come and clip the poodle [Susi, a little black dog that adopted the Hills] can't come until tomorrow because of the immense amount of poodle clipping appointments he has. Emily's main problem is how to blow up her water wings before she goes swimming in the pool every day. Martha's main problem is that she has no sun-tan lotion and too much free time. My main problem is that you keep writing me letters saying you are worried . . . The whole thing [the Easter Offensive] was about as far away from us as a fire in a tenement in the slums of Atlantic City is from you in Ocean City.

It was a good thing that Hill felt confident about his wife's mental state, because the arrival of Martha and the girls did not mean that he spent much more time at home. The Easter Offensive was still in progress, and he spent most weekends in the field, gathering reports from military officers on troop strength and the security of key towns. If the Americans ever hoped to withdraw completely from South Vietnam and expect the unsteady nation to remain intact, there was much work yet to be done. Hill, the "one-man Secretariat," would spend nearly every waking hour trying to do his part. The wife he left at home was proud of her husband, but scared and lonely.

While General Abrams continued his efforts to wear down the enemy and secure the South Vietnamese countryside, Henry Kissinger, then Nixon's national security adviser, led the American delegation at the Paris Peace Conference. The attempts to bring the war to a diplomatic resolution began in 1968. The talks over the next four years achieved little beyond a series of short-lived "understandings" regarding Hanoi's presumed self-restraint when Washington ordered bombing halts. In October 1972, after the failed Easter Offensive and President Nixon's decision to bomb and mine the North had given Washington more leverage, Hanoi tentatively agreed to a cease-fire— but President Thieu immediately rejected it and insisted on changes that outraged Hanoi. Kissinger was obliged to fly to Saigon to try to win over the stubborn South Vietnamese leader. Soon afterward the North Vietnamese were further incensed at the revelation in the American media that Washington planned to keep at least ten thousand American civilians stationed in Vietnam after withdrawing its troops. After Hanoi halted the negotiations, Nixon punished the North with the Christmas Bombings — twelve days of the most concentrated bombings in history. Still, Le Duc Tho, the masterful "adviser" of Hanoi's negotiating team, sensed that the balance had swung in his favor. Staffers of Kissinger's aide Alexander Haig stomped around the embassy muttering that Kissinger, the "Great Man," "has monumentally fucked up," noted Hill. "His ego made him try to do it all alone."

Hill's notes capture an irritated Kissinger returning to the embassy after a scheduled meeting at Thieu's Independence Palace was postponed, a red-faced herd of advisers trudging after him. While waiting for the summons to return for another meeting, they stared in disbelief as Thieu's motorcade cruised past the embassy — no one knew the wily president's destination. In a strange echo of the 1963 assassination of Thieu's predecessor, Ngo Dinh Diem, Thieu telephoned Bunker later that night to angrily charge that Al Haig's visits had been an attempt to prepare a coup against him. Kissinger realized the sad reality of Thieu's behavior: "the war would not end soon, or in a way that would heal the divisions in our country."

Talks resumed between Kissinger and Le Duc Tho in Paris on January 8, 1973. The destruction wrought by the Christmas Bombings had had some effect; Le Duc Tho was prepared to settle. After three months, almost two dozen changes in the text of the cease-fire agreement, and a threat to cut off American aid, Kissinger finally gained Thieu's acquiescence. On January 24, the Mission Council convened to hear Nixon's announcement of the peace agreement on ARVN radio. Rumors swirled at Katie's school that all Americans would have to leave Vietnam at once to avoid reprisals by South Vietnamese who believed they had been "sold out." Nothing of the sort happened. Mrs. Murtha, Katie's teacher, took the class out to her car where they could listen to the president on the radio.

The forlorn wail of a cease-fire siren cut through the air at 8 A.M. on January 28, 1973. On the first afternoon the cease-fire was in effect, artillery fire continued to crackle in the provinces north of Saigon—the peace agreement had allowed NVA units to remain in the South. Now it was left for the embassy to aid in coordinating the first joint session of the International Commission for Control and Supervision (ICCS) and the Joint Military Committee to supervise the cease-fire and lay the groundwork for some kind of coalition government. Hill helped orchestrate the arrival of North Vietnamese Army and political officers from Hanoi. The C-130s skidded into Saigon's Tan Son Nhut airport the same day the cease-fire was declared, but the Communists distrusted the Americans and refused to disembark. They stayed the night on the planes, with no windows and no latrines. The following day an intense diplomatic effort persuaded them to step outside, haggard in their shoulder boards, pith helmets with red stars, and rubber shoes. A few days later the Viet Cong arrived, ferried in by U.S. Army helicopters. They stepped onto the runway in jungle-green camouflage and sandals, with red, swollen sores about their ankles and necks from years of hiking through tropical undergrowth.

The atmosphere was tense. Hill and the rest of the embassy staff spent the week worrying about the pending release of the American POWs from their holding place at Loc Ninh. Finally, at eight o'clock in the evening on February 12, a few hundred reporters camped out on the tarmac since eight in the morning were finally rewarded for their patience. White Red Cross planes stood by to transport the released prisoners to Clark Air Force Base in the Philippines. All airport traffic had ceased hours earlier, and the runways were quiet. Hill hoisted Katie and Emily onto his shoulders. To the north, off in the distance, a string of seven red lights blinked in the darkness. The crowd was silent, their eyes fixed on the ballet of aircraft. There was no movement until the aircraft had landed and each set of helicopter blades came to a standstill.

One hatch opened and the crowd's first sight was a medical litter, sliding down onto the pavement, swelling and waving in the wind. Then the prisoners clambered off, all in Hanoi-issue gray hospital fatigues and sandals, "lean but healthy," Hill wrote. Some of the POWs waved. The crowd applauded and cheered but was oddly subdued. They were aware, Hill thought, of the historic moment. Part of him felt that they "should have been warmer, more emotional, but all there were professionals — press and military, and [there was a] sense of caution and care and awe in the face of so many prison years." In less than a half hour, every gaunt, weary figure was aboard a Red Cross plane; the plane and the helicopters were off, and the moment ended. Photographers turned and rushed toward Hill, snapping pictures of Katie and Emily in their pajamas and housecoats. "They sense some hidden story," Hill wrote. "Why were these little girls taken from their beds to see this?"

Hill spent Valentine's Day humoring Richard Waldhaus, the sole POW who elected to remain in Saigon. Hill escorted him by helicopter to Phuoc Vinh to look for an old girlfriend Waldhaus had left behind. She was nowhere to be found, although the villagers promised to deliver her to Saigon the following day—Hill cringed as they inflated his charge's hopes, especially as the embassy was hoping to get Waldhaus on a plane out of Saigon the next morning. The prisoner's mental state was rickety. He refused to change out of his Viet Cong hospital pajamas, shawl, and rubber shoes and throughout the day tried to give Hill the slip. When Hill took him to run some errands, Waldhaus drew a Viet Cong flag on his palm and flashed it to a shopkeeper, scaring the wits out of him. He confided in Hill that he thought all people in Saigon were secretly Viet Cong agents. At the Post Exchange, he chased girls down the aisles. The press was convinced the embassy was holding Waldhaus "incommunicado" and that he was a CIA agent—"but just loony," sighed Hill in his notebook. The girlfriend never showed up.

The last POWs would leave Vietnam by the first week of April. The newspaper stories covering their release provoked a brief flash of interest from an American public that had long ago grown sick of reading about the war. People like Charles Hill, who had the ugly job of trying to hold Saigon together while the South hemorrhaged troops and resources, were not heroes to readers back home. They had little reason to feel sympathy for American civilians in Vietnam. The *Wall Street Journal* portrayed the capital as a stoic city hardened by a decade of war and oblivious to the rising numbers of South Vietnamese casualties, preferring instead to decorate itself with victory banners and political propaganda. The lives of resident foreigners were, in a reporter's ironic phrase, "normal in the extreme," replete with show-riding competitions, Dada art exhibits and university lectures for the urbane, and girlie bars for everyone else.

Newspapers occasionally published colorful and sneering feature articles about the easy lifestyle of Saigon's diplomatic set. "The State Department may call it a hardship post and the Army classifies it as a combat zone. But no American in the United States mission here . . . is deprived of instant daiquiris or instant pizzas, lamb chops or steaks, Wonder bread or chocolate cookies," gibed the *New York Times*. The article went on to portray ambassadors and embassy wives cruising on the embassy yacht or lounging poolside while Vietnamese street urchins peered over the fence at their food and soldiers a few miles away fought and died. The average reader probably had no pity for Martha's plight: "Although American women are encouraged — but not prodded — into doing some form of volunteer work, most members of the [American Women's] Association stick together and play bridge," explained one smug passage. "One project of the group that seems to strike a warm chord is a cookbook of American recipes translated into Vietnamese, for the servants of Americans to read."

The embassy received a (much delayed) subscription to American papers. Martha read these articles and clipped them for her scrapbook. They pained her: "I didn't feel quite so frivolous when I was there," she said. She spent every spare hour in volunteer work — as much to keep herself sane as to contribute to the community. At Katie's school, Martha taught art classes and transformed the school library from a pile of discarded books on the floor in a bare room into catalogued shelves surrounded by that week's art projects. "I was not at my best there," she said. "But I kept busy."

Katie's school was a bright point in their life in Saigon. Dressed in a little white dress with an enormous, proud bow tied lopsidedly on the pinafore, she tramped off to begin first grade in the Phoenix Study Group on September 5, 1972. Katie's teacher, Mrs. Murtha, was a charismatic woman always flashing her Jackie Onassis sunglasses and wide toothy grin. Martha helped out on field trips and hosted the class Halloween party at the Hills' villa. She was an artist and an inventor in everything she did. She constructed a "haunted tunnel" in the dining room out of bed sheets, and the girlfriend of reporter Fox Butterfield, an old friend of Hill, dressed up as a witch to greet the kids at the tunnel's end. Afterward the children bobbed for apples, tripped over their costumes in races and relays, made Halloween-themed crafts out of construction paper, and participated in an ambiguous activity noted in Martha's scrapbook as "marshmallow grabbing," which could have ended only in an enormous mess. Martha received piles of thank-you notes for her efforts. "Dear Mrs. Hill, It is fun bobbing for apples. You went to a whole bunch trouble," wrote one perceptive little girl named Faith.

Martha felt a mother's instinctive guilt over bringing her small daughters to live in a dangerous place. "Katie and Emily have their ups and downs but I keep reminding myself we haven't been here very long," she wrote to Bridgeton on April 27, 1972. "Nothing is really very nice for them but I am hoping the play group will work out." The play group fell through — there were too few children to sustain it. Martha was grateful for the embassy pool. It was a safe place to take the girls every day to cool off and play, and as two of the very few children there, Katie and Emily were celebrities. They learned to dive and swim like little bikinied eels with the instruction of enthusiastic young military and embassy men who missed their families and were happy to play with kids for a change. Today, Katie and Emily have few memories of Saigon — except for the enormous cockroaches that crawled out of the villa's open drains and scared the girls from stepping out of their beds at night. At the time, the girls were too young to have any sense of the danger of the place beyond nightmarish creepy-crawlies. Katie remembers the guards in front of their house and their big guns. Emily will never forget the loud "whoop-whoop" of the helicopters overhead, and to this day a whiff of rotting garbage in a back alley reminds her of Saigon. But mostly they loved their new home for its big garden, climbing trees, and wizened nanny who played with them. Photographs taken at the time show the girls running about the yard, naked but for swimsuit tan lines and little striped shorts, out of breath and laughing.

The Saigon Zoo seemed like a safe place to introduce the girls to Saigon. By American standards, the zoo was shabby and poorly maintained, but it was the only peaceful green space (except for President Thieu's estate) amid the city's slums and screeching traffic. To *Wall Street Journal* correspondent Peter Kann, the zoo seemed the only place in Vietnam unaffected by the war; not since 1968, when a Viet Cong rocket struck near the aviary, killing two parakeets, had the conflict interrupted this patch of normalcy. Martha took her daughters to the zoo soon after they arrived in the country, but she did not share the reporter's reaction. Perhaps theirs was the difference of opinion to be expected between a seasoned war correspondent and an American housewife fresh from Cambridge, Massachusetts. To Martha, "the zoo was hell." The animals were hungry and mangy, much of their fur rubbed off. Martha and her girls stared as the beasts did the sort of disturbing things animals do when they're underfed and unhealthy. Martha regarded the other people standing around the cages, staring, like her and the girls, at these gruesome displays of sexual behavior. No one reacted — only watched. "This was another moment," Martha remembered, "where I said, 'I don't know what I'm getting into.'"

The class parties and field trips could never make Martha forget where she was. Even on the few occasions when Charlie had a little free time, the countryside was quiet, and Vietnam might have seemed like a tropical vacationland, the war was everywhere. In a letter to Bridgeton that May, she reflected on a three-hour motorboat tour she and Charlie took down the Saigon River: "It is such a strange thing — riding along a peaceful river in this war-torn land. Children jumping from trees into the water, water skiers zooming by, peaceful little villages, vacation homes being built for wealthy people to retreat to, housing projects going up, palms gracefully blowing in the breeze. And then you go under a bridge and each section below is heavily fortified and manned and you remember again where you are." Helicopters swatted continually through the air overhead, with soldiers' feet dangling over the sides. Explosions at a nearby ammunitions dump blew out the villa's windows in the middle of the night. All around her were signs that life here was disintegrating. There was a general laxness in the streets. The terrace bar at the Hotel Continental — where white-coated waiters once served genteel French officials and Somerset Maugham watched the sun set — was now crawling with transvestites, hippies, and ladies of the night. Martha knew she was "witnessing the fall of something."

The embassy, on the other hand, was a pristine place protected from the outside world by high walls and sharp-looking Marines. "The men stayed in there, working on cables, while the women had to live outside," Martha said. "They had no idea of the hell of the city. We got mad." She and Hill fought about the war every night over dinner—

Martha's second dinner of the evening, the one she or the cook re-heated on the stove late at night when her husband came home. The girls had long since been fed and put to bed. The fragmented dinner hour was just another sign of general deterioration. "Charlie and I evolved from two people who talked about everything to two people who talked about current events and the children—we subtracted us and the marriage from the conversation," Martha said. "He wouldn't drop it, defending [national security adviser Henry] Kissinger's inva-sion of Cambodia . . . we fought every night in Saigon about that war. I drank a lot in Vietnam, and so did he. I was coming out of Cam-bridge, where the press was counting body bags. I felt the war was just a futile exercise in killing young boys."

Martha had begun to drink in Cambridge, but it was in Vietnam that her alcoholism really took hold. She saw this, as most alcoholics do, only in retrospect. "The Foreign Service is a great place to be an al-coholic and not know you are one," she said later. "There are so many cocktail parties, dinner parties, and everyone is a drinker. As the mar-riage began to teeter, my drinking became alcoholic. It followed a pat-tern. We'd always have drinks before dinner . . . It was bad in Vietnam. That was a difficult place for women—it was not a family place." Hill did not see Martha's problem for what it was. The dinnertime fights, to him, were incomprehensible.

Martha literally lost her voice not long after she arrived in Vietnam. What began as a puzzling flulike virus that wouldn't go away became what Martha believed at first was just a protracted case of laryngitis. It reduced her voice to a brittle croaking sound and hurt when she spoke. After weeks she made an appointment with the doctor at the army base who took cultures and sent her to a psychiatrist, who "said what a man would say: 'This isn't a good place for you. You need to leave,'" Martha recalled.

The following spring, after nearly a year of struggling with her voice —a particular trial for a Foreign Service wife expected to make charm-ing conversation at all embassy functions—Martha was referred to a Johns Hopkins–trained doctor based in Bangkok, Thailand. After a day of lunatic taxi drivers, wrong directions, and a somewhat terrify-ing expedition through the streets of the strange city, she found the Bangkok clinic. He told Martha that she had a rare condition called spasmodic dysphonia, a neurological voice disorder marked by invol-untary spasms of the vocal cords that interrupt speech and cause the voice to break up or to have a tight, strangled sound. There was nothing the doctor could do for her. The condition was little understood and had no known cure. He recommended that she try to speak in a different register and seek out a speech therapist. "I guess I should be happy just barking and croaking at everyone," she wrote cheerfully to Bridgeton. Privately, she was less lighthearted. "It felt like someone had his hands around my throat," Martha remembered.

But Martha's broken voice, like the drinking and the loneliness, the crackle of firefights, the transvestites in the bars, the crippled beggars, and everything else that was wrong about Vietnam, became the norm of the place. Martha watched vigilantly for packages and letters from her mother and from Bridgeton—her vital link home—and waited out the year. One evening, as she was sharing a taxi with an American reporter, several men on motorcycles roared through the crowded street, shooting madly. The reporter instantly ducked his head into his lap. Martha just sat still, thinking, "My God, I'm getting used to this."

Martha lives on Cathedral Avenue, in the modest brick house the Hills occupied when they returned to Washington in the mid-1970s. Cathedral is a quiet street off MacArthur Boulevard near the old C&O Canal, lined with shady lawns and small children on bicycles. I rang the doorbell and waited, wondering if I would be thrown out after ten minutes.

Originally, Martha had refused to talk to me. She had responded to my letter with a polite postcard, the front printed with Robert Motherwell's abstract painting *Reconciliation Elegy:* "Time should have made me objective and lucid about the years, events, and life I experienced with Charlie," she wrote. "Instead my memories move toward the opaque and my perceptions blur in highly personal ways . . . I regret that I cannot be of help." But a follow-up phone call determined that she would agree to talk about, perhaps, impersonal subjects such as the life of the Foreign Service wife in general. We set a date for lunch.

Martha was much more beautiful than I expected. I had long been agog at the photograph that Charlie kept from their college days, the curves of her face as graceful as a Vermeer painting. The young woman in the photograph was visible in the woman who opened the door now. Martha was petite, neatly dressed and rouged, her hair colored a flattering soft blond. She seemed much younger than Charlie—until I heard her voice. The spasmodic dysphonia had aged it another fifty years. It sounded always afraid to break, as if she were about to burst into tears —an unnerving illusion for a biographer hoping to ask questions about her ex-husband. But as she invited me inside, her tone was warm and friendly.

The house was too big for one person. It appeared that Martha had moved her life entirely to the second floor. The ground-level living room into which I first entered was pleasantly furnished but dark and untouched. She led me upstairs, in the company of a persistent black-and-white cat. There the sitting room was more comfortable, carpeted, with armchairs and a sofa meant for curling up on. Along the walls were shelves of books and curios from the exotic places where she had lived, the remaining space decorated here and there with Chinese-style paintings of birds and waterfronts that, I knew, she had painted herself. Appetizing smells emanated from the small kitchen overlooking the back yard. She told me she had prepared a "South Jersey cheese pie" for lunch, a quiche recipe inherited from Charlie's grandmother. There were green beans too, and brownies à la mode for dessert. The menu was quite thoughtful, considering that the cook had barely consented to talk to me.

As she finished up in the kitchen I tried to make myself useful, carrying plates and glasses to the dining table. I can't remember what we chatted about at first, but I recall that it was not as awkward as I had expected. When we sat down, I briefly considered leaving my notebook in my backpack. Part of me still worried that Martha would ice over and dismiss me after a single question, and that to take notes would only be to ask for trouble. But I reconsidered and began in the logical place — Oak Park, Illinois, where she had grown up, not forty-five minutes from my own hometown.

That first coincidence was an omen. The more we talked — after I had raved appropriately about the cheese pie — the more I found myself identifying with her. I was myself very near to where she had been in 1957 when she accepted Charlie's proposal of marriage: a female graduate of an Ivy League college with her whole life ahead of her, fairly successful in her interests at school and hopeful for a career. Almost immediately, she was opening up, remembering stories about China and Saigon. She was a wonderful storyteller. She had an eye for the tiny details that could help me understand what it must have been like to be there. We hardly dwelt on "Foreign Service life in general." We soon moved from the dining table to the sofa — that first conversation lasted five hours. She answered all my questions patiently and without evasion, talking about herself and about Charlie.

The thing you have to understand about Martha Hill is that she is funny. Terrifically funny. This book cannot convey that. Her place in the biography of Charlie is mostly in the context of a failing marriage, not as a fully formed partner in his life, because their relationship didn't allow her to be that. In some ways it is hard to see how her life with him was much more than a humorless struggle. But when I met her, I saw how inaccurate that assessment was. She recognized the absurdity of doing laundry in her Zurich apartment building, where tenants signed up for a washing time and never deviated from it by a minute, and stood outside beating their rugs even in the rain. She told amusing stories about grocery shopping in Hong Kong and embassy parties in Vietnam. She laughed about it all and shook her head at herself. I did impressions of other friends of Charlie whom I had already interviewed, and she cracked up. I already knew that Charlie had a sense of humor — although dry and sometimes long in appearing — and as I sat laughing with Martha, I started to see that there must have been thousands of small, wonderful moments between them that no one had ever written down, or perhaps even remembered. The shared smile is the best reason to choose to spend your life with someone, and I believed now that Charlie and Martha once had that.

Martha liked me more than she had expected to, I think. She was also baffled by me. When I told her the story of interviewing Charlie's journalist friend from the Hong Kong days, the renowned *Washington Post* reporter Stanley Karnow, her eyebrows shot up. It was true that the interview had been a bit unusual. Karnow had told me over the phone to let myself in through the garage door when I arrived and find my way to his office. I did so, and found him surrounded by walls of books, piles of papers, and a fog of yellow cigarette smoke, hunched over an ancient computer at which he squinted through thick Harry Carey glasses and pecked with two fingers. I asked the age of the computer. "Ah, she's a spring chicken — fifteen years old," he muttered. He stood up and fastened his belt, which I suppose he had loosened while seated for reasons of abdominal comfort.

Martha was astounded. "A woman of my generation would never have just walked into the office of Stanley Karnow like that," she said. I hadn't thought twice about it at the time. In the course of getting to know Martha, I began to understand things I had always taken for granted about being female in the twenty-first century. I had never had much patience with feminism — the rhetoric embarrassed me a little bit. It always sounded whiny and self-absorbed, more interested in victimization than empowerment. But now I started to think about how I would have felt in Martha's place. When I considered the opportunities she had given up, and the disregard with which Charlie had often treated her, I found myself feeling angry on her behalf—and interested, for the first time, in reading books like *The Feminine Mystique*. And although I wasn't yet certain how meeting Martha would affect my relationship with Charlie, I knew immediately that there was a whole new dimension of his story that I had to tell.

While I stood on the doorstep preparing to leave, Martha hovered in the doorway, clutching her squirming cat. She smiled and hesitantly patted me on the shoulder. I think I detected in her a repressed urge for a hug, but I may be flattering myself.

7

HILL CAME HOME FROM VIETNAM IN JULY 1973. THE STATE
Department permitted him a brief vacation in Ocean City, then sent
him to China for two weeks to chaperone a group of inner-city Chicago
teenagers on a cultural exchange trip. They toured communes and assembly plants staffed by twiggy Chinese girls. They won a basketball
game against a team of factory workers in a huge Shanghai athletic stadium, ablaze with floodlights and packed with thousands of workers
clad in blue trousers and white short-sleeved shirts, pulsing and waving on all sides like fields of sea anemones. They paused for a day or two
in lush Suzhou on the Yangtze River, where a wizened Chinese restaurant worker, who remembered the U.S. Navy sailors stationed there in
his childhood, asked the kids to sing "Anchors Aweigh" for him.

This was Hill's first visit to the country that he had observed for so
long from a distance, but "China seemed perfectly normal and familiar," he recalled. "That was what I had done for all those years — I was
deeply informed, I knew the street maps, the personalities, the tone of
things. I didn't even think about it as my first time there." This is a
strange thing to say, to imply that looking in on a place is the same as
experiencing it firsthand. But the margin had always been Hill's preferred habitat.

After a slow few months back at the State Department writing
"think pieces" for the assistant secretary of Cultural Affairs and directing a Sino-American cultural exchange that culminated in an enormous Chinese archeological exhibition at the National Gallery of
Art, relief finally came. Ellsworth Bunker, now ambassador-at-large in
charge of Panama Canal treaty negotiations, swooped in to reclaim
his personal aide. For the next few months, as Bunker's team shuttled

back and forth to Panama to negotiate the treaty that would return the canal to the Panamanians after more than seventy years of American ownership, Hill served as Bunker's political counsel, adviser on domestic issues, aide, and speechwriter all in one. He sat alone with Bunker in the sticky August heat on Contadora Island, enjoying a drink and watching Armed Forces Television on a fuzzy black-and-white set, when President Nixon announced his resignation after the Watergate scandal brought his administration down. Hill was with Bunker during less weighty emergencies as well — there was, for example, that distressed phone call from the ambassador on a Saturday afternoon, asking what to do about a bee infestation under the front steps. Hill came over and burned out the nest. He was no longer just a conscientious aide but the person Bunker turned to by default.

Hill had learned that the best way to circumvent State Department bureaucracy, to free himself of the whims of the Foreign Service personnel department and position himself where his ideas would have the most impact, was to latch on to a Great Man and make himself essential. Adviser to the prince: Hill believed this was his destined role. Perhaps that feeling was shy and unfocused at the posts in Zurich and Hong Kong, where he stayed at his desk and made no effort at a relationship with the consul general — but he had also stayed up late poring over books about Confucius, the ancient Chinese sage and aspiring royal adviser. The ambition and instinct were there. In Hong Kong Hill still "had a great sense of social inferiority," he admitted. "I had no flare, no touch for the ability I perceived in the people at the top." The awakening came at Harvard. It was not lost on him that the most prestigious university in the country had battled the State Department to insure that he would come, and once he arrived, the faculty invited Hill to lunch every day and treated him as an intellectual equal. "I had the sense that I had something to offer," he said. "That they were learning from me." Then, of course, there was Vietnam. "Nothing makes you grow up so fast as going to war."

"Charlie always hitched his wagon to the right people," his Vietnam colleague Fred Brown once said. But Hill did not "hitch his wagon" in the traditional sense, riding up to higher echelons of policymaking on his boss's momentum. He was chosen because the big men recognized that Hill would be a silent but potent component of their generalship. More times than not, he did the job he was hired to do.

Bunker and the American delegation had years of work yet ahead of them, and negotiators wouldn't agree on key details of the Panama Canal treaty until 1977. Hill would not be on the team to witness the historic signing. He had long since found a colleague to take his place at Bunker's side, and he himself moved on.

Within the ranks of Henry Kissinger's Policy Planning Staff, a Foreign Service officer named Mark Palmer was angling to extract himself from his speechwriting position, and he had his eye on Hill as the ideal replacement.* "I just knew he wrote well," Palmer shrugged. "I had met him, and I recommended him to the Secretary's deputy, Lawrence Eagleburger." Nothing happened without Eagleburger's approval. But over the next few months — before Hill, working just down the hall, entirely understood what was happening—he had been duly vetted and was offered a position as speechwriter on Kissinger's Policy Planning Staff. It was the job he had dreamed of—rather, predicted for himself—just over ten years ago, when he wrote his career aspiration on a note card in a dingy classroom of the Foreign Service Institute.

One afternoon in the early fall of 2004, I sat in on the Grand Strategy seminar. Five days after the official death toll of American soldiers and civilians in Iraq topped one thousand, two days after the three-year anniversary of the September 11 attacks, two dozen students gathered around a seminar table to hear Professor Hill present "the optimist's view" of current world affairs. According to the course syllabus, they were supposed to have read Francis Fukuyama's *The End of History and the Last Man*. Fukuyama's famous argument that history had culminated with the rise of liberal democracy now seemed, to some in the room, less than convincing.

Paul Kennedy, who would lead the following week's class on Samuel Huntington and "pessimism," was away giving a speech at the National Press Club, and today the Gang of Three was reduced to two. Gaddis, resting his elbow on the back of his chair, watched the students gossip and find their seats. The extra chairs around the perimeter of

---

* Although Nixon was loath to allow any foreign policy authority to leave the White House, when it became clear that the Watergate scandal had destroyed his ability to manage the nation's foreign affairs, he asked Kissinger to assume the post of secretary of state. Kissinger, who writes in his memoirs that he had been planning to retire from government before Nixon asked him to take on the job, was sworn in during September 1973.

the room were packed with graduate students and anonymous gray-haired men auditing the course. Hill walked in at precisely 3:30 P.M., his suit surprisingly crisp for the end of a warm fall afternoon.

"Optimism is a stand-alone matter, a grand strategist's concern," Hill began. "It's a career matter as well. If you're going to be good at what you're doing, you need to be able to put yourself into the proper mood in any situation." He mentioned a few of the great diplomats he had known who could control their emotions rather than allow their feelings to control them—there was, for example, negotiator Philip Habib and Secretary of State George Shultz, both of whom would figure prominently in Hill's State Department career. A few students raised their hands and made the wavering, self-conscious remarks that always come with the first few minutes of a seminar. Gaddis interrupted. "Optimism sounds a lot like acting," he said.

"It is," Hill answered. "If you can't act, in your career you won't get past the stage of upper-mid-level bureaucrat." One girl raised her hand and asked if there wasn't an element of falsity in that course of action. Hill only stared at her and smiled. The class chuckled softly, and he continued with a maxim about the necessity, sometimes, of transforming oneself in order to achieve the best outcome. But the real answer to the girl's question lay in Hill's calm smile, the hint that he had been to grisly places and seen ugly things, and remained an optimist despite it all. Perhaps he even had to do a few of those things himself—it wasn't clear. Gaddis smirked, pleased with the choreography of the moment.

When Hill turned to the day's reading, part of the class was already murmuring skeptically about Fukuyama's thesis. The students who didn't buy it wondered about the validity of sweeping theories that ignore inconvenient details of history. "This is a Herodotean point," Hill interjected. "Whether you think history has a direction or it doesn't, a storyline or none, these big theories are out there, and people believe them. There is an importance in untenable theories," he said. Herodotus saw value in all the myths and hearsay that people told themselves, verifiable or not.

But who believes these things? "How do these theories get into the political and psychological bloodstream of the world?" Hill told the story of when he first met Francis Fukuyama, in the early 1980s, when Hill had just returned to the State Department from a post in Tel Aviv. Fukuyama had been hired by Paul Wolfowitz, then director of the Policy Planning Staff. When he first came to State, Fukuyama was "a diminutive, peripatetic Socrates, wandering around looking for a conversation," Hill said. "But he was becoming pessimistic—this was not the agora. There was no Euthyphro to talk to. So eventually he left." Fukuyama retained his friends and colleagues there, however. When a short article titled "The End of History?" appeared in the summer 1989 issue of *The National Interest* and a book by the same name followed three years later, powerful people paid attention.

A week later, a dozen Grand Strategy students sat around the heavy carved table in the Captain's Room at Mory's Temple Bar on York Street, not a block away from the classroom where they congregated once a week. A former speechwriter for President Nixon, Raymond Price, had come to Yale that afternoon to give a talk. This evening Hill was hosting an honorary dinner for him in the storied Old Blue gentlemen's club, where the dark paneled walls boasted hundred-year-old crew team photographs and the tables were gouged with generations of Yalie initials, where the Whiffenpoofs sang every Monday night while drinking unidentified brews from two-handled silver tureens. Tonight, Price sat across from Hill and students flanked them on either side of the great table, chewing politely on their Angus steak and green beans.

The two men traded stories like reunited members of a secret society. At its finest, speechwriting was the job that Fukuyama probably hungered for. It was the business of putting ideas into the bloodstream of the world. It was not just another Washington job but a brotherhood, a band of "Merlin-like wizards," Hill announced across the table, rhetorical magicians who hovered anonymously behind the words of Great Men. It had been decades since he wrote speeches for Henry Kissinger, but once Hill had taken on the frame of mind required for that job, he never shed it. From that time forward, his "optimism" was partly an expedient act but mostly an unrelenting faith that there are passageways between noble ideas and common existence, that a speechwriter is not a scribe but an architect of the political realm's occasional offering to civilization. He would have us all be speechwriters in our hearts.

The mortality rate among Henry Kissinger's speechwriters was unnervingly high. By early 1975, the colleagues who had shared Hill's office when he arrived a few months earlier had all left or been sacked. The speechwriters' office down the hall from the secretary's quarters was dismantled, and Hill moved around the corner to take up a small, plain room in the Policy Planning Staff's suite. Room 7330 was in the heart of the tumult, jostling corridors, staccato tap and ping of type-writers, and streams of coworkers in sweat-stained, wrinkled shirts hurrying around in the uproar that pervaded the seventh floor every day of the secretary's tenure.

Number 7330 suited its occupant. When a reporter from the alumni magazine of his alma mater finagled an interview with Hill, the several minutes she was obliged to wait while her subject finished up pressing business afforded her a chance to look around: "Resting on a table top near the door was a green army backpack that seemed to be serving as an executive briefcase." (Hill had been riding a motorcycle to work ever since returning from Saigon.) "Around the window, there was an abun-dance of hearty house plants. A red-and-black plaid jacket, the kind lumberjacks wear for a night on the town, was flung casually over a vacant chair. And, sitting behind the desk, was Charles Hill himself —dressed in blue jeans, a maroon turtleneck, and a sporty pullover sweater."

Neither the office nor the man was anything like the reporter had imagined them. Hill always selected his dress and décor for function rather than style, and his disposition did not change whether he was riding a Jeep in the Vietnamese countryside or sitting at a desk around the corner from the secretary of state's plush, chandeliered suite. The army rucksack, the flannel lumberjack coat, and the small, unadorned office all reflected the kind of man that Hill fancied himself to be: unpretentious, old-fashioned, and American. A European diplomat would never be caught in lumberjack gear, even in the privacy of his own office. The only significant wall decoration was a huge Audubon folio print of a bald eagle in full flight, clutching a rabbit in its claws. The print was as quintessentially Kissingerian as it was patriotic — one of the eagle's talons pierced mercilessly through the eye of its prey. Hill joked with visitors that he often felt like the rabbit.

The pace of the job was mercurial. Hill and his colleagues some-times had weeks to prepare remarks for a scheduled tour abroad; other times they had only a few frenzied hours before a deadline. Hill typi-cally worked on half a dozen speeches simultaneously, each in a differ-ent policy category demanding its own kind of thinking. Speechwriting was not merely a matter of enunciation. It was a dialectical process in which a statesman's political and ideological vagaries collided with the narrow-minded expertise of the administration's area specialists, and every subsequent draft transformed the secretary's broad visions into tangible policy statements. Kissinger's speechwriters enjoyed an exceptional degree of involvement in policy, as their boss was not afraid to meddle in other officials' jurisdictions or infuriate the bureaus' experts in the course of expressing himself. In subject areas where he cared to interfere but lacked a well-articulated position, his staff had to fill the breach. "It wasn't just about being a writer," Hill said. "That was what was great about the job. You became a policymaker." Some of the most furious fights that Hill could recall from his speechwriting years were feuds with the administration's resident Ph.D.s, who resented the meddling of shallow "generalists" like Hill who presumed to translate their charts and graphs into policy.

Often Kissinger did not know what he wanted in a given speech until he saw the right words on paper. Occasionally the bureau desk officers produced something useful, but more often the first round of memoranda that came back to the in box were "vapid, tired, cliché-ridden," Hill recalled. The bureaus' concerns usually lay in preserving the status quo rather than producing innovative ideas. Sometimes a meeting with the boss finally lit a fire under unimaginative desk officers. At any point during the day, without warning, Kissinger's secretary might call with an urgent request for the staff working on a particular speech to hurry down to Kissinger's conference room. There they would make quiet conversation and languish nervously for twenty to forty minutes, while no one had any idea why they had been summoned or how long the secretary would keep them waiting. Suddenly Kissinger would burst in, a crumpled draft clutched in his fist, and erupt, "'This is nothing! There are no ideas here! Why do we even have this bureau when they don't have any ideas!'" Hill recalled. "He'd be furious, screaming, 'This is nothing like what I want. Why can't you do what I want?!' and storm out of the conference room. On draft sixteen, he'd say, 'This is . . . good. Why didn't you do it this way the first time?'"

Kissinger expected his team to be intellectual and physical athletes who could work unending hours, blistered by his fuming reproof of their work, and still have the energy and self-possession at day's end to come up with the fresh ideas needed to seal a speech. "You lived off your intellectual capacity, but physical ability was paramount," said Lawrence Mead, a speechwriter who left Kissinger's staff not long after Hill arrived. It was a world of physical and intellectual overload. Just as if they were at a varsity crew practice, Kissinger's staff "had to know how to take orders, to do what you're told. It was a sort of WASP-culture athleticism, zero wasted emotion," recalled Mead. "You had to accept arbitrary, unreasonable demands and take hostile criticism." Kissinger was, in Hill's phrase, a "whirling dervish" whose outbursts reduced weaker staff members to cringing husks. Unlike Nixon, whose personal aides were skilled in separating their boss's temper tantrums from genuine orders that should be executed, Kissinger wanted no buffer. If a staffer displeased him on even one assignment, chances were good that the wretch would be packing up his office by the end of the day. It required backbone to withstand the secretary's fury, said Hill. "The insulting quality of it—'you are no good'—shattered people, because things like that are not usually said in the diplomacy and university worlds they were from. [In those places] there was plenty of back-stabbing and rug-pulling and backdoor things, but with Kissinger, it was frontal. He'd act on it, and devastate people—make them weak in the knees."

Hill was left as the last speechwriter standing primarily because he could withstand his boss's wrath unperturbed. It did not pain him to throw out pages' worth of effort at Kissinger's command; he had never hesitated, when he was a boy playing in the back yard at 30 Institute Place, to toss his painstakingly assembled cardboard airplanes into the burning rubbish heap. Occasionally he took the heat regardless of whether a poor draft was his fault. Knowing that if he told a bureau officer that his memo on the speech at hand was unusable, the colleague would take offense and refuse to contribute again, Hill often decided to present the bureau's ideas to Kissinger anyway. "Kissinger would shout at me, I'd take the blame, then go back and inform the bureau that he hated it," Hill said. He was the master of deadpan, the ability to maintain composure—if not outright optimism—in the worst circumstances.

Hill had not always been so invincible. In earlier years, sitting in a law school lecture hall among a herd of overeager classmates, he had fallen into self-doubt. However, it was never his professor's scathing (if Socratic) humiliation of the unwary student that intimidated him— only the omnipresent, low-grade feeling of inferiority, of being an unrefined Bridgeton boy far out of his depth. But even then—although a perceptive Martha sensed her husband's insecurities—he worked hard to conceal any anxiety. He channeled it into ceaseless note taking or concealed it during long hours in study carrels. He had never been one to falter under personal abuse. His father would not hear of such a thing.

Now, fifteen years later, he had the experience to trust his own abilities. He had scoured away any residue of self-doubt. His hometown newspaper had taken to printing feature stories about their "local boy made good"; Hill had not abandoned his roots, but they no longer bound him. Martha, for her part, had long ago noticed that Charlie had changed since their college days. It was sad, though hardly surprising, that the emotional distance slowly eroding their marriage had become an asset for Hill at work. He now preferred to spend most of his waking hours at the office, enduring Kissinger's furor rather than face subtler troubles at home. "I'm something of an emotional cripple anyway, and that served me well," he later admitted.

Kissinger was a whirling dervish by nature, but the caustic, distrustful atmosphere that surrounded the secretary of state during the mid-1970s made it all the worse. By the spring of 1975, the U.S. position in South Vietnam was collapsing. Hanoi had spent the past three years rebuilding its forces, and ARVN's ability to hold them off much longer looked doubtful. No one in Washington with the power to stop Hanoi's southward advance was inclined to intervene. Hill and the other Vietnam War alumni in the State Department "were agitated, rushing up and down the corridors, talking about what we could do to get the Administration to order action," he recalled. "But it was instantly clear that it wasn't going to happen." In those despairing final days of April, Kissinger campaigned hard for eleventh-hour aid to South Vietnam, but his pleas made no impact on a Congress galvanized against any further American involvement in Indochina. Berated for his Vietnam policy ever since he came to Washington, Kissinger was desperate to prop up Saigon and maintain at least the façade of the peace settlement he had negotiated in Paris. The New York Times's Anthony Lewis wrote that maintaining anti-Communist regimes in Saigon and Phnom Penh was for the secretary "a symbol of manhood in his diplomacy."

It was not to be. On April 29, 1975, the last 1,000 Americans and about 5,500 "high-risk" Vietnamese were flown out of Saigon by helicopter. It was the largest helicopter evacuation ever conducted by the U.S. armed forces. President Duong Van Minh, the head of the new South Vietnamese regime who had recently replaced the intractable

Thieu and was considered more "acceptable" by Hanoi, offered his unconditional surrender to the Communists the same day.

Most heartbreaking for Charlie and many of his colleagues, the war proponents' predictions about the human anguish that would follow a Communist takeover — ignored by liberal commentators — proved to be true. The floods of "boat people" clamoring for rescue by the U.S. Navy in the seas between Vietnam and the Philippines belied the media's claims about the welcoming attitude of ordinary Vietnamese toward Communism. So too, soon enough, came the genocide waged by the Communist Khmer Rouge in Cambodia. The administration's critics claimed that the genocide there actually began with the decision to launch the secret bombing of Cambodia in 1969, an operation that killed hundreds of thousands and further destabilized the country. Public horror at the bloodbath that followed the fall of Saigon and Phnom Penh was paralleled in America by a national sense of resignation to the inevitable outcome of "the illegal, immoral conduct of Nixon and Kissinger, as if it was divine retribution that had to come," Hill observed (the "retribution," of course, fell upon the people of Southeast Asia). During a decade of administration lies and media misinformation, the American public had become totally propagandized. Washington was populated by war criminals, the public had been told: America deserved to "lose Vietnam" and suffer an economic, political, and spiritual shattering in the process. The legacy of the war left the country self-lacerated. The wound festered in the national consciousness and in the minds of those who would govern in Washington. It infected every person who would hear the speeches crafted by Hill and his colleagues.

Saigon was only a symptom. The 1970s were a decade of extreme flux in the international order. Since the founding of the modern state system in the seventeenth century, world leaders had valued above all else a nonideological balance of power and increased productivity and strength for the nation-state. Advocates of global economic equity were now tearing down that model. The Third World was clamoring for equality in trade and international politics, and human rights issues found increasing resonance among peoples worldwide. As Arab nations discovered their control over the world oil trade, new market conditions altered the traditional economic equilibrium, and tiny countries amassed unprecedented ability to thwart the wishes of the superpowers. World leaders could no longer afford to ignore problems of inequity and shifting economic power balances. The growing political consciousness and economic potency of developing nations was forcing policymakers, including Henry Kissinger, to reevaluate their strategies.

In many ways, this paradigm shift was at odds with the philosophy by which Kissinger had always operated: the precedence of order over justice. This was the doctrine that marked the balance of nineteenth-century Europe crafted by his diplomatic heroes, Klemens von Metternich and Otto von Bismarck. More important, it was the traditional ethos of the cold war, in which Washington sought to strengthen its economy, extend its military complex, and solidify and extend its global influence faster than its Communist foes. During the cold war foreign policy trumped all other concerns in Washington, and a global landscape dominated by superpowers lent itself to — and required — a grand strategic vision. Pressures from the new international economic order came at a time when cold war threats from the Soviet Union and its surrogates had never been greater. Yet Congress blocked every administration attempt to control security threats, particularly in Central America.

Kissinger's vision of the statesman's task remained rooted in the Bismarckian traditions of diplomacy buttressed by the threat of force and realist manipulation of the balance of power. However, he understood that the international landscape had been transformed by the clash of the free world with that of the Communists. The consequences of that clash, coupled with America's internal cultural turmoil, had begun to erode the country's ballast. Kissinger feared that the American people — after more than a decade of civil unrest, Watergate, and the collapse of South Vietnam — were turning away from their responsibilities in the world at the worst possible moment. He felt a growing compulsion to speak to the American people directly. His message had to shift, and the individuals who crafted that message had to adapt.

"It was my fate to be in office," Kissinger later told James Reston in an interview, "when the United States had found a new approach to its foreign policy, one that understood the world's currents and its number of complexities." In his memoirs, he wrote, "The most important task of the second Nixon Administration was therefore psychological: to educate the American public in the complexity of the world we would have to manage . . . to ground American policy in a realistic sense of national interest and the requirements of the balance of power; American idealism would furnish the staying power needed for a long-term struggle that had no clearly definable turning point."

Kissinger, ever the Harvard professor, viewed his speechmaking as a pedagogical effort. The lasting success of his policies was contingent on convincing the American public that his goals were valid and his strategy the right one — despite failure in Vietnam, a cold war threatening to flame up at points around the globe, and the bleak state of the economy. He had to overcome the widely held belief that his diplomacy left American policy blind to human rights, the needs of other peoples, and his own society's restraints on executive power. He had predicted this task for himself two decades earlier, in his doctoral thesis on the crafting of the "concert of Europe" by Metternich and British Foreign Secretary Lord Castlereagh after the Napoleonic Wars. In one passage, the Harvard Ph.D. candidate foresaw his own future:

> The statesman is therefore like one of the heroes in classical drama who has a vision of the future but who cannot transmit it directly to his fellow-men and who cannot validate its "truth." . . . It is for this reason that statesmen often share the fate of prophets, that they are without honor in their own country, that they always have a difficult task in legitimizing their programs domestically, and that their greatness is usually apparent only in retrospect when their intuition has become experience. The statesman must therefore be an educator; he must bridge the gap between a people's experience and his vision, between a nation's tradition and its future.

Never, it could be argued, was the rhetoric of the U.S. secretary of state more critical — to American foreign policy and to faith at home and abroad in the United States' ability to remain the leader of the free world — than that of Henry Kissinger from 1975 through the end of his tenure. Never did a secretary of state take more seriously his words to the American people. Never was the task of the individuals who would craft that rhetoric more difficult.

The Heartland Speeches, Kissinger's roving attempt to rally the American public and make his foreign policy ideas stick, received only modest attention from the press. He began the tour during the summer before Hill's arrival and continued nearly to the end of his term in office in 1977. The speeches were an executive attempt to reach over the heads of an obstinate Congress in the manner of Woodrow Wilson, with faith that the people would understand Kissinger's policies once he explained them in person. The speeches were sweeping statements on foreign policy, typically Kissingerian, but they were exceptional because they were intended less for world leaders than for Americans. They aimed to present American foreign policy as a coherent system of ideas intimately connected with the citizens they meant to serve. In Bloomington, Minnesota, at a meeting of the Upper Midwest Council in July 1975, the secretary delivered the address often considered the most important of the Heartland tour: "The Moral Foundations of Foreign Policy." His speech emphasized the grand sense of purpose that Americans hold in common: "In a democracy, the conduct of foreign policy is possible only with public support. Therefore your government owes you an articulation of the purposes which its policies are designed to serve . . . to explain how our policies serve the American people's objectives. And those principles—freedom, the dignity of the individual, the sanctity of law—are at the heart of our policy."

In moments like this, Kissinger's speeches resonated with the spirit of American civil religion. A creed that had come under fire with the failure of American involvement in the Vietnam War, the traditional belief structure to which Kissinger alluded was rooted in two hundred years of American experience. It began with the colonists' sense of themselves as the new Israelites, escaping from Pharaoh George III, trekking into the wilderness of the New World to build their Zion. It evolved—even as the austere piety of the early American settlers waned—into nineteenth-century Americans' belief in Manifest Destiny. The deity of America's civil religion "is by no means a watchmaker God," wrote Robert Bellah in his seminal essay on the subject. "He is actively interested and involved in history, with a special concern for America." God had blessed the American enterprise, and the whole continent belonged to its pioneers to conquer and civilize, to fulfill the lot that Providence had laid before them.

America was to be, for the Old World and now for the developing world as well, a model of the virtues that Kissinger stated in Bloomington: freedom, individual dignity, and the inviolability of law. America's destiny was not only to serve as a "city upon a hill," as Massachusetts Puritan John Winthrop had written in his treatise "A Modell of Christian Charity" (1630), but to actively promote American ideals around the world. The two missions had long been intertwined, even before the reluctant end of American isolationism after World War II. Now, the Heartland Speeches came at a time when American national self-esteem and trust in government were at a nadir. They were, in the main, an attempt to convince the American public that Kissinger's foreign policy was a modern incarnation of their country's identity and founding moral principles. They were the attempt of a German-Jewish kid turned secretary of state to persuade his adopted countrymen of the majesty of their country, said Hill, to "convince them to be who they are."

When Hill or other writers used words like "freedom" and "democracy" in the secretary's speeches, they knew that these were not just innocuous entries in the civic vocabulary but religious symbols with sacred significance in American history. Such words had lost their clarity over the decades and now belonged mostly to the realm of political propaganda and rhetoric. As W. H. Auden observed in his acceptance speech upon receiving the 1967 Medal for Literature from the National Book Committee, "words like Communism, Capitalism, Imperialism, Peace, Freedom, Democracy, have ceased to be words the meaning of which can be inquired into and discussed, and have become right or wrong noises to which the response is as involuntary as a knee reflex." The Heartland Speeches took advantage of the emotional and psychological "reflexes" these words prompted, but they were also scrupulous efforts to treat such words with care. "Freedom" and "democracy" had unique meaning to American listeners, a meaning embedded in how they felt about their country's history and how they identified as Americans.

Hill further linked Kissinger's foreign policy objectives with the American civil religion—the same sense of mission that had inspired Hill himself to join the Foreign Service a decade and a half earlier—when he wrote under Kissinger's byline in an essay solicited for *Time* magazine's Bicentennial Essay series, "As the greatest democracy in the world, America is a reminder to all that there is an alternative to tyranny and oppression . . . The surest path to our own greater success, and the brightest hope for others, is to remain true to the American tradition—a heritage where reality is a point of departure but never our final horizon, and where ideas ennoble reality and enable us to shape our future."

The optimism in this prose is powerful. America remained a city upon a hill obligated to set an example for developing countries struggling to provide their citizens with civil rights and personal opportunity. But the message was not a passive one. Ideas would empower

Americans to shape their own destiny. Earlier in the essay, Hill described an agenda for America that could have come right out of one of the Heartland Speeches: America and its allies had to work together to maintain a secure peace, facilitate a mutually beneficial world order, and defend individual liberty. In the years to come liberal intellectuals would denounce Kissinger as a "war criminal" who — in policy decisions such as extending the Vietnam War into neighboring Cambodia and Laos and abetting the 1973 coup in Chile by brutal dictator Augusto Pinochet — consistently played power politics at the expense of human rights. To them, such noble declarations would sound hypocritical. But Kissinger cared less for what his political enemies thought than the legacy of his ideas. His public statements — whether a speech at a local Kiwanis Club or an article for a national news weekly — were intended to reverberate far beyond the time and place in which the secretary expressed them.

Kissinger never sat down with his speechwriters and explained to them at any length the nature of his mission in the Heartland tour. But his staff knew their boss well enough to realize how important these speeches were to him — his fulmination over each draft was significantly more strenuous. As was the case for every speech, he offered them no real guidance. But as he scanned the pages they submitted, savaged them with his pen, or tossed them across the table in disgust, there was an intensity in their boss's expression, a fresh blush in his gravelly Germanic diatribes, that made it clear these speeches were no stopgap enterprise. This was a search to articulate ideas that the secretary believed he had to express.

If Kissinger hoped to effect sweeping change in American public opinion in his Heartland Speeches and rouse the people to demand that their representatives in Congress cease their obstruction of the administration's foreign policy, then he certainly failed. His speeches moved those who heard them, but the numbers were too insubstantial to make a difference. Many legislators were all the more incensed by the thought of the secretary of state, who was already making enough trouble in the outside world, traveling to their home states to push his dangerous ideas. But no matter to what extent Kissinger intended it, his speaking tour did "increase the confidence of the average American in Henry Kissinger," Hill said. In these speeches, their secretary of state wasn't droning about esoteric matters of foreign affairs. He was talking about big ideas, like morality and the American mission. His language aimed at the hearts of his audience. "Before, people thought of him as this wizard of foreign policy, the guy in the cartoons in their newspapers, an impressive speaker on television," Hill continued. "But the Heartland Speeches made him seem to be an American statesman."

The scope and resonance of Kissinger's statements depended on the layers of meaning in his language. Speech craft at the highest policymaking level required an intimate familiarity with the subject at hand but also ease in the realm of ideas. Hill kept up the mode of writing he had developed in college and his early years in the Foreign Service, working at a desk surrounded by books, striding over to his shelf whenever he was strapped for ideas, pulling down volumes of literature, history, or philosophy, and reading a few paragraphs until he hit upon new inspiration. In the speeches that made Hill proudest, those inspirations lacked any specific attribution or signpost. Perhaps the speechwriter himself didn't realize at first what he had wrought. A reference might appear in the way he colored the words, or the inspiration for his tone—some passages had the ring of a seventeenth-century Plymouth Pilgrim pulpit, others the rhythm of a Roman oration. The language did not simply skate along the surface. It was rooted in something beyond itself.

Oratorical declamations constitute a unique genre of literature. They are, as Daniel Boorstin wrote, utterances pronounced on behalf of and for the community. They are distinct from other forms of human expression for their aural coherence and the intellectual echoes intended for a specific audience. The craft rewarded Hill for his habits of broad thinking and omnivorous reading, heretofore underused in his jobs writing diplomatic memoranda, and considered eccentric and curious, if admirable, by colleagues. He had always been a generalist by instinct. He was glad to trade in the narrow ideas and cold, telegraphic language of State Department cables for a vocation that made the most of his talents. "Speechwriting fit me," he said.

Late in 1976, after Jimmy Carter won the presidential election and it was clear that Kissinger's tenure was at an end, he began delivering "farewell addresses." He seemed conscious of the last impression he would leave before exiting the world stage. James Reston wrote that Kissinger was sounding more like a historian than a secretary of state, waxing philosophical on the obstacles facing the creation of a new world order, winning polite and appreciative responses from usually hostile audiences like the United Nations. Hill and the rest of the Policy Planning Staff worked furiously right up until the end of the Ford administration on January 20, 1977. The pace on the seventh floor only quickened as Kissinger's time in office grew shorter. Hill had no time to plan for what would happen at the end of the month, when he would be out of a job.

His years on Kissinger's staff marked a period of intellectual awakening to the world of high policymaking. In Henry Kissinger, Hill had found a Great Man who, for all his histrionics, took Hill's ideas seriously. Kissinger was the rare sort of prince who was smarter than his advisers, and so his Policy Planning Staff was a training ground of unusual challenges. But for all its difficulties, this was the job that transformed Hill. He became a literary craftsman. Assembling successive drafts of the same paragraphs forced him to be more attentive to shades of meaning than he had ever been. He had honed his ability to track cultural and political clues in public statements during his years as a China watcher, and in the role of the speechwriter he evolved from an analyzer to a creator. He possessed, however, no pride of authorship. On the contrary, he was rapidly learning that anonymity enhanced his effectiveness. Once only a note taker of unusual discipline and a composer of anonymous cables noted for his uncluttered mind, Hill was now a writer who thought with his pen and a thinker who had learned to write his ideas into history with quiet deftness.

The Grand Strategy course arose out of a desire to reaffirm the power of the big idea. It came from the professors' alarm at the rise of the "wonk," the Clinton-era policy expert with no concept of broad context. John Gaddis recounted to me "the infamous visit of the NATO briefing team" in late 1997, when he, Paul Kennedy, Charlie, and their colleagues reluctantly agreed to receive a NATO public affairs team that was touring intellectual circles to make the case for NATO expansion. After a long presentation on logistical minutiae and details of committee structures, Gaddis remembered, "one of us asked, 'Isn't there a danger that NATO expansion against the will of Russia, who opposes it, will drive Russia into the arms of the Chinese, recreating the Sino-Soviet entente?' There was a silence. Then one of the men slapped his forehead and said, 'Good God! We'd never thought of that!' That was a defining moment for us."

In a box of overstuffed manila folders affectionately termed "the

Grand Strategy archives," I found a memo that Charlie wrote to Gaddis and Kennedy early in 1998. In it he observed that the expectations policymakers and political scientists had expressed at the end of the cold war had all proved egregiously wrong. Among other things, the wonks had promised that Boris Yeltsin's Russia would align itself with the United States; that the 1991 victory against Saddam Hussein in the Gulf War would evolve into lasting security in the Middle East and peace between Arabs and Palestinians; that the end of superpower bipolarity would revivify the United Nations. What had gone wrong in their thinking, to account for such errors? Even more worrisome was that so few seemed to notice the glaring incongruity between reality and the world order they had predicted. The memo, with further input from Gaddis and Kennedy, evolved into a letter drafted in April 1998. The letter observed that policy is now made by "particularists": "These people are perfectly competent at taking in parts of the picture, but they have difficulty seeing the entire thing. They pigeon-hole priorities, pursuing them separately and simultaneously, with little thought to how each might undercut the other. They proceed confidently enough from tree to tree, but seem astonished to find themselves lost in a forest."

There are no great generalists in positions of authority today, the letter continued. Universities and think tanks are narrower and more specialized in their studies each year. Students are told that deep expertise in a single field is more marketable than a broad knowledge base or holistic intellectual scope. At Yale students were "voting with their feet," Charlie said later. Graduate students in history and political science were complaining about programs that trained them to be research assistants on tiny social science projects and forbidding them from writing dissertations on big ideas. The professors wondered whether the answer might be a new approach to the classroom, a class that was novel and old-fashioned at the same time. The letter proposed a Yale course that would view the world as a whole, from "an ecological perspective," where all ideas and challenges are interrelated. The curriculum would apply the ancient concept of "grand strategy" to modern-day problems. Gaddis and Kennedy cosigned the letter—Charlie chose to remain in the background—and sent it to a few dozen of the best minds they knew, their colleagues in business, government, journalism, and academia. A few months later two dozen or so interested parties, including a *New York Times* columnist, a member or two from the Council on Foreign Relations, and numerous academic types and graduate students, gathered for a weekend at a bed-and-breakfast in the Berkshire foothills to talk over the proposal. The conference produced few substantive ideas, although according to Grand Strategy lore, it was here that Paul Kennedy first sketched out the basic structure of the class on the back of an envelope. The professors left amid an encouraging atmosphere of excitement. The main lesson of the weekend, however, was that few people, even among these great minds, seemed to know what Grand Strategy was.

There was much to see in this seed of the Grand Strategy course, still in a barely embryonic state, long before the rise of the harrowing admissions process, the anxious rows of undergraduates eyeing their new classmates and sizing up rival résumés, the dinners at Mory's with former ambassadors and speechwriters. The founding mission of the course had much in common with Henry Kissinger's aim in his Heartland Speeches: the push to forsake bickering over issues for a discussion of political philosophy. The class, like those speeches, hoped to instill in its audience a unified worldview that was missing from coursework that students did elsewhere at Yale.

Kennedy and Gaddis would each develop their own approaches to the course. But Charlie's tack had its roots in his Kissinger days, where he first grasped the grand strategic worldview. At Yale, Charlie approaches all his teaching through the lens of civil religion. This is not to say that his lectures are anachronistic sermons reminiscent of John Winthrop's harangues, although his lessons often yield a fundamental faith in the righteousness of American power, properly wielded. Rather, in his awareness of the meaning inherent in every angle of culture, in his mission to teach his students to understand the matrix into which every part of their world fits, he builds his lessons on a global civil religion. In the Grand Strategy course, Charlie's colleagues have put him in charge of teaching the ancients, from Herodotus and Sun Tzu to John Milton and Dante. He treats the texts like scriptures. They offer ideas relevant to vast swathes of humanity, based not on common deities but common human experience. By linking all corners of culture together, by deeming everything worthy of class time and interpretation—from the military uniforms of World War I belligerents to trends of dress at today's United Nations—he imparts to it all a holy significance stretching well beyond immediate time and place. He is not just a professor but a priest.

Some students are eager—perhaps too eager—to embrace lessons that offer a way to make sense of their world. For them, Charlie's methods feel empowering. For other students, a professor who seems to have all the answers immediately provokes skepticism if not resentment. They sense that his classroom mission is broader and more presumptuous than that of most teachers. Yet it is hard to find students who will speak at length about why they dislike Charlie, even under the condition of anonymity. They prefer to brush him off as a "raving conservative" guilty of gray-haired crimes against idealistic twenty-year-olds. But his politics aren't the half of it. Something about his teaching style reeks of old Yale, the Yale of Jonathan Edwards and Timothy Dwight—a Yale whose ghosts today's students are happy to honor but whose reincarnation, they are conditioned to believe, must be a very bad thing.

It is sometimes a short jump from priesthood to sainthood, and most students know the risks of overexaltation. But in the secular world of the university, where there could never be a Great Awakening or religious renewal to fill the spiritual and intellectual gaps between what students see happening in their world and the explanations they are offered, Charlie's brand of education has met a real need. His professorship at Yale "fits" him for the same reasons that speechwriting did. Religion, even if it is only a metaphor for his pedagogy, is a powerful thing. History has proven that in the hands of mortal men, religion is very much like grand strategy. It has caused as much error and agony as it has led to good.

8

AFTER A FEW MONTHS WORKING AT A STOPGAP JOB IN THE office of the director general of the Foreign Service, Hill found himself mired in the Middle East. He spent the next several years in Israeli affairs, both in Washington and in Tel Aviv. He fell in love with the work immediately. After spending more than a decade holding out against the marching, chanting, blazing chaos of the American 1960s and 1970s, Hill saw in the Israelis a straightforward people who lived by a warrior code not far removed from the stalwart disposition of South Jersey.

Charlie belongs to what is typically classified as the Silent Generation, those conscientious, hard-working men and women born before 1946 who were shaped by the Great Depression and World War II rather than the civil rights movement and Vietnam. I wonder whether he was beginning to feel lonely in the places and among the strange peoples that had filled his life since he left Bridgeton in 1953. He found no allies in Europe and the Far East, nor among the kids at Harvard or the American people at large, who shrugged off the speeches he wrote for Henry Kissinger. I wonder whether Hill was drawn to the Israelis because the way they lived validated him. They reaffirmed his self-image as a man of honor who always knew the right thing to do.

I may be only projecting my own feelings onto my subject. My generation has never been interested in the things that Charlie and his peers sought when they were our age. We have no desire to grow up too quickly and join the ranks of responsible adults. Nor do we care to follow the example of our rebellious baby-boomer parents. I hesitate to speak too confidently on behalf of my peers in the newly christened "millennial generation"; evidence for how young people think and feel is always in flux and anecdotal at best. But I can speak from my own experience, and I know that I spent my college years trying to figure out where my roots were and what I ought to believe. I came from an apolitical, irreligious home located somewhere between Chicago and the cornfields of western Illinois. I was never dragged to church or made to think about God, discounting a single ill-advised attempt by my mother to confine my brother and me to the couch one Sunday morning and read us the story of David and Goliath. We squirmed away and ran off within ten minutes. For most of my life, visits to my grandparents were marked by fried chicken and impractical birthday presents. They were certainly not ventures into Old World traditions and stories of where my family came from. At the time, I did not feel the absence of heritage.

But at Yale, one of the great melting-pot universities prouder now of its racially diverse student body than of its Rhodes scholars, I felt like a rootless, white-bread mutt. Each year many freshmen come from places where everyone is just like them. At college, where they suddenly realize that not everyone is an Ashkenazic Jew from New York's Upper West Side or an Irish Catholic from Philadelphia, the diversity can come as a shock. My Jewish acquaintances who grew up in non-observant households suddenly began going to Shabbat dinner at the campus Hillel and sticking to the matzo in the dining hall during Passover. Children of immigrants ran off to join clubs of fellow Hyphenated Americans, chalking the sidewalks to advertise African dance festivals and Vietnamese *pho* soup fundraisers. To some extent, these were natural patterns of self-segregation. But more fundamentally, the first year away at college brings the realization of two things: we all saw that we had been cast together with people unlike ourselves, and we all now felt entirely at sea. We had to think, some of us for the first time, about where we had come from.

I began to nurture a bit of pride in my nasal Midwestern accent. But that was all I had to go on — no religion, no creed, and a mixed-up, boring ethnicity. I was jealous of my Jewish friends, my Greek Orthodox friends, my Irish-Catholic friends, who (it seemed to me) knew who they were and where they came from. I started casting about like a child in a costume closet. After two years of studying the Russian language and the Russian Orthodox faith, traveling to Russia, and (for an unfortunate three weeks) wearing Russian peasant dresses to class—

129

in search of the Slavic soul that I was convinced I possessed in a previous life—I realized that my behavior was weird and affected, so I gave it up. Then came the phase of genealogymania, when I pored over family trees compiled by great-grandmothers. I learned that I was one eighth German Jewish, one eighth Irish-Catholic, and one thirty-second Cherokee. The rest was an Anglo hodgepodge that ran all the way back, my father insisted, to the second governor of Plymouth Colony. I concluded that I must be English at heart. So I cultivated an obsession with the British Royal Navy and convinced myself to share Charlie's admiration for the Puritans and the rugged character of the British Colonial Service.

If I could have reprogrammed myself as a member of the God-fearing, self-assured, purebred Silent Generation, I would have done so in a heartbeat.

Perhaps I was a little more restless than most of my peers, but I was not unique. "Find yourself" would not be the cardinal cliché of the college years unless plenty of young people heeded that advice. But as I moved through Charlie's life story and tried to track his sense of self, I was surprised to find myself thinking about my own journey. When he found the Israelis, part of me cheered for him. The other part of me winced, wondering about the consequences of Charlie's tendency to oversimplify and idealize human beings. No matter the outcome, however, I marveled at his ability to identify with people so different from him. I have never been very good at existing on the margin and belonging to nobody, as my college angst testified. To Charlie, the margin seemed to be the most comfortable place of all.

It was during the pickup football games that Hill played with other members of Kissinger's Policy Planning Staff on Saturday afternoons that he first got to know Nick Veliotes, who under President Jimmy Carter became the assistant secretary for Near Eastern Affairs (NEA). Those ad hoc football teams had pretty much disbanded, but in the spring of 1978 Veliotes tapped his old teammate as deputy director of Israel and Arab-Israeli Affairs (IAI), the desk responsible for policy toward Israel and Israel's role in the peace process. It was an embattled place. Generally, NEA was one of the first-class bureaus in the State Department, famous for its professionalism and collegiality, staffed by officers who had spent their careers in the region, spoke the languages, and were invested—sometimes to an unhealthy extent—in the countries in which they served. NEA was aggressive about recruiting new talent, unlike some of the more lethargic bureaus. But it seemed to Hill that those superior management policies broke down in Israel and Arab-Israeli Affairs. When Hill arrived, NEA was almost entirely "staffed by a special creature called an 'Arabist,'" explained Harvey Sicherman, who would work with Hill on Middle Eastern issues during the Reagan administration. Many of the State Department's Arabists —a somewhat pejorative term denoting a specialist in Arab affairs afflicted with improper biases for the Arab position—did all they could to avoid contact with the Israel desk. Israel was by no means the sacred cow of American foreign policy that it is today, and careers spent earning entrée into the regimes of Israel's enemies left little room for the political risk—not to mention the patience for the Israeli point of view —required to serve at IAI.

Arabists considered the Israel desk and the American embassy in Tel Aviv professional dumping grounds. "If you served in Israel you were a *persona non grata* in Arab states," said Sicherman. "State had difficulty attracting people to the Israeli embassy. They tended to get political appointees, rather than career Foreign Service Officers, as ambassadors to Israel." For the lonely few in charge of Israeli affairs, NEA was a hostile place to work. Hill, with his aspirations to become a policy generalist rather than a specialist in the Middle East, had no worries about the impact of the post on the rest of his career, but the realities of NEA politics made his life difficult. "Everyone else in the bureau was pro-Arab, and no one liked us or would cooperate with us," he recalled. "We were like our own universe."

The anti-Israeli sentiments in NEA were not a new phenomenon. Thirty years earlier, most Arab specialists had objected to the founding of a Jewish state, in their minds a colony of immigrant usurpers who had overcome the bumbling efforts of British imperialists to take over Palestinian land, spreading and consolidating their settlements well beyond the bounds allowed by the U.N. partition of the former British mandate. In an incredibly brief time Israel's founders had built a flourishing democracy on their narrow strip of desert, boasting a relatively free and prosperous society and the strongest military in the Middle East. Israel was the sole outpost of the West in a region fraught with unstable, autocratic regimes, increasing Islamic radicalism, and creeping Soviet influence. Geopolitics combined with a powerful American sense of moral obligation (and an even more powerful American Jewish lobby) virtually to guarantee Israel an ally in America, much as the State Department's Arabists would have it otherwise.

The 1967 Six-Day War, in which the Israeli army advanced far into the Sinai, decimating Arab forces and short-circuiting their attempt to eliminate the Jewish state, proved how tough Israel was as a bulwark against the Arab onslaught. Following the cease-fire the U.N. Security Council passed Resolution 242, which called for the establishment of a just and lasting peace based on "withdrawal of Israeli armed forces from territories occupied in the recent conflict" and "termination of all claims or states of belligerency and respect for and acknowledgement of the sovereignty, territorial integrity, and political independence of every state in the area and their right to live in peace." The resolution's "land for peace" premise—which made no mention of the fate of Palestinian Arabs—would form the basis of Arab-Israeli peace negotiations for the rest of the twentieth century.

Under the leadership of Egyptian president Anwar el Sadat, the Arabs attacked again in October 1973 on Yom Kippur, the holiest day of the Jewish calendar. The war ended in another military victory for Israel, and in the following years Arabists in the State Department and many like-minded officials in the pro-Arab Carter administration came to see Israel as an arrogant regional bully. Neo-Revisionist Zionist* Menachem Begin and the rightist Likud coalition party came to power in 1977, insisting that the 1917 Balfour Declaration on a homeland for the Jews in Palestine legitimized their policy of sending Israeli settlers to build homes in formerly Arab territory occupied by Israeli forces since 1967. While the Israeli Defense Force's presence in the West Bank and Gaza would seem mild compared with the militarization of these regions that followed the Palestinian intifada during the next decade, no occupation is ever benign. Pro-Palestinian aid workers in the West Bank brought back tales of the corruption and brutality of the Israeli civil-military establishment there. As Wat T. Cluverius IV, a Near East hand who went to Israel as an economics officer, told Robert Kaplan, "Old Arab men were made to kiss the asses of donkeys in front of their families. Once the Likud came to power in 1977, they really

---

* Neo-Revisionist Zionism is the third and most extreme generation in the theory of Jewish land rights and state ideology. Theodor Herzl's notions of Zionism in the nineteenth century were first magnified by the ideas of Vladimir Ze'ev Jabotinsky. The goals of Jabotinsky's Revisionist ideology included mass demonstrations and other forms of relentless pressure to force the British to meet his demands: Jewish statehood on both banks of the Jordan River; a Jewish majority in Palestine; reestablishment of the Jewish military regiments; and military training for youth. Menachem Begin grew to embrace an even more inflexible political stance than that of his mentor Jabotinsky.

promoted the head crunchers. They put the toughest and poorest Iraqi Jews and other Sephardim in the West Bank, in order to really beat up the Arabs."

By the time Hill arrived, the Israel desk was more beleaguered than ever, its officers inundated daily with angry phone calls from legislators and staffers battling over U.S. arms sales to Israel and swamped with irate letters from their constituents protesting Israeli policy. IAI was constantly battling U.N. vitriol, as the United States vetoed resolution after resolution put forth in the Security Council proposing embargoes on the sale of arms and technology to Israel. Yet despite its isolated, understaffed, and embattled position, the Israel desk was "the center of the action," Hill said. Before Hill's tour at the Israel desk was out, the Camp David Accords would lay the groundwork for peace between Israel and Egypt. Despite continual outrage over new Israeli settlements and despite an Israeli invasion in retaliation against Palestinian guerrilla attacks originating from southern Lebanon, Israel and Egypt would sign a peace treaty in less than a year. Hill was fortunate to be posted at the desk when things were really moving, when American diplomats could see concrete results for their efforts. But that didn't make his job any easier.

For all the historic import of the events unfolding in the Middle East, the first challenges that Hill faced at the Israel desk were the mundane agonies of bureaucracies everywhere: troublesome personnel, paperwork, and office politics. Hill maneuvered around the personnel he couldn't change and recruited competent staffers as fast as he could. He was not so much a remarkable administrator or organizer as he was a shrewd delegator. For the most part, he worked as he had always preferred to, touching base with his staff at the morning meeting, directing them as they reported in throughout the day, and handling small catastrophes as they arose. He spent most of the day alone, among books and papers and a telephone permitted only by necessity, in the solitude of his office. Remarks on his personality in the workplace offered by one of his superiors in Hong Kong still held true a decade later at the Israel desk:

It is difficult to label Mr. Hill with any precision as either an introvert or extrovert. He clearly is not an exuberant back-slapper and appears to seek and enjoy interludes of solitude. Despite this tendency toward introspection, he is essentially a friendly person with a ready sense of humor . . . On a few social occasions I have noted in him a tendency to be blunt and sarcastic with individuals expressing uninformed or prejudiced views . . . In truth there is something to be said for an outspoken attitude towards pompous fools, but perhaps Mr. Hill too readily abandons tact and patience in dealing with such people.

Hill had no patience for incompetents and "was not warm or effusive," recalled William Bacchus, a colleague of Hill. "But this small staff—those folks would walk through walls for him because he wasn't going around back-slapping, but he didn't BS them either." He treated his staff like a team, insuring that they communicated with one another at the morning meetings and cultivating esprit de corps. One day while he was in Bridgeton on leave, he noticed a tiny ceramic blue jay sitting on a table, the latest antique curio his mother had picked up. At his request, she made another trip to the antique shack in Dutch Neck, New Jersey, that had sold her the little bird and ordered a dozen more, cleaning out the small company that made them. Hill brought the birds back to Washington and told his staff that if they did well on an assignment, they would earn induction into the Ancient and Honorable Order of the Blue Jay, and receive one of the birds to display on their desk. "We were blue jays at the Israel desk," he explained. "We'd go and steal things from the other birds, and if they challenged us, we'd squawk and fight. We were tough like Israelis, and blue and white, like the Israeli flag." The Ancient Order was an instant hit among the staff. Hill commanded them to keep it absolutely secret. IAI's alienated position within the bureau was now less a frustration than a source of unspoken pride.

IAI remained, however, the focus of low-grade, constant contempt. It is unlikely that the staff suffered any outright stonewalling or Kissingerian outbursts, but IAI was excluded from much of the bureau's Arabist-dominated stream of information, from departmental gossip, and from the casual coffee-break conversation that often yields more useful data than formal memorandums. Hill solved the problem by creating an unconventional intelligence system. Not long after he had arrived at the Israel desk, he called the staff together in his office and instructed them, each time nature called, to use a different bathroom on a different floor and corner of the building and to keep their ears open. "That's where you learn things," he explained. "It worked, and we had the best intelligence."

• • •

In late May 1978, about a month after his arrival at the Israel desk, Hill flew to Israel by way of Cairo, Damascus, and Amman, where he toured Jerash, the Roman ruins in the north. He had wanted to see the major Arab cities and had no choice but to go there first, since "the Arabs wouldn't let you into their world from the world of the Jews," he explained, "but the Jews would let you into theirs." From Amman he proceeded to Israel via the Allenby Bridge for a ten-day orientation visit. Late spring in Israel was warm and breezy, not unlike the weather in Ocean City that time of year. An officer from the consulate general at Jerusalem greeted him, and he spent the week accompanying American officers on their rounds and shaking the hands of important members of the Knesset and officials at the Ministry of Defense. He toured an Israeli aircraft factory, lunched with the blustery editors of Israeli newspapers, and began to get some feel for the people and the country he had heretofore known only from a distance.

He toured the West Bank and Gaza, regions today usually considered too dangerous for casual tourism. But in 1978, Prime Minister Begin and the Likud believed that these contested bits of land were part of the ancient Jewish homeland, Eretz Israel. There was no question that Jews and their guests should walk there freely, wade as they pleased through the bulrushes along the banks of the Jordan, and wander through their own settlements on the fringes of the golden Sinai waste. Begin's 1977 election platform declared, "Settlement, both urban and rural, in all parts of the Land of Israel is the focal point of the Zionist effort to redeem the country, to maintain vital security areas and serve as a reservoir of strength and inspiration for the renewal of the pioneering spirit." It was only natural to showcase the settlements and emphasize that spirit to a new American officer charged with dealing with Israeli affairs.

From that first trip to Israel, Hill took to the citizens instinctively. He had come to the job with only roughly formed opinions on Middle Eastern affairs, but he was soon known around the bureau as a strong Israeli sympathizer. "I admired the kind of people the Israelis were, their achievement of making a country, the superb spirit and professionalism of the Israeli military," he said later. "I saw this was a place that was admirable, democratic. I thought America should have a close, important relationship with Israel, that making peace between Israel and the Arab side was extremely important." The geostrategist in him admired Israel as the only good-faith participant in the international state system in a region of volatile autocratic regimes and anti-state terrorist organizations. The American Studies student in him, not to mention the South Jersey conservative, admired it as a lonely outpost of Western civilization in a premodern, radicalized desert.

Israeli soldiers took Hill sightseeing around the country by helicopter and treated him sociably, although their courtesy was tinged with the distrust that Israelis hold for everyone who claims to understand their cause but has yet to prove it. The Israelis had built one of the toughest military forces in the world precisely because their people had learned never to entrust their security to outsiders. Hill admired the discipline and strength of character he observed in the Israeli Defense Force (IDF). He couldn't help but compare them to the last soldiers he had seen, the unkempt and dispirited American troops in Vietnam. The IDF had its roots in the hardscrabble Jewish militias that terrorized the British and beat back Arab guerrillas before its soldiers could claim to fight in the name of a sovereign state. The individualist flair that Hill noticed in their dress had become tradition by default, for lack of funds to buy proper uniforms for ragtag immigrant troops during the austere early years. But that accidental individualism had become an essential element of the IDF's esprit. The army preserved "the democratic, feisty spirit of the [Jewish militia] Palmach commandos." Israelis meant to turn upside down the stereotype of the effete, cerebral, European merchant Jew who shirked physical combat. The military had become uniquely central to Israeli society, the source of its greatest pride and most beloved hero, the "fighting Jew."

In Israel, there was no need for fathers like Morton Hill to manufacture physical hardships to grind their sons into men. Since the state's founding, every able-bodied Israeli man and woman served a compulsory term in the armed forces. Youngsters joined the Pioneering Fighting Youth Corps, Noar Halutzi Lohem (NAHAL), where they learned to handle arms, went on scouting missions, slept in pup tents, and saw firsthand the realities of Israel's security situation — the responsibility of every Israeli citizen. Young Israelis were a species apart from the grubby, longhaired, draft card–burning kids Hill had encountered at Harvard.

When Israel's first prime minister, David Ben Gurion, established NAHAL, he envisioned a younger generation of "warrior-farmers" who would till and defend the Promised Land. The Defense Service Act of 1949 — still on the books, although not enforced — required every youngster to spend a year working the land in addition to military training. Ben Gurion knew that an individual bonds to the place where he works, sweats, and builds with his hands. Hill knew it too. That place for him was South Jersey—that unrefined, hard-up thumb of land, the butt of jokes and the spring of so many insecurities—but still the home he could never leave behind, not only because he had grown up there, but because houses still stood whose foundations he had laid during his summers as a young man, protected from the crashing Atlantic surf by bulkheads he'd help to build. South Jersey owned a part of him.

Hill admired the Israelis. He also saw himself in them, and that is the root of all empathy. It is tempting to wonder why he himself once fled from joining the military if he had such admiration for soldierly qualities and disdain for those who weasel out of danger and physical duty. The answer lay in the differences between the Israeli army, which he was free to idealize, and the unpleasant realities he had come to know in his own country's armed forces. Soldiers and officers of World War II had been the heroes of his boyhood, but upon his graduation from college and law school, right before the conflict in Indochina began to enter the public consciousness, there was no war on. There was no call to service. Later, when he encountered American soldiers during his tour in Saigon, there was little to admire in the U.S. Army, which had reached its nadir in morale and discipline during Vietnam. Some quirks of American military culture, perhaps inherited from the European military traditions of earlier centuries, stuck in his craw. Hill observed in the Vietnam troops a kind of

strange fastidiousness—it goes way back. They're trained this way—an overlay of manners, of sophistication that's learned. The idea is that because you live a rough, often dangerous life, when you're in your quarters, you should live well. In Vietnam, officers took great pains about the Officers' Club, their table manners and fine wines. I found it astonishing—they were only there a year, and yet they spent so much time making sure their surroundings were perfect, that they had the most gadgets. Israelis did none of that—they were very Puritanical. If I ever ran into Oliver Cromwell's New Model Army, it would have been like the Israelis'.

Hill believed he could do more for his country as a policymaker than as a private in combat boots. He had always been a romantic. He

137

was more at home in the world of ideas and ideals, where he could admire and glorify uniformed men and women from afar, rather than get dirty with them and expose himself to their unsavory humanity. This way the Israelis could remain for Hill unblemished by the dust of the present—much like those latter-day Protestant Israelites of his college days, the New England Puritans. The Israelis, too, shared the pioneering ideal that appealed to Hill. After all, three quarters of Israel was wilderness at the time of the country's founding. Both were "a people in search of freedom who were willing to undergo considerable hardship, to strike out for freedom and build a nation," Hill said. "When you think of 'virtue,' you think of the Romans—you don't attach that word to the Puritans or the Israelis. But there is a stalwart sense that they share—which I've always had, placed in me by my father and the men around my family—that hard times could come really fast."

The Israelis had a word for the quality of person Hill was trying to describe: *halutz*, pioneer. "A *halutz* does not exist for himself alone," said Prime Minister Begin's mentor Vladimir Ze'ev Jabotinsky, the Revisionist Zionist who created the Jewish Legion. The Israeli hero was the champion of the Old Testament: a believer, soldier, educator, and leader of men, a modern-day Joshua or Gideon. Jabotinsky had those heroes in mind when he spoke of *hadar*, the quality of physical strength and beauty, self-respect, loyalty, and honor: the transformation of a ghetto-born people into citizens of a proud nation. *Hadar* encapsulated the "antique virtues" that Hill mourned at the close of the 1960s, virtues that the Harvard brats thought obsolete but that were essential for a people who lived in perpetual readiness to defend their right to exist. "This is the fate of our generation," Defense Minister Moshe Dayan proclaimed in a eulogy for a young Israeli struck down in an Arab ambush. "And the choice before us is to be ready and armed, strong and hard, or to have the sword snatched from our hands and be cut down!" Preparedness lay more in the Israeli mental attitude than in weaponry. "That was the way you ought to be," agreed Hill. "Manly. I'd always had a sense that things could fall apart, that we're lucky to have a stable society. Who do you want to go with you when things crumble, when you have to pick up your squirrel rifle and go into the hills? Someone who's intrepid, who won't complain, who'll get the job done. That's Israelis at their best."

The Fighting Jew had become an Israeli cultural ideal, and this ideal, more than his limited face-to-face experience with individual Israelis, enchanted Hill. "This cult of manhood — I think that was what drew him to Israelis in the abstract," said Gil Kulick, a Foreign Service officer who would serve with Hill later in his career in Israeli affairs. "But for all Hill's Israeliophilia, I don't remember a single Israeli friend he had." Hill had few close friends of any nationality. The ideals that he saw in the Israelis were sustenance enough. He had spent much of his early career watching ideas fall apart: in China during the Cultural Revolution; at Harvard, where the brightest American youth tried to tear down everything he believed was important; in Vietnam, where the best intentions of his country went appallingly wrong.

The idea of Israel, stripped of the ugly realities of war, human suffering, and politics, has always been a seductive one. Hill never believed that the Israeli government was above criticism, but he possessed an instinctive faith in the idea of Israel. He spent most of his days at the Israel desk trying to articulate that faith to unbelievers, for this was the problem that lay at the heart of every one of the constant inflow of angry letters from Capitol Hill that preyed upon the minds of the NEA Arabists who strode past the Israel desk. After the 1973 war — against which popular acrimony swelled further when the Arab states declared an oil embargo against the United States and other "friends of Israel" — many Americans in the media, in Washington, and in the public at large were skeptical of America's special relationship with the tiny country.

In their letters to constituents and in conversations with colleagues in NEA, Hill and his staff did their best to lay out the reasons for America's "strategic partnership." Americans had a moral commitment to the Israeli state. That commitment grew from the legacy of the Holocaust, when the United States and the other Allied powers, despite reports early in the war of Nazi genocide, did nothing to intervene. As a nation built by displaced persons, whose abiding symbol was the open embrace of Lady Liberty, America had a responsibility to dispossessed Jews. The Jews had no organic connection to any other land, and if the purpose of giving them a territory of their own was to provide a homeland where they would no longer be dependent on the goodwill of others, then that homeland had to be Israel. No matter Americans' grievances about Israel's "undemocratic" actions toward the Palestinians, it was a fact — one that would become starker with the overthrow of the shah of Iran in 1979 — that Israel was the only democracy in the Middle East and the only reliable U.S. ally there. This was the conventional reasoning for the United States' special relationship with Israel: in effect, an alliance without a treaty. But Hill's support for the Israeli cause was, one suspects, much more than a matter of political logic. It was based in a notion of Israeli exceptionalism, in a special regard for a country that was, like America, founded on an idea. At its core, Hill's sense of duty and affection toward this people, their history, and their mission was rooted in his heart, not his mind.

His colleagues worried that his support of Israel went too far. "Charlie was isolated," said one official. "It was a combination of his aloofness and the fact that he came across as dismissive of the Arab world in general, although I don't think he ever was. But he was blunt, impatient. Most of what he knew about the Middle East, he knew from talking to Israelis." From the point of view of others in the bureau, Hill was an outsider. They weren't sure how to deal with him. Near Eastern Affairs was famous for its collegiality; most of the officers there had served together in embassies in the Arab world, and "that was no picnic," said Hill's colleague. "But Charlie was never a part of that. He didn't want to be. It wasn't his style. If people were standing around, laughing about [Syrian President Hafez al-] Assad's latest screw-up, Charlie might agree, but he didn't have much to add, because he didn't have the background . . . There was this perception that he was an Israeliophile."

Political and social isolation was hardly new to Hill. But during his youth and through much of his adult life, he had been a self-declared marginal character, observing more than participating mainly because of shyness. In NEA, for the first time he found himself isolated because of his actions and opinions. He embraced his isolation in the State Department. He transformed his role from a marginal, ineffectual position to a central one — the odd man out, but an odd man who had the ear of powerful people — because he now had the confidence to stand apart from others. He had discovered the advantages of being a lone operator.

Hill's loner personality affected his relationships with others in the bureau, but it is clear from the fond memories of so many of his staffers that the real explanation for his isolation was not an inability to work with other people. Nor was it the long hours he preferred to spend working alone in his office. The main reason was that his feelings about Israel were much too far to the right for many in the State Department. Hill's sympathies quickly became known around State.

His office featured a huge color poster of Chaim Weizmann, Israel's first president, tacked prominently on the wall. Harmless decorations were one thing, but his coworkers realized how effective Hill was at implementing his ideas. After the Palestinian uprising in 1987, one former American ambassador to Egypt would go so far as to say, "Charlie Hill is personally responsible for the *intifada*."

But he was a good manager, and even the Arabists in the bureau acknowledged that his experience in Israeli affairs was critical to the bureau's work. More important than what he knew about political issues or Israeli sentiments were the people he knew in his own bureaucracy. Other officers, who made their careers in the Middle East and never ventured out of NEA, often had little concept of the resources in their own building. Hill remained true to his philosophy of aggressive recruiting. "He's a great player-potential assessor, in sports terms," admitted one NEA officer. Hill brought in several staffers from other offices in the State Department who proved to be assets. But he remained aware of the sentiments around him. "Over the course of my work there, I think they found in me a more formidable competitor in the bureau" than his predecessor had been, he said later. "I think I was very good about it all, and that was revealed when I was moved up to be deputy assistant secretary [of NEA, during the Lebanon War in 1982]. But there was a sense that 'this guy is too pro-Israel for our good, and maybe for his own good.'"

While Hill and his staff were stamping out anti-Israel brush fires, they also had to battle the government they were trying to defend. Prime Minister Begin's claims to a Greater Israel were largely unacceptable to Washington, which refused to endorse his appropriation of the land Israel had seized in 1967, including the entirety of Jerusalem. More trivial problems arose constantly, and nearly every day Hill had some reason to trek down the hall to the small, locked closet — nicknamed "Attica" by staffers because it resembled both an attic and a cell in the New York State prison of that name — that held NEA's only secure phone. The phone was crammed into the back of the closet among boxes of ancient memoranda, telegrams, and other relics of an earlier communications age now withered and flaking to the floor. Inside, between rusty filing cabinets and stacks of papers, Hill exchanged news and predicaments with Richard Viets, the deputy chief of mission in Tel Aviv. Hill usually wanted intelligence on recent developments in Israel. Viets, for his part, knew the sympathies of the Arabist-run bureau and was constantly worried that pro-Arab operators in Washington were sabotaging the embassy's efforts. No other embassy maintained such frequent contact with its desk back home. Viets "thought it was critical for his survival," Hill said.

Viets was not paranoid, only realistic. To work at the embassy in Tel Aviv was perhaps the only position tougher than the Israel desk. At least Hill and his staff had the advantage of working in Washington, cheek by jowl with their Arabist rivals, positioned to watch the political winds, hear rumors, and keep on top of what Washington policymakers were up to. In Tel Aviv, the embassy's staff was thousands of miles away from the pro-Palestinian in the White House and the anti-Israel factions in the State Department and on Capitol Hill, whose decisions and remarks they had to defend to Israeli officials up the hill in Jerusalem. On the other hand, the embassy's relative proximity to the Israeli government was no guarantee that it could discern or influence its behavior. Begin had firm ideas about the world and Israel's place in it, and he heeded the Americans only to the extent that it suited his needs. Relations with the embassy's counterparts at the consulate in Jerusalem—Foreign Service officers who dealt with Palestinians living on the West Bank—were often less than smooth. Initially Hill was happy to remain in IAI. His job on the desk had placed him de facto in charge of Arab-Israeli affairs, and he couldn't bear the idea of trading his proximity to Washington policymaking for a Tel Aviv post "in the provinces." It was true that the embassy was something of an island. It was, however, an island without solitude. It was stormed on all sides by the Arab-Israeli conflict, the squawking and fighting that made most of its American staff retreat in unease and fear.

Hill's moment of reluctance was short-lived. He soon wanted to be there more than anything else.

Charlie's opinions on Israel are well known at Yale. His stance never fails to emerge during his lectures on international relations, and he is a perennial source for journalists—whether they write for an undergraduate publication or a national newspaper—looking for a sound bite on the Arab-Israeli peace process. His position is caricatured as blindly pro-Israel, further to the right than the ultraconservative Likud Party, utterly disdainful of the Arab viewpoint. Over the course of my conversations with Charlie he was occasionally critical of particular Israeli policies, but in essence, that caricature is not too far from the mark. His colleague Gil Kulick agreed. "I'd be interested in his take on the Israel of 2004," he mused in an interview. "The corruption of the Israeli way of life, the materialism. The occupation [of the West Bank following the 1987 intifada] has brutalized Israeli society to a shocking degree. Thirty years ago, it had the most egalitarian income distribution after Sweden. Now it has the greatest income disparity except for the U.S. Their founding ideal has been ground into the dirt."

When I challenged Charlie on these points, his response was calm, measured, and predictable. I imagine he was bored with my questions. He had heard them hundreds of times before. He believed the economic shift away from the socialist ideals of Labor Zionism was a good thing. His former boss and friend George Shultz had worked with Jewish industrialist Max Fisher to help mastermind the change during the 1980s. "From the American point of view, the government should be searching not for greater equality but for greater opportunity and freedom," Charlie said. It was the familiar conservative motto, the maxim that sounded so noble in theory but had such disturbing consequences for individual human lives.

The Israeli occupation of territories beyond the pre-1967 borders and the ruthless conduct of IDF soldiers were quite justified to Hill. The Palestinians, abandoned by the rest of the Arab world to fight alone for their interests, surrendered agency to a growing terrorist network operating against Israel and its allies in the late 1980s. The terrorists interpreted Prime Minister Ehud Barak's decision to unilaterally withdraw from southern Lebanon in the spring of 2000 as evidence that terrorism worked. A renewed intifada followed a few months later, and "Israel had no choice but to go back in—and did massive damage to the terrorist infrastructure," Hill explained. His arguments seemed reasonable. They always did—at least while I sat across from him in that uncomfortable chair in his office, scribbling notes faster than I could think.

But after I left his office, I had a chance to reflect. What bothered me about our conversation was not Charlie's assessment of the politics and motives involved in the Arab-Israeli conflict. I agreed with most of what he said. There was something else, an objection much less tangible that hovered at the back of my throat, nearly rising to "Wait a minute, Charlie . . ." but never quite making it out of my mouth. Nowhere in Charlie's office-hours chats or podium eloquence was there a sign that he thought about the individual human beings involved. "Peace process" is such a sterile term. It may as well describe a chemical reaction in a petri dish. But anyone who tunes in to CNN's bloody shots of "martyred" Palestinian boys and shrouded, wailing mothers realizes that at some point politics and reason defer to something more primitive. I didn't want Charlie to say that he thought the Palestinian terrorists were justified, or that Israel ought to capitulate. I wanted him to acknowledge only that human beings were involved — that the same Israeli army whose "superb spirit and professionalism" he so admired was capable of atrocity. I wanted him, just for a moment, to quit lending me books about the "Temperament and Character of the Arabs," and allow a flicker of admission that we were talking about individuals, not just ideas. The problem was that to Charlie, the two are so often one and the same.

This is precisely what is appealing and noble about Charlie: he is a man of ideas who exists above the fray, who is better suited to keep company with Henry Adams or Ralph Waldo Emerson than with most modern-day academics. His example is empowering for college students. It is enchanting to believe that the realm of ideas, our world in the classroom, is where power lies. We love to think that our elders have been corrupted and bogged down by the "real world" and the addled emotions of their mid-twentieth-century youth, leaving our generation of level-headed, well-read thinkers with the task of setting the world to rights. This is the self-image encouraged by the professors of the Grand Strategy course, particularly by Charlie. On a campus where political science and history courses urge their students to find the narrowest specialization possible, a Grand Strategy syllabus with headings like "The Romans," "The Founding Fathers," and "Kant vs. Metternich"(and that's only the first semester) has a certain audacity.

But the Dead White Men aren't really what bother the liberals on campus who disapprove of Grand Strategy. What eats at them, what disturbs them most profoundly, is the same thing that alarms the political scientists and alarmed me in Charlie's take on the Middle East conflict: that Grand Strategy is the study of ideas. Liberal intellectuals and political scientists — some of whom in their youth were captivated by big ideas — now believe that big ideas cannot be trusted. "I'm philosophically leery of Grand Strategy. It's a gross oversimplification of history," said one critic, Yale historian Gaddis Smith. "When you find a government with a grand strategy, watch out." He cited Napoleon and Hitler as examples of the dangers inherent in "thinking big." Ideas, runs this line of reasoning, conceal truth more often than illuminate it. Ideas place too much power in the hands of thinking men, and thinking men can make grievous mistakes.

Charlie has told me something about the students in the Grand Strategy class. Each year, there are those who "get it" and those who do not. There are also those who perch on the edge, some days appearing to grasp the essential lesson, some days backsliding into confused questions. Without stating what exactly is apprehended by the ones who get it, he has remarked that the left-leaning students have the most trouble. I must surmise that "it" is, first, the ability to see the connections between the big ideas of the world and their smallest manifestations. But it is also an essential comfort with the reality of power: the fact that there will always be a balance of power, and some parties will always possess more of it than others — so, Charlie teaches, it might as well be us, who have the best motives and are trained to make the hard decisions.

The Grand Strategy worldview implies inequalities among human beings and intractable traits in human nature. This premise often mortifies the modern liberal, who draws from his Enlightenment inheritance an appraisal of individuals as essentially equal, malleable, and interchangeable consumers and producers who would achieve social harmony if only the barriers of race, class, and gender were eliminated. Grand Strategy, on the other hand, searches civilization's seminal texts for an unchanging essence of humankind, the patterns that repeat across history. Whether or not the class succeeds in this endeavor, it does not take its cue from the Enlightenment but from Edmund Burke, Charlie's beloved British statesman and philosopher. Burke's understanding of man has even older antecedents. It is a cornerstone of the Christian doctrine of original sin. But for the purposes of Grand Strategy, Burke's articulation is most useful. He saw the Enlightenment's assertion of human nature's malleability as a grave error; only destruction and misery could come from forcing unique individuals to conform to an "ideal" society, as in the case of the abhorred revolution in France. History, it seems, has granted his point. Confidence in the tractability of the human species is one grand strategy that has failed across time.

Burke believed that the familial unit was the core of a person's life and the primary sculptor of personality. Charlie, too, has always been a great believer in the foregone conclusions of 30 Institute Place, in the personality that emerged on the sand in Ocean City, where ten-year-olds gathered for football each summer morning and fell into teams with the effortlessness of migratory seabirds winging into form. The years and adventures that followed had little impact on his essential nature, he has said. This is not to say that Charlie does not fear for the fate of human character. If it cannot be fundamentally altered, certainly it can be subverted, poisoned, and caked in barbaric accretions, as he saw in the cataclysm of the Cultural Revolution and the eruptions at Harvard's Memorial Hall. The task of the Grand Strategy student is to take such accretions into account, then strip them away: to see beyond complexity to simplicity, as John Gaddis likes to say.

Grand Strategy stands at the center of what has become, across the modern academy, a near-religious battle over what sorts of questions are permissible to ask. "Some left-wingers see the very questions that Grand Strategy asks as *a priori* immoral," said Mike Morgan, a graduate student who took the class. American students shouldn't be learning how to wield power, argue critics of the course. They should be learning how to empower less fortunate peoples. They should not be reading the Western canon and practicing the art of sweeping judgment, but rather digging claustrophobic holes in some untold corner of the human experience, perhaps the history of New York subway line number 9, or the changing role of laundresses in Jakarta. They should stick rigorously to tangible evidence. This pseudoscientific approach eschews troublesome questions of power, save the infrequent digression to demonstrate how leaders trample the common man. Statistical conclusions and narrow studies allow intellectuals to claim that every case is unique, that one must never pass broad judgments, that moral relativism is the only *logical* way to live. The result is ironic: their "scientific" approach to human problems obviates any obligation to find that Holy Grail of the scientific enterprise, the universal truth. So they never have to take the uncomfortable position that a group of people, a government, or a cultural phenomenon is "wrong"—a stance that Charlie is always willing to take.

Logic, it appears, has become the same thing as morality. Logic *is* the morality that emerged from the Enlightenment, the great call to universal human reason. It was then that liberal intellectuals first noted that logic might be safer than morality; human beings are less likely to hurt themselves with it. The Enlightenment's faith in rational human nature was razed in the nightmares of war, genocide, and suffering that humankind inflicted upon itself in the nineteenth and twentieth centuries. Yet today, if one shrinks the window of vision small enough, one can still claim to live by the rule of reason — perhaps not universal reason, but at least a kind of docile rationalism. There is nothing courageous about this philosophy of inquiry, but then, we live in the age of "Warning: contents may be hot" labels on coffee cups. The costs of liability have outpaced courage.

In some sense, "getting it" is a religious conversion. It is not just an intellectual adjustment, but a spiritual and psychological transformation that requires a student to exchange one means of understanding the world, one barometer of right and wrong, for another. It demands acceptance of a grand strategic morality above and apart from the personal morality that theorists often apply to international affairs, just as they would to individual lives. The Grand Strategy class is packed with two semesters' worth of intellectual history and strategic reasons supporting this worldview. But in the end there are plenty of things about the class that sit uncomfortably in the gut, that smack of placing abstract ideas above individual human lives. There can be no unassailable defense for what amounts to a vantage point, a way of understanding history, not a logical argument. As much as Charlie would cringe to hear me say it, students have to meet him with an act of faith.

There is much in Grand Strategy's mission that I find convincing. If I must take sides in academia's existential crisis, in this battle between the ideologues and the bean counters, the hedgehogs and the foxes, I throw in my lot with the hedgehogs. But a balance, an acknowledgment that both sides have something to contribute to human knowledge and compassion, would be ideal. So far, I had not found a balance in Charlie. Perhaps that is because a balance requires compromise and demands at least a small admission of weakness. No such infirmities are permitted in the Ancient and Honorable Order of the Blue Jay.

9

THE HOUSE ON CATHEDRAL AVENUE IN NORTHWEST WASH-
ington was a modest box of red brick on the quietest, shadiest of
streets. An ordinary-looking home, it was supposed to be a respite
from rootless, strained life overseas. But it failed to bring the relief it
promised. This house, for all its bucolic surroundings, was even more
unhappy than the villa in Saigon had been. At 47 Phan Thanh Gian,
the laughter of the two little girls who were then too young to realize
anything was amiss had partly drowned out the ugly scenes, long after
bedtime, between their mother and father. In Vietnam, the girls'
mother was too beleaguered by everyday life to think much about
the books she'd read and conversations she'd had with her feminist
friends in Cambridge. No one in Saigon talked that way, and not a
small part of her was relieved to sink fully into mothering the little girls
who needed her there more than anywhere.

Upon their return to Washington, Martha fell into the life she'd had
when the Hills were last stateside. She filled her days with Katie and
Emily and the endless school enterprises that needed volunteers, the
seasonal projects at her new church, Westmoreland Congregational
(she and the girls went every Sunday; Charlie almost never joined
them), and when she had a few moments, her art. She did whatever
struck her fancy—carefree collages or miniatures of famous master-
pieces. Westmoreland gave her an outlet, and she poured her creative
energy into the church's arts committee. She was grateful. After the
tour in Vietnam, "My whole psyche was so scattered," she recalled.
"That brought me back, under a roof I recognized." Soon after they returned from Vietnam Martha made one attempt to get a job, when the
church advertised an opening at its daycare center. She had to bring

Emily along to the interview, and "when I got to the door, Emily threw a tantrum like I had never seen—she roared, screamed," Martha said. "I looked at the woman and I said, 'you know, I don't think I should do this.' And that was that." She stuck to volunteer work a few hours a week. Although he wanted little to do with the church community, Charlie admired Martha's artwork. More than once he suggested that she start doing it seriously and make a business of it. She never did. She said later that she didn't know how.

She and Charlie communicated less and less. "We were in the habit —I don't know how people do this—certain topics we'd talk about, and certain topics we didn't," Martha remembered. They had conversations about Katie and Emily or world affairs. Everything else was off-limits. "We kept doing our own things. His jobs got worse. I got into that peculiar habit of having two dinners—one with the girls at a reasonable hour, and one at any time he got home—eight, ten, or later." Charlie tried to be home for at least one afternoon of family time each weekend, but often he could not be, for the reason he didn't need to explain to anyone: his life at the State Department wouldn't permit it.

On the days when he made it home at a reasonable hour, Charlie often found that Martha had spent the afternoon toiling in the kitchen to produce a brilliantly crafted dinner, all her recipes expertly coordinated, the dining table set with steaming platters and an old-fashioned homemaker's attention to detail. But three minutes after they sat down to eat, she would throw her napkin over her food and storm out of the room in a "self-induced fury." The cause, Charlie said, was never him —always some minor external irritant, a story on the evening news or an encounter with a snobby woman at church. They did not fight. Martha simply stormed off and went to bed. At dinner parties—usually after she'd had something to drink—Charlie recalled that she sometimes joined the other women in snapping loudly about the crimes of male oppression. Martha's retiring personality makes such public outbursts hard to imagine, and indeed they were rare occurrences. Most of Hill's colleagues recalled her as a meek presence at the few embassy parties the Hills attended. "I don't remember any outbursts," said Foreign Service officer Gil Kulick. "If she had an ounce of feminism in her, she never showed it." But the few times Martha did lose her temper in public left a strong impression on Charlie. "The first time it happened set the pattern," he remembered. Eva Kim, the redoubtable secretary of Ellsworth Bunker, then living with foreign correspondent George Mc-

Arthur, had invited the Hills for dinner soon after they returned to Washington from Vietnam. "Mid-dinner, while George was telling stories, Martha began sneering at him, denouncing him as a male chauvinist pig," Hill said. "We had to end the dinner, and we never saw them again." He never tried to talk to her about her behavior: "I didn't bring it up. I wanted to escape from it. I shut up. I never engaged in any conversation about it with anybody. I felt there was no way to deal with it . . . as a man, at a certain point you say, 'this is a woman thing,' and you stay away from it."

Social convention had dictated Hill's relations with the opposite sex from his high school years onward. He followed the lead of a bold high school girl because it seemed about time that he had a girlfriend. He married his college sweetheart because he loved her—and also because there was tremendous social pressure to marry upon graduation. But no traditional social protocol could tell him how to talk to women when they were angry, when the rules were eroding.

The outbursts always came when Martha had been drinking, when she wasn't aware or in control of herself, and that made it even harder for her to communicate how she felt. Fundamentally, she didn't have the time, the courage, or—a key ingredient—the ego necessary to upend her life and the family dynamic for the sake of her own happiness. Hill, for his part, had the same response to Martha's actions that he'd had when his mother-in-law imposed her opinions upon an otherwise snugly conventional marriage. He did not run, but politely walked away from the crisis, finding a rational justification (this time, the long hours in Foggy Bottom) for staying out of the house and refusing to meet the problem head-on.

Decades later, after describing at length his analysis of the troubles between men and women still with us today after the revolution of the 1960s, he added this disclaimer regarding the course of his own life: "This isn't me—I'm living in a paradise. I achieved it by turning things down, knowing what I want to do, and reducing my wants to the things I really want, in the manner of Thoreau." It would be glib to say that family life did not matter to Hill. A more accurate interpretation may be that the women's revolution and Martha's brewing discontent brought out a side of Hill of which he was not proud: the helpless adolescent who did not know how to conduct himself, the unhappy Bridgeton High student who didn't understand the rules of the game, and so proclaimed himself a "marginal character." He took control by withdrawing.

The Hills had been in Washington for six years, by which time Martha had long exhausted the chores and residual busywork required for making a new house inhabitable; Katie and Emily had fallen into ordinary schoolgirl habits; and Charlie had grown tired of the stateside bureaucracy, when the looked-for summons finally came from Tel Aviv. The American ambassador, Sam Lewis, served as deputy director for Henry Kissinger's Policy Planning Staff and remembered Hill from those Saturday morning football games. In the spring of 1979, although Hill's tour at the Israel desk was only half over, Lewis sent word that he wanted Hill back on his team as chief political counsel in Tel Aviv. He was to leave in July. Martha and the girls would finish packing up things at Cathedral Avenue and follow a few months afterward. They leased the house for the duration of Charlie's tour in Israel. It would be waiting for them when they came back.

The biography of a marriage is not just a matter of scrutinizing the backgrounds and motivations of two people in relation to each other. A marriage is more than the sum of its parts. The chemistry and common experiences of the bond transform both spouses and shape the webs of their lives in ways that neither person can control or predict. An outsider's access is limited, and not even the private view of either spouse yields a complete picture.

I first began to see how hard it was to comprehend a marriage from the outside at the end of the summer before my sophomore year at college. One afternoon, after a few sweaty hours spent squashing my essentials into suitcases and loading up boxes of clothes and books to ship back to school, my mother and I sat together on the back porch. After a sometimes testy and distant relationship during high school, we had become closer when I went away to college (funny how that tends to happen). When I was younger my mom rarely addressed me in anything but the various counseling and scolding modes with which motherhood is equipped, but suddenly, there on the back porch with lemonade in her hand, she began to talk to me like a friend.

My parents' marriage had always seemed idyllic and seamless to me. I had never witnessed any fights beyond an ephemeral few minutes of pointed glares from my mother or sarcastic retorts from my dad. But now my mother revealed that there had been serious disagreements, highs and lows that they'd struggled through together. Their marriage, while always charged with love, was sometimes a lot of work. As she recounted a moment or two when my brother and I were very

151

small, when their relationship almost collapsed, I was stupefied. I'd had no inkling of this.

Realizing that your parents are not perfect has always been part of growing up, but there was more to this revelation than learning to see my mother and father as ordinary human beings. I was shocked that I could have grown up in the same house, eating dinner with them every night and sleeping thirty feet away, and still had no idea what their relationship was really like. True, I was a little girl for most of that time, self-absorbed and busy with my dollhouses and slumber parties, but children are supposed to have a sixth sense about these things, I'd always thought. I came to the conclusion that a marriage, while it forms the nucleus of the family, remains a sovereign domain that only its two citizens may enter.

When it came to examining Charlie's marriage, I approached the subject with no small degree of caution and humility. No matter how many impolite questions I asked, in the end I would still know much less about their relationship than I had known about my parents' marriage, which I had so grossly misjudged. I dreaded broaching the subject. There is nothing more unpleasant or perilous than asking a person about things that pain him and are none of your business. The hubris inherent in the biographer's objective is colossal. In the case of the subject's married life, it is not only particularly offensive but also an enterprise likely doomed to failure, even if disguised in enlightened psychobabble.

Charlie tried to kill the subject with kindness. When I worked up the nerve to ask a personal question about his relationship with Martha, he never demurred. Nor did he approach the subject as he did all the others, with intricate description and thinking out loud. On this topic he answered with blunt, abbreviated sentences. "I was close-minded," he told me in the Charles Hill monotone. "I was a bad husband. By the nature of what I was doing, I was making her a single mother." I didn't have to prod. He went straight to the cruel final analysis. He said things that had crossed my mind, but I never dreamed I would hear him say them out loud.

I didn't question the honesty of Charlie's confessions. As much as I was beginning to feel protective of Martha and appalled by how my supposedly all-knowing professor could have made such hurtful mistakes, I was impressed by the frankness of his self-condemnation. But it was also a brilliant tactical move on his part. By pleading guilty straightaway — before I could delve into the charges — he headed me off at the pass. What more could I want from him, now that I had his signed confession? Did I expect him to wallow in the details of every quarrel and heartbreaking gaze? Charlie knew that my questions needed to be asked. He had admitted as much when he lectured me, prior to the story of Mary Anne Gbur and the first kiss, on the biographer's task of presenting a balanced portrait of a life. But he had never been one for groveling or hand wringing.

I have to admit that his tactic worked. I hated treading this ground in the first place, and I fled back as quickly as I could to the safe territory of his glamorous career and all the Great Men that he'd known. The realm of Grand Strategy is a seductive place for biographers, whose essential goal — as much as we try to deny it — is to make a life adhere to a storyline. I thought at the time that Charlie's succinct illumination of the story was enough — that I had gotten all I came for.

Tel Aviv was built on the sand dunes along the shore of the eastern Mediterranean just north of the old Arab town of Jaffa, on a strip of land where no one had believed that houses, roads, and spirit could ever last. It was built by pioneers, sixty Jewish families who set out in 1909 to found the first entirely Jewish modern city, and it had always been a youthful, incoherent, unromantic place, an unfinished metropolis permanently under construction. Zoning laws were virtually nonexistent until the 1960s, and so settlers had built whatever dream houses they liked. Small European-style dwellings with red tile roofs mingled with Oriental architecture along the tangled streets of the old neighborhoods, while the newer, more orderly sections of the city stretched northward toward the Yarkon River. Tel Aviv had none of the historical or religious ballast of Jerusalem; it was materialistic, unspiritual, even "American" to many conservative Israelis. "Tel Aviv is and remains a rather shapeless European settlement at the edge of the Orient," author Henry Zoller, who had lived in the city since its founding, wrote a few years before the Hills' arrival. "[T]he pioneers' urban showpiece in the Jewish state is, in the last resort, nothing but a small shopkeeper's capital, a city of people driven by their own personal ambitions."

Tel Aviv was "a short-sleeve town" in the words of Dorothy Kahn, hot and ugly, although probably no hotter or uglier than most other human metropolises. Martha was struck by the machismo of the city. As

Israeli Defense Force troops strode past her on the street, they wore their khaki shirts open at the neck, their sleeves rolled up over muscular arms, and caps tucked into their shoulder epaulets. She called it "the 'pioneer' look." "Very macho, as is this whole place," she wrote to Morton and Alvenia not two weeks after her arrival. Most women Martha's age "wear literally vibrating colors. I looked like a nun [when she first arrived] but now I look OK. There is a real macho-physical quality to people in Tel Aviv. The men wear open-necked shirts, gold chains, a lot of hair, sandals and often shorts. The women wear tight pants, high heels, baggy billowing tops or tee shirts, longish swishing skirts . . . quite a lot of makeup—in a way it is a kind of chi-chi resort-type look—a lot of bare skin. And it seems that everyone has a cigarette dangling out of their mouths."

Martha's remarks about the Israelis reminded Charlie of the way she had seen the insufferable Foreign Service snobs on the voyage to Zurich as play-actors, or dolls in a dollhouse—another time when he had mistaken her anxiety for enthusiasm. Despite her apprehensions Martha warmed to the country quickly, as did the girls. The Hills found a house north of the city in Herzliya Pituach, a quiet suburb split between the original settlement and the younger, seaward side of town, now home to resorts and green residential neighborhoods. The house was spacious and sunny, much larger than their home in Washington. Martha found the most appealing feature to be the covered porch, "which catches sea breezes and looks out on a pretty garden which surrounds us with green and provides a peaceful quiet place," she wrote to Bridgeton.

The neighborhood was unfriendly, however, populated mostly by Israeli families who fenced off their yards and kept angry, barking Dobermans. Martha was quick to try and make it her home, reconstructing the busy lifestyle she had done her best to keep up at every post. After settling in, she registered for Hebrew lessons at the American embassy and rose at 5:30 each morning to rouse Katie and Emily, who rode with their parents part of the way to classes at the American International School. After Hebrew class Martha returned home, wending her way through one of the neighborhood markets to pick up the day's groceries. Charlie had to take the car to work, leaving her with no way to get around. Other officers' wives often spotted her trudging home, struggling with her loaded shopping bags.

She occupied the remainder of the day with her standard cavalcade of volunteer commitments and household chores. Even when the cleaning lady came to help, Martha could not force herself to take a rest: "Whenever Adele, Pearl of Israel, comes to clean I feel I should chug along beside her to keep her spirits up—and lower my own. However, since I have been chugging since 6am I will stop to refuel and say hello. I haven't written for a while since we are in the usual desperate Halloween-Thanksgiving-Christmas run. If I do any more things I will explode in all directions and disappear." One wonders if Martha manufactured this hectic pace for herself, filling her days with the virtuous occupations to which she had grown so accustomed, because they had become her profession since she gave up the possibility of a career outside the home.* "I still have a hundred things to do from my 'list' of things to definitely get done today," she wrote in November. The laundry proliferated, she groaned in another letter, "like mushrooms in a forest." In her account to Bridgeton of a fifteen-person dinner party she hosted at Thanksgiving, Martha sounded overcome with fretting over whether the extra chairs she needed would arrive on time, last-minute preparations for kosher meals, and the politics between food caterers. "I still get into a hysterical turmoil inside over all the uncertainties we live with but on the outside I can be cool (almost)," she wrote.

The daily violence of life in Israel upset her, and perhaps the familiar anxieties of entertaining were preferable to worrying about her new home's fragile peace. Moreover, boredom, or even just a bit of unoccupied time to herself, was in a small way terrifying. Undoubtedly, part of her knew that. She had read Betty Friedan. But what else could she do? If she poured her creative energy into "running a perfect house and supervising her children and sharing her husband's career in such omnipresent detail that she [had] . . . no time for serious larger interests, who is to say that this is not as important, as good a way to spend a life, as mastering the secrets of the atoms or the stars, composing symphonies, pioneering a new concept in government or society?"

As long as a housewife had jobs to do and other people's needs to fill, she could avoid facing up to the empty restlessness inside. Martha's letters from Israel remained carefully glazed, as always, with the

---

* Betty Friedan explains the tendency she found in many housewives to extend their housework needlessly to fill the day and disguise the problem of boredom. See *The Feminine Mystique*, Chapter 10, "Housewifery Expands to Fill the Time Available," 233–257.

veneer of cheerful forbearance. But much more than her correspon-dence from Hong Kong or Vietnam, they betray exhaustion with the re-sponsibilities of Foreign Service life, and exasperation and anxiety over the two daughters who were just hitting the most enervating strides of adolescence. To Charlie, in Israel Martha seemed the happiest she had been since their year in Cambridge. It is more likely that he conflated her ability to maintain a state of harried occupation with genuine con-tentment. In that note to his parents from Vietnam he had, after all, joked that Martha's "main problem" was "too much free time." Charlie was always happiest when consumed with his work. It was only logical that his wife should feel the same.

When they arrived in Israel, Emily was in junior high and Katie was ready to enter high school. They were at the ages marked in many households by constant fighting and self-inflicted misery. Emily in par-ticular was aggressive and intractable. Her "favorite gesture now is the finger," her exasperated mother wrote to Bridgeton. "Everybody gets the finger. She fits right into this society. We suspect she once walked into the world as a Jew and then was reincarnated as a Chinese girl." An older, wiser Emily explained that when she and her sister were small and living in Vietnam, they were each other's only friend. "People said that Katie was Lucy and I was Linus, because I sucked my thumb constantly, and she was bossy, like Lucy," she said. "But we started get-ting our own friends and going our separate ways — when we went to Israel, we were on different tracks." They kept out of each other's way most of the time, but the occasional fracas was inevitable. After one skirmish, Emily slammed a door so hard that plaster crumbled down from the ceiling.

When they sat in the living room decades later and recalled the girls' teenage years, both Martha and Katie laughed them off as the typ-ical sibling battles and trials of adolescence. Emily's rebelliousness was credited to her friendship with "two of the naughtiest little blond girls," the daughters of other families in the American ex-pat community. "Both Katie and Emily at times wanted to be blue-eyed blondes," Mar-tha said. "Emily found two blond girls, and she was fascinated by them. They were bright, but wild." Charlie and Martha were less concerned about Katie, who was doing better in school and spent most of her free time with a mild-mannered "geek-like" boyfriend, an Iranian Jew who went to great lengths to ingratiate himself with Martha. Katie was always busy, acting in school musicals and putting on small plays with other Foreign Service kids. "Emily, more than Katie, really went berserk," Hill said. "If you said, 'What did you do today?' she'd fly into a rage and scream, 'Stop hounding me!' For a few years, it was impossible to communicate. Any statement or assertion was taken as monarchical oppression."

One evening, while Charlie was away on embassy business in Egypt, Martha was waiting for Emily to come home. She had a test the following day and had been instructed to come straight home after school. The sky grew dark and still there was no sign of her. Finally, just as Martha was beginning to panic, her daughter stumbled in, her corduroys ripped open and bloody at the knee. She told her mother that she'd been riding her bike with a friend (not on her way home, it soon came out), when one of the neighborhood guard dogs, a vicious German shepherd, lunged at her and bit her leg, puncturing the skin and bruising her calf. "Whenever Charlie goes away we always manage to have a domestic crisis," Martha calmly wrote to Morton and Alvenia. She did her best to sound unruffled: "Fortunately she had on long corduroy pants. If she hadn't her leg would have been shredded instead . . . There follows a long, long story of confrontation with the owners, doctors, tetanus vaccine which had to be purchased by us and then a shot, and then calls to the Embassy and finally a trip to the Ministry of Health . . . The lady showed me the shot card (in Hebrew) and if I had been less upset I would have asked for it to have it verified."

When she recounted the story decades later, it was clear that this was one of her ugliest memories of Israel. It was also one of her most vivid. Martha grew animated as she told the story, and the listener couldn't help but see that the incident with the dog had broader significance than merely as one of Emily's more dangerous transgressions. "Once again, Charlie was not there," she said. "This was an unraveling time for me—how to handle this? It was the Sabbath, so everything was closed. I was mad at the Israelis, mad at Emily for not coming home. I felt out of control. There was so much to do, and I lacked the perspective I have now. Things were out of control, and our family was too small to have a father so rarely there."

To some extent, Martha and her daughters are probably right to brush aside the anxieties of those years as mostly normal. But in Martha's recollections of Israel it is hard to ignore the correlation between Emily's troubles and Charlie's chronic absences.

Hill found Emily's behavior baffling. His daughters had no apparent cause for dissatisfaction. They were well occupied. Katie was studying ballet twice a week and became "locally famous" for her dancing ability, according to one letter her proud mother wrote to Bridgeton. Emily was taking piano lessons, and although she struggled in school, she did win first place in the science fair. "It made no sense to me," Hill said later. "They were living in a nice house with a big yard, in a country where people were friendly. The American International School seemed perfectly okay, and they had sports, music. My conclusion was that adolescent girls go insane for five or six years, and you do your best not to have to incarcerate them." He rightly concluded that his daughters' bickering and Emily's outbursts were a call for attention, but he brushed it off because this was "just a phase" that all teenage girls went through. It did not occur to him that his daughters' cry for attention could have been a message to him, personally. "I don't think the girls cared about him having an important job," Martha said later, when neither daughter was around and the conversation turned more serious. "They wanted to see him more. I think they needed more attention than they probably got—a sense of cohesive family."

Hill took over the post of political counsel in the wake of a predecessor who was a gifted analyst but harsh manager. Robert Blackwill was a talented political officer and a skilled writer, but "he was so nasty and tough on his staff," Ambassador Sam Lewis said. "I didn't pay as much attention as I should have, and morale was bad. Charlie had a reputation as a good supervisor, a person who could manage staff. He had to get the team spirit back."

Hill's position was third in command at the embassy (subordinate only to the new deputy chief of mission, Bill Brown, and the ambassador) at a critical point in the Arab-Israeli peace process. Shortly before the Camp David talks began a year earlier, in the fall of 1978, Gideon Samet, correspondent of the Israeli newspaper *Ha'aretz*, had come to talk with Hill in Washington to say he was worried about whether piecemeal negotiations were in his country's best interest. He told Hill that he had once asked Henry Kissinger whether step-by-step negotiations were not ultimately weakening Israel. Kissinger said no, adding, "That's the idea of those who see diplomacy as a chess game and think that they have all the moves thought out far enough ahead to win. But it doesn't work that way in practice. Each step has a life of its own."

Samet retorted that interim agreements meant chaos and unreasonable risks for Israel. "You give up reality — territory — for an intangible, peace settlements — which can be retracted easily, while you can't get territory back easily," he told Hill. "And the closer you get to getting the ultimate peace, the less territory you have to bargain with." The Arabs, for their part, distrusted any negotiations whose outcome they could not guarantee beforehand. Before they began talking, they wanted to be certain of winning all their demands. "Arab view really pre-modern," Hill wrote in his notebook. "Hierarchical, status-determined, inflexible; no comfort with situations of flux or change."

When Camp David ended on September 17, 1978, Begin and Sadat signed a statement of general principles on future negotiations to determine "transitional arrangements" and the final status of the West Bank and Gaza. Jordan was invited to represent the stateless Palestinians in future negotiations with Israel on the basis of the Camp David framework. A second agreement pertained to the goal of concluding peace between Egypt and Israel. Israel would withdraw troops from the Sinai and abandon some settlements, while Sadat agreed to allow three years for the withdrawal, monitored by the United States and the United Nations, and committed to normalizing relations with Israel. Sadat had chosen to negotiate directly with Israel at the price of isolation from the rest of the Arab world. He had elected a separate peace, an incomplete beginning to a gradual solution to the Arab-Israeli problem, rather than insisting on "the whole loaf," as Hill put it. This was the essence of Camp David's historic significance.

The road from accords to treaty six months later had not been smooth. Arabs throughout the region were furious. When President Carter sent Hill's boss at the time, Assistant Secretary for NEA Harold Saunders, to Jordan to assure King Hussein that his hopes for the ultimate removal of Jewish settlements from the West Bank were not in vain, Begin retaliated by "thickening" the Israeli settlements in the West Bank by one hundred or so families. Meanwhile the Jordanians refused to participate in negotiations for Palestinian autonomy, and Palestine Liberation Organization (PLO) agents terrified all local Palestinians into silence. When it came to answering the irate phone calls and letters that had immediately poured into Hill's office in Washington, the truth was that the United States did not have a clear position in the Arab-Israeli peace process. "The primary thing was for the U.S. to remain involved," said Foreign Service officer William Kirby, who worked with Hill on Israeli affairs in Washington. But when Hill arrived in Tel Aviv, the personal conflicts and political disagreements that nearly derailed the peace treaty still remained and were all the more intractable for having been washed over after its signing.

The embassy operated as a facilitator, a contact point between Washington and Jerusalem and a watchtower for the Carter administration. The place of Charles Hill in all this is difficult to discern because he was primarily an adviser, an observer, and a delegator, not a principal actor. Moreover, the medium of diplomacy obscures the process of political progress. As Hill explained later, "This is how diplomacy works, and people don't understand it. It works in tiny increments. It comes from and is expressed through an endless series of small perceptions and intellectual angles of approach. Often that approach is negative; your job is to be a gatekeeper. Ten ideas may come up in the course of a day, nine of those are bad, and no one knows which one is good. You have to be able to say why something's not a good idea, and get it put aside."

Hill was a quiet presence at most meetings, "touching the rudder" lightly when he believed arguments were moving in the wrong direction. He believed he was most effective inside, as the political section's command center. "The Ambassador had a lot of confidence in Charlie as his alter-ego," said Ted Feifer, a Foreign Service officer who worked with Hill. "If an issue came up, he knew Charlie could handle it." Over the course of his career, particularly during his last year at the Israel desk, Hill had developed sensitivities to attitudes and undercurrents in Washington on which the ambassador came to rely. "It's one of the biggest problems for the embassy in Israel when you're involved in high policy," Lewis said later.

> There are a lot of crosscurrents in the State Department, among the principals, between the Department and the White House, the political world outside, Congress, and the Jewish community. We'd get echoes of all the crosscurrents, different sets of guidelines and instructions. It was very important, using the secure phone, to keep a sense of the mood in Washington, how to handle the delicate balance of support for Israel and concern over Begin's government's behavior on some issue. So one of the embassy's jobs was to understand Washington, to keep the Ambassador sensitized to concerns that weren't in the telegrams, weren't stated publicly. Charlie was instrumental in that. He was instinctive in maneuvering between the raindrops.

A critical example was Hill's role in handling President Carter's human rights initiative, spearheaded by the brand-new Bureau of Human Rights and Humanitarian Affairs. Although the bureau swiftly declined in influence as Carter's idealistic campaign promises gave way to a more pragmatic view of foreign policy, its feisty secretary, Patricia Derian, still demanded rigorous human rights reports on every country each year. The embassies were responsible for providing the first drafts, and in Israel's case Derian battled hard to call attention to the plight of the Palestinians. "Israel was extraordinarily sensitive to this project of criticizing their human rights behavior in public documents," said Lewis. There was a tug of war over every word used to describe human rights violations. In the end the Bureau of Human Rights usually lost its battles, and the human rights report had a negligible impact on American aid to Israel or Washington's stance in the continuing negotiations. A central reason why so few front-page headlines came of the reports, why what little hostile transatlantic bluster they did produce seemed to evaporate before causing permanent damage to the latest tentative progress toward peace, was that Hill was doing his job.

It was an insider's job. It required a second-nature instinct about Washington and offered no glamour or public recognition. In fact the job was mostly negative: if he had misread the tenor in Washington or fumbled the battles over the human rights report, the consequences could have been disastrous. But if these were properly handled, the best one could hope for was that nothing would happen at all. Despite Hill's quiet presence at senior meetings, despite the absence of obvious positive advancement in the daily bureaucratic cease-fires he marshaled, no one was fooled. "Charlie was Lewis's intellectual guru," Gil Kulick said later. "I think he had a huge intellectual impact on policy. Lewis relied heavily on Charlie's judgment—not always to the benefit of policy."

Kulick was not the only one on Hill's staff who parted ways with his boss in political philosophy. The section was staffed almost entirely by liberal Jewish Americans, a noteworthy development in itself, as until this time the State Department had a firm unwritten rule against assigning Jewish Foreign Service officers to Israel; only during Lewis's tenure as ambassador did that taboo begin to give way. Most were loyal to Israel's Labor Zionist roots and believed the Likud government was betraying the country's founding vision. Hill would have butted heads with them no matter who the Israeli leadership had been. But Prime Minister Menachem Begin was the uncompromising Irgun hardliner, a lecturing zealot who even on the occasion of the signing of the Egypt-Israel peace treaty refused to relinquish an opportunity for Neo-Revisionist Zionist rhetoric.* Hill's staff did not dismiss Begin's accomplishments at Camp David or in the peace treaty with Egypt, but they feared what his vision meant for the country. Hill, on the other hand, came to know Begin personally during his tour in Israel. Among the meetings he attended with the ambassador were occasional interviews with the prime minister himself. Those meetings were the only occasions on which Hill—in exception to the casual intimacy of Israeli culture—donned a coat and tie. Begin too wore a suit—a visible departure from the open-collar Labor Party prime ministers.

Hill, a man oblivious to so many basic truths about the wife and daughters who shared his home, seemed to "get" the people of this strange country in a way that eluded most foreigners. He admired Prime Minister Begin—a leader whose violent past in the Irgun, an underground Jewish militia that resorted to terrorism, horrified most Americans. His steadfast refusal to negotiate his people's right to inhabit the entirety of Eretz Israel, the ancient homeland promised to the Jews by God, baffled and frustrated world leaders and many of his own people. Yet Hill would approach Begin at the end of his tour in Tel Aviv and ask the prime minister to autograph a portrait of himself. "I have that photo he signed to me, and that's odd, because nobody ever wanted one," Hill said. "No one would have thought to ask for one." Although his personal contact with the prime minister was limited to the formal meetings he attended with Ambassador Lewis, Hill glimpsed in Begin that rare kind of statesman who "saw history on a vast scale, and felt that what he was deciding upon on a given day had monumental significance for the course of history." Hill had encountered one other figure in his career thus far who possessed the same broad perspective of his own place in the course of the human narrative: Henry Kissinger, another figure many reviled.

---

* As the *Wall Street Journal* reported, "Begin produced acute discomfort in some parts of the audience when he said what many did not wish to hear at the moment, that this portion of peace for his country had been bought only with the blood of its soldiers and that in the past, when Jews had no armies of their own, the good offices of the West had not been used to save them from Hitler's ovens or Stalin's prisons."

Charlie made his mother sew sergeant's stripes on his T-shirts. Here he wears the insignia of First Sergeant, Air Corps. 1942.

Unless otherwise noted, all photos courtesy of Charles Hill.

Charlie and his father, Morton Hill, at Ocean City. 1940.

Charlie, age four, in the bushes beside a neighbor's house.

A serendipitous stroll across the quadrangle during the spring of his freshman year landed Charlie (left) in *Brown Alumni Magazine*. He was every inch the image of the 1950s Brown undergraduate that deep-pocketed alumni wanted to see. November 1953. *Courtesy of Brown Alumni Magazine.*

Charlie Hill weds Martha Mitchell at the First Congregational Church of Oak Park, Illinois. August 31, 1957. *Courtesy of Charles and Martha Hill.*

Morton and Alvenia Hill visit Charlie and Martha in their stateroom on board the SS *Constitution* before the couple departs for Genoa en route to Zurich, Hill's first Foreign Service post abroad. February 1962. *Courtesy of Charles and Martha Hill.*

Martha, Emily, and Katie at Martha's mother's home in Oak Park, just before their departure for Saigon. April 1972. *Courtesy of Martha Hill.*

On one trip back to the United States from his post in Saigon, Charlie was given charge of eleven Korean babies on a flight from Seoul to New York. Here, just after the flight landed at JFK Airport, he cradles one of the anonymous bundles. 1972. *Courtesy of Martha Hill.*

"Base Ops," Saigon, ca. 1972. Military and civilian officers await a dignitary's arrival. Deputy U.S. Ambassador Charles Whitehouse (left) talks with Robert Mossler, director of the Joint U.S. Public Affairs Office, while deputy mission coordinator Charlie Hill stands off to the right. Over Whitehouse's left shoulder is U.S. Ambassador Ellsworth Bunker.

Ambassador Philip Habib arrives at Ben Gurion Airport, near Tel Aviv, Israel. 1979. Behind and to the left of Habib is the U.S. ambassador to Israel, Samuel Lewis.

A farewell song for Hill upon his departure from Tel Aviv in the fall of 1981, performed by his daughters, Katie (with guitar) and Emily. Two State Department officers look on while Martha holds lyrics she wrote to the tune of "Take It Easy" by the Eagles: "Charlie's goin' down the Haifa / Tryin' ta straighten his life out / He's got lotsa problems on his mind . . ." Martha later said that Charlie hated all the attention, "but the kids were really cute, and people were watching, so he had to be polite."

During a stop on his Latin American tour in February 1976, Secretary of State Henry Kissinger embraces Miguel de la Flor, foreign minister of Peru. In the background, Charlie Hill (second from the top) disembarks. *Charles Hill collection, Hoover Institution Archives.*

Charlie Hill and executive secretary Nicholas Platt enjoy a moment of levity during a briefing session in Secretary of State George Shultz's study, where Shultz preferred to work. Through the door to the left is Hill's office. 1986. *Charles Hill collection, Hoover Institution Archives.*

One of the approximately twenty-two thousand pages of notes Hill took during his tenure as George Shultz's assistant. Dated November 5, 1986, the day after the Iran-Contra scandal broke, the dense paragraph at the top of the page is Hill's record of NSC Adviser John Poindexter's message to Shultz, which begins: "At some point we will have to lay out all the facts . . . I do not believe that now is the time to give the facts to the public." Next, the heading "S=CH 0630" is followed by a verbatim record of Hill's 6:30 A.M. meeting with the secretary to discuss U.S.-Soviet relations.

Left: Aboard Air Force One, en route to Bitburg, Germany, where President Reagan would pay a controversial visit to a German military cemetery. As they posed for this photograph, Reagan noted to Hill that they were almost exactly the same size. May 1985. *Above:* Secretary Shultz admires souvenirs purchased during a trip to Africa, while Charlie Hill broods over matters of grand strategy. January 1987.

Hill leaves a characteristic scene on the tarmac at Ben Gurion Airport, Tel Aviv, during a Middle East peace initiative. Upon arriving at the airport at the conclusion of a trip, the secretary of state would give a press conference (visible in the background), which Hill always skipped, walking alone to the aircraft to read the incoming cable traffic and prepare for the next leg of the trip. April 1988.

Charlie Hill and Norma Thompson, recuperating after a tennis match at George Shultz's ranch in Mendocino County, California. Norma, as usual, beat Charlie. July 2004.

Students in Yale's Grand Strategy class tackle another emergency in the year-end Crisis Simulation. December 2003.
Courtesy of Andy Scott.

At breakfast with Grand Strategy students at the Yale Club of New York in 2003, Henry Kissinger expounds on a fine point of foreign policy while Professor John Lewis Gaddis and student Andrew Klaber look on. Kissinger, Hill's former boss and also a friend of Gaddis, has shown a keen interest in the Grand Strategy class since its inception. *Courtesy of Minh Luong.*

A moment of reflection during a trip to south China with the secretary of state. March 1987.

Begin was concerned not with Kissinger's grand design for world order but with the peace and security of his tiny country. He had little time for Kissingerian philosophizing or intellectualizing. Begin believed his duty was to fulfill the destiny of the Jewish people as the Old Testament had proclaimed it — a secure Jewish state that would occupy all of Eretz Israel. Few modern world leaders have relied on the Bible as their central foreign policy document. Begin was not oblivious to twentieth-century concerns of political strategy and security, but in the main he chose not to inhabit the intellectual framework of the policymakers who tried to work with him, fraught as it was with conflicting interests and moral confusion. Begin made no move without feeling the weight of history. His foreign policy was part mystical eschatology and part realistic appraisal of his people's story. To Hill it was an honorable grand strategy.

The prime minister knew Hill and liked him. Although Hill assumed the role of silent note taker during Lewis's meetings with Begin, he had more active relationships with Begin's personal aides. They must have reported favorably to their boss. "They told him about me," Hill said. "They must have said, 'He's a good guy, he understands us.'" In the course of afternoons spent waiting for a meeting with Begin in the prime minister's offices, Hill befriended one of Begin's cronies, a balding, sharp-featured man named Yehel Kadishai. Hill showed him the latest collection of Yiddish stories he'd bought at a Tel Aviv bookstore and allowed Kadishai to tell him endless numbers of Yiddish jokes. When Kadishai got in to see his friend Begin, he probably had good things to say about the quiet Foreign Service officer outside.

One Saturday afternoon during the latter half of Hill's tour in Israel, the State Department contacted Lewis in an uproar over the latest Israeli military assault in Lebanon. Although embassy work always shut down on Shabbat, Washington ordered Lewis and diplomatic envoy Philip Habib to seek an interview with the prime minister. They took Hill along to Jerusalem. No other staff accompanied them. Begin had agreed to receive them at the prime minister's residence, a spare, modern structure faced with Jerusalem stone, like most of the city's buildings. Begin invited them into the sparsely decorated living room, where a crowd of his friends was beginning to disperse. Apparently they had been told that their holiday socializing would have to resume later in the afternoon.

When the room was nearly empty, Lewis began the readout of

American concerns he had been instructed to relay to Begin. The prime minister interrupted: the conversation couldn't proceed, because he could not ask his aides to take notes on the Sabbath. Most Israeli diplomats were fanatics about their record keeping. They relied on meticulous accounts of every conversation, organized and maintained, Hill recalled, by "wonderful Israeli grandmotherly figures who kept the files and could find anything . . . the Israelis could go back and say, 'You said this five years ago, and you can't change it now.'" American policymaking might have benefited from half as much exactitude, even if it seemed to those in Washington less a virtue than a ploy of fastidiousness intended to hamstring Israel's adversaries.

Lewis looked perplexed. There was a moment of uncertain silence. Then Begin spoke: "Mr. Hill can take notes for me."

When the meeting concluded and the Americans had returned to the consulate general in East Jerusalem, Hill went upstairs to find a desk in one of the empty offices and write up the memorandum for Washington. Then, like a chess master playing a match against himself, he wrote a separate account for the Israelis. "I did it twice," he emphasized later. "I didn't just send a copy of the same cable. I wrote theirs as though I were an Israeli note-taker. Both were accurate, but from different perspectives — what you take as being the serious points, stresses on what's important, different commentary. For example, at one point the American report might have said, 'think we made an impression on the Prime Minister'; at another point, the Israeli one would say, 'think we effectively cut short their argument.'"

Begin sensed, or had been told, that Hill's cast of mind and political sympathies set him apart from other Americans. "Charlie was someone that Begin admired, there's no doubt," agreed Lewis. The incident also demonstrated the seriousness with which Hill now approached the art of note taking. Although his personal notebooks from this period contain mostly brisk tasking notes, his afternoon as Begin's "*shabbas goy*," his effort to think like an Israeli in order to craft the Israeli version of his account, proves that note taking was no longer just the harried, verbatim drudgery it had been for him in law school. Recording the words of others was much more than mindless transcribing. As fifteenth-century monk Johannes Trithemius instructed his followers long ago, the dutiful scribe copying out his work "is gradually initiated into the divine mysteries and miraculously enlightened." He steps into the minds of those who spoke or wrote the original words, and he makes their words his own, if only for a brief moment. For Hill, note taking was becoming a state of mind, a near-mystical act.

Ever since childhood Hill had been an instinctive observer. By the time he reached Tel Aviv, he had become a scholar of observation whose analytical assets came from watching, missing nothing, and noting it all down on his steno pad: his leadership strengths lay chiefly in his talent for grasping the whole landscape of his office and detecting the best ways to coordinate the men and women he supervised. He was on his way to becoming not a household-name policymaker but the policymaker's anonymous, essential adviser and witness.

The most powerful adviser is an entity wholly apart from his prince. He is no slave to a single model of statesmanship and understands his prince in his proper context among his peers in history. Hill's career in the Foreign Service was an education to this end, and by now he had learned crucial lessons in the two most masterful models that he had encountered so far: Henry Kissinger and Menachem Begin. For all of the faults that observers have assigned to the secretary of state and the prime minister, failure to ponder the meaning of history was never one of them. Theirs was the class of mind that Hill had toyed with as a boy, scrambled for as a student, earned in his career, and now begun to exercise—quietly, often in the shadow of Great Men—but with no less potency.

In observing Kissinger grind through the Paris Peace Agreement negotiations while he was in Saigon and later in working with him on speeches to the world, Hill was in a good position to grasp the ambiguities of Kissinger's philosophy. The secretary's most prominent side, much attacked by critics because it was so easily caricatured, was his preoccupation with power politics that seemed to deny any higher good. It was this image of Kissinger as a heartless skeptic that Hill and others labored to correct in the Heartland Speeches. It was true that Kissinger's essential aim throughout his reign as America's foreign policy czar was to persuade troublesome states to buy into the international system as the best means of achieving their goals—because in that system, the United States reigned supreme. But his geostrategic calculations were infused with a vision for a new world order, for transcending history. Kissinger was an instinctive cynic. His faith in humanity's ability to rise above horrors like the Holocaust was ambivalent at best. Yet he told a German journalist that as a policymaker, one had to act on the assumption that history's failings could be transcended: "I have never said that I have a pessimistic outlook. I have said, what is after all empirically true, that most civilizations that we know anything about have eventually declined. All you have to do is travel around the world and look at the ruins to confirm that fact. As a historian one has to be conscious of the possibility of tragedy. However, as a statesman, one has the duty to act as if one's country were immortal. I have acted on the assumption that our problems are soluble."

Kissinger's attempts to render all problems "soluble" brought him into conflict with the Israelis during his 1975 attempt to negotiate an Israeli withdrawal from the Sinai. Many Israelis came to consider Kissinger an enemy of their state and a traitor to his people. To them he was exactly the sort of self-hating Jew whom Begin blamed for abetting the Holocaust. But no matter what the two statesmen thought of each other personally, it was clear to Hill that Menachem Begin's worldview was predicated upon a sense of history just as deeply considered as Kissinger's. Rather than look toward the future for vindication of his public service, Begin's gaze was fixed on the past. To him history was an obligation as much as a lesson. His abiding mission was to secure the ancient homeland for his people. "The bond between our people and this Land is eternal," he said on the occasion of Sadat's historic visit to Jerusalem in 1977. "It was created at the dawn of human history. It was never severed."

While Kissinger believed that history was an unending process, Begin's policies were predicated upon a final historical destination: a secure Jewish state occupying all of Eretz Israel, the "Myth of Return" whose fulfillment was all the more dire since the Nazi genocide. In the United States, the tendency was to treat Begin as an "ideologue— some would say a primitive—who has the luxury of indulging old dreams and the lazy slogans of the opposition." Many of his own compatriots perceived him this way. In 1978 and 1979 polls showed that nearly 70 percent of Israelis were willing to give up the West Bank and Gaza in exchange for secure borders, rejecting Begin's myth of Eretz Israel. Hill would have disagreed with most of them. "Charlie seemed to have a lot of affection for Begin, or at least a great deal of respect," Gil Kulick said. To Hill, the greatness of both Begin and Kissinger arose from the fact that they had beneath every policy decision and every diplomatic maneuver a philosophy of history and the statesman's role in it. They occupied the world of ideas.

Years later, in explaining his "theory of Great Men" to a student who was reading Kissinger's memoirs, Hill described the historical mentality he perceived in Kissinger and Begin as "a deeply pondered, well thought-out product of a silent dialogue with oneself . . . This produces a near-absolute and calm certainty that one has the correct approach on the fundamental questions of life and great affairs of mankind." But in Kissinger and Begin, as well as in other Great Men he had encountered, Hill detected a "dissonant strain" as well:

> a deep, abiding sense of potential inferiority, or of not measuring up, or of being disparaged as somehow inadequate to the task . . . This takes the form of a hyper-sensitivity to the attitudes and assessments of others on oneself. This hyper-sensitivity is well-hidden in some great men, and rampantly displayed in others. The ability to make this sensitivity work as a propulsion mechanism for greater achievement, as against letting it show too clearly to others (thereby stimulating the disapprobation that the GM fears) is one gauge of successful GM-ship.

For all his concern for historical legacy, Kissinger was also well known for an acute sensitivity to personal criticism. Begin suffered from what was probably manic-depressive disorder throughout his life, sinking into long periods of gloom and insecurity to which his wife's attentions were the only antidote. Although it took Hill several more years of experience with diplomacy's Great Men to fully form his conclusions, by the end of his time in Tel Aviv his theory of leadership was well developed. He concluded, from the paradoxical personality traits he perceived in men like Kissinger and Begin, that while their sensitivities produced a nervous energy, their intellectual confidence "stabilizes the personality and displays itself in the self-assurance that in fact draws ordinary people to look to the GM for leadership, especially at times when no one else seems to know what to do." In a fit of psychoanalysis, he continued: "This also propels the GM to seek the kind of high offices in which this certitude can be exercised in an appropriate arena. This [intellectual self-assurance] usually has been engendered by upbringing, as when a father or father-figure has been influential. Sometimes being an 'only child' brings it to a higher pitch. But there has to be some 'born in the bone' aptitude for it."

It is not clear how much Hill really knew about Kissinger's childhood or Begin's relationship with his father. Nor is it certain, given his avowed distaste for looking back upon his own past, whether his mind wandered at all from Kissinger and his peers as he expounded to the student. What is clear is that, inadvertently or not, he had described himself. The question is why Charlie Hill never stepped out from the shadows of Great Men to join their ranks.

Much of this chapter, in Charlie's opinion, would qualify as shamelessly ungrounded displays of pretentious, pseudopsychological erudition. When he assigned my class to read Herodotus's *Histories* so long ago, he admonished us to resist the urge to psychoanalyze. We were to read the text on its face, as the author presented it. Charlie probably would have preferred that his students stay out of his own head too.

Earlier in the course of writing Charlie's biography, the idea of psychoanalyzing my professor felt to me like violating a sacred boundary. It seemed impossible, or at least very rude, to impose the standard rules of human behavior upon a man whom I knew in the context of the pristine university classroom, a place absent of worldly background noise beyond the boom of the lecture and the immaculate scratch of pencils. But the turning point came months ago, when I first met Martha. As I listened to her take on my subject, I had begun to see that Charlie the Foreign Service officer and professor was inseparable from — and unexplainable without — Charlie the person: the eccentric introvert; the human observer who, for all his watchfulness, sometimes missed the obvious; the man possessed by a strange (but perhaps not uncommon) mix of self-assurance and private anxiety.

Part of me, however, remained intimidated by Charlie's dismissal of the psychoanalytic enterprise. When he spoke of his daughter's visits to a therapist during those troubled teenage years, he brushed them off as a fad, even a strange ploy to achieve a status symbol among her friends. In one of the rare instances when, unprodded, he delved a bit into his own motives, suggesting that his affection for the Israelis was related to his penchant for the Puritans, I answered that I had already thought of that. He smiled. "Maybe someday you can take me out to lunch and tell me all about myself," he joked. Despite his teasing, I could not put aside the question that was rapidly emerging as the greatest mystery of Charlie's psychology: why, despite all his intellectual confidence, his love for the bird's-eye view, and his fierce desire to stake a place in history, he never became a Great Man himself.

The easy answer came up in our conversations all the time: he hated the public eye, the ceremony, the trappings of fame and trans-parency that hamstring a world leader. But I wasn't satisfied. History's roster includes plenty of misanthropes and recluses who nevertheless ruled effectively from the throne, the dais, or the White House. More-over, I had come to know Charlie as a charismatic professor who com-manded the attention of packed lecture halls, submitted to press inter-views, and even (after a martini or two) charmed listeners at academic social functions on a regular basis. He was a quiet man who disdained small talk and sometimes came off as aloof, but by no means was he a hermit incapable of functioning outside his walls of books. I knew him in the classroom. To me, he was a leader.

He has the ego required for the job. He rarely entertains the possi-bility that he might be wrong about anything. "It does put you off," said one student, Bryan Cory. "Although I'm shocked that he isn't more ar-rogant. I think the reason is that he was always the number-two man. He always wanted to be number one, but never dared to be. Rather than put himself out and risk failing, his attitude was more along the lines of 'do the best I can, go as high as I can, without taking a risk.'"

Charlie asserts that from the beginning he aimed to stay in the background — as a new Foreign Service officer he named the Policy Planning Staff as his aspiration, not the office of secretary of state. Even at the university, the world of ideas and perhaps the only place where a man of ideas could become a Great Man, one might have ex-pected Charlie to assume the bookish, aloof lifestyle that he chose dur-ing past stints in academia. But in spite of his retiring personality he has become a public figure at Yale. What, then, accounts for his cult following, the dozens of students who sign up hungrily for his classes, line up at his office hours, and agonizingly interpret his every word and glance — is it all a lucky mistake?

Yale students are shrewd people who do not select their mentors lightly. In Charlie's case, they refuse to believe that anything could be accidental. The armchair psychologizing runs rife. "Psychologically he's basically a shy, insecure person," mused Mike Morgan. "I think most academics are at base shy. You have to be, to enjoy being in the library. It's solitary work. His is a quiet aggression, a way of crafting his personality around his shyness — as if he said at one point, if he could embrace this discourse of manliness, toughness, aggression, that's a way of compensating. It's no coincidence that he always tells people the last movie he saw was *Patton*."

The Great Men that Charlie has described to me were often calculating and self-aware in their ascent, but there was always an element of heedless audacity in their personalities, an ability to barrel onward when the moment required. Perhaps Charlie was too deliberate, too worried about the details. Yet his mission here — shaping young leaders, animating their latent antique virtues — requires him to be an irresistible professor, a guru, a local Great Man. That is his role in the Grand Strategy class. His colleagues know it too. "If there is a cult of personality around Hill, it's actively managed by Gaddis and Kennedy," observed Aaron O'Connell. Charlie drops enough hints about his career to make clear his experience in the halls of power, just enough to "create the mystique of the intellectual warrior, the statesman warrior," Aaron said. I thought of Charlie's childhood heroes, the World War II soldiers and generals on the cardboard trading cards — had his life been one long process of self-scripting?

My classmates were not alone in their conclusions. People who had known Charlie for many more years — and in a much different capacity — agreed. Most memorable was my conversation with Joe Evans, Charlie's childhood friend from the summers at Ocean City. I arrived at his house late in the evening, after a long day of interviews and driving lost around the Philadelphia area. We sat on the sofa in a living room carpeted and upholstered in the faded oranges, browns, and reds that were trendy thirty years ago. The room smelled musty. Probably the curtains, the curios, and all the furniture besides the sofa, with its friendly, concave cushions and balding armrests, had sat untouched since Evans's wife passed away more than ten years earlier. Evans himself was lean and energetic in the face. He was dressed in faded jeans and loafers, and he seemed just a bit younger than Charlie. He sat on the far end of the couch and leaned into the backrest, folding his hands over his belt buckle and stretching his thin legs out onto the floor, like a garden rake. In an afterthought, perhaps inspired by a flash of the beloved wife and hostess whose presence still glowed faintly in the house, he offered me something to eat. I had the feeling there wasn't anything to be had, so I declined. He asked me if the house smelled funny to me. I said no.

Evans had lost touch with Charlie long ago. The prolonged drifting apart now appeared permanent, although Evans remained close with Martha. He had hardly spoken to Charlie in decades, but the conclusions that he reached long ago about his old friend echoed those of my classmates. "Charlie has made himself somebody he always wanted to be," Evans said. He spoke like a man explaining truths he had realized twenty years ago, not thinking out loud in response to a question. He sounded a lot like Charlie, actually. "The person he's made himself into is very different. Slowly but surely, starting when he was young, he tentatively but intuitively embraced a cultural ideal," Evans continued. "It's the notion of how one perfects—purifies—oneself, puts aside the contaminations of common, everyday life." Evans sounded faintly pleased with himself, satisfied to have figured out a subject that eluded scrutiny. That subject, although one would be hard-pressed to know it from these detached intellectual observations, was a best boyhood friend who had pulled away and hurt people who meant something.

When I mentioned Charlie's account of Martha's "outbursts," Evans scoffed. "Often after some drinks, Martha would voice discontent; she'd ask, 'why are we living like this?' She wasn't a gullible female. But she's a person that gives everything she's got. This is a quality that will do you in. Charlie preferred to be oblivious to her alcoholism. Her stand—'why are we living like this'—meant the whole picture: Why are you working twelve hours a day? Why don't I ever see you? Why am I raising the kids?" I asked Evans what he thought about the sacrifices Charlie had made. "One loses what one wants to give up: the manifestation of the human," he answered, falling back into philosophy professor mode. "Being entangled too much in people's lives, being subject to doubts and uncertainties . . . He's relegated the more human stuff to the incidental and uninteresting. The way he talks to his family—that has to come from something profound, something that he's decided." All this time, a piece of me had kept hoping that the way Charlie treated his family was, at least partly, unintended.

Before setting off for Philadelphia, I had asked Charlie for some guidance on questions to ask Evans, and what had happened between them since their childhood at Ocean City. Charlie offered that some decades ago, when Joe was having a midlife crisis, he had suggested that his friend go back to school and get a Ph.D. in philosophy. That is what Evans did, and like so many who have followed Charlie's advice, he was infinitely better off for doing so, Charlie claimed. Charlie made no mention of their drifting apart, but then he had also confessed that he had almost no true friends anyway, so the break with Evans probably seemed to him insignificant for biographical purposes. Their parting was not insignificant for Evans. Maybe it was partly the darkness outside, the stale odor of the house, but he seemed to me like a very lonely person who had made peace with his old friend by vivisecting him.

As to Charlie the Great Man, Evans conceded that his old friend had at least one thing in common with the statesmen he served. Charlie, too, could never have been who he was without an invisible staff, the shadow crew that managed the mundanities of their prince's life so that he could reside in the realm of ideas. Alvenia and Martha fed him, clothed him, and gave him a home, all in such a selfless manner that even Charlie, the invisible man himself, the one on whom nothing was lost, took no notice. Evans pointed out the puzzlement of Charlie's daughters at this arrangement. "Katie worships her father," he told me. "She'd prefer to be him, and has his capacity to denigrate the common man, but she's perplexed by the difficulties such a life imposes on one. That's not something Charlie knows. She doesn't realize the reason her father gets away with it is that he has a ton of people propping him up. He's 'forward-looking'—this is a conscious conviction that he's detached, but really he's less detached than most people. Emily doesn't buy it. Still, it's a great credit to Martha that she presented him in such a way that they could admire him."

I had long been fascinated by the idea of Charlie the mastermind, Charlie the unerring sculptor of his own grand strategy. But I was also repelled. His was a frigid way to live. I could find no way to relate to him as a human being. Initially his persona made it easy for me to maintain the scholarly detachment appropriate in a biographer, and moreover Charlie's inaccessibility was what captivated me (and so many other students) in the first place. But awe is always proportional to distance, and as I came closer the mirage began to fade. In the classroom Charlie seemed to us a man who had made all the hard decisions decades ago and now stood by what he believed, unflinching. It was easy to feel intimidated and inspired. It never occurred to us that for every decision made and every spark of doubt extinguished, there had been a sacrifice—a victim, a casualty, a road not taken. The more I explored the hidden dimensions of my professor's life, the more I saw that his aura of transcendence was only his brightest, smoothest, most visible side. The moon had blinked. I began to wonder if the very idea of Grand Strategy, and of Great Men, was a fraud.

10

THE GRAND STRATEGY CLASSROOM HAS A REPUTATION FOR being more than a place of learning for learning's sake. Past classes produced a memorandum on the future of reform in the Foreign Service that ended up in a speech Charlie wrote for George Shultz. The students met with one of the principal authors of the Bush administration's National Security Strategy two weeks after the document was released and later drafted a mock Iraqi constitution that Charlie faxed to his colleagues in Washington. This sort of contact with power does not happen every day — as the overexcited students admitted this year found out — but the possibility saturates the culture of the class. There is an abiding sense that their discussions tackle the same problems facing policymakers in Washington. "For me, GS offered a chance to transition from the point in my life when I was learning just because it was neat to learn and play with ideas, to where I was thinking as a real individual in the world who could be in a position of responsibility," Sky Schouten explained.

Charlie may not care about getting credit for his ideas and drafts, but he is training students who do. Grand Strategy applicants are not drawn to recruitment posters printed with pictures of Roosevelt and Churchill because they crave a career in the shadows. From the looks of things, they will not be content to emulate their professor's life behind the scenes of policymaking. They want to be Great Men and Women themselves. The culture of the course encourages their ambitions. After class students sometimes dine with famous guest speakers; they make occasional junkets to New York to meet with notables; they spend their summers in high-profile research and government internships. In the spring and fall there are fundraising banquets, and Professors

Gaddis and Kennedy hold festive barbecues in their adjoining back-yards so that students can load paper plates with ribs and fried chicken, bask in their own society, and schmooze with the Old Blue alumni who donate funds to the Grand Strategy program. There is nothing like free food and alcohol to cement the comradery of budding statesmen.

Not only does the class work, dine, and socialize together, they are also constantly on display, paraded around to impress the old men in bow ties who write the checks to International Security Studies, the umbrella organ that pays for all these perks. Even in the classroom Grand Strategy students are usually surrounded on all sides by observers. Typically these are graduate students or postdoctoral fellows auditing the course, but one often spots grown men sitting in on the class. Sometimes they are an impressive lot—I've seen university trustees, vice presidents from British Petroleum, Iraqi political scientists spending a term at Yale to study the teaching of democracy, and an assortment of other pensive, bearded faces squished into the old-fashioned wooden desks. Grand Strategy students are conditioned from the beginning to perform for an audience. It should come as no surprise that a certain pride of purpose arises, a sense of election, and a profound self-consciousness. "Certainly it is a fairly select group, but the cult that surrounds it is one of almost religious fervor for elitism. In a way that's okay, because it gets people to perform," said Aaron O'Connell, who as a former Marine knows something of the value of esprit de corps. "But the problem is that once you think GS is not just a class, but an adventure, the role of the teacher becomes almost iconic." A professorial icon: a sacred personage, to be adored and beseeched for guidance, and above all a model of what the student might achieve. And with a little more elbow grease and emulation, perhaps they can even surpass Charlie and reach the ranks of the world leaders that he served. Grand Strategy quickly becomes all-consuming. The professors encourage this: "by the end of the year, you will forget you attend Yale University," they say. Grand Strategy University will have replaced it. Unsaid, but always implied, is that this university confers its final degrees not on the quadrangle between ivied halls, but in the corridors of power. This message makes for heady motivation, but it can also set the stage for disappointment.

When the kids in the Grand Strategy class got wind of what I was up to, they started to talk—ceaselessly. Not only the students whom I sought out for an interview—although there were plenty of those—

but others too. GSers past and present began stopping me on the street, cornering me at parties, and poking their heads inside my office doorway. Many of them complained that the class failed to live up to its reputation. I got the impression that they came in expecting instant access to summer jobs at the CIA, regular audiences with Washington insiders, and riveting seminar-table debate. What they found was, in many ways, an ordinary undergraduate course. I'm not sure what they thought about me or my project, or my unsettling habit of sitting against the wall during their class and scribbling notes. I do know that the reality of the classroom proved tougher to pin down than the Grand Strategy myth with which I had begun.

During the course's first year, in the days when word about what the Gang of Three was up to had only just begun to spread, the students who applied were a self-selected, curious bunch. The professors, still fine-tuning the syllabus and getting used to sharing the stage, clashed and argued more often. Alumni who took the course in those early years tell stories of rousing debates featuring a red-faced Paul Kennedy quivering in his chair while one of his colleagues spoke, turning to the student next to him to hiss, "I disagree! Make certain your notes reflect that!" The excitement was real, and when the professors and students sensed a growing esprit de corps, they did everything they could to strengthen the bond.

Left-leaning Kennedy is still prone to closing his eyes and wincing softly when Charlie talks, but the days of those fiery debates seem far away. Like any college seminar, Grand Strategy has its good days and its bad. On some days discussion is lively and self-directed, but on others I observed the professors choreographing leading questions, passing the baton from one to another while the class remained quiet. I wondered if this year's GSers, intimidated by all the hype, were more wary of raising their hands than their predecessors had been. It seemed the professors had decided early on that this year's crop weren't the alpha specimens of years past and therefore required more lecturing, prodding, and tugging. I wondered whether Charlie would complain that they just didn't "get it."

The life of a classroom is a slippery thing. I knew that, as in the subtleties of diplomacy, things happen just beneath the surface of class discussion that an outsider cannot always perceive. I felt like an anthropologist seeking out conversations with informants, observing and occasionally participating in the rituals of my research community, but always coming away with the feeling that I didn't quite have it right. There is nothing more difficult to capture on a page than what exactly goes on around a seminar table. Even a verbatim transcript of the conversation would miss the nuances of the interplay between professors and students, the ebb and flow of a discussion's momentum. Pedagogy is much like diplomacy. A good teacher must know how to touch the rudder of the class discussion to keep the conversation on course without disturbing the unfolding of students' ideas. Depicting the Grand Strategy class at work was almost as hard as describing the actions of my subject, the anonymous, invisible Foreign Service officer Charlie Hill. For all the student complaints and my own criticisms, I was still wary of selling the Grand Strategy class short. A dangerous hubris comes with watching from the margin. Things are never as clear in the fray as they are from the sidelines.

The question is what kind of training the class really provides — whether, for all the prestigious trappings, Grand Strategy accomplishes anything more than do a dozen other challenging Yale seminars. Perhaps it does. When I describe some of the class activities as self-aware performances, I do not mean to deride them as empty, egotistical theater. As Charlie told the class when he spoke on the subject of optimism in foreign affairs, sometimes one must act the part first in order to transform oneself when the moment counts.

Still, I wondered whether grand strategy — that of a classroom, a life, or of a government — ever exists in the moment or only in retrospect and fantasy. That would make it no less powerful. As historians love to say, history is all we have. I would add imagination too; as Herodotus knew, these two capacities are the only tools human beings have to understand themselves. Self-perception is at the heart of life, not objective fact. If that amounts to grand strategy — well, then, there is nothing more real.

In the fall of 1981, Hill returned to the State Department to direct his old desk, Israel and Arab-Israeli Affairs. The military situation in the Middle East was alarming. Most observers predicted that the next flash point would be Lebanon, where civil war between Arab factions and Maronite Christians had crippled the central government and allowed the PLO, headed by Yasir Arafat, to become virtually a state within a state. PLO terrorists had been bombarding northern Israel from their sanctuaries in the south of Lebanon for more than a decade. By the time of Hill's tour in Tel Aviv, Israeli reprisals for the terrorist strikes threatened to escalate into full-scale war. Hill spent considerable time accompanying special envoy Philip Habib in Jerusalem as he tried to broker a cease-fire. Habib got both parties to agree to a tenuous cease-fire in July, but Menachem Begin's government was now more radical than ever. He had been reelected by a narrow margin owing partially to a political deal with Ariel Sharon, earning the hawkish Israeli Defense Force (IDF) general the post of defense minister. On June 6, 1982, on the pretext of retaliation for an assassination attempt on the Israeli chargé d'affaires in London,* Sharon launched his offensive into Lebanon. The IDF decimated PLO forces in the south within a week, destroyed Syrian air power, and soon trapped the remnants of the PLO in Muslim West Beirut.

With the onset of the Lebanon War, Hill took over the position of deputy assistant secretary for Near Eastern affairs and spent most of his time single-handedly running the State Department's communication with Habib in Beirut. The PLO had destroyed the American embassy, in the western half of the city, so Habib and the other American officers had moved their operations to a villa in the hills of Christian East Beirut—where they were safe from Israeli and PLO artillery fire but had no means of communicating with Washington. The only link was by way of an old-fashioned tacsat,† which looked like a simple army field radio and transmitted a crackling signal via satellite to a dish the size of an umbrella on the roof of the State Department. Hill spent a good portion of every day and night alone in a closet-sized room on the eighth floor, talking with Habib over the tacsat. By the time the secretary and other State Department officials got into the office around eight o'clock, Hill already had been on the tacsat for two or three hours. Most days he went home between midnight and four in the morning. Since his time in Israel he had honed the ability to subsist on these few hours' dead sleep, supplemented by catnaps on his office floor whenever a lull in activity afforded the opportunity. "There was no communication other than that," he said later. "Three or four times a day I

---

* The attack occurred on June 3, 1982. It later proved that a separate Palestinian terrorist organization, led by Abu Nidal rather than the PLO, had been responsible.

† Now largely obsolete, tacsats were satellite communication repeaters with small-surface terminal communication equipment originally designed by the U.S. Air Force for highly mobile land, sea, and air forces.

would talk on the radio to Lebanon, and that was the only way to do it —I was the guy. I would go downstairs—I was there almost 24 hours a day—and since only I knew what was going on, I'd brief [Secretary of State Alexander] Haig. Haig was a general, and he ordered people around, scared people, raised his voice, but I was used to that from Vietnam. I just kind of lashed back at him, and he liked me, I think, because I didn't take any crap from him."

Phil Habib, the youngest son of Lebanese immigrants who had grown up in Brooklyn and, improbably, graduated from the University of Idaho School of Forestry, was one of the toughest, shrewdest, and noisiest officers in the Foreign Service. He began his career with posts in Canada and Vietnam, where in 1965 he made a strong impression on a Harvard professor who was there on a trip with Ambassador Henry Cabot Lodge Jr. to assess the conflict. "Professor, I'm a busy man and you don't know a goddamn thing about Vietnam," Habib had told Henry Kissinger. "I'll give you a couple of my boys, you go spend two weeks flying around the country, come back, and then maybe I'll talk to you. In the meantime, get the hell out of my office." A little more than a decade later, Kissinger appointed Habib his undersecretary for political affairs. "Phil was my conscience even if he brutalized me from time to time," Kissinger said later. "I might not do what he said, but I wouldn't make a move without finding out what he thought."

Negotiating a peaceful conclusion to the Israeli siege of Beirut was probably the greatest challenge of Habib's long career. His job became more complicated when it emerged that he and Secretary Haig disagreed over the fundamental facts of the conflict. Haig was convinced that Habib was overdramatizing the severity of the Israeli bombardment, and he believed that PLO attacks on northern Israel were much more serious than Habib claimed. Despite Habib's efforts to get Sharon to halt the Israeli advance, Haig wanted the Israelis to push onward. Throughout the siege, from June to September, Hill was caught between the general and the diplomat. A significant element of his job was "trying to control Habib, because he was so volatile," he said.

> Habib had a tremendous temper. He would yell, scream, and rage at what the Israelis and Americans were doing. So a lot of it was psychotherapy—I would just listen to him . . . It was also about trying to get him off certain things that I knew we couldn't change. The main one was the incompatibility of what Israelis and Americans felt had to be done, and what the Lebanese could take. The Lebanese would

tell Habib they couldn't deal with him—and they were an avenue to Arafat—because the Israelis were shelling the city . . . But as soon as we stopped the Israelis, we'd see the Palestinian position harden, so we had to shell—which would prevent the Lebanese from negotiating. That was the major battle.

The well-known disagreements between Haig and President Ronald Reagan nearly brought decision making in Washington to a halt —but Habib, the consummate professional diplomat, always wanted formal instructions. The meteoric pace of the war, the hour-by-hour changes in the situation on the ground, made it difficult to obtain formal authorization properly vetted by the bureaucracy. Technological marvels like the tacsat meant decisions and events moved faster than cable traffic, so there was no paper documentation of Habib's reports or Hill's responses to route through the State Department for approval. An attempt was made to write cables after the fact, for the sake of providing some record, but they did not capture the real story and were of little use to Hill at the time. Often, when Habib proposed what he wanted to do in his next approach to Sharon or the Lebanese, Hill told him to proceed without checking with his boss first. "I'd simply tell him—because I knew how the Secretary would respond—I'd say, go ahead," Hill said.

On June 25, after Haig had irritated the president and his cronies once too often, Reagan announced his secretary of state's resignation. Hill got into the office that morning at 5 A.M. and missed the news. When he came downstairs from the tacsat room around eight, one of the women who worked on the Lebanon desk spotted him in the hall and started laughing at him. "She said, 'your time has come to an end —Shultz is coming in, and he's pro-Arab,' " Hill recalled.

Reportedly, Yasir Arafat was equally exultant about Haig's successor. George Shultz, who had served in the Nixon administration as secretary of labor, later as director of the Office of Management and Budget, and finally as secretary of the Treasury until 1974, was now president of the Bechtel Corporation, an international construction concern with interests in the Arab world. "In contrast to 'pro-Israel' Haig, I was being stereotyped as an 'Arabist,' because Bechtel Corporation had big construction jobs under way in Saudi Arabia and around the Persian Gulf," Shultz wrote in his memoirs. It wouldn't have been hard to find a replacement that could be considered "pro-Arab" compared with Al Haig.

Shultz came in for his first day of work—mostly to observe and learn, as he was still unconfirmed by Congress—and found Larry Eagleburger, then undersecretary for political affairs, waiting in his office. Shultz recalled that Eagleburger immediately "got on the phone and with exaggerated profanity, and in tones of mock irritation and impatience that were his trademark, summoned Charlie Hill, a foreign service officer who apparently was good at writing things down. The appearance of this hollow-eyed figure in a sawed-off sweatshirt, who had obviously been at it all night, and his sidebar briefing of Eagleburger on what was happening at this moment in Beirut underscored that I had walked into a hands-on operational outfit in the midst of a crisis."

The crisis persisted through the rest of June and July, as Habib tried to work out a plan to evacuate the PLO that was acceptable to all parties. Finally on September 1, the ship *Mediterranean Sun* departed for Syria from Beirut harbor with the last Palestinian fighters and Syrian troops onboard. Although IDF snipers held Arafat in their crosshairs and Israeli foot soldiers spat on members of the multinational force that had come to escort the PLO, the evacuation went forward. The siege was over.

In discussions between Shultz and his staff during the waning days of the siege, "we were saying that we're going to succeed or not in getting the PLO out, but either way we will have people with bruised mentalities and bodies and blood on the floor, and we need to think about what we can make out of this when the war is over," Hill said. "It was the end of a crisis, a chance to do things differently." At Reagan's request a policy review was conducted in the tightest secrecy, but "according to most accounts, Hill wrote the first draft version of what became the nationally televised speech that Reagan delivered on September 1," wrote John Goshko in the *Washington Post*. A later report called him the speech's "principal author." The speech, which Reagan delivered from his home in Burbank, California, was one of his most important foreign policy statements to date. It had become clear that an aggressive U.S. proposal might be the only thing to induce the Arabs and Israelis to recommence negotiations. The propositions that Reagan outlined were bold: a freeze on Israeli settlements and a five-year transition period in which the Palestinians of the West Bank and Gaza would gain full autonomy "in association with Jordan" to prove that "they can run their own affairs and that such Palestinian autonomy poses no threat to Israel's security."

Hill's speechwriting role was vital, although he later emphasized that his role in formulating the plan itself was a subtle one. He was not the originator of the ideas. Those had been part of the peace process dialogue for years; then Secretary of State William Rogers had first enunciated "the Jordanian option" more than a decade earlier. Hill's role was making sure that the State Department experts retained control of each meeting, often chaired by National Security Council (NSC) staffer Robert "Bud" McFarlane or another one of Reagan's deputies—in whom Hill had begun to share Haig's distrust. Hill and his staff ensured that a wide range of minds from the legal adviser's office, the NSC staff, and the relevant State bureaus attended each meeting, in order to balance the Reaganauts. Hill usually sat quietly at the end of the table. He rarely intervened, "but if I felt that it was going in the wrong direction—not that I had this authority—I'd touch the rudder of the conversation to bend away from something," Hill said. "Or sometimes, that meant just letting the conversation go in the hopes that the meeting would result in nothing but cacophony. Then my gang would put it back together again in our offices. Others in the meeting may have had more authority, a more muscular role in the meeting itself, but they had to go do something else when the meeting was over. We didn't. We could go do the work. That's how it came out."

The Reagan Plan was supposed to be the coda to cap Habib's negotiations in Beirut as the administration's first major victory in the Middle East. At stake was Reagan's credibility as an American leader who could continue to advance the peace process. "The Reagan Plan was supposed to allow the Arabs to say that the U.S. was compensating for Lebanon. The fact that it was a surprise to Begin made it better, because it was supposed to persuade the Arabs that we were serious," said former State Department aide Harvey Sicherman. But on September 9 at the Twelfth Arab Summit Conference in Fez, Morocco, Arab leaders unanimously rejected every one of Reagan's propositions. Shultz saw that "the would-be beneficiaries of the Plan had killed it," said Sicherman. "That turned Shultz [from his pro-Arab sympathies]. Israel had nothing to do with it . . . He suffered an epiphany on the road to Damascus." The new secretary of state so many had hailed as pro-Arab was, by the war's conclusion, thoroughly disillusioned with the Arab heads of state in the Middle East. Shultz surmised, drawing on his own experience, that the success of America's policies in the region depended upon close cooperation with Israel. In the years to come, many who resented Hill's growing influence on the secretary of state would blame Hill for brainwashing Shultz with his pro-Israeli bias. "People around the Department couldn't stand his relationship with Shultz," said one former official. "They were convinced that Charlie was making sure no pro-Arab thought ever darkened Shultz's doorway." But the truth is that, whatever Hill's overall impact on the secretary's thinking, Israel was a subject on which they came to see eye to eye.

Hill had been haggard and unwashed when Shultz first encountered him during a Lebanon War briefing the previous June, but the secretary liked the look and sound of Hill immediately. Shultz took Haig seriously when his predecessor recommended that he take on Hill for his personal staff. In the winter of 1982, Hill moved into the office of the executive secretary, L. Paul "Jerry" Bremer, where he worked as Bremer's deputy until taking over the office when Bremer departed early the following year. The job put Hill at the head of the Secretariat, a bureau of about 125 people in charge of overseeing every one of the department's regional bureaus and country desks and controlling communication between the bureaus and the secretary's office. By the time Hill inherited it, the position was critical to the balance of power between the State Department and the president's inner circle. He worked closely with Ray Seitz, Shultz's executive assistant and closest aide. Managing the Secretariat required attention to a dozen things at once, demanded sharp administrative skills, and allowed little time for deep thinking about grand strategy or big ideas. The job was his most important yet, by the standards of the department's organizational chart.

In the summer of 1984 Seitz was tapped as deputy chief of mission in London. In his farewell letter, he urged Shultz to demand a "free hand in staffing your own operation . . . you must have the rein to select the best people to get the job done." Shultz had long been contemplating a counterattack to wrest authority over foreign policy from the Reaganites in the White House. In a November meeting with the president, Shultz secured Reagan's acquiescence to a personnel overhaul that would go down in Washington lore as "the Christmas massacre." By the end of the year, Shultz had purged the State Department of many of Reagan's political appointees, appointing career Foreign Service officers in their stead. "Reaganites high in the president's confidence doubt that he fully understood what he agreed to," observed the *Washington Post*. Three of the key Reaganites — presidential counselor Edwin Meese III, CIA Director William Casey, and ex-NSC adviser (now interior secretary) William Clark — scheduled hasty meetings to discuss how to fight the putsch, but it was too late. The *Post* wondered if Shultz's worst adversary might lie instead in Senator Jesse Helms, who had lost a former aide in the turnover and was eager to bolster his foreign policy image in the eyes of his right-wing critics by interfering with Shultz's appointments. Although Hill did not yet know it, one day Helms would have his revenge. In the meantime, it appeared that the State Department had regained control of American foreign policy.

The personnel takeover had been swift and elegant, but observers on the inside had an inkling as to who had masterminded Shultz's counterattack. "The secretary's critics inside the administration privately blame two young Foreign Service officers in Shultz's secretariat — Charles Hill and Jock Covey — for playing a central purge role, partly by their control of the paper flow," reported the *Post*. Hill later acknowledged the accuracy of the *Post* article with a silent nod. His part in engineering the expurgation was only another sign of the increasing influence that had earned him enemies in the State Department and the administration at large. The quiet officer who had always preferred to keep to his office, who professed no desire for the ambassadorships and glitzy accolades most of his peers desired, had finally begun to draw attention to himself. Many of Hill's colleagues recognized his clout and moved to finesse their relationship with him. But others — a few probably noticing him, from their lofty White House view, for the first time — noted Hill as an emerging obstacle, an influence that might embolden the secretary in ways they had never expected.

When the dust settled, their fears were confirmed. Shultz had made Charles Hill his executive assistant.

Most of his coworkers advised him to turn down the offer. The executive secretary was in the top echelon of the State Department pyramid; the position of executive assistant was not even on the bureaucracy's organizational chart. But Hill had never been one to make career decisions based on job-title prestige. He had long observed that while the executive secretary controlled the material that went into the secretary's office, the executive assistant, sitting inside with Shultz as he read through memoranda, shaped what came out. The job would make him the gray eminence of the State Department, the one who assisted the secretary in assembling the information he needed and guided him in his decisions. He would control the secretary's agenda and advise him more intimately than anyone else.

Hill took the job. He carried his few boxes of belongings from the Secretariat's suite to his new place of work, the only office in Foggy Bottom directly adjacent to the small, plain room where Shultz usually worked. In an inconspicuous *New York Times* article noting Hill's promotion, an insider remarked that Hill knew "more about what's going on there than anyone else." Former ambassador to China James Lilley, who had known Hill since Hong Kong, said that "everyone got the sense that [Hill] was very powerful. Charlie may deny this, but people talked about it. He was the second most powerful man in the State Department. He governed access to Shultz, and Shultz trusted him."

For the next four years, Hill would advise the secretary on policy matters and manage his staff. He would develop a friendship with Shultz that would last long after both were out of government. "Since turning to full time duty as my Executive Assistant, Charlie pretty much runs the show from here while I am in meetings with foreign visitors, up on the Hill testifying, or otherwise focussed on one particular problem," Shultz wrote in a memorandum on Hill's performance.

> He gives guidance, makes decisions, and pitches in to help solve fast breaking problems. So far there doesn't seem to be anything that he can't fix or improve, from the quality of speeches, to protocol problems, to helping shape substantive policy . . . Charlie's personal style is informal but authoritative. He has the respect and confidence of high officials in and out of government including some former Secretaries of State. They feel able to deal with him when I am unreachable, a quality that is invaluable here. And Charlie does all this without inserting his own ego into the picture. In fact, he is a model of Ronald Reagan's favorite saying, "There is no limit to what a man can do if he doesn't mind who gets the credit."

One last duty must, by now, go without saying. Hill would take verbatim, contemporaneous notes on every conversation he shared or heard.

When George Shultz named Charlie as his executive assistant, my subject reached the summit of his backstage power in foreign affairs. Everyone I spoke to confirmed this, referring ominously to Charlie as "the gatekeeper," "the right hand," "the alter ego." He had great power; he shaped historic decisions; and, they insinuated, he made dangerous enemies. Finally I had arrived at every biographer's dream: the point at which you prove to the most skeptical reader that your subject is fascinating, worth writing about, and surely worth reading about, because your subject made an impact on history.

The problem arises when your subject's mark is almost invisible. The task of writing Charlie's narrative was like trying to depict the dark matter between every star and planet, which we cannot see but which, scientists insist, is everywhere, moving the universe. It began to feel like an exercise in futility, as if I was trying to paint with water.

How do you narrate the actions not of the prince, but of his adviser —whose duty is to operate invisibly? Nearly fifty years before Charlie Hill rose to the post of executive assistant, a presidential study commissioned to investigate administrative reform in the executive branch suggested standards that Hill took to heart—and that so frustrate the biographer. The 1937 Brownlow Report recommended that ideal aides to the executive would possess the "ability to discharge their functions with restraint. They would remain in the background, issue no orders, make no decisions, emit no public statements . . . They should be possessed of high competence, great physical vigor, and a passion for anonymity."

That passion had been evident in Charlie from youth. It showed itself in his bookish boyhood, his quiet place in the shadow of the record player at Brown fraternity parties, his love for crafting anonymous cables from Hong Kong. Now, when I asked him what he had accomplished in the State Department, he described quietly coordinating his staff, controlling meetings with his silence, and having conversations over the tacsat with Phil Habib that were as ephemeral as they were historic, leaving no reliable record. His notebooks from the Shultz years, all twenty-two thousand pages of them, were a rare and tremendous asset. But the steno pads, crammed with his meticulous verbatim records of nearly every conversation that took place in or around Shultz's office during their five years together, lack one needful component for the biographer of Charles Hill: what, in all these high-pressure meetings and quiet talks in Shultz's office, was said by Charlie himself.

There is hardly any record of this. Charlie rarely wrote down his own words as he was speaking, and the conversation moved on too quickly for him to pause and note what he had said. His analysis and reactions to events appear occasionally in the notes, but these are of only limited use. They give some indication of the ideas that passed through his mind, but they are not proof of what he actually advised Shultz to do, or whether these notepad musings had any impact at all in the end. Charlie was indeed Shultz's alter ego. So much of his impact and voice in those years is lost because he preferred to work in the secretary's shadow. When Shultz left the building for a high-profile opening statement before a summit or a photo opportunity with foreign dignitaries, Charlie did not venture from his Foggy Bottom burrow into the daylight where the press might seize upon him and leave the historian something to work with. He remained inside, playing the role of the secretary while Shultz was away. His door was kept closed, his small office usually quiet. But about that I am only guessing—there is no record one way or the other.

The notebooks of that "Foreign Service officer who apparently was good at writing things down" would be the central source for Shultz's memoir of his years as secretary of state, but in this 1,138-page tome there are only two dozen brief references to Charlie himself—usually only a note that he was present at a given meeting. This is as it should be. Shultz's subject was the turn of events on the world stage, not the subtleties of his inner circle. But that gave me no comfort. Moreover, what little Charlie could tell me about his own influence remained hard to pin down. Every day in the State Department, according to Charlie's memory, was such a blur of overlapping crises and misinformation that he could hardly sort through it all well enough to provide me with a step-by-step account. He could only direct me back to his notes.

When I embarked upon a narrative of Charlie's years as executive assistant, I had at my disposal a more voluminous record than I'd had for any other segment of his life so far—the photocopied notebook pages filled several cardboard boxes the size of packing crates. But those years that ought to have been the easiest to describe would prove to be some of the hardest. In the end, the solution lay in teaching myself a new category of description: a method of describing the describer, of looking over Charlie's shoulder as he observed everything and noted it down. To capture Charlie, I had to watch for things most historians might have the luxury of overlooking. I had to find the subtleties of the notebooks, the scribbled stars in the margins and emphatic underlines—the hints at what the observer really saw in the scenes he wrote down — and the way it all coincided with the active descriptions of events that I did have, such as Shultz's memoir and Charlie's recollections in interviews. I would learn to speed-read just as well as I nitpicked. Tedious close reading was incompatible with the sheer volume of material I had at hand. Forward motion in diplomacy would prove to be as Charlie described it. It is an endless series of small perceptions, of which a truly accurate record requires what is almost impossible for the historian: that nothing be lost.

11

THE WRITTEN WORD IS THE GEAR AND LEVER OF FOREIGN affairs, the small, often unnoticed mechanism by which policy becomes action. The world of policymaking has little time or inclination to thank its draftsmen, the individuals who write the public statements and correspondence that propel history forward. It has even less care for the chroniclers who will, one day, immortalize it. For the historian, this world pauses for only a moment of loathing or stifled trepidation, if anything at all. Charles Hill, who would prove in his own way to be both a drafter and a recorder of history, was an easy resident here. He was not interested in displays of gratitude. They would have only embarrassed him. They would have rudely assumed that his aims were like those of all the others and distracted him from the watching and the writing that were his job. Long his trademark and unnerving to some of his colleagues at first, Hill's compulsive note taking had quickly receded into the background when he returned to the State Department from his tour overseas. People grew used to his silent presence at meetings, often motionless except for the quiet scratch of his pen.

He took notes in small, careful handwriting, the clean font of a medieval scribe concerned to produce a manuscript that would live for centuries. He wrote on unremarkable steno pads that filled quickly and piled up in stacks in his office. Other officials in Washington kept end-of-the-day diaries or reflected on their work in PROFS notes* on their office computers, but Hill was unique in his verbatim records of every conversation. His predecessor as executive assistant, Ray Seitz, kept notes, but his were not so meticulous. Nick Platt took "operational

---

* The IBM Professional Office System, a predecessor of today's electronic mail.

notes" that focused on the outcomes of meetings and tasks that needed doing, but he rarely recorded conversations word for word. At summits, where foreign delegates knew Hill primarily as a silent note taker, Hill's records of high-level meetings often included *nota bene* remarking on shifts in the tone of conversation, chance hallway encounters that no one else bothered to record, and pages of cultural musings upon what he saw in the streets and faces of the country. They frequently ended with the analysis Hill would offer to Shultz later in private—advice the secretary almost always took. Hill's notebooks are meticulous professional records, but they are also acutely personal documents. "He's much more in the diary tradition of some of the great diplomats who sat down at the end of the day to write," said Hill's colleague Jock Covey. "Except Charlie did it all day long. It's fair to see him as a diarist. This wasn't what the rest of us did. He had a different sensibility." Shultz believed a scrupulous record was an important managerial tool—but Hill was so relentless in his note taking that it made his boss nervous at first. By January 1989, however, when the Reagan administration left office, Hill would cover more than twenty thousand pages with his tiny, professional script.*

These thousands of pages are a main reason why Charles Hill's story is different from the biographies of countless other talented Foreign Service officers. He was an anthropologist of foreign affairs who watched and recorded the history that he worked to shape. That intellectual quality would prove to be the most valuable asset he would bring to the university classroom as a teacher.

It is also an element of foreign affairs that is mostly overlooked by those who write about it. American foreign policy during the Reagan administration has been documented exhaustively. The unauthorized biographies, self-indulgent memoirs, and international relations tomes spawned by the Reagan years are enough to keep any student occupied for decades. Even the basic facts provided by Charles Hill's own notebooks have already been well mined, many of their verbatim State Department dialogues forming the raw material for George Shultz's prodigious memoir, *Turmoil & Triumph*. But all these choose to neglect the anthropology of diplomacy, because this would require the examination of diplomats as human beings. It would demand that the historian or

---

* Comparison with the record of Hill's close colleague Nick Platt, who produced 4,500 pages of notes in a similar time frame, gives some sense of Hill's singularity.

memoirist embrace quotidian routines and internal politics, each day's endless series of telephone calls, coffee-break rituals, meetings among the principals and their staffs, as well as general atmosphere, mood, and other intangibles of human life. On the rare occasion when the historian has these kinds of data, it remains a struggle to reach a verdict of progress or failure, or a general lesson that applies to the diplomatic realm at large. But this is the stuff of what diplomacy actually is. As Harold Nicholson wrote in the introduction to *Peacemaking 1919*, his famous account of the Paris Peace Conference:

> Of all branches of human endeavor, diplomacy is the most protean. The historian and the jurist, relying upon the protocol and the *proces verbal*, may seek to confine its lineaments within the strict outlines of a science. The essayist may hope to capture its colours in the vignettes of an art. The experts — and there have been many experts from Callieres to Jusserand, from Machiavelli to Jules Cambon — may endeavor to record their own experience in manuals for the guidance of those that come after. The journalist may give to the picture the flashes and interpretation of the picturesque. Yet always there is some element in such accounts which escapes reality, always there is some aspect which refuses to be recorded or defined.

Charles Hill was valuable to Shultz because as his executive assistant he was also his chief foreign affairs anthropologist, recording endless pages of observations in his close, neat script and helping the secretary sift through it. For all his ability to grasp the philosophy of a moment, Hill was a student of cultural detail first.

Uncolored, verbatim transcriptions of conversation make up roughly 90 percent of Hill's notes. But more unusual entries permeate the notebooks like algae on a summer pond, floating quietly across the pages with a life of their own. They testify to the kind of observer that Hill was. These are his occasional expositions on culture, for example, which consist of a page or two filled in the long hours onboard an aircraft on the way to some diplomatic engagement abroad, often inspired by the armload of books he invariably brought along on such trips. For example, there are his July 1985 thoughts during Shultz's Asia tour. On one page we find a long discourse on Furio Colombo's *God in America* (1984), Hill's plane reading on the way to Hong Kong. Hill was inspired to categorize himself and his fellow passengers: "I am a

Roundhead + NP [Nick Platt] is a Cavalier . . . and S[hultz] is a Lutheran
pastor with Luther's earthy and direct speech." Roundheads were the
Puritans who fought on the side of the Parliamentary Party during the
English Civil War in the seventeenth century (named for their custom
of wearing their hair cut close to the head); a Cavalier was an Anglican
and a Royalist. Hill was ever a student of American Studies, even at
moments of leisure, looking about the cabin at his dozing colleagues.

Later Hill pondered the philosophical differences between Austra-
lians, whose founding philosopher was the utilitarian Jeremy Bentham,
and Americans, who took their cue from John Locke. He remarked on
Australian humor: "the sardonic, savage flavor of a disenchanted, embittered people, who knew the one certain thing in life was defeat and
failure." He scrutinized their public buildings: "Architecture of parliament is markedly utilitarian by contrast with the confident classicism
of US Congress." For two and a half tightly packed pages his thoughts
wandered on, over Australian bureaucracy, citizenry, and intellectual
climate. When they stopped over on Hawaii, he was still at it, devoting
another page to his vision for redesigning the Australian flag in green
and gold, to symbolize "the blooming and development of a once arid
land . . . and the golden beauty of its deserts."

Sometimes his jottings might be mistaken for poetry. At another
point on this (prolific) Asia tour, Hill described the hospitality on the
Pacific island of Fiji:

> *Fiji*
> the Methodist hymns. Amen Amen Amen
> the warrior dances. Spear + calabash thrusts
> Ratu Mara 6'6" dignity and wisdom. A real leader.
> The farewell tune: sung + played by the band
> Give the pig to the villagers
> the Daimler ceremonial vehicle
> The clouds + wind threatening. Blowing the thatch.
>   The huts with no walls
> the sugarcane train seen from the airport
> clouds of smoke as the cane is burnt off
> the hemp rope holding the old whale's took
>   (you can buy a farm with it)

It is not clear whether Hill intended these notes to sound like bits of
poesy or whether they simply issued from his pen that way. What is ob-

vious is that his note taking had evolved since he became Shultz's executive assistant. Now there were fewer bulleted tasking notes and more verbatim records of conversations, strange musings and observations like those above. All these reflect the thoughts of a man whose primary job was no longer to manage paper flow, but to watch, and to think.

This was not how most diplomats spent their free time. On the plane rides that Hill spent sketching out pages of cultural analysis (some of which future students would recognize in his lectures two decades later), most of his colleagues spent a few minutes pretending to read memoranda and then goofed off or fell asleep. Hill recorded one such scene on the way to the November 1985 summit with the Soviets at Geneva. The president, Chief of Staff Don Regan, and Shultz practiced their golf stroke on a portable putting green. Later some of the staffers quarreled among themselves, and Nancy Reagan and Paul Nitze gossiped about the Soviet leader's famous birthmark and Nancy's instinctive dislike for Gorbachev's wife, Raisa:

> 11/16 Saturday 1030
> On AF 1—roll out golf green strip. P + DR + S take putting shots . . .
> On acft, PN [Paul Nitze], McF [Bud McFarlane], [Pat] Buchanan all knock Ikle [undersecretary of defense Fred Ikle]. McF "I see you got your story in the paper. A hell of a way to do business,"* turns + walks up aisle, FI stands after then quits. (golf strip had been removed) . . .
> 1st lady talks to PN about Q [question] of any medical significance to Gorba's birthmark. And psychology of Mrs. Gorba—conscious of status. [She] Can't believe other countries don't have *nomenklatura* [Soviet bureaucratic class]. A professional intellectual + philosophy student/teacher when all other Sov women we meet talk only of children, holidays + meals . . .
> Night falling, dark coming alarmingly fast as we into the 5 hr mark. People stop pretending to read memos + start reading books (PN: May *Know Your Enemies*). Shoes off, stocking feet up on bulkhead. Sweaters + jogging suits (1st Lady's is scarlet). Speechwriters doze off w walkman headphones playing tapes in their ears.

---

* McFarlane was referring to a letter from Secretary of Defense Caspar Weinberger just published in the *New York Times* and *Washington Post* in which Weinberger urged the president to refuse Gorbachev any commitment that the United States would continue to abide by the second Strategic Arms Limitation Treaty, as well as to reject a narrow interpretation of the Anti-Ballistic Missile Treaty, so that Strategic Defense Initiative research could continue freely. See George Shultz, *Turmoil & Triumph*, 598.

Hill's pen was never at rest. Sometimes he recorded the smallest social encounters, even those whose significance was lost on him in real life. At a meeting in July 1985, he noted his own inadvertent snub of State Department staffer Robert Oakley: "Oakley comes late, opens doors which pushes up rug + starts to tear up rug. CH pushes door shut + straightens rug + opens door. Oakley gone—undoubtedly offended. The delicate sensitivities." Most people would think before slamming the door on a person entering a room. Hill's instinct was not to observe basic etiquette but to do the practical thing to fix the rug. It matters less whether he recorded the moment out of amusement or chagrin, than that he wrote it down at all.

Occasionally he took notes at dinner, while others were eating and chatting. At dinner in Helsinki in November 1985, Mark Palmer, Hill's predecessor on Henry Kissinger's speechwriting team, told a story of how Kissinger once rejected a draft of a speech proposing the establishment of an International Fertilizer Institute on the grounds that the press would undoubtedly dub it the "Kissinger bullshit initiative." So, Palmer said, the speechwriters retitled it the "Comprehensive Research in Agriculture Program" and Kissinger went for it. The team went through more drafts, then someone finally admitted to Kissinger's deputy, Larry Eagleburger, that the speech was intended as a joke; the acronym spelled CRAP. But Eagleburger was afraid to tell the secretary, so the drafting went on: "It got to be only a few days before the speech and we finally all agreed that we had to tell HAK; it no longer was funny. So we went to him + said look it's a trick your speechwriters have played on you—it spells CRAP. He was enraged, furious. He shook + waved his arms. It was too late; he had to give the speech. So we changed the title back to Int'l Fertilizer Institute—and it was a big hit—it got lots of support + millions in contributions. And even today in Tennessee there is a functioning IFI turning out the . . . [ellipsis in original]."

When the team flew on to Moscow, Hill recorded dinner conversation there as well, and some of the amusing anecdotes he captured would provide color for George Shultz's memoirs. But others, like the priceless story above, would slumber unnoticed in his notebooks. One wonders whether the other guests around the table stole odd glances at him over their wine glasses as his pen scribbled while his fork remained beside his plate. Probably he held the steno pad discreetly in his lap, and no one really noticed.

These are the notes of a compulsive observer, an outsider who preferred to record the world with his pen and react later, on his own terms, rather than surrender to the spontaneous ebb and flow of conversation as it happened. These are the notes of a man who never allowed himself to be off-duty, nor allowed others the luxury of slipping beneath the radar. The patterns and perceptions found in his notebooks beg comparisons with many anthropologists, journalists, and scholars. But there is a broader comparison that is useful, for all its outlandishness: it might be fair to suggest that Hill fancied himself a Herodotus of State Department affairs, preserving the stories that individuals or states told him about themselves. It mattered less whether the stories were factually accurate than that, true or not, they filled the minds and mouths of the world's decision makers.

Within Hill's own building, every State Department bureau was a tribe with its own rituals, band of elders, and culture, and their memoranda and diplomatic communiqués were cultural products that expressed volumes about the human beings who created them. Hill would remark upon the quirks of State Department culture in reminiscences years later, but many of his observations also come out in the notes, in the layers of talking points, bull sessions, memoranda, and counter-memoranda.

Hill's notes were a professional tool, like those of every Foreign Service officer. But they were also the chronicles of a man who felt instinctively the same insight that moved the ancient father of history: that time was a destroyer. That no one who was not there when it happened would ever be able to get the story right. That the truth was in the ephemeral details, the conflicting accounts and motives, the countless interwoven stories that made up each day in foreign affairs, rather than in some academic's attempt in decades to come at setting down a single definitive history:

> I, Herodotus of Halicarnassus, am here setting forth my history, that time may not draw the color from what man has brought into being, nor those great and wonderful deeds, manifested by both Greeks and barbarians, fail of their report, and, together with all this, the reason why they fought one another.

While it would be misguided to flatter Hill too much or draw an excessive comparison between the Persian Wars and the final years of the cold war, Hill's history, like that of Herodotus, is fundamentally a story of two conflicting civilizations. Hill would not have documented the events he witnessed unless he believed, like Herodotus, that if details and contradictory accounts were not set down, then statesmen—or worse, posterity—would draw dangerous generalizations, miss crucial points, and repeat history's mistakes, or simply forget. Herodotus's *History* remains useful to students today less for historical accuracy than for his timeless commentary on human nature. Hill was concerned with both, but he was, there is no doubt, most interested in the latter.

Hill's historical sensitivities as a note taker are undeniable. There are occasional jottings that make his historical consciousness explicit, such as his exclamation, a bit melodramatic, during one eventful day on the seventh floor: "This is as important a moment as Sir Thomas More and Cardinal Wolsey, or in Gibbon's works, or Henry Adams. Realize that tomorrow is a big day in the history of the USA."* But Hill was writing in the first place for George Shultz, not for the historian. He took scrupulous notes because it was his job to be a good reporter, to create, in the stacks of notebooks in his office, a vault of information to which the secretary could refer at any moment. Shultz tapped Hill as his closest adviser because he trusted him to do this. Shultz had trusted him instinctively ever since the disheveled Foreign Service officer trudged downstairs after a night on the tacsat with Phil Habib to brief the new secretary on the progress of the Beirut siege. He had no choice but to trust Hill then. "I was the only one to tell him. I had a monopoly on the information," Hill said later. "And my appearance was authenticating. I looked like such a bum—the other Foreign Service officers were arriving in the morning in their suits, and I was looking like I just came in from playing sandlot football."

Accurate reporting was at the heart of Shultz's trust in Hill. Their relationship would grow stronger as time passed and other members of the administration repeatedly deceived the secretary and excluded him from important channels of information. Hill's reports, oral and written, were disciplined and methodical. He included details that most officers left out. Reporting, like note taking, was an art in which the slightest thing mattered. It was more important to watch and record what others were doing than to dwell on one's own reactions.

---

* Hill note, December 12, 1986. The statement, written a month after the Iran-Contra scandal broke, probably refers to the revelation that the CIA had kept a channel open with "moderates" and arms traders in Iran.

Decades later Hill likened the sloppiness of his colleagues' briefs to his seminars with overeager college freshman:

> Most people report in a gestalt manner — "Pow! This happened!" This is the thing I'm constantly working on in class. Everyone wants to talk about the whole text all at once. When that's what you do, you're smearing it all over the lot, jumping from page 280 to page 10, things that don't go together. There's no sense of progression. You don't read it the way it was written. You can think about it as an entirety, but not yet — you have to prove to me that you can do it. Most people's reporting is one-size-fits-all, "that's the impact it had on me." I'd report in the real order, and Shultz recognized the importance of that approach, of getting it straight.

Hill's frustration with his students arose from his sense that extracting real meaning from a text required a perfect grasp of the sequence of ideas and attention not only to the main points but to the intellectual filaments that linked them. Insights made without proper regard to context might sound clever but were invariably distortive. Hill strained, always, to perceive reality correctly. Throughout his notes, as well as in his commentary long after the fact, the failure of other decision makers and historians to "get it" is a constant theme, just as in his classes at Yale. Rare indeed is the published account with which Hill will unequivocally agree (although perhaps this is true for most who must bear the judgments of academics and reporters upon their firsthand experiences). One perceives in him a degree of frustration, a desire to "set people straight" about the history they think they understand so well. But for these few years with Shultz, he had the ear of a policymaker who trusted him absolutely. He had unparalleled access and ability to set his ideas in motion.

Hill was not careless with this power. He was just as attentive to the context in which he was reporting as he was to the details of the information itself. When he ventured out of the secretary's suite for a meeting or conference, he always paused to consider what mood he would project. Eventually, he got Shultz to realize the importance of mood as well. "It's like setting a thermostat," Hill explained. As he came to know his boss better, he saw that Shultz understood this because he had the same sensitivity to criticism that Hill had observed in other Great Men, although Shultz's sensitivity was well hidden behind a famously calm exterior. The secretary was better off for his self-consciousness, Hill believed. Confidence was good, he said, "but it's better to be able to project self-confidence while not being utterly self-confident, because if you're self-confident you will let your guard down — which is what you never want to do." This quality was important not only for the statesman in the spotlight; if a note taker forgot himself even for a moment, he might miss something crucial. Worse, others might observe him and understand *him*, without his permission. He would become visible, and he would lose control.

Hill's notes provide an unusual lens through which to study what was perhaps the most important foreign policy arena during the Reagan years — one that occupied much of Hill's attention and would have a profound impact on the international relations theory that he would teach students in years to come — U.S.-Soviet relations. The notebooks, their ink strokes like a physician's radioactive dye, do much to render invisible forces discernible. Soviet affairs also provide a useful context in which to examine evidence of Hill's active part in the subtle movements of diplomacy: his role as speechwriter, draftsman of every manner of foreign affairs document, and mastermind of talking points.

By 1985, when Hill had settled into his office next to the secretary's on the seventh floor overlooking the Lincoln Memorial, the Reagan administration was fractured. Reagan took office in 1980 with a mission to confront the Soviets and rescue the globe from the encroachment of Communism, heretofore countered only by the détente approach of three American administrations. This cold warrior tenacity was a cornerstone of what it meant to be a "Reaganite" in the first Reagan administration. But shortly before Reagan was elected to a second term, his mindset began to change. Shultz convinced him that now that Washington had achieved a military buildup and proved to the Soviets that the United States would never bend to their will, it was time to negotiate. The president's March 1983 announcement of his revolutionary Strategic Defense Initiative ("Star Wars"), a protective shield that would defend the United States from nuclear attack via antiballistic missiles, had shocked the Soviets and radically changed the framework of arms talks.

The press was rife with reports declaring that Reaganites in the White House and the Defense Department did not trust the State Department to handle Soviet affairs. Secretary of Defense Caspar Weinberger and Director of Central Intelligence William Casey led the battle against Shultz: "their view was that it was a fundamental violation of Reaganism to negotiate with the Soviets," Hill said. "Negotiating would be taken as a sign of weakness. Negotiations would get State into things, and [the State Department was thought to be] soft on Communism." The Reagan administration had always been an uncomfortable place for diplomats. Reagan and his advisers had already demonstrated their black-and-white worldview and their distaste for diplomacy in their policies for undermining anti-American regimes in Central America, their sneering denouncements of the Soviets, and their near-destruction of relations with China by selling arms to Taiwan. Describing the disturbing pattern of Reagan's foreign policy, foreign affairs commentator Leslie Gelb observed: "It is difficult to accept the Administration's description of these swings as a new realism and sophistication . . . The condemnations are too sweeping and the concessions are virtually unilateral. Rather, the very extreme nature of the acts suggests a view of the world as a simple struggle between good and evil and a keenly developed sense of domestic politics."

Reagan and his advisers were not interested in the subtleties of diplomacy, Gelb wrote, because they weren't interested in dealing with "bad guys" or "devils." Reagan's closest advisers were his political allies from California. Their backgrounds lay in domestic politics, and they were more interested in protecting their president's electability than in schooling themselves in the political and historical intricacies of far-off lands. It was simpler to frame these conflicts "in the only context they felt they did understand, that of East-West struggle," Gelb wrote.

Charles Hill had risen to the highest ranks of the State Department in part because he had the temperament of the perfect diplomat. He was patient, more concerned with observing than with making a statement. He had a genius for subtly directing dialogue and an abiding interest in the historical context of each political issue at hand. He was, in short, everything that Reagan and his cronies in the White House and on the National Security Council staff were not. In the Reagan administration, the art of diplomacy had become a last resort, and a mismanaged one at that. "Thus, diplomacy is undertaken with reluctance," Gelb continued. "It becomes something to be pursued episodically rather than continuously. The essential ingredient of diplomacy, persistent contact, is lost. The genius of diplomacy is to keep things moving, to generate pressures for compromise, to look for openings, opportunities, possibilities, where none previously existed. The temperament and understanding for such a long and arduous process seems to be missing from the Reagan Administration."

Hill has called Ronald Reagan one of the most brilliant American presidents of the twentieth century. He has cited Reagan's instinctive ability to sense the mood of the American people, as well as his skillful handing of the Soviets, American political scandals, post-Vietnam malaise, economic stagnation, and academics' warnings of "the decline of the West." Yet a quintessential diplomat like Hill was bound to be frustrated by the culture and policies of the Reagan administration. What felt in these early years like constant, low-grade animosity between the diplomats and the White House would, at a time not so far off, prove the root of a scandal that would nearly topple the administration and come close to destroying Charles Hill's career. But no one, not even the most observant note taker, could know that yet.

At the time, Reagan yielded to Shultz's urging and agreed to engage the Soviets diplomatically. When Hill took over the position of executive assistant, the State Department was in a flurry of preparations for Shultz's upcoming meeting with Soviet foreign minister Andrei Gromyko in Geneva, scheduled for January 1985, where the two diplomats would prepare the way for the planned November summit.

In what would prove to be Shultz's technique for staffing every major summit, rather than choose among the factions in Soviet affairs throughout Washington, he simply brought them all along. There were so many staffers from departments and agencies throughout government that the secretary's entourage required an extra plane. Hill flew with the secretary in a battered 707, the same plane on which Lyndon B. Johnson once stood beside the newly widowed Jackie Kennedy and took his oath as the thirty-sixth president of the United States. Hill first flew on the secretary's plane when he traveled with Kissinger during his days on the Policy Planning Staff. When George Shultz assumed the job, plane rides were more orderly than they had been during Kissinger's reign. Back then, transatlantic flights throbbed with energy. Prince Henry roamed the aisles, stuffing his face with handfuls from strategically placed candy bowls, shouting at his aides and pontificating to the press while his staff clambered over one another in an unending state of frenzy, photocopying memoranda and briefing books on primitive, dumpster-sized copy machines. But even during the calmer Shultz years each flight was a strange scene, a source of ir-resistible fodder for any anthropologist.

The press sat in the back of the cabin, which was brightly lit and fur-nished with a lot of blondish wood and plastic—a style Hill christened Eisenhower Modern. They spent their time writing, sleeping, playing "liar's poker," arguing, drinking, and nagging staffers to talk to them so they could file their stories. Shultz, unlike Kissinger, never went back to the media cattle car to court them. In front of the press sat a few rows of security agents, young Diplomatic Security professionals in plainclothes, drowsily reading adventure books. Shultz's staff, when they weren't up and about, occupied the seats ahead of the bodyguards. His secretaries sat in front of them: four neat women working over Shultz's schedule, pounding out last-minute memoranda on their typewriters. At the front of the plane, separated from the cabin bustle by a bulkhead, was the secretary's office. That was where Hill usually sat, in the big reclining chair behind a teardrop-shaped desk once meant for the president. Shultz preferred to remain in his cabin, leav-ing Hill free to take the office as his airborne command center. He sat surrounded "by all kinds of fancy-looking things on this desk in front of me, telephones and stuff that made it look like you could communi-cate with anybody from inside the plane. None of it worked," Hill said. "It was all basically phony. You looked like you were controlling the world, but when you picked up the phone, you'd get the Air Force tech sergeant up in the front of the plane."

Much of the equipment was original to the aircraft, making it nearly twenty years old and well beyond its functional lifetime. There was a telephone that could, in theory, connect the plane with a caller any-where on the ground, but in practice it almost never worked. If the sec-retary wanted to send a message, usually he would dictate to Hill, who cleaned up the phrasing in longhand on his notepad and called the ser-geant up front, who would hustle back to fetch the message and type it in Morse code over a telex. The message was decoded at Andrews Air Force Base, where it was reconstituted as hard copy and sent via cou-rier to the intended recipient. The plane was also equipped with small television sets with rabbit ears, which received a picture only on the tar-mac. There were call boxes intended to link different parts of the plane, but no one was ever seen using those.

For the most part, Hill conducted business the old-fashioned way, steno pad in hand, other staff members offering their ideas from the bench seats along the walls of the office. His job was to tell people what to do, to assure them that what they were doing was indeed what the secretary wanted, to evaluate latest drafts, and to keep track of the pulse of the delegation as it hurtled toward its destination. He frequently absented himself from the bustle of the office to sit in the secretary's cabin, volunteer his thoughts, and spend long minutes watching Shultz stare at the wall, contemplating, speaking when he felt like it. These occupations were hardly aided by modern technology, perhaps even impeded by it—the work of an army scout who leaves behind sophisticated radar and reconnaissance equipment to walk the terrain himself.

The antiquated plane could not cover the distance from Washington to the European continent without refueling. Typically, en route to a destination like Geneva, the plane would land in the frosty hours of the early morning to refuel at a tiny airport in Shannon, Ireland. There everyone onboard filed off the plane to peruse the mass-produced Irish fisherman's sweaters, elaborate Celtic crucifixes, Irish whiskeys, and other tourist items sold at kiosks inside the airport (except for Hill, who remained in his seat and made more productive use of the time). The American plane was usually alone on the Shannon runway. Planes stopped there at odd hours, according to their own schedules. But often, Hill recalled, their refueling coincided with the arrival of a giant Soviet Ilyushin, full of Soviet workers on their way to or from Cuba for their annual weeklong vacation. "When they came in, it was like an emergency, as if sirens would go off: 'The Soviets are coming!'" Hill remembered. "And the Irish would shut down the whole place, the iron screens like you see on jewelry shops in the city would come clattering down, hurricane fences would go up—because the Soviets would steal everything. The money they had was no good, and they would just stuff things in their pockets—and the Irish couldn't stop them."

The Soviet vacationers would swarm into the tiny terminal, overwhelming the place with the smell of body odor and cigarettes. There were fair European faces and round, weathered Asiatics—the passengers came from across the Soviet Union, all dressed in bland, mass-produced clothing and plastic shoes, their hair (the men's and the women's) tinted with cheap dye. "Their whole being—you just wanted to get away from it," Hill said. "'Here they come!' Like hordes of Gadarene swine. The Irish would say, 'Please forgive us, but you have to leave now.' We didn't want to hang around there with the smell of the

Soviets, so we got back on the plane." These occasional tarmac encounters were both banal and profound. Each was a chance confrontation
between two sparring civilizations, a terrifying whiff of foreignness,
and an uncomfortable sight of average individuals when one was prepared only for rehearsed dialogue with statesmen.

The Soviet mission in Geneva, where Shultz's delegation met with
Soviet Foreign Minister Andrei Gromyko in January 1985, made a vivid
impression on Hill. The building was grand and spare. An imposing
portrait of Lenin stared out from a wall in the receiving room. The furniture was nondescript but adequate, the shades of tan and brown wood
selected primarily to wear well without showing spots. The vodka, the
furniture, and all the other logistical matters lay in the hands of a squad
of frumpy Soviet women who rustled around the rooms in house
dresses, "interchangeable-looking, potato-faced women," Hill recalled.
They never spoke.

On January 8, as Shultz prepared to give the Soviets a draft of the
joint communiqué, Hill urged him not to present it as the Americans'
formal draft. "It will make it harder for them to accept it as watchers
back in Moscow would see them taking our language," he said. "Instead, just say we have some thoughts and pass it out. Stay silent on
the transcript." The statement that came out of Shultz's January meeting with Gromyko—Hill's first summit as executive assistant—was
big news. In an agreement that ran contrary to the theology of the
first Reagan administration, the Americans and the Soviets agreed to
resume arms control negotiations—a process that culminated at the
Reykjavik summit in October 1986, when the leaders of the world's
two superpowers came within a hair's breadth of eliminating strategic
nuclear weapons. That historic meeting, which the leaders modestly
called a "pre-summit," has been scrutinized by historians in the years
since. Most have concluded that while the press dubbed it a failure,
Reykjavik marked a turning point in the course of U.S.-Soviet relations. Hill described the summit as "a total, shocking collapse of the
[Soviet] façade, as though a mask had dropped away. To me, that was
the end of the Cold War."

It is clear from Hill's notes, however, that while Reykjavik was radical, dozens of signals presaged its outcome. There were minute shifts
in mood, strangely thawed "un-Soviet" encounters, and enough talk
of eliminating nuclear weapons—long the foreign policy goal that
Reagan held most dear—to suggest that what occurred at Reykjavik

should not have come as such a surprise. These were the tiny shifts in tone, the incremental stirrings of diplomatic affairs that Hill specialized in recording, and in manufacturing himself.

There was ample evidence that in the months since Gorbachev came to power, Soviet diplomatic style had changed in subtle but essential ways. No matter their claims to revolution, the Soviets remained of a Byzantine mindset. They were long-winded obfuscators, deceivers, and mystics, historically alienated from the Western style of communication. Diplomacy, for most of Russia's history, had meant defending its borders against enemies. Their brand of negotiation, wrote George Kennan,

> like that of the Orient in general, is concentrated on impressing an adversary with the terrifying strength of Russian power, while keeping him uncertain and confused as to the exact channels and means of its application and thus inducing him to treat all Russian wishes and views with particular respect and consideration . . . We would find it much easier to deal with Russia if we would recognize frankly in our minds the fact that its leaders are, by their own choice the enemies of all that part of the world they do not control, and that this is a recognized principle of thought and action for the entire Soviet machine.

American negotiators had always found the Soviets difficult to deal with. To the Soviets, negotiation, like politics, was essentially a continuation of war by other means. Beyond their perpetual hostility and suspicion, Soviet diplomats were conditioned to be the automatons of Moscow, incapable—for fear of losing their jobs, or worse—of deviating from the party line. "Every line of Bolshevik conduct is either prescribed or forbidden," wrote Nathan Leites. "It is prescribed if it will maximize the power of the Party. It is forbidden if it will not. There is little behavior that is merely tolerated, or recommended."

Mikhail Gorbachev, however, seemed to bring a fresh wind into Moscow. How different from his predecessors Gorbachev really was is up for debate. The State Department craved a leader who would be a productive negotiating partner, and so State preferred to believe that Gorbachev was what they wanted him to be. The intelligence community and many in the Defense Department and the White House, on the other hand, believed that Gorbachev's liberal policies of perestroika and glasnost were nothing but a ploy to dupe Washington. Hill's analysis fell somewhere in between. Just as Henry Kissinger's policy of détente had been a necessary strategy in light of the unprecedented weakness of America's economic, social, and geopolitical circumstances in the 1970s, it seemed to Hill that Gorbachev's policies were a Soviet version of détente. During his first term in office Reagan bolstered the American position in the cold war, particularly through the deployment of Pershing missiles in Western Europe and his announcement of the Strategic Defense Initiative in 1983. By the time Gorbachev came to power, the Soviet economy was collapsing, Moscow's strategic position was slipping, and he had no choice but to take some liberalizing measures in relations with the enemy.

Hints trickled into the State Department that things were changing. On the afternoon of September 5, Shultz met with Kenneth Bialkin, a prominent Wall Street lawyer and chairman of the Conference of Presidents of Major American Jewish Organizations. Bialkin reported that in a recent conversation with Soviet ambassador to the United States Anatoly Dobrynin, he had asked why the Soviets continued their repressive policies toward Soviet Jews. "It's irrational," Bialkin had said. "I personally agree," Dobrynin told him, "and I will lobby my government on it." Such a response would have shocked the Sovietologists. The ambassador's use of the word "personally" is a remarkable departure from standard enunciation of the party line, let alone Dobrynin's admission that the party line could be wrong.

The following day Rozanne Ridgway, assistant secretary for European and Canadian affairs, and her deputy Mark Palmer met with Shultz. In Hill's notebook, the conversation is headlined "contrary to common wisdom of moment." "I think the Soviets are signaling. It's *not* all media blitz. Gorbachev is trying to define research," said Palmer. He was probably referring to the research and development of weapons systems, particularly SDI. There had been a recent surge in Soviet pre-summit propaganda, which included a deluxe full-color mailing entitled "'Star Wars': Delusions and Dangers," published in Moscow and circulated around Washington, as well as Gorbachev's recent well-received interviews with *Time* magazine and U.S. senators. The extent to which research and development outside the laboratory (particularly American efforts toward SDI) was permissible under the existing Anti-Ballistic Missile Treaty was a central point of contention in the negotiations. The fact that Moscow seemed to be examining the issue suggested that there might be room for movement.

A few days later while Hill was in New York City, where the secretary was scheduled to address the U.N. General Assembly on the occasion of its fortieth anniversary, he received an unexpected phone call from Henry Kissinger. The call came in when Hill was away from his desk, so he hastily took down Kissinger's remarks on a piece of scrap paper. Kissinger's description of a Soviet diplomat's approach to him about the upcoming visit of Soviet Foreign Minister Eduard Shevardnadze (who had replaced Gromyko earlier that year) was remarkable enough to warrant Hill's taking the time to transcribe it into his notebook in a cleaner, less staccato format than most of his transcriptions. Kissinger's report attests to an atmospheric change in the Soviet approach to negotiations, and for that reason it is worth reproducing at length:

9/23 *Kissinger=CH* telephone call 1045 (at UNGA)
[Soviet propagandist Georgi] Arbatov came to see me and we had an unusual conversation. I try to avoid him because he's a hack. But he has been pursuing me, assaulting me to ask for a meeting. Insisted we have breakfast. In every conversation I've ever had with him Arbatov just takes the Party Line and says everything is going to be a disaster unless we change. This time he didn't do that. He came with a list of questions and took careful notes. He said he was going to report our conversation directly to Gorbachev.
Our talk was so out of the ordinary that I thought I should report it to the Secretary right away.
First, he said that Shevarnadze [sic] would be coming with specific detailed proposals. That was interesting but more unusual was that he wanted to talk about a "formula" for SDI . . . He asked what my "formula" would be? I said there might be an agreement to keep negotiating about SDI side by side with offensive limits, and we would leave ourselves limited to SDI research, but keeping a future deployment open.
He said that was *"possible."* I said my view is that the US should never give up SDI but that we should negotiate limits on it just as we negotiate limits on offensive weapons. He said perhaps each side would state its view about how it would negotiate on SDI but it would not be settled. He asked a lot of questions about how to put limits on SDI . . .
He said that Gorbachev believes the US and Soviets can have "a very close relationship" within 15 years. He claimed he has direct access to Gorbachev. I can't believe he would have come to me like this without specific authorization. Usually he says we have screwed everything

up and it's all hopeless. This was totally different demeanor for him. I never before saw him in a negotiating mode. His tone was very soft and not at all threatening. Not like his current TV appearances.

He asked about regional issues. I said there ought to be some political understanding. A code under which each side would stick to its principles and interests but agree to avoid or hold back on specific cases that are particularly aggravating or alarming to the other—like Nicaragua. He said how about Afghanistan? I said I thought so but their troops would have to get out. His tone was very soft on Afghanistan. He said he did not think some agreement on Afghanistan was impossible.

On SDI he said again that we could continue to negotiate about it. Each side would give its own version in public to what that meant. Research would go on.

He said he hopes the President doesn't quote from Lenin's writings as he did the last time.

All through this I told him repeatedly that I did not speak for the Administration and had no influence with it.

Arbatov's approach to Kissinger was a big deal for a number of reasons. No matter Kissinger's pro forma insistence that he "had no influence" with the Reagan administration, it is clear that Gorbachev had sent his envoy to Kissinger because he wanted Arbatov's message to reach the ears of the administration outside regular channels. An official communication, via the Soviet ambassador or other visible government figure in a meeting with his American counterpart, could have easily leaked to the press and upset the diplomatic minuet. There was, it appeared, a widening gap between the Soviets' public obstinacy and a private willingness to negotiate seriously.

The content of Arbatov's statement would have been astounding to outsiders observing the negotiation process. For all of the Soviets' blustery rejection of SDI research (which Shevardnadze would reiterate when he came to Washington in a few days), here was Arbatov intimating that Moscow might consider some kind of "formula" for "limiting" SDI rather than refusing any compromise outright. Even more striking —as Kissinger notes—is the about-face in Arbatov's tone. The party line had retreated into the background. Arbatov wanted a real conversation. Hill got off the phone in a hurry and reported Kissinger's call to the secretary.

. . .

Shultz left for Moscow in the first week in November to prepare the way for the summit between Gorbachev and Reagan planned for later that month. Hill recalled that he spent the long flight furiously writing and rewriting talking points the secretary would use with Gorbachev, refiguring the arguments nearly twenty times before Shultz was satisfied, "draft after draft all the way across the Atlantic." He ended up with a series of talking points that presented not "a call for freedom that would lose govt [government] control over people but increase peoples allegiance to the govt," he concluded in his notebook. "Your human rights paper is a hell of a good piece of work," Shultz told Hill when they stopped over in Helsinki. "Finally we've got something to work with." In a rare moment of self-adulation, perhaps prompted by his pen's arrival at the final page of this particular steno pad, Hill wrote that his human rights talking points were one of the most important "CH achievements this term."

In a chapter in his memoirs entitled "Classroom in the Kremlin," Shultz describes the conversation that resulted from Hill's talking points. On Shultz's first day in Moscow, his argument with Shevardnadze over human rights was the "longest ever," Hill noted. Normally the Soviets refused to tolerate any prodding on human rights and shut down the conversation immediately. Contrary to what the State Department's Sovietologists had predicted, Gorbachev agreed with much of what Shultz had to say, although his tone was hot at times. His "approach was to *repair* his system, not *replace* it," Shultz realized. Backchannel thaws to the contrary, Gorbachev remained stubborn and deeply ideological. "S[hultz] invited here in order to be frightened by Soviet approach," Hill wrote. But when Shultz got back to Washington, in another unusual departure from Soviet diplomatic form, Ambassador Dobrynin came into Shultz's office alone and offered "something of an apology" for Gorbachev's harsh treatment of the secretary. "And the Soviets *never* apologize," Shultz wrote in his memoirs.

The Geneva summit later that same month ended with both parties still in vehement disagreement over SDI. However, both leaders had come to like and respect each other. The big story was the long period of time Gorbachev and Reagan spent alone, walking down to the boathouse on the lake where a fire crackled in the fireplace, talking for hours while Secret Service agents shivered outside in the bitter weather. On November 21, the two leaders issued mutual invitations to Moscow and Washington for further talks aimed at seeking a 50 percent reduction in nuclear arms. In January 1986 Shultz received a letter from Gorbachev, via Dobrynin, addressed to the president. Dobrynin informed Shultz that Gorbachev would go public with the letter on Soviet television shortly. The letter was "full of barbs," but the "essence is — *lets go to zero* [nuclear arms]," Hill noted. After Shultz got off the phone with NSC adviser John Poindexter, he turned to Hill. "This Gorbachev letter is a big deal," he said. Hill recorded his own reaction: "A dilemma for P; he loves SDI, [but] he's determined to get to zero." He set to work on talking points for Shultz to use in discussing the letter with the president.

Hill's notes suggest that Shultz relied on him to supply most of his talking points for important meetings, both at home and abroad. He was by no means the secretary's ventriloquist — his drafts resulted from hours of conversation with Shultz — but Hill had the task of articulating their brainstorming sessions into a usable product. He drafted the cables Shultz was often obliged to send back to Washington when rivals in the White House or the Pentagon tried to undermine State Department policy.* In February, after a fraudulent presidential election in the Philippines led to a popular uprising and ultimately the ouster of corrupt (but anti-Communist) Ferdinand Marcos in favor of Corazón Aquino, Hill drafted the statement of recognition that Shultz carried to the White House. In a heated meeting with the president and his top aides, Shultz persuaded a reluctant Ronald Reagan to deliver it. "Charlie, thank you for getting that written up. Something written up always saves the day," Shultz had told him. Two months later, when the secretary's staff learned of the Chernobyl nuclear disaster while they were abroad in Asia, Hill whipped out his pad and pen and sat in the airplane during a refueling stopover on Guam (while Shultz and Chief of Staff Don Regan practiced their putts on the roll-out green), drafting a message for the president to send Gorbachev offering American assistance. Poindexter was initially reluctant to send the message, but according to Hill's notes, he contacted Nick Platt late that same evening

---

* There is, for example, Hill's note of June 20, 1986, which details an incident in which Poindexter protested a cable explaining the most recent Soviet arms negotiations proposals, which the State Department had sent to multiple embassies for distribution among allied NATO governments. Poindexter protested providing this basic information on the grounds that it didn't include "an appropriate U.S. assessment" and so only advertised the Soviet position without providing the president's response.

and the message was cabled from Bali to Moscow while Shultz's entourage was still abroad.

The "Daniloff affair" is a notable case in which Hill operated as agile draftsman of policy statements. In August 1986, when the Soviets arrested American news correspondent Nicholas Daniloff in Moscow on charges of spying and proposed a "swap" for a Soviet spy, Gennadi Zakharov, recently arrested in New York by the FBI, Hill drafted talking points for Shultz to use "for getting a decision from the P on Daniloff." At first it seemed that the Soviets had fabricated the charges. But Shultz soon learned that although Daniloff had never been used or paid as a spy, the CIA had indeed provided the KGB with all the evidence they needed by discussing Daniloff (who had useful connections and access in the Soviet Union) over a wiretapped phone. Reagan seemed to favor a trade, but he didn't have all the information. "P is poorly informed and people don't want him informed," Shultz told Hill. The decision was complicated by the scheduled arrival of Foreign Minister Shevardnadze on September 19, who brought with him a letter from Gorbachev proposing a meeting in either Reykjavik or London to lay the groundwork for a future summit in Washington. Reagan could not agree to such a meeting until the Daniloff affair was settled. On the second day of Shevardnadze's visit, Hill intercepted Shultz in his office at 7:20 A.M. with a draft of a "strategy proposal" outlining what the secretary ought to say to Shevardnadze. Hill recorded his explanation:

0720 CH=S (hands over paper that says we would agree to Gorba prop[osal] for mtg soon in London + Reykjavik—but atmosphere so bad that it difficult to put such a positive response into effect. Thus all the more important to resolve the immediate problem (D [Daniloff]) asap.
• The paper I drafted has some implications for our strategy. If you go through this big block of mtgs w Shev and at end there is no symbol of movement on D, media will call the round for the Sovs . . . you might start by presenting *this* paper then asking whether Shev has a response to our list [of other Soviet dissidents whom the U.S. urged Moscow to allow to emigrate]. He will say no—that will take time.
• You then say but our positive reply to Gorba makes sit[uation] urgent if it is to occur . . . Then you break so he can transmit our msg [message] to Moscow + request authz [authorization] to nego[tiate] on D.

209

The clear, full-sentence character of this summary suggests that Hill drafted what he would say to Shultz before his boss arrived at the office in the morning. Hill was always in the building before nearly anyone else. Although this notebook entry represents one of the rare moments in which Hill records his own words (or intended words), it is characteristic in other ways. He was ever the draftsman, aware that control of a crisis came to whoever could get something down on paper first. This entry reflects his constant awareness of the media as a pack of hounds ready to pounce on any foreign policy initiative and spoil it if the administration didn't act carefully. It indicates an anthropologist's sensitivity to how the Soviets operated—Shevardnadze would need permission from Moscow before he could proceed with negotiations for Daniloff's release. Shultz read over Hill's proposal and at 8:30 A.M. he picked up the secure phone and read Hill's paper to Poindexter. "I am certain if we don't leak the proposal [by Gorbachev], they [the Soviets] will, and soon," Shultz said. "So we can gain by responding and making a public statement along these lines." He reread Hill's paper again, more slowly, as Poindexter took it down on paper at the other end of the line.

Hill's proposal formed the basis for discussions among Shultz's staff throughout the day. Later that day Shultz turned to Hill, and in his notes we find a record of gratifying recognition: "S=CH *Your draft gets us in sustainable posture.*" Hill took the encouragement to heart and, based on his notes, drafted nonstop through the afternoon. By 2:30 P.M. he had produced for Shultz a draft of the president's announcement accepting Gorbachev's summit proposal, a possible statement to the press, a "schematic way of looking at a [spy trade] deal," and, as a possible add-on, a drafted statement announcing that the Soviet spy would be released without trial. He updated these drafts throughout the day, as the American position on the issues shifted. When Shultz's late-night meeting with Shevardnadze at the Soviet mission to the United Nations proved inconclusive, Shultz left a copy of Hill's paper with the Soviets before he departed for the night. "We were almost there," he told Hill that night. "Then, just at the end, it started to fall apart. I left your paper, which was an excellent job, because they started to act like they didn't understand [the U.S. position]." Undoubtedly, Shultz also realized that it would be much easier for the Soviets to transmit the language of the American proposals to Moscow than to report the American positions in their own cables. A written American position, according to Soviet protocol, had to be reported, while an oral argument could be rejected outright.

In the end, the Soviets agreed to let Daniloff leave Moscow. Zakharov was permitted to plead nolo contendere and was expelled, at which point the Soviets were to permit the emigration of Yuri Orlov, a Soviet dissident, and agree to reduce the size of their U.N. mission by twenty-five people. The meeting at Reykjavik—chosen in the hopes that its remoteness would discourage hype and press attention— would be announced at the end of September.

The leaders' choice of the isolated island capital heightened the drama of the summit from the start. The delegations convened at Hofdi House, a stark, unwelcoming pile on the edge of the sea, the walls of its upstairs sitting rooms hung with improbable oil paintings of American astronauts and moonscapes. On October 11, the first day of the summit, Reagan argued for large cuts in the warheads on strategic arms. Gorbachev responded with a long presentation of his scheme on strategic and intermediate-range arms, nuclear research, and space and defense. He proposed to cut strategic weapons in half, including the total elimination of all Soviet and American missiles in Europe. He pushed Reagan to halt SDI research, scoffing when the president offered to share American findings with the Soviets.

While their principals slept, the two delegations worked to lay the groundwork for productive negotiations the next morning. Through the night and into the next day, the American note takers worked in shifts. Hill covered the afternoon meeting between Gorbachev, Shevardnadze, Reagan, and Shultz on the last day of the summit. Although Hill later asserted that the note-taking task was no more difficult than on an average day at the State Department, these notes are sloppier. One is hard-pressed to identify them with his normal handwriting. Perhaps despite his modest memory of the event, the pace of conversation was faster or his own hand a bit less steady than usual. He captured the mood at the meeting's beginning: "G + P banter + argue as Shev ponders + S drafts to try to find a formula." After the morning session it appeared that they had achieved the general shape of an agreement on intermediate nuclear forces (INF) in Asia and some movement on the more troublesome issues of space, defense, and nuclear testing. But by the end of the afternoon session, it was clear that Reagan was not willing to give up SDI in exchange for a reduction in nuclear arms. Gorbachev would settle for nothing less. Talks collapsed in the early evening. Back at the American ambassador's residence, Hill recorded Shultz's assessment: "This wd have been the most sensational agmt [agreement] *ever reached* if we had got it. What next? We better protect ourselves by seeing that SDI protected. We will cont [inue] to struggle."

It became clear that Gorbachev still hoped for an agreement. A few days later he sent a message to Shultz via his U.N. ambassador, Yuri Dubinin. Dubinin had been instructed to report that Gorbachev had appreciated the "good atmospherics" and "real progress" made at Reykjavik, and to push on the issue of SDI research, reiterating Soviet flexibility: "a 'test range' could be part of a definition of a laboratory," Hill noted from the Soviet statement. "It just means no testing in space. D [Dubinin] said the 2 sides shd get together soon to clarify their views." By Shultz's account, Gorbachev's message was a near-desperate attempt to salvage something from Reykjavik. There is no record of this conversation in Shultz's memoirs, and indeed no indication that the message, if passed on to the president, did much to change Reagan's mind. "I talked to P today w (CH) tps [Hill's talking points on the results of Reykjavik]," reads Hill's note of Shultz's report that same morning. Reagan had no intention of responding to Gorbachev's offer anytime soon. But, said Shultz, "We can plough along . . ."

Even though no treaty emerged from the Reykjavik summit, Gorbachev could not retract the willingness he had expressed to make concessions toward the American position. As Hill said, "a mask had dropped away." The terrain of American-Soviet relations was forever changed. But the events in October 1986 in that drafty mansion on a rock in the North Atlantic were less surprising to those who had been watching the details over the previous few months. And Hill, surprised or not, continued to operate as he had always done, carrying a notebook with him always. No matter the changing landscape of foreign affairs or the unsteady fits and starts of the Information Age, Hill adhered to the antique virtues he knew were important in a diplomat. He tried to read everything, perceive everything, and write it all down, anonymously if he could. He rarely permitted himself a down moment. He was a professional, just as he had been since the day he entered his country's service. Nothing, not even Reykjavik or the eventual end of the cold war, would change that. Professionalism, in the words of Mr. Stevens in Kazuo Ishiguro's *The Remains of the Day*, requires that one must "not be shaken out by external events, however surprising." For Hill, there could be no greater indignity than to be surprised. To be surprised would mean Hill somehow failed, that the anthropologist had been outsmarted by his informants—that he had been a person upon whom something was lost.

The biographer, for all her interest in her subject's conduct for its own sake, must eventually try to determine the historical impact of his actions. At some point, it is not enough to say "my subject spent great amounts of time in the company of power." One has to draw specific links, corroborate moments of agency. Nothing could be more maddening than discovering that the subject doesn't really know the nature of those links, or care all that much.

It is difficult to evaluate the ultimate impact of the endless numbers of talking points, memoranda, speech drafts, and bullet points generated by Charles Hill during his tenure as executive assistant. In many cases, although he sketched out his ideas for talking points and speeches in his notebooks, the actual drafts that he handed to Shultz do not survive. Shultz's published account of what he said and did corresponds with the talking points and advice recorded in Charlie's notes, but this proof is circular, since Charlie's notes were the primary source for most of the book. In cases where independent evidence does exist, such as published statements or archived memoranda that Charlie's notes indicate he had a principal hand in drafting, there is no way to be sure how closely Charlie's version resembled the final draft. When I asked him how I might determine this, Charlie was of little help:

> I never paid attention to the final drafts of my statements—with [President Reagan's recognition of] Aquino, we said this is what we had to do, Shultz said 'we have to have something on paper to make it work' So I went away and wrote something. He'd come back later and say, 'this is how it happened at the meeting'—writing is what makes things happen, although I'm sure at the meetings they'd fool with the words.
>
> As with everything else, the fundamental principle is that you never look back. You keep going forward. If you give someone a memo, never thereafter say, 'did you look at that? What did you think of it?' It becomes annoying if you do. The Secretary of State doesn't want to have to justify himself to you . . . Following up is important,

but if you're in an idea-producing status or situation, you just throw ideas in and move on to the next problem. If something works, you'll hear about it in some form.

There is little that Charlie cares about more than his impact on history. But what interests him is the manufacture of the ideas that move world affairs, not the bureaucratic dexterity required to make sure that he got due credit. The essential fact—which I never felt the need to corroborate, as I have seen its proof in real life, in the classroom and the workplace—is that transmitting ideas into written words is hard, and people do not like to do it. A person who is willing to do so, and does it as quickly and reliably as Charlie always has, in most cases ends up the default author, the quarterback to whom others start to turn, out of habit, for the play.

In the end, the meaning of Charlie's notes in historical terms is debatable. But there can be no doubt about their significance for his students at Yale. The art of diplomacy, after all, has much in common with the art of running a college seminar. In both contexts, heavy-handed control can kill an idea while it is still in utero. True genius lies in deftly "touching the rudder" without others realizing what has happened. The parts of the notebooks that deal with Soviet affairs—I would guess that fully half of these thousands of pages are concerned with relations between the superpowers—are of particular interest to anyone who has studied international relations with Charlie. In those final years of the cold war he hardened in his ardent belief, rooted in his foreign policy reading during his years at university, that one of Communism's great evils was its intention to mastermind a global revolution that would force the state to "wither away." Today his beliefs are updated for the post–cold war era, but they remain fundamentally unchanged.

The notebooks' significance goes beyond foreshadowing Charlie's hobbyhorses as a professor. From the reflections on Australian culture to his commentary on the problems in the American media, Charlie's notes are packed with the seedlings of his favorite lectures and chalkboard diagrams, in which anthropology crosses into international relations, history, or literature. The meticulous reporting, the crisp, logical sequences of ideas in his notes echo the way he runs his class. "He has a very linear thinking style. He likes causal connections, clarity, simplicity," said Amia Srinivasan, who studied literature with Charlie. "He gave me a D on my first paper . . . He circled all the abstract terms in my paper, and said an essay should be like a U.N. document. I had written a paper on modes of literary criticism, and he said writing like this doesn't prepare you for life. In life, you don't write like this."

Many students would also find, in the notes' merger of poetry with fact, cultural review with verbatim transcription, a portent of the holistic scope of Charlie's teaching, as well as the work he expects from his students. "I appreciate his grasp of historical trends. I value his synthetic insights, his capacity to relate tiny details or random quotes he has in his head, to start writing on the board in German," Amia continued. "He embodies a really strong belief in the importance of the relationship between literature, politics, history, and philosophy. That's the one thing missing in modern political life . . . the death of the Renaissance man in the civic arena."

Effective diplomacy is not just a matter of liberal arts education and careful observation, however. Over the course of his career, Charlie perfected the craft of unassailable logic chains and immovable judgment necessary in his fast-paced, unforgiving profession. Some students are put off by a diplomat-cum-professor who does not see the difference between the security bubble and the seminar room. Charlie's self-assured teaching style is a far cry from the hand-holding pedagogy they encounter in most Yale classrooms. "In his career, it was a crucial skill never to be stumped," Aaron O'Connell said. "It demands that you know what you want when you walk in the door. In a negotiating sense, what you don't want to do is to challenge your assumptions or see if you can come up with a new way of thinking about [the problem] . . . The classroom should be collaborative. There's no collaboration in his teaching approach."

Many veterans of the Grand Strategy course, as well as professors who have observed from the back, note that only a handful—often non-American students, interestingly—take Charlie's assertions to task. Those few who do usually find, as his State Department colleagues have, that they can never convince him he might be wrong. Aaron explained: "What I saw in him was 'I've been there, I know the answers, I know how to solve problems, I will tell you my answers and entertain questions.' There were a few of us who were not intimidated, who would occasionally challenge him, but only about four people. He was never stumped. That's part of the problem—to be stumped means to say, 'gosh, I've never looked at it that way.'"

To be stumped, it seems, would be un–Grand Strategic, and entirely unprofessional.

At Reykjavik, the world's two superpowers entered the twilight of the cold war. As that war came to an end — with only five years remaining until the Soviet Union's fall and the final collapse of the bipolar paradigm that had framed world affairs for half a century — a new war was beginning. The first salvos were fired not by an enemy state but by faceless bands of terrorists in the Middle East. Hill's notebooks record his role in the back-channel diplomatic efforts to rescue American hostages from terrorists' clutches. They describe largely unreported nuances in the Reagan administration's scramble to adjust to the country's new enemy. The notes prove that the Iran-Contra scheme — the infamous legacy of the Reagan administration's attempts to win freedom for American hostages — was not the only strategy employed. But it was, sadly, the one that would outlast all other, more sensible efforts. Hill's notes contain unparalleled documentation of that affair, just as they had documented so many others. Iran-Contra would be a stumper — a case in which one wonders whether he later wished that he had, for once, set down his pen and allowed the past to dissolve behind him.

12

ON JUNE 14, 1985, HIJACKERS THOUGHT TO BE SHIA MUSLIMS
stormed Trans World Airlines flight 847 fifteen minutes after its departure from Athens. On board were 153 passengers, most of them Americans. Shortly after the plane landed in Beirut, witnesses watched the
body of a young navy diver named Robert Stethem drop onto the tarmac, beaten and shot in the head. "You see. You now believe," said a hi-
jacker over the control tower radio. His voice was thick with a south
Lebanese accent. "There will be another within five minutes."

The hijackers, reportedly led by members of the terrorist organization Hezbollah, had already announced their demands: the release of
Shia Muslims captured by Israeli forces during the invasion of Lebanon and international censure of the Israeli incursion there. They had
chosen a plane full of mostly American passengers as retribution for
Washington's support of Israel's war effort. After tossing Stethem's
body out of the plane, the terrorists took off in the ensuing confusion
and headed for Algiers, where the plane now sat parked at Algeria's
Houari Boumedienne Airport. A growing swarm of television cam-
eras, satellite news vans, and packs of reporters surrounded the plane,
all seething for the story, the Reagan administration's first hostage crisis with American victims onboard.

Terrorism against American targets in the Middle East reached a
crisis point during Reagan's years in the White House. Bombings and
hijackings ripped through the cities and skies of the region with increasing frequency, and more recently a shadowy network of terrorists,
apparently directed from Tehran, had seized several Americans, most
now held somewhere in Lebanon. Despite the administration's public
refusal to deal in any way with terrorists—a policy known as Opera-

tion Staunch—the terrorists were gaining momentum. The president felt an acute sense of responsibility for Americans in trouble, and he was losing patience with his policy. "Officially, we were not dealing with terrorists," Hill said later. "And as far as the open, official conduct of the [TWA 847] crisis was concerned, we were maintaining that policy. But in fact we really couldn't. We realized it was just too much to do—when someone has a hostage and is going to kill them, you can't say, 'go ahead, we're not going to do anything.'"

The Reagan administration faced a dilemma. The Israelis, through various channels public and private, made it clear that even before the hijacking they had decided to release some of the prisoners and would now do so at Washington's command. At a meeting in the Situation Room on June 16, Shultz had to convince the president that to take up the Israelis' offer would mean a swap of hostages for prisoners, a direct violation of Reagan's announced policy. But repeated Israeli offers to release the prisoners were creating the public perception that Israel and the United States disagreed on antiterrorism strategy, and that if the hostages were killed, President Reagan was to blame. Even more dangerous, the standing offer from the Israelis to comply with the terrorists' demands would certainly embolden them further. Shultz considered communicating directly with Israeli Prime Minister Shimon Peres, but he decided that any official communication would be interpreted as preparations to make a deal with the terrorists. So the job fell to his executive assistant and Israel's ambassador to the United Nations, Benjamin Netanyahu.

The State Department's central concern was getting through to the Israelis in order to coordinate their public statements while appearing to stand firm. Shultz ordered Hill to call Netanyahu and say that current Israeli statements were undercutting the Reagan administration's policy on terrorism. "Maybe you should call Netanyahu and let him have it," he told Hill.

Hill called him that same morning and tore into the public position of the Israelis, per Shultz's instructions. Netanyahu "loved it. That's terrific. Will transmit back [to Israel] that we shd *stand together*," Hill recorded. He kept in touch with Netanyahu throughout the day, working to align the announcements issuing from their respective governments. No one knew about the link between Shultz's executive assistant and the Israeli embassy—not even NEA or the Secretariat—and both sides preferred that it remain that way. "We should keep this channel so there are no leaks that the U.S. and Israel are consulting on how to deal," Hill told Netanyahu that afternoon. There is no indication that word of this critical communication ever got out, within the State Department or in the American media, even after the hostage crisis was resolved.

Meanwhile, Reagan sent a private letter to enlist the help of Syrian President Hafez al-Assad. No one mentioned that Syria, currently in control of the Lebanese bases and supply lines used by the Shia terrorists, had almost certainly endorsed the hijacking. In the morning press briefing on June 18, White House spokesman Larry Speakes horrified the State Department and confused the Israelis by affirming that the United States did want Israel to release the prisoners — an announcement that immediately rocketed around the world via CNN. Netanyahu called Hill to report that he had received a call from Peres, who wanted an explanation for Speakes's statement. Hill called national security adviser McFarlane and warned him that "Speakes is beyond guidance. The President needs to straighten it out." McFarlane vowed to "get on it." Hill called Netanyahu back and promised him prompt clarification. At a press conference that evening, Reagan reiterated his vow never to make concessions to terrorists.

The next day several State Department staffers gathered for a brainstorming session. It went nowhere. "The thrust: wavering, at cross-purposes, ideas that won't work, *helplessness*," Hill reported in his notebook. Hezbollah seemed to be in control of the crisis, and Washington's attempts to work through Lebanese Shia middlemen and the Syrian government did not appear promising. Everyone worried that if progress was too long delayed, the terrorists would move the hostages to the Bekaa Valley in Lebanon, where other American hostages were already being held, transforming the hijacking into a permanent crisis. At the meeting Hill's colleagues concluded that there remained a narrow window in which President Assad might be able to intervene, but if his efforts fell through "we should consider going to *Iran* as the ultimate source of control, not to blame them for this specific act, but to hold them responsible," Hill noted. "*Then* we can consider pressure on a *state*." Iran was known to be the main financial supporter of Hezbollah, and although Tehran was hostile to America, at least it was a sovereign government that, unlike the terrorists, might respond to international pressure.

The next day, Shultz learned to his horror that the CIA had communicated (via the Israeli intelligence agency, Mossad) with Prime Minister Peres without the State Department's knowledge, undermining the special channel Hill had established with Netanyahu. Shultz reported the unauthorized back channel to Reagan and did his best to insure that everyone in the White House acknowledged Hill's link with Netanyahu as "the best channel to Peres." The Israelis, for their part, preferred to communicate via Hill. "Charlie, you are the most coveted American personality in our government," an Israeli Foreign Service officer told him, urging that he continue to "talk to us in the embassy." Word had gotten out in Israeli government circles about Hill's conversations with Netanyahu, and the Israelis seemed to think they were getting somewhere. "We went back and forth and back and forth, all offline," Hill said. "Nobody knew about it, or had anything to do with it . . . so that plausibly we could maintain deniability—we could say we were not doing deals. But after long, bitter negotiations with Netanyahu, the two governments agreed that after a decent period of time passed, Israel would release some of the prisoners." Meanwhile a deal was struck with the terrorists—via the Syrian government—to release the hostages in exchange for guarantees on Israel's part regarding the release of the Shia prisoners. No leaks of the agreement reached the press before it was publicly announced. Hill had become thoroughly embittered with the news media over the course of the TWA 847 crisis. In a few lines of reflection written the day the hostages were freed, Hill remarked that the administration's decision to refuse to participate in the media frenzy—after a few hiccups from Larry Speakes—was the most important judgment made throughout the crisis. "The most effective tactic we used was putting the *lid* on any comments by Admin officials," he wrote. "Never since WWII has it been done. It must have been astounding to the terrorists—and alarming to our allies."

Hill code-named his communications with Netanyahu "Nebraska." The State Department had long used an official code system for sensitive business, but there was nothing official about "Nebraska"—no one knew about that code name except for Hill and one or two others. When he was still executive secretary, Hill and colleagues Jock Covey and Jerry Bremer began to make up their own code words to control access to materials. They used the code when they spoke on open phone lines, where anyone could listen. The National Security Agency and other arms of the intelligence community had recently begun to use voice-activated computer programs that monitored open microwave transmissions for key words. "Netanyahu," for example, might have been flagged, but the program would pay no attention to a word like "Nebraska."

Similar code words pepper Hill's notebooks. He was always involved in one or another offline, classified negotiation or project. To some extent any officer with Hill's level of access to the secretary of state could expect a role in back-channel operations, but Hill was involved more than most because the schemes suited his personality. He was perceptive and discreet. He gave away nothing, even in the rare moments when he found himself somehow the focus of attention, like a mirror-eyed cat caught by the flashlight. Most important, if anything good came of his work, he had no care for credit.

It was a given part of the executive assistant's responsibilities to receive numbers of incorrigible "unofficial" — and usually unbidden — ambassadors. These were typically high-powered American businessmen, Washington schemers, think-tank sages, and Capitol Hill staffers who returned from travels abroad carrying "very important secret messages" from one or another foreign insider. Hill, who unlike his predecessors was dependably available in his office at most hours, had to tolerate more of these characters than did most State Department staffers. The vast majority of these supposed breakthrough channels of communication that well-meaning citizens brought to his attention were useless or, at best, only an extra move in the obfuscating game played by the Soviets or regimes in the Middle East. Very rarely, one yielded something more — and the Reagan administration could not afford to brush off any contact that might lead to the release of American hostages. "In general the hostage-taking situation was ongoing, and we were flying blind," Hill remembered. "We didn't have a working embassy in Lebanon, we had no relations with Iran, and hostile connections with Syria and Iraq. So what were we to do here, with Americans being taken?"

His notes record at least one case in which the activist wife of a hostage, in her trips to the region to work toward her husband's release, connected Hill and Shultz with an independent agent who kept in touch with Hill for years. The agent checked in often with tidbits of vague information about the Iranian and Lebanese terrorist networks, but he was most useful as a pair of informed eyes and ears that could travel to places and meet with shadowy characters as no State Department official could do. Increasingly, however, it seemed to Hill that despite the agent's optimistic reports on his meetings with sheikhs and clerics, he would never deliver any progress of consequence. To a historian reviewing Hill's notes of their conversations, the agent's reports seem pollyannaish. In one rosy portrait of the Iranian street he reported that "in a factory, I saw a U.S. flag on the ground—you have to step on it to walk in. Children and old people walked around it. They said they've had enough of it. No fundamental differences [with the United States], as they have with the Communists. Each time [Soviet-supported] Iraq bombs Iran, the Soviet Union is called 'Great Satan.'" Hill always listened, even if he did not act on these accounts. In 2004, long after Hill had left government service and almost fifteen years since he had last had contact with this man, the agent telephoned him to report that he was traveling in the region once again, meeting with his contacts in Lebanon, Syria, and Iraq, and nothing was as terrible as the American media made it out to be. The Iraqi people were excited, energetic, and hopeful to move on with their lives, he said. Hill, who always leaps at any chance to prove the American media wrong, embraced the news, despite the proven biases of his contact. After all, the only way to uphold a grand strategy is to pick and choose one's reality with care.

Hill spent a good portion of his stint as executive assistant engaged in the quiet, backdoor diplomacy that his boss was unable to do, whether because of other commitments, media scrutiny, or both. The case of his link with Israel via Netanyahu during the TWA hijacking suggested that going offline to communicate official to official was often necessary in this age of unrestrained media encroachment upon diplomacy. But as to unofficial agents operating in the Middle East, "you may be getting a minuscule amount of information or intelligence of value, but it's very small, with a great risk of getting yourself into a stupid, deleterious tangle," Hill said. He admitted that the intrigue of it was attractive. "But those things are a waste of time. The reality is that official-to-official, ministry-to-ministry, diplomat-to-diplomat is the right way to do it. All other sideshows are bad."

Hill and Shultz knew this for sure. A particularly poisonous sideshow, a stupid, deleterious tangle that would nearly bring down the White House, was going on right under their noses.

The Iran-Contra affair grew out of two covert foreign policy initiatives created by top officials in the Reagan administration and buttressed by the president's strongest moral and emotional compulsions: his knee-jerk sympathy for "democratic freedom fighters" defying the spread of Communism, and, as past hostage crises had proven, his compassion and commitment to American citizens in trouble. In December 1981 President Reagan authorized a covert Central Intelligence Agency operation to support the Contras, a rebel force in Nicaragua. The Contras were using guerrilla tactics to oppose Marxist president Daniel Ortega and his Sandinista National Liberation Front, which had overthrown dictator Anastasio Somoza and taken power in 1979. Alarmed by the possibility of escalating American involvement in "another Vietnam," Congress moved in 1982 to restrict U.S. aid to the Contras through an amendment to the 1973 War Powers Act proposed by Representative Edward Boland of Massachusetts. The Boland Amendment was riddled with potential loopholes. The National Security Council staff* would try to exploit one ambiguity in particular: the law did not specifically name the NSC staff among the "United States Government intelligence entities" prohibited from helping the Contras.†

Through Israeli intelligence channels and Iranian middlemen, members of the CIA and the NSC staffs arranged arms sales through Israel to "moderates" in Iran who promised to engineer the release of hostages and prepare the way for friendly relations between the United States and the post-Khomeini regime. An operation headed by NSC staffer Oliver North then diverted the arms sales profits to aid the Contras in Nicaragua, along the way depositing some of the money in private Swiss bank accounts.

This was the context of the State Department's deteriorating authority over American foreign policy, the battle for power between State, the White House, and the intelligence community that Hill had long known firsthand. Hill's notebooks document that loss of control, the frustrated efforts to take it back, and the broader question that remained: Why was the NSC staff able to hijack foreign policy in the first place?

---

* Under the National Security Act of 1947, the National Security Council's statutory members are the president; the secretaries of state, defense, army, navy, and air force; and the chairman of the National Security Resources Board. The term "NSC staff" refers not to the official members but to aides in the council's employ. In the context of the Iran-Contra affair, this staff was primarily under the direction of the NSC adviser.
† This "loophole" stands on very shaky ground and has been dismissed by most knowledgeable sources as wishful thinking on the part of the NSC staff. The Boland Amendment was intended to apply to all U.S. government entities, the NSC staff included.

George Shultz was President Reagan's only close adviser who would emerge unscathed from the congressional inquiry into the Iran-Contra affair. Former national security adviser Robert McFarlane would suffer a nervous breakdown and attempt suicide. NSC adviser John Poindexter, Chief of Staff Don Regan, and Secretary of Defense Caspar Weinberger would resign. Central Intelligence Agency Director William Casey was to die of a brain tumor when the investigation was barely under way. Shultz, however, had the benefit of his executive assistant's voluminous notebooks. When a member of the NSC staff challenged a claim Shultz made in his testimony, Hill's contemporaneous notes were usually ample refutation—Shultz's enemies "realized there was powerful evidence to support a story they were reluctant to tell."

Unlike the secretary's reputation, the practice of good record keeping in government would not survive the scandal. The Iran-Contra affair heralded the coming of an age in which all records—from Post-it notes to electronic mail—would be discoverable under law. All citizens, top government officials most of all, began to think carefully before committing anything to paper or hard drive. The investigation would prove that the wrongdoers in Iran-Contra did not let history unfold behind them. They actively administered the historical record and kept most of it "plausibly deniable." Charles Hill's notebooks are the last relics of the classical diplomat's devotion to a thorough written record. Thereafter no one would keep notes like his.

The first inklings of the Iran initiative appear in Hill's notes from the summer of 1985, just before the TWA hijacking. On June 1, State Department staffer Jock Covey told Hill that an NSC consultant named Michael Ledeen had asked national security adviser Robert McFarlane for permission to travel to Israel to explore a lead on possible Israeli intelligence connections in Iranian domestic politics. Hill and his colleagues had never taken Ledeen very seriously. Hill recalled that "Ledeen would call me infrequently and say something opaque—he was just being a mystery man—like 'Charlie, something's happening . . .' —and I would say, 'Thanks Michael,' and hang up. He was one of a large number of people who . . . drop out of Ph.D. programs, don't get tenure, but they get into Washington politics as staff aides and wheel and deal around town . . . Michael was one of these, but he was especially involved in international intrigue, and it was a joke, because he was being more intrigue-ridden than the world really is."

Hill may have rolled his eyes at Ledeen's phone calls, but the NSC adviser gave this "mystery man" a plane ticket and authorization to tell the Israelis "we want to plug into your product." When Hill and Shultz discussed McFarlane's meddling in talks with the Israelis and his authorization of Ledeen's trips, Shultz remarked that McFarlane was probably pursuing the connections through private parties and "cutting out the Ambassador, making him look foolish. This all goes back to Bud's [McFarlane's] notion that the NSC should be the center of foreign policy." Hill's offline channels in the Middle East were acceptable to Shultz because Hill reported directly to him, satisfying the secretary's notion of the proper chain of command. One always feels more favorably toward back channels when one is in control of them.

In July 1985, while Shultz and his staff were traveling in Australia, McFarlane cabled that an Israeli emissary had informed him of contacts in Iran who, according to Hill's notes, "were confident that they cld [could] achieve the release of the 7 hostg [hostages]. They sought some gain in return: 100 TOWS* from Israel — but the larger purpose wld [would] be the opening of the private dialogue w[ith] a high level American official and a sustained discussion of US-Iranian relations." Shultz told Hill to "do a cautiously positive reply to say ok." He and his aides were skeptical that the channel would lead to anything, but they agreed it would be irresponsible to reject out of hand a chance to secure the release of hostages. The recent experience of TWA 847 suggested that some conversation with unsavory characters might be a necessary fact of life. Later that day, Shultz wired a hesitant message to McFarlane suggesting "a tentative show of interest without commitment." He agreed that they should convey interest in private dialogue, but he reminded McFarlane of "the fraud that seems to accompany so many deals involving arms and Iran."

At a meeting after Shultz returned to Washington, McFarlane told him that after several conversations with his contact in Israel, Foreign Ministry Director General David Kimche, as well as with a cadre of anonymous Iranians, he believed the time was ripe for overtures toward "moderates" in Iran. Hill recorded: "Irans [Iranians] see IR [Iran] in shambles. See new govt as inevitable. Mil[itary] + people still pro-American. Want a dialogue w[ith] Amers [Americans]. Want arms from

---

* A guided antitank missile system. The acronym stands for Tube-launched, Optically-tracked, Wire-guided Missile Weapon System.

us. Want 100 TOWs from Israel. All totally deniable. Say they can produce 4 or more hostg [hostages]. Want a meeting somewhere. So Bud
is pursuing it." The deal McFarlane described was a trade of arms for
hostages, "totally deniable" to supervising bodies such as Congress.
Hill was candid about his opinion: "We are being had. Isr[ael] desperate for a big arms trade relationship w[ith] Ir[an] that the U.S. permits.
They have finally hit on a way to do it." Shultz agreed the sale was a
mistake and told McFarlane that the deal had to be stopped. That same
day, unbeknown to Shultz and his staff, McFarlane briefed the president on the Israeli proposal to sell American missiles to Iran via Israel.
McFarlane later claimed the president personally approved the sale.
Reagan agreed with McFarlane's claim at first but later said he could
not remember. On August 20, 1985, Israel shipped ninety-six antitank
missiles to Iran. No hostages were released.

The opposition of Shultz and his aides gave McFarlane and company incentive to cut them almost totally out of the information loop.
When the subject of the arms sales did arise in meetings or telephone
conversations — Hill's notes indicate this happened intermittently —
Shultz and his staff continued to express their disapproval but sensed
their arguments fell on deaf ears in the White House and on the NSC
staff. By autumn Shultz felt "as though my standing in this administration is less than zero." Nearly every conversation with McFarlane left
him feeling uneasy and isolated. He mused about resigning.*

Although 1985 witnessed three shipments of American arms to
Iran through Israel, it is not clear from Hill's notes whether Shultz
and his staff knew that either sale was consummated. While Shultz
believed McFarlane's operation — which Hill dubbed "Nightowl" and
"Bud's Folly"† in his notes — should be stopped, judging by the scraps
of information he received, he later told the congressional committee
that he thought McFarlane had been unsuccessful so far. However,
Hill's notes indicate the secretary had evidence that McFarlane was serious about the arms sales, that the sales were involved in negotiating
the release of American hostages, and that the NSC staff was not

---

* Hill note, November 12, 1985. Shultz threatened to resign multiple times during his
tenure as secretary of state. The first was in 1983 after discovering no one had informed
him of a secret trip McFarlane made to the Middle East.
† After the November 1986 revelations revealed Oliver North's role and the diversion of
arms sales profits to the Contras, Hill referred to both operations under the code name
"Polecat."

telling him everything. In mid-November he remarked to Hill that "Bud asked Cap [Secretary of Defense Caspar Weinberger] how to get 600 HAWKS* + 200 Phoenix† to Iran. Its highly illegal. Cap won't do it I'm sure. Purpose not clear. Another sign of funny stuff on the Iran issue. Pdx [Poindexter] not leveling w[ith] me." In December, when Poindexter told him that the most recent attempt to coordinate an arms sale and hostage release had foundered but that the president still backed the initiative,‡ Shultz told Hill his strategy was to "let them [the NSC staff] post me. I will not pursue or ask. But will take over when it gets messy."

Investigators would later criticize Shultz for failing to ferret out the facts of the Iran operation, suggesting he was more concerned with keeping his own record spotless than stopping the arms sales. Hill's notes indicate that Shultz did object to being left uninformed, and whenever McFarlane or Poindexter raised the subject, he said he was emphatically against it. A December telephone conversation that Shultz had with new NSC adviser John Poindexter, recorded by Hill,§ reveals the secretary's frame of mind:

(1505)# I am basically uninformed although Bud told me about it at the start + I sd [said] no. ##### Does that require notific[ation] to Congr[ess]? # What does a TOW do? #### (1517) ##### This is far more info than I ever had before. I have been skeptical about this op[eration] + uncomfortable from the start. If we can better our rels [relations] w[ith] Iran that's clearly desirable. Separate from hostg [hostage] deal. This is paying for hostg [hostages]—so we have broken our principles . . . If—+ when—it leaks, fact we have broken our principle will be clear + our effort to bloc[k] arms from others to Iran will be seen to be perfidious. But we have gone so far that I think no

---

* Surface-to-air missiles. The acronym stands for Homing All the Way Killer. The HAWK missile system has been the Marine Corps' primary method of air defense since the early 1960s.

† A radar-guided, air-to-air weapon. The Phoenix is the navy's primary fleet air defense long-range weapon for the F-14 Tomcat fighter and is one of the world's most technologically sophisticated tactical missiles.

‡ On November 24–25, the CIA arranged to ship 18 HAWK missiles from Israel to Iran. Iran rejected the missiles, saying they did not meet Iran's requirements. Hill note, December 9, 1985.

§ Hill recorded the time the conversation occurred, as well as how much time had passed at regular intervals, in military time (i.e., [1505]). He used the symbol # to indicate speech by the party on the other end of the line.

way but to go on. But I am very uncomfortable with it all. ### That's subterfuge. And Isr[aelis] have incentive to leak this. They want to sell to Iran + we have been banging on them not to. It's one probl[em] w Iraq. In long run working w Iran is important (1530) ## all right. I'll be there at 10 Sat [for a meeting with the president]. This thing has got to be stopped . . . ### We've been upset by being cut out of cable traffic.

Shultz was worried about congressional notification, but he knew the president could make the arms sales legal simply by signing a piece of paper. He was more concerned about breaching American policy against selling arms to a nation that sponsored terrorism or negotiating with terrorists for the release of hostages. Shultz had spent most of his tenure as secretary of state trying to convince other nations to adopt this policy. The idea that his own government might be flouting it alarmed him. But Poindexter, who had just replaced McFarlane as NSC adviser, insisted the emphasis of the arms sales negotiations was on building a relationship with Iranian moderates who might lead Iran after the Ayatollah—not on the release of hostages. For the moment, Shultz was unconvinced, but he believed Poindexter would keep the State Department informed. Poindexter stopped short of telling Shultz that on that very same day, President Reagan had signed a Covert Action Finding authorizing an arms shipment to Iran.

The Iran initiative was worrisome to Shultz and his aides but by no means all-consuming. Most of Hill's notes dart across the myriad of other foreign policy issues the State Department faced at the time, such as the Middle East peace process and the upcoming summits with the Soviets. Relative to other foreign policy concerns there is strikingly little discussion in Hill's notes of the arms sales to Iran, and there is almost no mention of the Contra funding project. Hill's notes do indicate more contact between the State Department and the arms sales than the secretary would later volunteer under oath. But of the thousands of pages of notes Hill took during this time frame, only several dozen entries are relevant to the Iran arms initiative. This context does not negate what Shultz and his aides did know about the operation, but it may confirm what they would later tell investigators: they lacked the information to understand the scheme and had little time to focus on its shadows.

The arms initiative continued to move ahead with President Reagan's explicit approval. Hill's notes suggest that even in cases when the secretary was never told outright that the arms deals went through, he often had enough information to surmise they may have. By the summer of 1986 Hill and Shultz were concerned enough about the NSC staff's operations to begin brainstorming possible means of wresting control of backdoor communications with Iran. In a notebook entry headlined "a way out of Polecat," Hill recorded a plan to use the Pakistani foreign minister, Sahabzada Yaqub Khan, as a channel to the Iranians. Failing that, the Japanese government had expressed interest in serving as an intermediary. "This would get the Iran business out of the Ollie North/McFarlane channel," Shultz observed hopefully. They were grasping at straws. A few days later one of Shultz's staff raised the question of CIA channels to Iranian middlemen reportedly close to Khomeini and Imam Musa al-Sadr, the uncle of the infamous Moqtada al-Sadr, whose militia would cause American forces in Iraq so much anguish almost twenty years later. But Hill predicted that the CIA link was already a corrupt "outgrowth of Polecat." He was right. State Department efforts at reasserting control amounted to nothing. By the first day of November, when Shultz and Hill got word of another arms-for-hostages exchange, Hill's notebook entry sounded angry and somewhat resigned: "we provide wpns [weapons] for Iran as part of the [hostage] deal (so we are as bad as the French in dealing with the terrorists)," he wrote. "It *reeks*. Let WH [White House] do the press guidance on it. S[hultz] has deliberately kept uninformed about it." Maybe Hill sensed that within days the entire operation was to crash down upon them.

On the afternoon of November 4, 1986, Shultz, Hill, and the rest of his staff were in flight somewhere over the Atlantic, en route to a conference of foreign ministers in Vienna. The mood was tense. The rumor was already buzzing among reporters in the back of the plane that the White House was trading arms to terrorists in exchange for hostages,* and the secretary was shut out of it. News of the arms sales had begun to break only the day before. A Lebanese weekly, *Al Shiraa*, published an exposé of covert missile sales by the United States to Iran, describing a particular mission in May of that year by McFarlane. The story was that McFarlane and three other Americans had arrived secretly in

---

* In some cases, the "moderates" in Iran made good on their word. Reverend Lawrence Jenco's release in July 1986, for example, was the result of a $24 million arms sale.

Tehran on a plane carrying military equipment. They carried Irish passports and brought as gifts a Bible signed by President Reagan and a chocolate cake made in the shape of a key—baked to symbolize the "key to Iranian-American friendship." Revolutionary guards at the airport poked fun at the cake, then devoured it.

During his regular mid-flight press conference, Shultz said little and directed all questions to the White House. He sent an angry cable to NSC adviser Poindexter in which he stressed the need to get all the facts out. The next day, Poindexter's reply proved that reporters' conjectures about a cover-up were right: "Thank you for providing me with your perspective on our problems with Iran. I share your desire to find a way to prevent further speculation and leaks about U.S. policy in Iran . . . At some point we will have to lay out all the facts . . . I do not believe that now is the time to give the facts to the public."

Even before their aircraft touched down at Andrews Air Force Base, Shultz told Hill and Executive Secretary Nick Platt to begin reviewing what he had known about the operation and when he had known it. According to Hill, the mid-flight effort to reconstruct a chronology was not an attempt at self-defense. They were not worried about protesting the secretary's innocence. "We were not thinking that way," Hill said. "The issues were first, that McFarlane and Poindexter had actually carried out this stupid thing, and we were stunned. Second, it was disastrous for our anti-terrorism policy. Third, it could do vast damage to the Presidency, because the opposition would try to turn it into another Watergate. Our view was 'here's what we knew, that's the best we can do'—not to say Shultz is innocent, but to say he opposed it because it was wrong . . . and all the information should come out."

No historians have ever reviewed Hill's notes before. If they did, they would probably have a hard time understanding how Shultz and his aides could have been stunned by the extent of the arms sales to Iran. I myself felt this way initially. Hill has explained repeatedly in interviews that in the bustle of their daily work, brief conversations with the NSC adviser—which clearly spell out arms deals when culled from his notebooks and read together, with the benefit of hindsight—simply did not register as they should have at the time. "It's not an excuse, but it's a fact of life," Hill explained. "The stuff goes by you like the flashbulb of some camera . . . [the Iran initiative] just wasn't in the forefront of our thinking."

To the historian, several entries in Hill's notes seem particularly unforgettable—such as the news from McFarlane and Poindexter in December 1985 that a shipment of missiles might have prompted the release of a hostage three months earlier, or President Reagan's explicit authorization of the extension of "Polecat" in the January 1986 NSC meeting. Such reports, no matter how brief, still meant a major breach of U.S. policy. If Shultz and his aides were stunned when they heard about McFarlane's covert trip to Tehran, why weren't they disturbed enough by earlier hints of the operation to begin keeping track of the snippets McFarlane and Poindexter provided and draw the story together? "Whatever the record shows, we were shocked," Hill said.*

The secretary continued to duck questions. He said he had not asked to be cut out entirely but had requested that McFarlane and Poindexter tell him only what he needed to know in order to do his job. After all, the White House was concerned about leaks of sensitive material, and the easiest way to curb leaks was to limit the transmission of information. But Hill told Shultz that "the line of not saying anything won't last much longer." He was already working with Platt and the State Department's legal counsel Abraham Sofaer to build a chronology of the secretary's knowledge of the arms sales so that he could answer some of the media's pressing questions. While Platt kept notes as well, Hill's notes were the most voluminous of the materials they used. The chronology they wrote was to serve as the basis for the secretary's interview with Attorney General Edwin Meese and, later, for his interview with the Tower Commission† and his testimony before the congressional committees. Hill could not take time off from his regular duties to comb through thousands of pages of notes for references to the arms deals. He has said that because in the preliminary investigations no one insinuated any wrongdoing by the secretary—people be-

---

* Charles Hill, March 1, 2003. Hill's explanation of the State Department's surprise at the extent of the Iran-Contra scandal evokes Roberta Wohlstetter's "signals versus noise" argument in *Pearl Harbor: Warning and Decision* (Stanford, Calif.: Stanford University Press, 1962). Wohlstetter writes that the Japanese attack on Pearl Harbor was presaged by many signals, but these were obscured by contradictory and competing information, or "noise." "To discriminate among significant sounds against this background of noise, one has to be listening for something or for one of several things," she writes. "In short, one needs not only an ear, but a variety of hypotheses that guide observation." (56)

† Named for its chairman, Senator John Tower of Texas, the commission was appointed immediately after the scandal and issued its report in early 1987.

lieved Shultz when he said he opposed the arms sales from the start—
he did not feel pressed to comb through every page for evidence to buttress his boss's reputation. Rather than go through the notes page by
page, he focused his review on the meetings or conversations Shultz
remembered on his own. If the aim of keeping notes in the first place
is to compensate for the gaps in faulty human memory, Hill's review
strategy seems flawed, but the basic fact is that he had no time. He
knew there had been other unremembered moments when the Iran
initiative came up in conversation, and the notes cited above indicate
some of those entries referenced specific arms shipments and presidential approval. But at the time Hill's recollection was that "the other
references were pretty unmeaningful, i.e., 'Bud says it's still alive.'"

In late November, while the attorney general was finishing his inquiry, the Justice Department issued a call for all records pertaining
to the scandal. When Hill briefed Sofaer about the relevant notes he
had collected, one entry in particular caught Sofaer's attention: Hill's
record of a November 1985 conversation between Shultz and McFarlane in which McFarlane told him HAWK missiles were to be shipped
to Iran in exchange for hostages. During the briefing, a CIA official arrived with a copy of the testimony CIA Director William Casey planned
to deliver before the congressional committees the next day. Reading
the draft, Sofaer noticed that Casey was planning to claim that the NSC
staff and the CIA thought the November 1985 shipment contained oil-
drilling equipment, not weapons. Sofaer also noticed that the airline
that transported the missiles, Southern Air Transport, was the same
company whose cargo plane had been shot down over Nicaragua while
carrying supplies to the Contras only a month earlier. "To me," he said,
"it was a red flag indicating a possible connection to Central America."

Sofaer told Hill he wanted to contact the attorney general with his
concerns about Casey's proposed testimony. Hill, who was worried
about granting Sofaer free rein with his notes, agreed only "with great
apprehension." After Attorney General Meese brushed off Sofaer's suspicions, and Assistant Attorney General Charles Cooper showed him
a sworn statement from Oliver North denying that he or anyone else
on the NSC or CIA staffs had known the shipment contained missiles,
Sofaer produced Hill's contemporaneous note. According to Sofaer,
Cooper "expressed shock in a way that would not be polite in a public
record."

The revelation of Hill's note—and the Contra connection that Sofaer had surmised—set off a quiet panic in the White House and

changed the tenor of the attorney general's investigation. At a press conference five days later, Meese announced the diversion of arms sales profits to the Contras. It is possible that the attempted cover-up might have succeeded, at least for a time, if Sofaer had not been so dogged in pursuing it. Hill had not opposed disclosing the November 18 note in particular; he certainly saw the necessity of forcing Casey to correct his testimony. He was worried, rather, about the fate of his entire collection of notebooks once Sofaer got excited and the investigators got wind. He noted his reaction to the possibility that investigators would seize the whole corpus of his notes, much of which was sensitive material unrelated to the arms sales: "CH [Charles Hill] raises hell. Stop Abe [Sofaer] for shit's sake!" Although Sofaer was negotiating with representatives from the FBI and assured Hill the "notebooks will not be taken out of your possession," Hill was worried that persons who read his record would not understand the difference between clear hindsight and the reality of top-level diplomacy, with its layers of simultaneous international crises and bureaucratic chaos.

When Sofaer saw the chronology Hill and Platt had prepared from their notes, he questioned whether Shultz ought to testify before Congress at all. They had given relevant records to the FBI, and public testimony would be damaging, he said:

> A mistake to give the testimony. Revelations are spectacular. Not analytic. Porno material. Jagged. Not thoughtful. Public articulation would raise real question of law and ethics. You can't quote from secret cables and NSDD [National Security Decision Directive] drafts. P[resident] has released you from executive privilege but not from the need to keep sensitive things within the Admin. And you reveal intelligence sources and methods. And the story you tell will temporarily distract attention and satisfy press's crude need for sensationalism. But an incomplete story . . . Doesn't say why you failed to act. Doesn't tell your view of P's knowledge at critical points or his statements. You have no added rationale for making this statement on Monday. No utility to it. You have given it to the FBI. You would be making a statement that separates you from P when he is coming closer to you . . . You would be defending yourself at P's expense. And it is an inadequate effort to explain your role as it raises more questions than it resolves.

Sofaer was an attorney by training, and Shultz was a client he had to defend. He had reconstructed a narrative from the chronology of Hill's scattered notebook references to the Iran initiative, and he thought that narrative would hurt his client. Shultz, however, was outraged by Poindexter's proposed cover-up, and he argued for getting his side of the story out: "Charlie and I smelled an arms deal from the very first we heard of it. Not fair to say I was cut out and deceived," he said. "I was an advocate of saying that info should be confined to those who need to know. I had to assume that a Constitutional* officer like Pdx [Poindexter] or North would act properly. An assumption I was entitled to make." Shultz wanted to tell everything he had known about the arms sales as a matter of honesty. And although the advantages of claiming ignorance were obvious, Shultz probably had no desire to appear foolish and impotent.

Hill disagreed with both men. He believed the narrative Sofaer had constructed was dangerous not because it was "porno material," but because it did not reflect reality. Sofaer's narrative implied reasoned links among the fragments of information that Shultz and his aides simply had not understood at the time:

> CH: (Shrieks! Abe trying to put picture together from current NYT [*New York Times*] and S[hultz] contemporaneous record. Stop!) . . . *Shriek!*
> Sofaer takes CH chronology of S record and balloons it up to point where it is virtually coextensive with the documents — why not just transcribe the documents and hand them over? This is not a court. Abe is handling this like tomorrow is the first day of a 9-month-long criminal prosecution of Ariel Sharon.

Sofaer was using the series of Iran initiative snippets harvested from Hill's notes to construct Shultz's testimony in the same way that newspaper reporters were trying to pull together a clear sequence of events for their readers. But Shultz and his aides had never understood the piecemeal information they received as a coherent story. When Hill reviewed his notes, "the most astonishing thing was that when you went back, you'd see things that you didn't see until you scooped them all together . . . but now Abe had the chronology and he was telling Shultz 'you knew A, B, and C,' and Shultz was saying, 'Ah yes, I guess I did,' and I was saying, 'No, you didn't.'"

---

* This word is illegible in Hill's notes. If Shultz did indeed refer to Poindexter and North as "Constitutional officers," he was mistaken, because the Constitution makes no provision for the NSC adviser or his staff.

Hill's notes presented a unique interpretive problem because, for the most part, they were hand-recorded transcripts of casual conversation. Therefore they did not fit neatly into either the category of written text or spoken word. His notes were both forms of speech at once, and yet not really either one. Comprehension of oral speech is not just a matter of processing words; the listener has the advantage of vocal tone, gesture, and environment to help him understand the speaker's meaning. A writer putting words to paper knows his reader is without these aids and so contextualizes his ideas to help the reader understand. The reader of Hill's notes is without either set of clues, and Hill probably feared the consequences. The director of the FBI, William Webster, agreed to let Hill meet with agents and go through relevant notes he had found, explaining the context of each entry as he went along. The meeting lasted an hour and a half. Afterward, Hill noted that the agents were "astounded at the detail of fact" in his notes. There was "much that was new to them. [They] said, personally, 'if only the WH [White House] had taken the Shultz advice.'"

For the purposes of piecing together Iran-Contra, Hill's notebooks were as capable of distorting as clarifying. One is reminded of the curse of Ireneo Funes in Jorge Luis Borges's short story "Funes, the Memorious." In the story, Funes is known "for certain peculiarities such as avoiding contact with people and always knowing what time it was, like a clock." He would sound familiar to anyone who knew the noiseless executive assistant or glanced through Hill's finely calibrated notebooks, every page marked with the hour and minute. After a throw from a horse paralyzes Funes, brain damage turns his memory into a "garbage heap." His mind was less organized than Hill's stacks of notebooks, but like the note taker, doomed to remember everything: "not only every leaf of every tree in every wood, but also every one of the times he had perceived or imagined it." Such a boundless memory, without any means of navigation, dissolves the rememberer's grasp of reality. Funes effortlessly amassed details, learning foreign languages with ease, but "he was not very capable of thinking. To think is to forget differences, to generalize, make abstractions. In the teeming world of Funes, there were only details, almost immediate in their presence."

In Hill's notebooks lay an ocean of details. They would drown the outside reader in misperceptions. Years later, such readers would drag Hill and Shultz down with them.

.   .   .

The testimony that Shultz gave the next day in an open hearing before the congressional committees was not as revelatory as one might expect, given the heated argument that preceded it. Shultz's testimony—which both won him sympathy and provoked accusations of disloyalty to the president—focused more on what he did not know than on what he knew. Generally, his audience was approving. Senator Daniel Inouye, the Democrat from Hawaii who headed the Senate committee, said Shultz came across "very clearly, very credibly, very clear and bright." In pointed contrast to Poindexter's testimony, which was fraught with "memory lapses," Inouye observed that "Mr. Shultz doesn't hesitate in his recollection." Hill's notes do not record a happy ending to the battle over the testimony, but its positive reception suggests that Hill won a few of his points.

Shultz's testimony succeeded because Hill controlled most of the material used to write it. Years after Shultz and Hill had left office, independent counsel Lawrence Walsh would seize Hill's notebooks and publish glaring omissions in the notes Hill had supplied for Shultz's testimony. Walsh would devote nearly a whole chapter of his final report to arguing that Hill withheld evidence. There he sets forth a compelling case that not only were Hill's exclusions responsible for significant errors in Shultz's testimony, but that Hill *intended* to omit relevant entries—the omissions were not an accidental result of the rushed review process, as Hill claimed. Hill wrote down entries of interest and thoughts that struck him as he was reviewing his notebooks in late 1986, and in examining these notes on notes, the independent counsel found references to Iran-related entries that Hill did not include in the final compilation he provided the FBI. For example, a note from November 10, 1986, references the entry regarding the connection between an earlier arms sale and the release of hostages Rev. Lawrence Jenco and Terry Anderson of the Associated Press:

From CH [Charles Hill] notebooks
7/28 *Jenco* release (July) was Polecat $24m [$24 million] in wpns [weapons.] next will be [Terry] Anderson

The fact that Hill included this entry in his personal review of the notes, but did not include it in his final compilation, suggests he made a conscious decision to withhold it. Hill defended omissions like these by claiming that he had either simply made a mistake in his review or decided some notes were based on rumor and not sufficiently reliable. He added that many of the notes did not reflect action on Shultz's part, and his "impression before the testimony was that [Shultz] wanted to confine himself to what he had actually done." All these excuses may be valid in some instances, but not in the case of the Jenco information, which Hill used in preparing talking points for Shultz's meeting with the president two days later.

Sofaer, when asked whether Hill had done wrong, said Hill met his legal responsibilities by preserving all notes and making them available to investigators upon request. But he believes Hill ought to have been more careful when he collected relevant entries. Sofaer said he and Shultz were under the impression that the chronology Hill gave them was all-inclusive. They treated the excerpts he provided as "the Bible," and were surprised to learn they were incomplete. He explained the gaps by citing a fact of Hill's personality: "Charlie's not a humble guy. He might have said to himself, 'this is what happened, these are the things that were important. I'm going to give them all these things, and these other things weren't important.' I wouldn't be surprised if Charlie made that judgment."

Today, Hill's students at Yale admire his integrity as much as his colleagues in the State Department did, and this is an important reason for his effectiveness as a teacher. But another reason why students flock to his office hours and carefully trace his chalkboard diagrams into their notebooks is the quality that Sofaer describes: Hill's ability to subtly control the facts of an argument so that, by the end of his line of reasoning, it is nearly impossible to disagree with him. Hill honed this persuasive skill over the course of his diplomatic career. His ability to translate his editorialized version of fact into a conclusive logic chain was a central reason for his rise to the highest tier of the Foreign Service. This was why Shultz hired him and why Hill was an outstanding adviser and an invaluable asset in the aftermath of Iran-Contra.

The fact remains that the professor whom so many of today's students see as a paragon of ethical judgment did, whatever his rationalizations, withhold evidence from federal investigators. Hill would claim that—like the Yale students who don't buy into the mission of the Grand Strategy class—those who accused him of willfully concealing evidence in the Iran-Contra investigation were those who did not "get it." On this point, Oliver North and Bud McFarlane might have agreed with him. The question then becomes: Who is the more dangerous, those who fail to get it, or those who are certain they are the only ones who do?

• • •

It is true Hill was pressed for time when he reviewed his notebooks, and he did not conduct a comprehensive examination. It is also true that he knew Shultz and his aides had argued against the NSC staff's initiative all along and could have probably done no more with the little information and access they had. Moreover, they were shocked when the full story came out. For Hill, this was the essential "truth" of the State Department's role in Iran-Contra. Had investigators examined every single note relevant to the Iran initiative, Hill feared that entries like those cited above — information and events that Shultz and his staff lost track of or could do nothing to change — would take on meanings that they did not have at the time they occurred and could distort the State Department's role. The adviser to the prince, whose very reason for relentless note taking was to empower the Great Man he served, had in the end produced a document of missed opportunities and impotence. He decided to neuter the record so that the details he had worked so hard to capture could not be turned upon him.

The question of which is more "true" — a historical record that includes all available facts or an account of what decision makers knew and believed at the time of their actions — would dog Hill long after the Iran-Contra affair. In Shultz's memoir of his tenure as secretary of state, Hill and Shultz deliberately confined the narrative to what Shultz knew in the moment, often excluding facts that came to light afterward. Policy analyst Theodore Draper criticized this approach in his review of the memoir, asserting Shultz's account was "hopelessly distorted" and "untrustworthy." Hill and Draper engaged in a hostile exchange of letters to the editor of the *New York Review of Books,* in which Hill defended the memoir as a unique historical document that "reveals a reality that 'memoirs' invariably obscure: decisions of statecraft must be taken on the basis of partial and sometimes erroneous reports." Draper retorted that "what Shultz knew at the time" is distinct from a truthful historical record. Perhaps the two categories of knowledge are distinct, but in an accurate memoir they should not be mutually exclusive.

In the memoir and in his notebook review for the Iran-Contra investigation, Hill tried to tell a story that an all-inclusive string of facts would not convey. In the case of the notebooks, it is hard to determine whether his approach was a conscious decision or simply his instinctive sense of what really happened. Regardless, Hill's impulse to filter his record raises the question of why so many signals of the NSC staff's operation went undetected by Shultz and his aides. How could the secretary of state, the most important foreign policy official in the U.S. government, have been so disengaged from a major operation that he was reduced to arguing in vain against schemes he only vaguely understood?

The State Department had suffered marginalization before. During World War II, Franklin Roosevelt ran his foreign policy through an informal assembly of loyal aides, routinely bypassing Secretary of State Cordell Hull. With the rise of the Central Intelligence Agency following World War II, ambassadors were sometimes cut out of intelligence traffic sent from CIA headquarters in Langley, Virginia, to CIA station chiefs in embassies abroad via side channels that used the embassies' cable equipment but were handled by CIA technicians. During the Nixon administration, diplomatic wizard Henry Kissinger hijacked this system, using it routinely for his own diplomatic traffic. The existence of unofficial side channels was no secret. Heads of state and their appointees had been using them for years. What made the Iran-Contra affair disturbing was that in this case, the back channels did not depend on the president's personal authority and discretion. Instead, control of the initiative lay in the hands of an anonymous, unaccountable staff that could bypass all constitutional safeguards and run their own policy from a separate communications center. The Reagan NSC staff's operation had no precedent. Oliver North was a lowly staffer to the NSC adviser. Michael Ledeen was a freelance consultant with no formal staff position. Yet they had manipulated the most powerful government in the world. It was a bureaucratic coup d'état.

A simple fact of geography goes a long way toward explaining the NSC staff's control over information that reached Reagan: the NSC adviser's suite was right down the hall from the Oval Office. While Shultz worked in a separate building and had to make an appointment to meet with Reagan, Poindexter and McFarlane had frequent, informal access. Moreover, recent political disagreements had cooled Shultz's relationship with the president. Some Washington observers believed the discord began with Shultz's decision to replace many of the president's political appointees with career Foreign Service officers like Hill. From Hill's perspective, Shultz's and Reagan's "wavelengths started to diverge" in February 1986, when Shultz had to work hard to convince the president to urge his old anti-Communist ally, Ferdinand Marcos, to step down from power in the Philippines. The White House and the

NSC staff stepped into the breach. They began deriding Shultz and the State Department at meetings, interfering in an increasing number of foreign policy issues, and in general trying "to demonstrate how important they were and how they could overrule State."

Shultz and Hill were intensely loyal to Reagan. Even after the disastrous press conference on November 19, 1986, in which the president misstated key facts about prior arms shipments and denied that other countries were involved, they viewed him as a tragic hero, not a villain like McFarlane or Poindexter. He remained, to Hill, one of the twentieth century's transcendent Great Men. In "historical notes" Hill recorded in his notebook a few days after the conference, he wrote that the scandal was

> 1. a tragedy (near) in the real sense. Not like overused word for plane crashes. Hero who achieves, but is flawed. And flaw brings him down. His aides did not protect him against his flaw, they played on it (concern for hostages).
> 2. a pattern seen in the past. (King Henry and Becket)* The leader says ok boys, let's see some results. So they produce results—but don't tell him how they got them.

Reagan may have been a "tragic hero" motivated primarily by concern for Americans in trouble. But it is almost certain that Reagan understood and approved of more of the operation than Hill wanted to believe. Reagan fulfilled most of Hill's Great Man requirements. The president's firm worldview was "a deeply pondered, well thought-out product of a silent dialogue" with himself. To the eternal frustration of Reagan's opponents (and plenty of his advisers), he governed with a "calm certainty" that his approach to humankind's affairs was always the correct one. But Reagan lacked the counterbalancing trait that Hill

---

* In 1162 King Henry II named as archbishop Thomas à Becket, his loyal adviser and the archdeacon of Canterbury. But when Becket interfered with Henry's attempts to extend his court's jurisdiction over the Church, legend has it that he shouted in a rage, "What sluggards, what cowards have I brought up in my court, who care nothing for their allegiance to their lord. Who will rid me of this meddlesome priest?" His words inspired four knights to murder Becket by splitting his skull with their swords while he knelt at the altar in Canterbury Cathedral. The death of Becket distressed the king, who may not have intended anyone to take his outburst literally. Several miracles were reported at Becket's crypt, and he was soon canonized. Four years later, the king atoned for his sin by donning a sackcloth and trudging barefoot through the streets of Canterbury while eighty monks flogged him with branches.

had observed in leaders like Henry Kissinger and Menachem Begin. He had little sensitivity to criticism. He was never bothered by contrary points of view. His self-confidence — some might call it obliviousness — was unassailable. Reagan was a Great Man, but he was the most dangerous kind.

The president's self-assurance combined with his work habits to exacerbate the disconnection between the State Department and the White House. The hypotheses that have come out over the past decade suggesting that Reagan may have been suffering from Alzheimer's disease while he was still in office are too numerous and disputed to discuss here. Regardless of medical diagnosis, Reagan was isolated from the daily business of policy planning. In February 1987 Shultz remarked to Hill that he had heard "people around P say he has lost it. Not in real contact." A few days later, after a conversation with Chief of Staff Don Regan, he elaborated:

> I asked DR how P operates. Don talked for long time. He feels frustrated + alarmed. P is detached. We have good pkg [package] on welfare + catastrophe ins. [insurance] + on competitiveness. But P *hasn't read any of it. He's not in it.* His work schedule is start at 0900. Meets DR + VP [Vice President Bush] on days sched[uled], FC [new NSC adviser Frank Carlucci] at 0930 for 20 mins . . . Meetings at 1100 like NSPG [National Security Planning Group]. 12 sharp lunch. Once in a wk w VP — other than that he's alone at lunch. We tried an issues lunch or outsiders but didn't register much. Then once a week a cabinet mtg. Then mid aft [afternoon] Admin time: photo ops. [opportunities] Day ends 1630. Back to Residence . . . He spends *huge* amt of time watchg [watching] TV. That's where he gets his info. He doesn't have content in his mind beyond a few minutes. He's not really working at the job + not in touch w reality. It's a lousy picture . . .
> I sd a Pres has resp. [responsibility] Can't be P + not work hard than that. He sd NR [Nancy Reagan] watches sched avidly + won't let him do much.
> So a picture of *nothing much.*
> But you can't stand w a Pres who won't work. Someone has to get him to go to work.
> CH: He won't shift his views on Iran + he won't suddenly start to work. He's *beyond* stubbornness.

The fact that a description of Reagan's work habits was secondhand information to Shultz is further proof of his distance from the president. If this is an accurate portrait of Reagan's daily routine, it is easy to understand why it was hard for Shultz to get through to him. There were logistical obstacles: unlike Shultz and his aides, who arrived at work well before 8 A.M. and often stayed nearly to midnight, the president spent comparatively little time in his office. He did not read all briefs prepared for him. Don Regan's description hardly portrays the "Great Man of ideas" that Hill typically admired, but President Reagan was well known for having reasoned out his positions on major policy issues well before he took office. Perhaps there was something appealing to Hill in a leader who appeared to have fused ideas with instinct. But Regan's account suggests that any information that contradicted what Reagan already believed was often a hard sell. The NSC adviser's duplicity notwithstanding, formal channels of communication between the State Department and the president could work only if Reagan was easy to reach, open to what the secretary had to say, and plugged into accurate and thorough intelligence. He was none of these things.

The NSC staff was empowered by President Reagan's personal leadership style, but they were able to take control of foreign policy because they were quick to harness the broader development that disoriented and frustrated many of their colleagues: the rise of the Information Age. Shultz recognized early in his tenure that technology was making it harder to limit sensitive information to the inner circle of top officials, as Kissinger had done. The State Department lost command of foreign policy in large part because it lost exclusive control over official communication in the name of the U.S. government to foreign agents. Advances in communications technology meant that any party that so desired could establish a direct line to foreign governments or agents, circumventing traditional State Department channels.

Hill pinpointed the moment when the NSC staff realized they no longer had to bow to State. It happened during the summer of 1982, when Hill was manning the tacsat link with Phil Habib during the Israeli siege of Beirut. Secretary Haig was away at a summit in France when a phone call came through from Oliver North at the White House. It was four o'clock in the morning and Hill was nearly alone in the building. North ordered Hill to send a cable to Israel stating that the U.S. position was that Israeli forces must stop their invasion of Lebanon. Hill knew such an order would violate Haig's strategy. He refused on the grounds that a cable to Prime Minister Begin required

Haig's authorization. North said he was instructing Hill to send the cable anyway. When Hill told him that would violate the chain of command, North slammed down the receiver. Twenty minutes later John Poindexter, then an NSC staffer, was on the line. He told Hill to send the cable without Haig's approval. Hill retorted, "I'm sorry, that's the way it is."

Until then, the State Department–to–U.S. embassy line (in this case, to the American embassy in Israel) had been the communications system for the U.S. government for diplomatic matters. But North and Poindexter used the new technology that had just arrived in the White House to break State's monopoly and fire off the cable to their contacts in the Israeli government. Hill did not learn of it until the following day. When they sent that cable, "that was the point where the NSC staff—McFarlane, Poindexter, North—realized they could run their own foreign policy," Hill explained. "Jock [Covey] began reporting to me that North and McFarlane were putting together a room in the basement of the Old Executive Office Building. We concluded—this was in the spring of '83—that they were creating their own vest-pocket State Department because they had the communications technology to do so."

The "vest-pocket State Department" was known to those who used it as the crisis center. Located, ironically, in a room in the Old Executive Office Building once occupied by secretaries of state until the State Department moved to Foggy Bottom, it was fitted with three VAX computers* and the latest communications equipment. A year before the first overtures toward "open dialogue" with Iranians and almost three years before North began engineering the diversion of arms sales profits to the Contras, the NSC staff was building the communications infrastructure necessary to bypass the State Department. There was nothing Shultz could do but tell the president he was worried about this backdoor communication. In the end, the secretary of state has no constitutional right to a monopoly on foreign policy. But in a well-ordered government, he does have the political right to be consulted.

The increasing ease of communication, especially by paperless means like tacsat and telephone, exacerbated the most serious obstacle

---

* Released on October 25, 1977, by the Digital Equipment Corporation, the VAX was the first commercially available 32-bit computer. (Source: "The VAX Computer." http://www.internet-tips.net/Misc/VAXhistory.htm.)

Iran-Contra investigators faced when they tried to piece the story together: the dwindling written record. In the months following the first news of the scandal, Oliver North became infamous for "shredding parties" in which he and his devoted secretary methodically destroyed thousands of pages of relevant documents. But the record of Iran-Contra was in jeopardy from the beginning of the operation because the NSC staff fully intended to leave behind a deficient record that would allow "plausible deniability" in the event of discovery.

As the congressional hearings progressed, it became clear that Poindexter, North, and Casey had worked together to construct a bogus Iran-Contra chronology and falsify relevant documents. There was little if any documentation of NSC staff meetings — few summary memoranda turned up, let alone verbatim records comparable to Hill's notes. Shultz was infuriated when he learned the NSC staff had kept "no memcons [memoranda of conversation]. Shows they wanted no advice. Memcons are a way to get help — because not everybody can be in meetings. You get expertise, a record to evaluate — and it keeps you honest. ON [Oliver North] kept no memcons." The congressional committees were obliged to concentrate on PROFS notes North thought he had erased and the rare memo or two that escaped the shredder — instants of unintentional history where North and others revealed facts they meant to destroy. When chief counsel for the House select committee John Nields asked North why he destroyed his records, North replied: "Part of a covert operation is to offer plausible deniability of the association of the government of the United States with the activity; part of it is to deceive our adversaries. Part of it is to insure that those people who are at great peril, carrying out those activities, are not further endangered. All of those are good and sufficient reasons to destroy documents. And that's why the government buys shredders by the tens and dozens. And gives them to people running covert operations. Not so that they can have convenient memories."

"Plausible deniability" was not original to North. The concept is as old as the idea of covert operations. More recently, increased interference by Congress in White House deliberative processes in the aftermath of the Vietnam War and the Watergate scandal had changed people's notion of the written record. Officials no longer saw a good record as a useful managerial device, internal reference, or obligation to posterity. A written record was a liability. "This was the beginning of the age when papers deliberately don't say things," Hill said. "A memo is now a sanitized statement, not a historical record." The paucity of the NSC staff's written documentation stands in contrast to Hill's notebooks. During the second phase of Lawrence Walsh's independent counsel investigation, those notes would be a curse.

Attorney Jeffrey Toobin from the Office of the Independent Counsel first visited Hill in January 1987, in the company of an FBI agent. Hill recalls telling Toobin that he had compiled a summary of notes Shultz wanted to review. Toobin asked whether there were additional references to Iran or the Contras in his notebooks, and Hill said there might be. When Toobin asked where the notebooks were, Hill pointed to the security cabinet in his office and said, "You can have them, but the references to Iran and the Contras that you're after are going to be like 19 needles in 40 haystacks." According to Hill's recollection, Toobin said he'd get back to him on the matter and left. Toobin does not remember the details of their conversation, but he later emphasized that as a junior member of the prosecution team, under no circumstances could he have given Hill "any sort of waiver from producing his notebooks." Hill said he did not understand the conversation as an oral waiver, but he did believe he had given the independent counsel sufficient notice of the notes in his possession. No matter what Toobin said or how Hill understood him, the result was the same. Hill did not turn over his entire cache of notebooks, investigators did not yet realize they were missing relevant documents, and that would be the last of Hill's contact with the independent counsel for three years.*

Meanwhile, Walsh's investigation was fast becoming a disaster. It would be unfair to confuse the job of the independent counsel with that of congressional investigation, and by no means was Walsh responsible for solving the systemic crisis of the NSC staff. His own experience in government also made him more attentive to the unique context of high policymaking than other attorneys might have been. However, by paying insufficient attention to the central issue of the renegade NSC staff, he had the wrong theory of the case and ended up

---

* The transcripts of Hill's interviews with the independent counsel, housed at the National Archives in College Park, Maryland, are classified above top secret and were unavailable for review at the time of this writing. I was told that if I filed a Freedom of Information Act request for declassification of the transcripts, I could anticipate waiting several years for a reply. Therefore my account of the interviews is based primarily on my conversations with the participants.

trying to criminalize legitimate elements of the policy process. The independent counsel's problems were compounded because the House and Senate select committees, in a rush to write a definitive history of Iran-Contra and put the scandal behind them, granted immunity to some of the central wrongdoers to persuade them to testify—so what they said in their testimonies was unusable for Walsh. The administration's refusal to declassify certain information also hamstrung his cases against some of the defendants. Three years after Toobin left Hill's office, Walsh had spent millions of dollars of taxpayers' money with only minor convictions to show for it. His most significant victories, including the convictions of Poindexter, North, and McFarlane, were later overturned by the courts, or the guilty parties were pardoned by President George Bush.* Walsh constantly tried to end the investigation, but he could not responsibly do so until he had extracted evidence from Poindexter, North, and other defendants in the first wave of prosecution. As more documents were discovered or made available and more people chose to cooperate or confess, the investigation had to continue. By 1990, Walsh had launched the second phase of his inquiry, in which he turned his focus onto the State Department and the secretary of defense. Hill's read on the independent counsel was more personal. He has theorized that Walsh was frustrated and embarrassed by his failures and was looking for someone to blame—someone who concealed evidence with which Walsh could have locked away the entire NSC (maybe even the president himself) if only he had the proof in time.

After Shultz and Hill left office with the end of the Reagan administration in January 1989, they were appointed as fellows of the Hoover Institution, a conservative policy research center at Stanford University. Soon after Hill moved out to California, John Barrett, a youthful, well-dressed independent counsel attorney following up on disclosures

---

* Political fundraiser Carl Channell; former CIA officer Thomas Clines; Albert Hakim, a businessman who helped arrange Iranian arms sales and delivery of supplies to the Contras; Richard Miller, a Reagan campaign worker and aide to North; and Richard Secord, a retired air force major general hired by North, all pleaded guilty to various crimes relating to the Iran-Contra operation. The major players in the affair escaped: North and Poindexter were convicted, but their convictions were overturned by the courts. On Christmas Eve 1992, President George Bush pardoned five others: Robert McFarlane, former State Department official Elliott Abrams, and former CIA officials Clair George and Alan Fiers, along with Caspar Weinberger, who was indicted but never tried in court.

from Oliver North's trial, made an appointment to go through Hill's notes, primarily to look for references to the Contras. During two sessions, each lasting two days, Hill reviewed his notebooks with Barrett and another independent counsel attorney. He answered their questions as best he could, although Barrett recalled that Hill was "unhappy we were there. There was a tension in the room." Not long after the lawyers returned to Washington, word reached Hill that Walsh "had exploded in anger" at him, charging that Hill had withheld pertinent documents from investigators. Barrett does not remember such a severe reaction, but he admitted that over the course of late 1990 and early 1991, the possibility arose that Hill and others had deliberately withheld evidence. "We were realizing that we were had—partly by virtue of our own choices and assumptions, and partly by others' withholding of relevant documents . . . there was a general ire."

The independent counsel demanded Hill's notes in their entirety.* In February 1992 Hill was summoned to a formal deposition in Washington, D.C. The independent counsel interviewed other members of Reagan's State Department too, including Secretary Shultz, but Hill believed they focused on him because he possessed the largest, most tantalizing written record. The notebooks, by now infamous in Washington circles, were subpoenaed. The FBI instructed Hill to bring them in person to the National Archives, where they would be sealed pending the conclusion of the independent counsel's investigation. Sofaer briefly considered whether Hill should plead the Fifth Amendment, but after Sofaer extracted a written guarantee from the independent counsel that Hill was not a target of the investigation, he flew east for the deposition without even contacting a lawyer. He made only one preparation before he left. He and one of the Hoover Institution archivists stayed up until early morning photocopying every page of the stacks of notebooks he had filled over the past five years. He locked them in a vault below the building's basement. There they would sit dormant, their existence known to only a handful of people, for more than a decade.

---

* The FBI classified Hill's notes in absentia, and later agents examined the notebooks and redacted portions that did not pertain to Iran-Contra. The Office of the Independent Counsel had all necessary clearances and reviewed the documents before redaction, first in a secure facility at the Hoover Institution and then in a secure area of the National Archives and Records Administration building in Washington, D.C. The OIC photocopied all relevant material for future review and use in depositions.

Upon arriving at the Office of the Independent Counsel on 13th Street, Hill was directed to a nondescript room on an upper floor. Venetian blinds blocked the sunlight—a security requirement to protect classified interviews. He sat down at the table, facing the deputy independent counsel Craig Gillen, with Barrett at his side. An FBI agent sat observing on one side of the room, and in the corner a stenographer murmured softly into a face mask—"the kind of stenographer where you talk into the thing? A peculiar kind of stenography," recalled the consummate note taker.

Craig Gillen was a short, solidly built attorney from Atlanta whose prosecutorial zeal had earned him renown over the course of the investigation. Gillen's discovery of discrepancies in the independent counsel's record had steered the investigation toward the former secretary of state and his staff. He led each of Hill's depositions, and Hill found him hostile and snide from the outset. Although Gillen recalled nothing unpleasant about Hill's deposition and said he does not remember "any emotional exchanges I'd term antagonistic," Hill's perception was different: Gillen exuded "a kind of jovial hostility, a menace . . . that Southern way of appearing courtly and friendly, but every word has an extra twist, as in, 'I'm being friendly, but I could ruin your life.'"

Paging through a fat binder of notes, Gillen asked Hill to explain nearly every instance of suspicious words like "Iran" or "Contras." "It was clear they'd taken things and made huge extrapolations to say 'you knew all' when it was just Shultz being told something, or us pondering, or Shultz saying 'I'm frustrated with Bud,'" Hill said. "They translated that into an Iran thing." Before Gillen began interrogating Hill on each new entry, he announced for the record, "Now I want to turn to your note of June 3, 1986, not produced," meaning that Hill had not provided the note to the independent counsel. Hill, who thought he had fulfilled his legal obligation in 1987 by offering his notebooks to Jeffrey Toobin, insisted on stating for the record every time that the note was produced and describing in detail his conversation with Toobin. This ritual slowed the deposition to a glacial pace and infuriated Gillen. He suggested they insert the "not produced"—"yes, produced" exchange into the record and stipulate that it applied to every entry so they could skip the formality and move more quickly through the binder. But Hill preferred to say the words himself. "It was really just a tremendous amount of fun," Hill said. "I had the time of my life because I just drove these people crazy."* This process persisted through several more depositions "until eventually it was my feeling — although Gillen never said it — I just wore them down." The interviews ceased shortly before the court released Lawrence Walsh's final report in 1993.

Hill's notes had a substantial impact on the independent counsel investigation. A single entry from August 1987, in which Shultz told Hill "Cap takes notes but never referred to them [in interviews with investigators] so never had to cough them up," led to the independent counsel's discovery of Caspar Weinberger's diary (which he had "hidden" in a closed collection in the Manuscript Division in the Library of Congress). The independent counsel subsequently indicted Weinberger on five felony counts, including obstruction of a congressional investigation and perjury. Although the independent counsel did not indict Hill, the final report's evaluation was harsh, substantiated by relevant notes that independent counsel investigators found after they demanded all his notebooks in 1990. In Chapter 24 of the report, "The Investigation of State Department Officials: Shultz, Hill and Platt," Walsh is skeptical of Hill's "multi-layered explanation" for his exclusion of relevant notes from the excerpts he collected to prepare Shultz's testimony in 1986 and 1987. Walsh never declared Hill an official target of the investigation, but in these pages he essentially accuses Hill of obstructing justice. Walsh's explanation for why his office did not prosecute Hill does not dull his basic accusation: Hill was "a subordinate to Shultz who had delivered that testimony and who was not the subject of a prosecution himself. Additionally, Hill's assertion that he was given an oral waiver from full document production by Sofaer could raise an issue of fact regarding events several years old that might create a reasonable doubt in the minds of jurors. Finally, the passage of time itself weighed against the prosecution of Hill, who promised little in the way of further investigative developments beyond what was contained in his extensive notes."

---

* Hill, November 15, 2002. Gillen offered a more neutral account of the series of interviews with Hill. He said he could not recall the hostile "produced" — "not produced" exchange. Although he believes Hill deliberately withheld relevant notes, he expressed great respect for Hill: "He has an amazing mind, to be able to write down, verbatim, complicated interviews and participate in them at the same time. It's almost like he has two minds. I've never met anyone like that, and I don't expect to." (Gillen, March 28, 2003)

The newspapers picked up the report, and the invisible adviser was forced into the media glare, a spotlight too brief and bright to elucidate Hill's nuanced definition of an "accurate" record. Judgment had been rendered. But the more profound conclusion observers reached was that guilt clung to people who kept a good record. To Washington insiders who followed the investigation, Hill's example taught a powerful lesson: don't write anything down.*

Charles Hill took notes because the habit was ingrained in his personality and because he felt a duty to record the raw material of history: the stuff that captured the relationship between what actors knew at the time and what scholars would later uncover in retrospect. He felt that both elements were crucial to understanding human events. Most fundamentally, he kept his notebooks because an accurate record was necessary to do his job. He would later insist that he and George Shultz remained professionals while others in the government ignored protocol and did not respect traditional codes of consultation. In his arguments with President Reagan about Iran, Shultz made his feelings clear but respected the boundaries of his advisory role. He could argue for only so long. All final policy decisions rested with the president. Shultz respected the organization he worked for and always trusted the system, even when he doubted the honesty of the personnel. Perhaps his faith seems foolish in retrospect, but Shultz was an experienced administrator who had learned over the years that if you do not follow procedure, the system will break down. The failure of the NSC staff and the CIA to do so—and the catastrophe that followed—proved him right.

It seems, however, that Hill remained a professional only so long as

---

* Hill's interaction with the Office of the Independent Counsel was not unique. In Elliot Abrams's memoir about his experience in the Iran-Contra affair, *Undue Process: A Story of How Political Differences Are Turned Into Crimes* (New York: Free Press, 1993), Abrams writes that although Craig Gillen refused to declare him an official target of the investigation, he was treated as one. He describes Gillen as "a killer with a choir boy face" (79) who asked him "caricature questions, Perry Mason questions." (77) When the investigators zeroed in on a note Abrams had made to "monitor Ollie," like Hill, he too learned the dangers of keeping a record. During a conversation with college students years later, he told them, "Notes are things people will use against you five years later when no one, not even you, can remember exactly what they meant. Notes are small time bombs you set for yourself, at least with guys like Walsh walking around they are."

it was safe. Once "the system" demanded that he surrender his notes, he fudged his professionalism. Today, Hill defends his actions. Professionalism is a combination of proper protocol and priorities, and the top priority, for Hill and Shultz, was loyalty to the president, his policies, and the legacy of his administration. "The system" had broken down long ago, contaminated by careless, self-serving investigators, no longer an adequate standard for professional conduct. Loyalty to Reagan led them to have more faith in his decisions than they should have, but their devotion also compelled Shultz and his staff to fight for control of foreign policy after the scandal broke. Hill drafted pages of talking points for Shultz to use to try to convince President Reagan that "the lesson to be learned is keep the NSCS [NSC staff] out of operations + foreign policy," he wrote. ". . . And don't give me any more of those 'don't worry it'll be alright, no need to do anything' letters," Hill urged Shultz to add. Hill has said repeatedly in interviews that his and Shultz's principal aim in the scandal's aftermath was to restore professionalism to the administration's foreign policy system while forcing the NSC staff monster back into its cage. The most distressing part of the story is that they failed.

There was some comfort in Shultz's survival of the scandal. It was the State Department, buttressed by Hill's copious notebooks, that maintained long-term credibility. Yet Shultz's victory could not change the fact that Charles Hill's notebooks were a lucky aberrance in a political community that routinely shredded documents, erased files, and obscured history. As Hill would tell his students in International Studies years later in a lecture on diplomatic note taking, the record was in shambles. In Washington, to treat one's record "professionally" had come to imply careful self-editing and excruciating concern over every word put to paper, not conscientious documentation. This is the ultimate irony in Charles Hill's notebooks. He was caught between two professional cultures: the classical diplomat's historical sensibility and the modern executive's fear of outsiders' judgment. His experience in the Iran-Contra affair proves the latter paradigm won out. The written record was now a weapon, not a tool.

I have written that to be a professional means adhering to the proper combination of priorities and protocol. That is not a bad definition for Grand Strategy either: a guiding system by which one renders judgments, a philosophical approach to problems, a way to live and act that tries to take everything, long- and short-term, into account. For the professional, after all, nothing is more important than a bird's-eye view that allows not one detail to slip by unnoticed. The Iran-Contra episode caught Hill and Shultz by surprise because they had lost track of the details, the scraps of evidence that leap off the page when one reads Charlie's notebooks in retrospect. "When you don't have a grand strategy mentality, your radar won't swing 360 degrees. It will paint the area in front of you, but not on the sides or in the back. Iran-Contra was one thing we didn't attend to," Charlie later acknowledged. "We weren't looking in every direction." For him, the affair underscored the value of the vigilance that he had long believed crucial to the business of world affairs—but it was also evidence of grand strategy's practical limitations.

These limitations were to Charlie not intrinsic flaws, however, but an unavoidable component of policymaking in a protean, crisis-ridden world. His faith in the enterprise of grand strategy, if altered at all, only grew stronger. He had toiled for a grand strategy all his life. He thought that he had it while working in Kissinger's office, and he almost did, but back then he was still new to the business of gazing down upon the globe. By the end of his years with George Shultz, he had found his footing and the landscape clicked into focus. He grasped the single problem that encompassed all the perils of the Shultz years: the emboldened media, the vanishing record, and the Information Age. That problem was the rise of nonstate actors in the international system.

Traditionally traced to the Peace of Westphalia, which ended Europe's Thirty Years' War in 1648, sometimes granted a pedigree stretching back to ancient Greece's assemblage of city-states, the international system of sovereign states replaced the notion of empire or tribe as Europe's paradigm of international relations. It is the foundation of the way states have interacted with one another for centuries, and it is rooted in mutually accepted codes of conduct and official channels by which national governments behave and communicate. It is a system of protocol and priorities, the rules by which states keep their relationships professional.

Iran-Contra was not only an unbecoming scandal of shady Iranian agents and shredded documents. The backdoor dealings of Oliver North and the NSC staff were a direct result of the empowerment of the media and congressional investigative bodies in the wake of the technological revolution and the American public's plummeting trust in Washington. The all-seeing public eye of the late twentieth century crippled modern diplomacy by forcing policymakers out of the official network that had long served as the framework for state-to-state communication. To keep their dealings private, diplomats turned to unsupervised back channels and middlemen with, at best, uncertain links to legitimate governments. The TWA hijacking, the hostage crisis, and Iran-Contra all testified to the corruption of communication between sovereign governments. Charlie had come to know this breakdown well. The international system was eroding from the inside — and with it, the old model of cold war grand strategy.

There was another dimension in the foreign policy challenges of the Reagan years, one that Charlie did not perceive until later. There was more to the terrorist acts of the 1980s, the hijackings and kidnappings that left Washington feeling helpless and set the stage for the Iran-Contra mess, than a gang of angry extremists willing to go to horrifying lengths to win freedom for their comrades in prison. World leaders grimly realized that they had entered, in the phrase of James Reston, the age of fanatics. But Charlie told me over and over that, back then, they did not yet perceive the cultural force that was fast binding these lone radicals together, that would threaten the ruling ideas of the age: the drumbeat of Islamic fundamentalism.

This is old news now. But it was unheard of then. The rising wave of terrorism at the hands of faceless, antistate entities augured ill for the mores and unwritten global standards that had governed international society over the past centuries. The traditional tools of diplomacy and deterrence on which modern policymakers and their predecessors had always relied now seemed worthless. As John Gaddis has written, "The terrorists struck, as states can never do, from the sanctuary provided by anonymity: how does one negotiate with a shadow? Nor were they interested in their own survival: how does one deter someone who's prepared to commit suicide?"

After Egypt's President Sadat was assassinated in 1981, Charlie recalled that the television news networks broadcast images of the assassins, members of the Muslim Brotherhood, in their Cairo prison cells dressed "all in white robes and white caps, shrieking and wailing about Allah — we looked right through them." Most in the State Department, like the rest of Washington and indeed most Western governments, concluded that Sadat was assassinated by secular extremists fighting for Palestinian land rights. But Islamic fundamentalism, which desires not only the destruction of Israel but a return to traditional pan-Islamic rule, an effective revival of the Caliphate, was the fire that drove and united the terrorists. Fundamentalist leaders preach that the plight of Muslims is due to their abandonment of shari'a, Muslim religious law, in favor of a compromised existence according to the rules of greater global society, an arrogant world that will decimate Islamic culture if holy warriors do not destroy it first. Some of Charlie's colleagues are reluctant to attribute such a grand design to terrorists, to credit them with anything more sophisticated than animal retaliation. Charlie would answer that ruin of the international system is indeed a big idea, and that it remains the fundamental premise by which terrorists plot, destroy, and die—whether the teenage martyrs and thugs among them realize it or not. Human beings live according to big ideas, even if they don't "get it." When he reminisces about the attempts he and his colleagues made to cultivate a dialogue with those dark figures who pulled the strings of the terrorist networks—or failing that, to combat them through conventional means of trying to hold a state, like Iran, responsible—his voice sounds chagrined. He seems incredulous that they could have ever been so blind, or blindsided.

"When terrorism strikes, civilization itself is under attack," Reagan proclaimed at a press conference on the last evening of the TWA 847 standoff. "No nation is immune." The international system is one of the great achievements of Western civilization, and as a young man joining the Foreign Service, Charlie told himself that he was there to help defend the ideas for which his civilization stood. This new threat surpassed anything that his heroes, the old cold warriors, ever considered. For despite the Soviets' Marxist-Leninist rhetoric about the state's fate to "wither away"—not to mention both superpowers' unfortunate habits of ignoring neighboring countries' sovereignty, flouting treaties, and bulldozing past the United Nations in pursuit of their own interests—Washington and Moscow always behaved like states. They negotiated at summits and exchanged ambassadors. They maintained a professional relationship. The radical Islamist terrorists would prove a more terrible threat to the United States than the Soviet Union ever was. When the cold war came to an end, Charlie remained a thinker formed in an antique age, and fundamentalist Islam now replaced the Soviet Union as the evil force whose ideology ran counter to all that is, to him, human and rational. But the terrorists' aim to destroy the international system—and America, that system's unchallenged leader—

is not just ideology. It is demonstrated reality. If there is to be any hope for a grand strategy in this chaos, it must focus on restoring the world order that the terrorists seek to decapitate.

For Charlie's students and for his biographer, these are the years that explain and encapsulate him. He is a thinker of traditional discipline and traditional philosophy of international relations rooted in ancient Greece and Westphalia. He is an anthropologist who saw fit to note down human details, and eventually recognized the danger of fundamentalist Islam, a force even stronger, perhaps, than the religious energies European statesmen tried to eradicate from world affairs in 1648. Charlie's tenure alongside George Shultz was in many ways the blueprint for his lesson plan at Yale.

He and the other Grand Strategy professors end their course on a note that drives home modern urgencies and forces students to put to practice what they have learned. They spend the final semester drilling professionalism into the students, who divide into teams and work intensively to prepare "policy briefings" on subjects like economics, religion, and national security, of the caliber and seriousness of mind that the great World War II general and secretary of state George Marshall would have expected from his staff. They dress properly for the occasion and prepare PowerPoint presentations—for since the days of Cicero, every proper statesman's education has included rhetoric. When the teams take the floor, their professors and classmates try their utmost to rip their arguments to shreds. The presenters must stiffen and bear it, "undismayed by disaster," never "shaken out by external events, however surprising." Many Grand Strategy graduates recall their policy briefing as the most brutal day of their lives.

Having survived the rigors of the semester, the students then face one final test before the year ends: an event that is both ridiculous and deadly serious, the Crisis Simulation. Justin Zaremby, a precocious graduate of the course, was given charge of designing the scenario for the students who came after him. For two consecutive Saturdays, he held the whole class captive in the basement of one of the largest classroom buildings on campus. He could do with them as he wished. The point was to force them to construct a grand strategy of their own, then test how it worked—to see whether they had learned anything since they first gathered nervously for Gaddis's speech a year earlier. The crisis was titled, with some melodrama, "The Newark Nightmare."

The students had little idea what to expect. They were told only to appear on the appointed morning, when they learned that the president had raised the national security alert to level orange. The imagined enemy was shadowy and amorphous, removed only a few degrees from real-life reports from the Middle East in the newspapers. The rules of the international system failed to prescribe a response, so they would have to come up with something of their own. The object of the first day was to draft a letter to the NSC providing a national security strategy for dealing with weapons of mass destruction. They had to be ready to brief national security adviser Condoleezza Rice at 11 A.M. At the briefing, the professors, playing the roles of Condi and her colleagues with great relish, pounced on poor public relations, lack of concern for congressional support, and use of military forces on American soil. The basement classroom began to feel cramped.

In the midst of a scramble to mitigate embarrassing press leaks, the students were told to elect a president from their midst. They chose a history major named Jack who was levelheaded but prone to pompous declarations of goodwill. By the end of the day, all the students had specific roles, from White House press secretary to assorted U.S. ambassadors and director of the CIA. The real challenge would begin the following Saturday, when they would convene for a presidential press conference at 9 A.M.

Following the press conference, the president was informed of an outbreak of the Ebola virus in Newark, New Jersey. The NSC and CIA dispersed to collect intelligence, responding to leads about an unknown virus on a Disney cruise ship and a reported dirty-bomb attack on the American embassy in South Korea. Such interjections would arrive periodically throughout the day, most emanating from the "control room" in the corner of the building, where Gaddis, Hill, and Kennedy sat chuckling to themselves and thinking up new and improved catastrophes. The Ebola outbreak was traced to an Al-Qaeda cell operating in southern Syria, in conjunction with a Hezbollah cell in Lebanon. "Intelligence," provided by Justin and his collaborators in the form of irregular and insidious e-mails, was a source of continuing frustration. There followed a series of exasperating exchanges with the Syrian ambassador, played with flourish and authenticity by Charlie, who took great offense at the way the Americans treated him and at one point stormed out of a meeting "because there was no coffee." Later, when the participants requested a meeting with the Saudi crown prince,

Charlie informed them smugly that "the prince was resting and could not be disturbed."

Justin mobilized a gang of diabolical *Yale Daily News* reporters to descend on the crisis, publishing "leaks" about a coup against the president planned by the director of Homeland Security and misrepresenting the encounter with the Syrian ambassador. At one point, the president was informed of a *New York Post* report that alleged he was having an affair. As the game drew to a close, the U.N. Security Council convened. The American ambassador confronted the Syrian delegate to the United Nations and demanded his help in destroying the terrorist cell. Characteristically, the Syrian ambassador refused to negotiate. The death toll from the virus continued to mount, and the game concluded with a surprise Israeli strike that wiped out the Al-Qaeda operatives.

The lesson of the whole experience, the students agreed afterward, was the extent to which mundane details interfered with their grand visions of strategy (this class's calamitous ending was hardly an exception—the following year the Crisis Simulation would end in nuclear winter). Outside the classroom, they were forced to act decisively well before they understood the situation. They had no time to ponder what Clausewitz or Machiavelli would do. One student was shocked at "how little time was available in the middle of everything as the crisis took shape." Having spent the past year immersed in the craft of grand strategy, encouraged to embrace it as a worldview and their ticket to success as leaders, students now had to recognize its limitations. Long-range objectivity proved much more difficult in the moment of crisis than from the position of the historian in the ivory tower, as Charlie, veteran of the lessons of the Iran-Contra affair, could have told them. At zero hour, priorities and protocol often fall apart.

From an outsider's vantage point, there is something disconcerting about the Crisis Simulation. On the one hand, it is at times a comic spectacle, and the students enjoy themselves. In this way it fits the tongue-in-cheek tone that Grand Strategy occasionally assumes. There was, for example, the year-end party I attended at which a student with a well-connected father in the Marines presented a tacky four-color diploma decorated with flags and federal seals, supposedly bestowed by the Marine Corps upon the Grand Strategy students in gratitude for their intellectual contributions to the nation. Afterward I tried to get a consensus on whether the gesture was serious or intended in jest. I was relieved to find that most students hoped for the latter. There has also been talk of ordering custom-designed Grand Strategy ties and scarves. These would be emblazoned with the logo of a squirrel and nut—for, goes the running joke, Squirrel & Nut is the Grand Strategy secret society that will take its place next to Skull & Bones. Charlie, who once described a conference of the American Political Science Association as "a zoo where all the animals are squirrels," deserves credit for the name. These occasional chuckles of self-mockery, like Charlie's rare quiet smile, remind one that at some level, these students are just normal kids.

While the Crisis Simulation is partly self-deprecating parody, it is disturbing that students who have absorbed themselves all this time in grand strategy suddenly, in the event, pull back with a smile and resist taking themselves seriously. The final lesson seems to be that in the end, grand strategy falls down. However, the impact of this concluding caveat to the class is not clear. The students see the Crisis Simulation as fun, a bit stressful, yet not really part of the education they have received. It is more like a separate end piece, an amusing going-away party that has little to do with the high-minded discussion and book learning of the previous year. The simulation is a series of absurd surprises, flying at the students as if from an off-kilter pitching machine. This year's class knew that Justin and the professors were deliberately trying to think up more monkey wrenches to undermine their strategy, and so it became a game, a match of wits, rather than a sobering taste of the real world.

To remain undismayed by disaster may, it seems, put one at risk of losing touch with reality. But Charlie would never say so. His obsession —there is no better word for it—with grand strategy, with the current plight of the international system, is rooted in his psychology. Islamic fundamentalism was the uniting force behind the terrorism of the 1980s that he and his colleagues had failed to perceive. It crept up on them. It was a horrifying, colossal surprise, made all the worse because they had been looking straight at it for so long. Charlie Hill, the professional watcher, thinker, and note taker who has desired all his life to be the hedgehog, in this case remained a fox. Lost in a multitude of little things, he had missed the one big idea. He would not let it happen again.

13

IF THERE WAS A PLACE WHERE CHARLES HILL OUGHT TO
have been able to escape the long shadow of the Iran-Contra investigation, it was the Hoover Institution on War, Revolution, and Peace at
Stanford University in Stanford, California. A cluster of buildings in
the middle of the yellow sandstone arches and Spanish terra cotta tile
roofs of the main campus, the Hoover Institution is a cloister of conservative political thought on one of the most liberal college campuses
in the country. The think tank's Hoover Tower rises 285 feet into the
air, well above the manicured quadrangles and palm-lined thoroughfares. Its red dome and cupola are visible for miles around, the main
landmark used by tourists driving in from the interstate to find their
way to campus — much to the dismay of generations of liberal students
and faculty. It was a long way from the media vultures and political intrigue roiling around Washington. Indeed, it was perhaps a little odd to
find Charles Hill, a career minister in the Foreign Service and one of
the brightest stars in the State Department, suddenly so far from the
action.

Hoover had not been wholly his own choice. Shortly after George
H. W. Bush won the presidential election in November 1988, it became
clear that the ascent of the vice president, no matter past loyalties and
working relationships, would be a hostile transition. A degree of coolness was natural, for Bush had to establish independence from his old
commander in chief to be effective in the White House. The attitude of
the Bush staff, however, caught many of their colleagues from the Reagan administration off-guard. The incoming secretary of state, James
Baker, had always seemed to hold a negative opinion of Shultz and
Reagan, but the incoming staff's sullen hostility was "strange, surpris-

ing," Hill said later. "It was suddenly clear that this would be an adversarial transition. The new people were not friendly. The signals were: get out of here as fast as you can."

In the rare free moment in which he had indulged a daydream or two about his future after George Shultz left office, Hill mulled over the posts he might seek (or, preferably, be sought for) in the Foreign Service. Despite his avowed disdain for ambassadorships, a few scribbled notes and career-path diagrams survive that betray at least a moment's rumination on running his own embassy somewhere. He considered the possibility not because he had lost his distaste for embassy ceremony and social life, but because an ambassadorship was the only seemly direction to go after serving at the top of the State Department. There was little chance, however, that the Bush administration would consider him for an ambassadorial appointment. Additionally, while the Iran-Contra investigation—which had already come within a hair's breadth of snaring the president-elect—still seethed in the Washington headlines, Hill knew the danger contained in his notebooks. A leave of absence, a quiet year or two far away from the ill winds in Foggy Bottom, seemed increasingly attractive.

Shultz, who lived in California and had been affiliated with Stanford and Hoover before Reagan tapped him to replace Al Haig, wanted his executive assistant to come back with him. Together they had books to write and intellectual legacies to forge. Hill was the perfect partner, already a good friend who knew Shultz's mind and—just as important—happy to do the thankless research and writing in which Shultz had no interest. To start with, over the last months of the Reagan administration, Shultz and Hill had worked up a plan for a television series that would render the world of diplomacy intelligible to the viewing public. It was Shultz who initially pushed for the television medium. Hill soon came around, and they envisioned a documentary series modeled along the lines of Milton Friedman's *Free to Choose* (1980) or Kenneth Clark's epic *Civilization* (1969). Theirs would be called *Statecraft*, the name of their true medium, Hill had always thought, but a word that incited blank stares even around the State Department. If their own colleagues so poorly understood the grand strategy of foreign affairs, the public's ignorance was surely frightful. Hill would get to work blocking out every episode of the twelve-part series, as well as the companion book they envisioned, as soon as he got to Hoover.

Second, there was the memoir that everybody was urging Shultz to write. He did not want to do it and neither, particularly, did Hill. But it had to be done. All in all there was plenty to do for a year or so in California, to pass the time while the new administration found its sea legs, Lawrence Walsh ran his investigation aground, and the storm in Washington subsided. Hill notified the Director General's office, requesting leave without pay.

Shortly after he submitted his request, the director general, George Vest, came to see Hill in a panic. "He said, 'you mustn't do this, I don't want you to do this, it would be awful,'" Hill recalled. Vest told him that as Shultz's executive assistant, he was the epitome of what a Foreign Service officer should aspire to be, and it would look terrible if Hill packed up and disappeared into the West. Couldn't Hill go to Stanford as a diplomat-in-residence, remaining on the State Department's payroll? Hill argued that it would be better if the work he planned to do with Shultz remained unconnected with the State Department, but Vest would not relent, and Hill finally agreed. He and Martha found an apartment in Palo Alto and departed at the end of January, shortly after Bush's inauguration. They had barely settled in when he received notice from the inspector general of the State Department that Senator Jesse Helms of North Carolina was on the attack.

Senator Helms, chairman of the Senate Foreign Relations Committee, was the scourge of the State Department. He was a "spoiler Secretary of State," according to Washington insiders. The State Department, having no voting constituency, was easy prey for Helms, a bald, bespectacled, beady-eyed man with impeccable Southern manners and a drawl that curdled the blood of policymakers. He routinely mobilized his staff to launch offensives against one or another State Department or White House policy or office to bully them into submitting to his demands. Often his true aim—such as the appointment of one of his henchmen to a State Department position—was entirely unrelated to his ostensible target. "I just have my opinions and my agenda. I just take a swipe at the ball when it comes over the plate, and I do the best I can," he chuckled to the *New York Times*.

Helms's latest target was the diplomat-in-residence program, which he claimed was too expensive and too often exploited by Foreign Service officers who used it as a cover to pursue their own selfish interests at taxpayers' expense. Hill was a high-profile officer, a colleague of Shultz who had gone off to Stanford more to help with Shultz's pet projects than to contribute to the university. He was an easy mark.

The trigger, it later came out, was a July article by David Streitfeld in the *Washington Post*'s Style section entitled "Shultz's $2 Million Book Deal." Helms could not have dreamed of more damning evidence. The following day two officers from the State Department's Office of the Inspector General told Hill that the article, which cited anonymous sources familiar with the bidding on Shultz's book project, had Helms "in a fury! He's called in a rage," Hill recorded in his notes. Although others in the State Department assured the senator that Hill was not helping Shultz make any money yet, "CH in bad position," one of the Inspector General men told him. "GPS looks like he's getting free services of USG [United States Government] employee to rake in dough. DIR [Diplomat-in-Residence] program in jeopardy. The *facts* don't matter. The truth is irrelevant. The appearance of impropriety exists + that's all that matters."

Hill never met Helms personally. It is quite possible that Helms himself hardly knew who Hill was. Helms's staff, a savvy cabal of ex-journalists and Washington veterans, were well known for launching attacks without informing the senator of every detail. When an officer from the Inspector General's office went to California to investigate the case, he left convinced that Hill was teaching, advising students, and generally behaving as a diplomat-in-residence ought to. Hill had not yet done any work on the memoir, and the publishing deal, despite what the *Post* article claimed, was not even signed yet. When the contract was finalized, Hill did not receive a penny. The *Statecraft* TV series was expected to lose money, if anything. The inspector general told Hill that none of this mattered. Helms could still exploit the way the situation looked. When Hill again requested leave without pay, the Inspector General officers told him it was too late for that. Hill was frustrated. "I'm an FSO. I want to be told my orders," he said.

Everyone seemed to have a different opinion. Irritated with their lack of professionalism, Hill asked them to go back to their supervisors so they could give him a unified State Department position. Later that afternoon he telephoned Larry Eagleburger, his old boss from the Kissinger speechwriting days who was now deputy secretary of state, and explained the dilemma. Eagleburger responded with characteristic furor and theatrics. Hill recorded:

LSE: It's a goddamn outrage. We can't lose top FSOs like you. Jesus! You shd write a letter saying what it is you are doing there + do it + the hell with them . . .

I'll tell you, here alone, w the door closed, that it is clear Geo Bush does not like Geo Shultz. I don't know why. Maybe Iran/Contra (yes), but Bush has a little list of those he doesn't like + Shultz is on it. As you know *you* were my choice for NEA [Near East Affairs] but it was killed in WH [White House] + [I] think by Geo Bush. Not because of you, but because of Geo Shultz. After a while I think that won't be a problem for you, but it will take time. These guys are not exactly anti-Semitic but what they are are Texas oil men. They like Arabs. And they think Reagan + Shultz let Israel get away w murder.

Further conversations with Henry Kissinger and Paul Nitze confirmed Hill's suspicions that if he went back to Washington, the best he could hope for was a job in "some parking-lot place, the board of personnel or some Admin job," he said later. Despite Eagleburger's protestations, Hill told him that he was leaning toward leaving the service. "I don't have 2 options. I have one — R [resign] or not," he told Eagleburger a few days later. "I have to seriously consider R as my talks in Dept [State Department], including to you, do not fill me w hope that there is interesting or significant work. I don't want to be Amb to Norway. Israel, Panama, Cambodia is where I could help do some undesirable + difficult work. You tell me you want me to get rid of the Khmer Rouge for you, I'll be there tomorrow."

Hill's dilemma was, at its essence, how to behave professionally in unprofessional circumstances. It was a disturbing indication of the Foreign Service's internal erosion. American diplomats were no longer members of a professional service, but a political one. Hill went home to Bridgeton to mull over his decision. In his notebook he wrote scornfully, "CH is actually highly enjoying this demise of his own career by stringing out the days in order to Jesuitically, casuistically, equivocationally point out to the FS nabobs the self-contradictions + fallacies of their own positions and precepts." There is little doubt that the choice was harder than these tart lines suggest.

In August 1989, M. Charles Hill of New Jersey, career minister and Foreign Service officer for twenty-seven years, submitted his resignation. It was the only honorable thing to do.

The Foreign Service was the only profession that Hill had ever known. It was his life. "Looking back it was a remarkable thing, kicking away a career," he said later. "I did it without anguish or thought. It seemed to me the whole thing was a fouled-up administrative mess, politically colored, and what was going to be the result for me was some lower administrative job from which I would have to find a way to climb back up, and that would be difficult in the new administration. But I did it very quickly, without agonizing."

Hill prided himself on never looking back. Besides, there was no use in looking back when he had already begun to turn his gaze toward what lay ahead: the university, the earthly kingdom, the place where he had always wanted to belong.

The *Statecraft* project and Shultz's massive memoir were to be the cornerstones of Shultz's legacy, and they were prodigious endeavors. When they first got to Hoover, "Charlie and Shultz were still behaving as if they were in Washington, as if everything's important," said Grace Hawes, an archivist who worked closely with both men. "It was a crisis atmosphere. It took them a while to settle down." Hawes recalled that Hill came in at 6:30 A.M., earlier than everyone else in the building. Through those quiet morning hours, before Shultz came in and he got the usual call to come to the former secretary's big corner office for an hour or so of mulling ideas, Hill sat at his desk writing. Hawes got used to odd requests for an obscure literary reference or a copy of a certain passage from Thucydides. At noon, he went off to play basketball; no one in the office seemed to know whom he played with. He returned to write and work with Shultz until the dinner hour, when — for the first time since his sabbatical at Harvard two decades earlier — he usually went home for the day.

Statecraft required hours of fundraising, writing and research, and drudgery in the unfamiliar fields of audio and visual production. For the memoir, Hill had to set aside his distaste for revisiting his own past and immerse himself in his notes again, finding some way to pull together a coherent story from those thousands of pages. It is remarkable that he had any time left to teach and advise students. But he did: he taught a lecture course on the Vietnam War and another based on the work he was doing for *Statecraft*. Professors from the Stanford Business School asked him to address their classes as a guest speaker on risk analysis of business ventures abroad, a field in which he had no training but plenty of educated suggestions. As word of his and Shultz's arrival filtered through the Stanford community, undergraduates trickled into his office for academic and career advice, as did admiring female graduate students who wanted to flirt more than talk foreign affairs. The Hoover archivists recalled one young woman who sat in Hill's office, theatrically reciting her poetry, while Hill shifted in his chair and blushed—although the color would have been imperceptible to the untrained eye.

By early 1990, the *Statecraft* series was ready to take off. Hill's personal files contain detailed production plans complete with narration, onscreen images, and expert interviews for each segment of the series, peppered with quotations by history's great strategists, from John Quincy Adams to Machiavelli. A glance at the table of contents reads like a greatest hits list of Hill's favorite foreign affairs themes. The *MacNeil-Lehrer Newshour* expressed interest in producing the documentary, and they had obtained a promise from IBM to underwrite production to the tune of several million dollars. Everything had fallen into place. Suddenly in the spring of 1990, only a few weeks after all the logistics had been arranged, the funding fell through. It is hard to believe that Shultz, a powerful Bechtel businessman well connected in the corporate world, could not have found other parties to fund the series. And it seems a terrible shame that Hill would abandon a project that had been the focus of tireless work for over two years. But the IBM disappointment brought to the surface doubts that had been festering for a while. Earlier Shultz and Hill had tested Kenneth Clark's *Civilization* series on a roomful of undergraduates, only to watch the students squirm in their seats after fifteen minutes. "They were antsy, not used to it," Hill said later. The model that Shultz and Hill had used for their series was starting to look obsolete. An intricate twelve-week documentary, *Statecraft* was too epic and too interested in grand ideas —a bit of an antique, really—to captivate a modern audience. The plans slipped quietly into the bottom of filing drawers, where they would remain, mourned but soon forgotten.

Shultz, who always had a dozen commitments on his calendar at once, moved on painlessly to other things. Hill was soon absorbed in excavating his notebooks for the raw material that would form the body of *Turmoil & Triumph*. Despite his initial reservations, once he began going over his notes he found he enjoyed the work—much more so than the hasty review he was forced to conduct when the Iran-Contra scandal first came to light. Foiled in his admirable and heartbreaking attempt to embrace modern American culture and express all he had learned of foreign affairs through the adventurous medium of television, Hill retreated willingly into the world of the pen, so much more familiar to him.

He worked rapidly. He mused in his notes that the memoir had to be a classic, to tell an accurate story while also addressing "a small core of eternal questions." "It became clear that this would be *the* book of the 1980s, the end of the Cold War, the biggest, the most authoritative and factually based, with the most integrity in writing about what you knew, when you knew it—almost no other memoirs do that," he said later. The fat, tediously comprehensive volume would come out in hardcover in 1993, to reviews that, while not soaring quite to the altitude of Hill's own appraisal, were still mostly friendly (with the glaring exception of Theodore Draper's upbraiding in the *New York Review of Books*). *Turmoil & Triumph* earned a bestseller listing in the *New York Times* and, perhaps improbably, a place on the *Times* list of "Books for Vacation Reading."

In all his researching and drafting, brainstorming and lecturing, in lecture halls as well as in publishing houses and in endeavors both failed and flourishing, Hill was becoming a teacher. He had been one off and on for many years—from his halting start correcting Harvard graduate students on details of the Cultural Revolution twenty years earlier to his increasing skill in directing his own staff during his later years in the Foreign Service. But Hoover was a more formative classroom. It was a place that forced a teacher to take sides. The radically conservative think tank—for many years directed by fiery cold warrior W. Glenn Campbell, who worked hard to politicize the institution and increase Hoover's influence in Washington—had enjoyed unprecedented power during the Reagan years. The president, who as former governor of California had many ties to Hoover, essentially imported the institution's economic and foreign policy doctrines to Washington wholesale. But now the glorious Reagan Revolution had come to an end, and Hoover was left isolated on the West Coast, an obstinate island in Stanford's sea of vengeful liberals who wanted to check the think tank's power and reshape the university's curriculum to reflect the politically correct trends of the early 1990s.

No intellectual battle could have energized Hill more. These were the days of Jesse Jackson's pilgrimages to Stanford and the protest rallies crying "Hey ho, hey ho, Western Civ has got to go!" To Hill, the crisis ran deeper than university politics. In an October 1992 letter he wrote to the institution's new (and more reasonable) director, John Raisian, Hill expressed sentiments that would be the groundwork of his own pedagogical mission. The letter ran for many pages, and a few lines merit quotation at length:

> By now it has been widely demonstrated that the 1960s leftist genera-
> tion of student radicals became the 'tenured radicals' of university
> faculties in the 1980s. The jest was that having failed to take over
> Congress and the White House they took over the English depart-
> ments . . . If this were simply a matter of aging hippies trying to pass
> the torch of SDS [left-wing Students for a Democratic Society] along
> it would be exasperating but less than ultimately determinative. Far
> more significant, a powerful, far-reaching new school of social phi-
> losophy has come into being in the course of the past decade . . .
> There is a philosophical elite today . . . Their work is left as against
> right, equality as against liberty, and communalism as against indi-
> vidualism . . .
> *Now comes the struggle over who and what will define the meaning of*
> *democracy itself.* Why? Because this is *not* a mere matter of tinkering
> between benign varieties of democracy. If the momentum of the
> 1980s is not recaptured, the winners of the Cold War will fail to col-
> lect their winnings; the liberal agenda, which already has returned to
> life, will entrench itself. Private enterprise and individual intellectual
> creativity will be regulated and suffocated by bureaucratic systems . . .
> Unless this new battle is joined, with Hoover in the lead, the collapse
> of the Soviet model will be followed by the discrediting of the Ameri-
> can vision for the future. A neo-Marxist, restored liberal-leftist social-
> ism will take root.
> . . . in one word, I would select 'Education' as our primary task . . .
> The crucially lacking dimension in American life — and the life of the
> West today — is that the people do not understand the fundamental
> arguments for freedom.

This was a letter a long time in the making. Its composition began in the back of Hill's mind when he was a young Foreign Service officer, born ten years too early to forsake the tight-lipped order of South Jersey for the seductive turmoil he encountered in China and at Harvard. As he watched the Red Guards and the SDS rallies, he realized the power of young people.

But there is more at work here than a conservative harangue against "aging hippies" corrupting youth. Hill notes bureaucratic systems among the weapons of those out to destroy "the momentum of the 1980s." Bureaucracy was a force that Hill had long labored against, or at least held at arm's length. He viewed it as a fundamentally leftist entity, a faceless organizing principle devoted to limiting executive power, betraying secrecy, pasteurizing individualism, and turning creative human beings into cubicled drones—a diagnosis not unlike William F. Buckley's indictment of the university in *God and Man at Yale*. Hill's own bureaucracy had, in the end, abandoned him to the ruthless jaws of a self-serving politician. Bureaucracy, to Hill, was passive, dithering, and headless. It ate away at the American character. To the son of Morton Hill, it was unmanly.

Therefore conservative political coups and rollbacks of Washington bureaucracy would be impossible, or at least of minimal effect, without reeducation of the American personality. The letter that Hill wrote to Raisian was a rough battle plan for what he understood to be a war for democracy, the cornerstone of America's civil religion. In these pages he was describing an enemy line whose salient he first tried to blunt in his work on Kissinger's Heartland Speeches, that early and little-known effort to reunite a country already drawing the lines of today's culture war. It was now a battle not for politicians but for thinking men. It was a job for teachers—at least teachers of the elite, the next generation of leaders, for we know Hill's distaste for the plebian.

He had always adored university life. But at the University of Pennsylvania in the early 1960s, Hill saw in his mentor Anthony Garvan a life of self-indulgence and isolation. In the cloister of academia he had found insufficient higher mission; the call to duty lay elsewhere. Now he had come round, from graduate studies through the ranks of government and the lessons of the real world, and found himself in academia again. It had been a circuitous but necessary journey. The civic consequence of clearing and shaping the minds of the young was probably no greater now than it had ever been—for it is always a first principle—but Hill had reached a moment of clarity in his own intellectual career. To the wonderment of a growing cadre of Hillophiles, to the dismay of many an aging hippie, Charles Hill would be a teacher.

The move to California was for Hill the most consequential life change yet—mostly because it failed to deliver many of the opportunities it promised. It did not save him from the clutches of Lawrence Walsh's investigation. Nor did it prove fertile ground for the television documentary ambitions he and Shultz had brought to Hoover. Rather than insulate him from the tempest in Washington, it left him more exposed than ever, forcing him to end the career he loved. His last hope was that his new life on the West Coast would succeed in at least one respect, the most important and the most daunting—that it would breathe new life into his marriage to Martha.

At the Hoover Institution, for the first time in her life Martha found a job that made her happy. Toward the end of their time in Washington, she had enrolled in a master's program in library science at the University of Maryland. She hated it, but when they moved to California the degree qualified her for a position assembling exhibitions at the Hoover Archives. After decades of channeling her artistic ability into hobbies, church projects, and her girls' schools, she had an outlet at Hoover for using her talent professionally. "I finally found my perfect job, in my fifties," she recalled. The girls were out of the house. Katie had graduated from the University of Chicago in 1988 with a degree in English literature and was still living in Chicago, volunteering and taking graduate courses at Northwestern. After academic struggles at the University of Pennsylvania, Emily had transferred to the University of Rochester and was now thriving in the nursing program. Charlie came home every night at a reasonable hour. Both he and Martha were intellectually engaged in their work. Their lives were more balanced. It seemed fair to hope that now they would have plenty to share over dinner conversation—that they would have time to slowly restore the marriage that, however atrophied, had lasted through so much.

The Hills had stopped going to parties almost completely sometime in the 1980s. After one or two of the outbursts that came when Martha had too much to drink, Charlie concluded, during the silent car rides home, that they might as well avoid altogether the social events he found miserable anyway. In their last years in the house on Cathedral, Hill detached his life from his marriage, and he was unable to rebuild the link here. In California, in the modest apartment among the palm trees and vibrant bougainvillea on Sand Hill Road, things only got worse. An air of barrenness hung about its rooms, like attic dust. He focused wholly on his work, retreating into what he sometimes called his "strange South Jersey character." "I wasn't there," he said later. "I was an occluded person. I didn't realize this. I'd virtually never been to a restaurant before. I'd never been to a bar. I didn't do the things people did. I never went to restaurants because that was the way I was brought up; my family didn't. I didn't realize people had a recreational life that was social—dinner parties back and forth, informal family things, or that you'd go out with your wife to a restaurant on your anniversary, or watch the end of a baseball game at a bar. I never did any of that. I was a very narrow person."

This was how Charlie had chosen to live his life and interact with those closest to him, not only Martha. He was the same way when they went to visit Bridgeton, the cradle of that strange South Jersey character. Hill later said that he enjoyed every trip home. They were easy and relaxing; the neighborhood around Institute Place was somehow immune to Bridgeton's creeping urban blight, perennially "comfortable, pleasant, and warm." But it seemed to others that over the years, visits home became a burden. He could never pull his mind away from his work. "When we'd go there, Charlie had other things on his mind," said Martha. "He took to carrying a clipboard with him everywhere. He used to be writing on that thing, and conversation would just go on around him. It was hard for me to talk [because of the condition in her vocal chords], but I'd be talking with his parents while he had the clipboard. I ended up as the chief conversationalist."

Even when they went to the Jersey shore, the one place where he found freedom as a little boy, "he was always working," recalled Emily. "He was always on the phone, and it was always ringing. We learned very early to answer the phone very politely, 'This is Emily speaking, just a moment please . . .' The shore kind of took him back to his boyhood, but I don't know if he was happy there." Martha chatted endlessly with Alvenia—in Emily's words, a "cozy, have-a-cookie kind of grandma"—the girls played on the beach, and their father withdrew more and more.

As much as Charlie had always admired his dad, they were never great friends. Charlie shared few of his father's interests in gardening, cars, or the stock market (Morton's passion after he retired from dentistry), although Charlie would pick up the latter hobby later in life. And however much Alvenia nagged him to call up his childhood buddies, he had little patience for those few relics of his Bridgeton life who stopped by for an afternoon. Martha recalled that one evening Hill's old friend Bill Doherty came over, and Hill spent the entire evening in a book. "Bill is a talker, and the evening went on and on, but Charlie never looked up," she remembered. "Finally Bill got up to leave and said, 'Nice talking to you Charlie,' and left. This was at a time when Charlie began to stop talking to old friends who had nothing to say to him and didn't agree with his politics. He was closing down, totally preoccupied with what he was doing."

Doherty was a coarse, gabby "pain in the ass" who, although he drove the women in the Hill family crazy, was always welcome and was one of the few old friends still a part of Charlie's life. Charlie shrugged off Martha's account of that evening: "I would pay attention or not as I chose to — often not," he said. "But others, being civilized people, felt they should attend to him and pay attention, not be rude." Hill had no compunction about dropping out of a conversation that had nothing to offer him and consuming himself in a book or scribbling on his clipboard. He felt no duty to social etiquette in the small encounters and connections of life. Yet it remained important to Hill to pay homage to the idea of Bridgeton. He came for vacation and walked about the town not as a resident, but as an anthropologist and American Studies student, impassively observing the urban decay — or alternately as a duty-bound Foreign Service officer, speaking to local classes when teachers invited him. He was also there to spend time with his parents, as a proper son should. But he wanted less to do with the town's realities: the high school acquaintances who had never left and the long afternoons with the family and friends he cared for, but who had no idea of the weight on his mind every day. To them, frankly, he had little to say.

He and Martha had stopped having real conversations long ago. They still loved each other, but love was not enough. In Washington, Hill later admitted, he had been unfaithful. The women were fellow Foreign Service officers. He gave in to their advances. Years later he wondered aloud whether women have antennae for sensing when a man is having trouble with his marriage. It is a strange question from a man so concerned for the honor and integrity of the American male character. He did not want Martha to find out, but she did.

"I thought all this would be cleaned up if we could go to California," Hill said. "So that's what I did — to try to get into another society, another atmosphere. At first it seemed to be workable, transforming. The girls were away at this time. But she became alcoholic and the explosions continued — never at me, from no cause I could imagine." Never at him. Their age-old patterns continued. When Charlie (and now Martha, too) came home from work, they would sit, crunch peanuts, and drink cocktails, even though Martha "was less and less able to do that" without alcohol ruining the evening, she said later. "But we never talked about it." Charlie still understood Martha's behavior in terms of the specter of her mother, which forever reminded her what a mistake she had made with her life. "I was a bad husband. I didn't understand it, or try to talk it over," he confessed. "It seemed built into her. It came

271

about in a slow rise over the years. I was stupid. I didn't see it as a sudden problem. I just thought, that's how she is. My number one conclusion was that marriage, to be married, was something she didn't want. I was so tied up in work, I didn't think about things. My eyes were veiled."

According to Charlie, it was he who first used the word "divorce." But it was a bluff to him, at first. He had not planned to separate from Martha. He thought he could never go through with it. The idea of divorce horrified him. It is tempting to brush off this noble sentiment as that reflexive South Jersey sense of duty—duty to the letter of the law, at least. While that assessment holds some truth, Charlie still loved his wife. Nevertheless, life at home had gotten only harder after their move to California, and his hopes for renewal evaporated almost immediately. After one blowup he went out for a walk and ended up at the office of their landlord, where he put down a payment on an apartment in another building only a few hundred yards away. He would move out after Martha's next explosion.

In the Hoover Archives, where Hill deposited his vast collection of papers after he left the Foreign Service, there is a set of notebooks that tell the story of the last years of his marriage to Martha. These are nothing like his State Department steno pads. They are fine leather daytimers, the kind that have oversized calendar pages punctuated occasionally with black-and-white *New Yorker* cartoons, probably Christmas gifts from a relative who was happy to hit on a present that Charlie would enjoy, or at least put to good use, year after year. For the most part the pages are filled with banal notations of Hill's days at Hoover: meetings, phone calls, early-morning runs and rowing, football scores, and dinner appointments. Interwoven with the mundane rhythms of his daily calendar, Hill recorded a narrative of his broken marriage that sometimes contradicts his own recollections. Some of those discrepancies are probably meaningless tricks of memory; others might reflect the version of reality that Hill came to prefer. But what is more important about these notes is their portrayal of a side of Charlie that he rarely permitted anyone, even himself, to see.

On July 26, 1989, after a cookout and swimming party at Shultz's house described in Hill's day-timer with only an ominous frowning smiley face, there is the stark beginning to the notes' story: "M: 'I think we should get divorced.'" If Charlie had brought up the end before Martha said it now, he did not record it. A few days later, on August 31, he noted their thirty-second wedding anniversary. It appears from the day-timers that Charlie continued to share the apartment with Martha through the rest of the year. On November 5 Martha talked again of separation. On the fifteenth, there is an entry that contradicts Charlie's claim that they never had real fights:

M monologue. CH roar. M scratches C face hard.

Three days later, Martha noticed the laceration:

M: "How did you get your face so badly scratched?" (You did it) (shock)

She had been drunk during the fight. She did not remember anything.

The implications of the "CH roar" note notwithstanding, Hill later emphasized that his refusal to engage Martha emotionally persisted even in the death throes of their relationship. "This is important, to me at least," he wrote in an e-mail after I brought this diary entry to his attention. "I never fought, or fought back, verbally or physically; I was silent and passive on every occasion. The event happened when I was sitting (in that "captain's chair" now in this office) and M. was in the bedroom. She walked up behind the chair and gripped my face with her nails and raked them back. And then went back to the bedroom. The whole thing was done in total silence, and I returned to reading." It is not clear which does more damage to the link between two people: the fog of illness or a wall of willed indifference.

Now, when it was too late to salvage their relationship, Charlie's notes suggest that he and Martha were beginning the conversation they should have had decades earlier. In early January, Martha pleaded:

M: "I wish I could talk to you about the deep things you are thinking about, but I can't." (a tear) writing, life, discontent

The fact that he noted it in his day-timer proved that, this time, he listened to her. A little more than a week later, after a long harangue from Martha while Charlie was in the bathroom, he told her, as they lay in bed, that he was leaving. The next morning she demanded a better explanation. "You're just throwing people away," she told him. He repeated the reasons he gave her the previous night, recording them in parentheses, the format he usually used for his own speech: "(bitterness revealed when drunk) (need to see if I'm a person. It's all in a box)." That last remark, strangely introspective for the forward-marching Charlie Hill, must have sounded to Martha like a flip attempt at reducing emotions to shorthand. "Have seen this in you for a long time. What you must do you must do. You're [an] only child. Never learned to share," is the recorded response. A few days later she told him to sleep in the other bedroom. That weekend, according to the notes, it was Martha, rather than Charlie, who proposed that he get a studio apartment elsewhere in the neighborhood.

Charlie moved out in February. He slept poorly, his unconsciousness pocked by nightmares of gunfights and bad haircuts. Some days Martha called him and they convened in her apartment to attempt civil conversation, but more often than not these visits ended bitterly. Martha was having trouble at work. In March she received a scathing performance report from her supervisor. "God is hurling every bolt he has at me right now—and I don't think I deserve it," she told Charlie during one visit. She was "totally weak and shaking from first day taking Artane [a muscle relaxant] for muscle spasm," he wrote. "Life collapsed, marriage, health, career." Years of surgery and treatments had done nothing to help her voice, but at least now Charlie seemed to hear her. He had ignored her before: "The worst thing was that you knew how I felt and you were not there for me," she told him a few days later. "I have no motivation, no enthusiasm for this job. Anything this past year has meant to me is gone. I'm finished. There is no me. None. I should go back east. It's gone."

Charlie never took notes like these before. While the sudden implosion of a marriage is much harder to ignore than its steady erosion, even for the most phlegmatic South Jersey character, there is more to it than that. Amid the notes of painful encounters with Martha a degree of self-awareness emerges, an emotional candor totally unfamiliar to those who knew Charles Hill. The notes record things he never before deemed worthy of record. Like the notebooks he kept during his time with Shultz, these day-timers capture things that would be otherwise lost, details forgotten or sanitized, even in Hill's candid recount of his divorce in interviews years later. Unlike the history contained in his professional notes, the day-timer entries capture something more elusive, a dynamic quality that even a faultless memory could not recreate. They are artifacts of personal change.

Divorce forever alters a person, leaving a lasting crimp after the knot has been cut. But so does love. Charlie soon yielded to an unexpected love that made him like wet clay, softening and reshaping him, just when the old love was admitting final defeat.

As the end of the Reagan administration approached, Hill had felt an urge to reconnect with the academic world. In late 1988 he received a winter-term course catalogue in the mail from Georgetown University, and he decided to enroll in a class on Herodotus, taught by a young professor named Norma Jean Grima. She was a University of Chicago Ph.D. candidate now teaching continuing education courses at Georgetown. She was a pretty brunette with shrewd sea-green eyes, more than twenty years his junior. Back then she was married to a successful, impeccably groomed lawyer, a graduate of the University of Chicago Law School who now practiced in Washington. When Hill signed up to take her class, he thought she would be a stereotypical Chicago graduate student — "dark, a smoker with thick glasses," he remembered. "I was quite amazed, because she wasn't that image at all . . . She was immediately distinctive because she was coming out of a deeply, profoundly, almost humorously exaggerated intellectual atmosphere, except she was not the Chicago type. She was an athlete, a beer-drinking, all-American-girl kind of person."

Norma Thompson grew up outside of Providence, Rhode Island, in a pleasant suburb that offered more shopping malls than hometown roots. Her family was large, churchgoing, and Irish. She studied history at Bowdoin College, where she began as a tentative liberal, joining feminist groups on campus and reading Marxist literature. She felt increasingly uncomfortable in those circles, drifting toward something else. A prescient professor pointed her toward Hannah Arendt, in whose writings Norma found an appealing union of history and political theory. Arendt had taught at the University of Chicago; Norma followed suit and matriculated there for graduate school, where she was earning a Ph.D. from the Committee on Social Thought.

She thrived immediately in the bleak, gray confines of the Hyde Park campus and was now devoted to the Western canon and bewitched by the charms of David Grene — dairy farmer, Greek scholar, and indomitable authority on Herodotus. Having completed her classes, she followed her husband to Washington when he found a job there. Here Norma was trying to finish her thesis on the value of Herodotus for modern readers. She was struggling with it, drowning in her research and unsure of her own voice. It was a terrible idea for an insecure graduate student to teach a class of uninterested laymen on her thesis subject, the object of such obsession and misery, but she was doing it anyway.

Although Norma was typically just as shy as Charlie, she walked up and introduced herself to him on the first day of class as he stood quietly by the door, clutching his motorcycle helmet. From the start, he became her ally. The class was awkward, populated by eight ordinary citizens and retired seniors (the minimum enrollment that Georgetown would permit) who never really understood what their teacher was talking about. When the class greeted her questions with ponderous silence, increasingly it was Hill who leapt into the breach. He wrote a paper on the Alcmaeonidae, the powerful Athenian noble family traditionally blamed—although Herodotus disputes this in his account—for treacherously raising their shield at the battle of Marathon as a signal to the Persians. His essay impressed and devastated her, she remarked later. He had bested her years of work in a paper that, she was certain, took him half an hour to write.

But she was not intimidated by Charlie, and he, strangely, felt at ease around her. They were both uncharacteristically themselves. "He had wonderful eyes," Norma said later. "I just knew by his eyes." Knew what—she was not yet sure.

When the course ended, they saw little of each other. Once, some months later, he invited her to come to the State Department for lunch. "It was a very interesting conversation because I had read a lot of stuff over the years in fairly wide-ranging fields, and we had a lot in common in that regard," he recalled. "I'd had no one to talk to like that." He started to call her Nori. It is not often that two Herodoteans stumble upon each other, two thoroughly sophisticated premoderns. But if Herodotus teaches us anything at all, it is that people who speak the same language, and tell the same stories, will find each other.

When the Hills moved to California and Thompson moved back to Chicago to finish her degree, they kept in touch over the phone. Thompson's own marriage was quickly deteriorating. Although Charlie later maintained that back then his relationship with Norma was not romantic, the documentation of their long-distance friendship, sparse as it is in his notes, reads like the playing of lovers discovering each other. In one entry, Charlie noted that Norma, while rooting around in the Regenstein Library at the University of Chicago, had found a first edition of Henry Adams's nine-volume *History of the United States of America During the Administrations of Thomas Jefferson and James Madison* (1889–91). While reading one of the volumes, she came upon a pressed four-leaf clover that looked to be a century old. It seemed fated; the nickname of Adams's wife, Marion, was Clover. Norma carefully removed it and mailed it to Charlie two weeks later. A more fitting sign that Charlie had found a soul mate is difficult to imagine.

Norma finished her work in Chicago, and shortly after Charlie had settled into his own apartment she found a job at Golden Gate University, flew west, and moved in with him. She had just been through a rough divorce from her first husband, and she and Charlie were in the same emotional place, even if they were far apart in age and career trajectories. Norma was the only person he found he could talk to. On February 3, 1990, they celebrated the two-year anniversary of their meeting in the Herodotus class.

A day-timer entry suggests that Charlie first told Martha about Norma in early June, but it is likely that this note marks only their first substantial conversation about his new relationship. Norma and Charlie were living in an apartment just down the block. It is hard to believe that almost five months could pass before Martha learned there was another woman. In an entry from a Saturday in late March, Hill recorded a confrontation with Emily that suggests his younger daughter at least suspected her father was in a new relationship months earlier. The lines read like an anguished poem:

> 0830 tennis with Em. Desultory. Not focused. Talk by pool M [Martha is] totally insulted (not heartbroken?); wrong time. 20 years ago or never; slime you are; paddling after great men. A shame; unresponsible [sic]; your parents will be crushed; why didn't you tell us; are you having an affair; all those pretty interns you hire . . . Are you sick?; can't believe your father w another woman; how can you destroy the family? . . . you come first, so who cares what others feel; will you be home for the holidays . . . Em: [on Sunday] Yes, heartbroken. Depart at 1130. I love y[ou] mommy (not to me)

There on the tennis court, Emily clawed at her father in the places where it hurt him the most. He was tearing the family apart, she told him. He was shirking his duty as husband and father. All his masterful work at the side of Great Men meant nothing to Emily, compared with this. She was not proud of her father—she was angry. Her definition of a Great Man, it seems, was not the same as his.

Martha slammed the receiver down the first few times she called Charlie's apartment and Norma answered, but she was doing her best to adjust. On July 20, when she phoned to tell Charlie that she had joined Alcoholics Anonymous, he recorded her strained courtesy when Norma answered: "Hi. May I please speak to Charlie for a couple of minutes?" But a month later when he stopped by the old apartment to see her, she offered him vodka. She was off the program. They talked about Emily's anger at him. Then, a heartbreaking parting line, a sentence that sums up Martha's most painful ache—

I never had the chance to be a Nori.

Three days later, Emily told her father not to contact her anymore. Charlie had no choice but to back off from her for a while. In September, when Martha asked him about his Thanksgiving plans, he lied and said he planned to be in China—so that his parents, who were used to chatting more with Martha than with their son during holidays, could invite her to Bridgeton.

Two days later Martha called him at 8:30 in the morning: "I need to talk to you. I'm in big trouble." Charlie offered to come over that evening, but Martha told him to come the following night. At eleven o'clock she called back and told him, "You don't have to come tomorrow. I have to handle this by myself." "I'd like to talk about it," Charlie told her. "Can I ask you tomorrow?" "Yes, but you don't need to come." He was worried for her. When he didn't hear from her, he went over after work two days later: "5 at M's. M goes to AA everyday. IS an alcoholic. Went to work in the evening thinking it was morning after passed out about 5:30pm. Said she wanted to apologize. The end of our marriage was brought about by 'this' (points to vodka). AA said alcoholics filled with resentment. She thought there wasn't, then wrote out pages of her bitter resentments starting with law school and on through Kissinger, etc."

When he went to visit her a couple of weeks later, for the first time the vodka bottle was absent. Martha asked him to explain again "how it happened." He talked about the oppression of her mother and the feminists in Cambridge that gave Florence Mitchell's lectures legitimacy. He recalled her outbursts at dinner parties and the "nightly tirades" that had only grown worse in California. Martha apologized. "This is first time M indicated she wished it hadn't happened," Charlie wrote.

At the end of this day-timer entry is a line that the South Jersey stoic never thought he'd write:

Back with N, CH cries.

At the end of the month, Charlie stopped off at Safeway for groceries and bought two pumpkins for Halloween—one he dropped off at his apartment, the other he took to Martha's garage and left it in her car for her to find. A few days later, he gave her an airplane ticket to Philadelphia so she could spend Thanksgiving with his parents (her own had passed away). Later that month, when she and Charlie were going over divorce papers, she asked him, "What if I changed? Would you come back?" He told her no.

Charlie doesn't remember that encounter today. "If she'd called once and said please don't do this, please come back, I love you, I would have. But she didn't," he said later. "I could not have withstood that. I was not approaching this with bravado or assurance. It was the most horrible thing, in my mind, to do—utterly grotesque and hideous." His notes prove he was torn apart inside. "In car on way back see M going to parking lot. I love her and this hurts so much," reads an entry from November 13. His heartache combined with fear for Martha's life. There were a few terrifying occasions when she lost control and came close to seriously hurting herself. The death of their relationship was agonizing. The divorce paperwork required nearly two years. The process was made easier because Charlie gave Martha everything —the house in Washington and his entire pension. It was the only honorable thing to do. At times they had cordial, even pleasant interactions, but alcohol seemed to be winning its war of attrition. There were many drunken, angry calls that Martha did not remember the morning after. There were just as many moments when Charlie spotted her walking down the street or lunching with friends on the grass outside his office window, and felt his heart pinch.

The nadir for Martha came in the spring of 1992, shortly after the divorce was finalized and Charlie and Norma were married in San Francisco City Hall. After a near-deadly night that ended with a trip to the emergency psychiatric ward, she finally understood that alcoholism was killing her. She immediately enrolled in a treatment program that met five times a week. She began slowly to recover for real. Despite her love for the job at Hoover and the friends she had made there, Palo

Alto was too expensive for a single woman, and she "needed more roots than I had there at the time," she said later. In late 1992 she packed up the apartment on Sand Hill and planned to move back to Washington, to Cathedral Avenue. The house had not changed since they first moved there almost twenty years earlier, only now, with the girls and Charlie gone, it was much too quiet and much too big. Sometimes the house stank with memories, but it was still home, as was Westmoreland Church, to which she was happy to return. She bought a cat, black and white, and named her Lila.

Charlie and Norma started their own life anew back east. Norma received her doctorate in February 1991 and had been furiously sending out résumés since then, but the job market was rotten. Out of the blue came an offer from Yale University, where she had applied months earlier at the suggestion of Yale political science professor Steven Smith, who had watched Norma defend the Western canon against a panel of left-wing academics at a recent American Political Science Association event. Fortuitously, a few weeks later Charlie got a call from U.N. official Jean-Claude Aimé, whom he had known casually when they were both posted in Israel. Aimé wanted to know whether Charlie would like to work for the new secretary-general, Boutros Boutros-Ghali, in the capacity of "special policy consultant." Without much sense of what exactly he would be doing, Charlie took the job. He and Norma left California in the summer of 1992. In New Haven they would first live in the house of a professor on leave, then as residential fellows in Berkeley College at Yale. Soon they bought a 160-year-old white clapboard house on Bradley Street in New Haven. Charlie would commute to New York.

Martha had not yet left for Washington, and shortly before he and Norma were set to depart, he met Martha for a goodbye lunch. She wished him well but broke down in tears. Although there had been tears of anger before, to him this seemed like the first time she cried from grief. "Took 2 years to cry," he wrote. "If she had at the time I would never have left." Once Martha was out of sight, Charlie cried too.

Charlie's second marriage, to Norma Thompson, was the lifeboat that made his years in California bearable. In her he found a partner who shared his political values, matched his intellect, and broke through his withdrawn personality. His relationship with her has been a rather astonishing personal discovery that carried him through the divorce and into a wholly new phase of life, but for the outside reader it makes this part of the story even sadder. Martha was never the intellectual that Norma was, but it is hard to escape the feeling that even if she never could have "been a Nori," she certainly could have "been a Marty"— successful and independent, deeply engaged in her own medium, art —if she had continued to pursue her own passions as she had in college. Some of the fault lies with the demons of alcoholism and the fragile fits and starts of women's liberation, as well as with Martha's own inability to put herself first, to seek out what would have made her happy. However, one cannot help but blame Charlie, who said over and over that he loved her but boxed that love away in a corner, where it would not interfere with his work and his life of ideas. Years of time to think and seek counseling have made Martha admirably diplomatic in her reminiscences about her ex-husband, but now and again bitter realism creeps out:

> What Charlie doesn't realize is that his entire life has been enabled because of women—his mother and me. Our entire marriage, he didn't buy one pair of shorts. His mother and I clothed that boy. It's a huge gap in his knowledge—that there was this staff of people who made his life possible. But that stuff is uninteresting, mundane . . . That's one of his flaws. He doesn't take the mundane stuff, rejects an integral part of people's lives, partly because of the way his life has been. The women in it have enabled him to work all night. He can afford these giant concepts because he's allowed to live without having to pay attention. Katie tells me that now he has a credit card for the first time, and when he loses it, Nori gets it replaced.

Martha is right. In New Haven Charlie continues to shirk mundanities as much as he ever did. He still hates parties and small talk. He still claims that the last film he saw in a theater, and the last one he ever plans to see, was *Patton*, which came out in 1970. But beneath the familiar exterior something fundamental has changed in him, and that is what makes the jottings in those day-timers remarkable. A note taker's mind is laid bare in his notebooks, and these are a mixture of personal confession, self-flagellating records of life's most painful conversations, and the familiar eye for detail others would miss. The last characteristic is probably the most bizarre, because in these notes that eye for detail yields not armchair anthropological musings, like those Charlie recorded while at the State Department, but careful records of what Martha and Norma were wearing almost every time he saw either woman. One day we find Norma dressed in a "green jumper, white blouse, necklace . . . next day N (tapping fingers) Chi[cago] Bears sweatshirt and sweatpants." Two days later, it is a "wht turtle [white turtleneck], gold earrings, big brown sweater CH gave . . . big brown skirt, boots." On Halloween 1990, Martha "comes up in witch's costume, big hat, short black skirt, very sexy." One day the following summer she "looks like dish of ice cream in white shirt, lime pants, white shoes, woven Guatemala belt." These observations remind one of the astute commentary on the outfits of Charlie's female classmates that charmed Mary Anne Gbur in Bridgeton long ago. But these precise notes on Norma's and Martha's wardrobes, interspersed with heart-wrenching quarrels, accusations, and moments of regret, strike the reader as very strange. Perhaps, as Charlie scribbled down in odd corners of his day-timers entries that would come closer than he had ever allowed to personal reflection, this precise notation of what the two women in his life wore was an unconscious attempt to remove himself from the situation. It was a small effort to counter the emotion pouring onto the page with a dose of the old Charlie, the impassive observer who misses no detail, no matter how minor.

But that is only speculation. The fact is that even though for most of his life Hill had been unwilling or unable to exercise the "feminine ability" of intuition and observation upon himself and his personal life, he was always astute—and self-aware—in employing that mode of thinking in his work. Years after he left the Foreign Service he assessed what he considered the cornerstone of his relationship with George Shultz and his impact on policy: his sensitivity to the undercurrent and context of every diplomatic encounter, the nuance and attention to detail in his diplomatic reporting.

> It goes back to whether or not you think everything matters—whatever this is that you're doing, does it make a difference. Most would say yes, but they don't believe it. It's a feminine quality. Women are more attuned, but men have to be so in diplomacy if they are to be effective. Men are, almost by definition, not this way. They are genetically programmed to be oblivious to things because if they weren't, they'd be diverted from their duty. Women can read invisible signals, sense things, catch a word out of place, a hesitation in answering a question, an answer too short or too long, changes in clothes, appearance, or posture.

He noted Martha's and Norma's clothing because, in small but important ways, it mattered. The way a woman dresses is a signal to the man she is going to meet. It was a detail he had noticed instinctively since he was a boy; old habits of mind do not die easily. He collected details in the lines of his notebooks as a butterfly collector pins his finest specimens in a box. But what makes his quirky fashion commentary more remarkable is that it offers such personal, detailed images of the two women he has loved. These entries provide the scenery for a story of breakdown and rebuilding.

It is a story that any reader of Charlie's notes over the years, usually so antiseptic, is surprised to find him willing to tell. Maybe we had been selling him short all this time. Or maybe he had changed.

There was a time when I hated Charlie. It was brief but fierce, the kind of feeling that possesses you entirely and makes you think you will never be able to touch its source again, like a bout of terrible food poisoning.

It began with Martha. He first told me about the end of their marriage when I was just beginning to work on the biography, and I was surprised and troubled. I had a hard time believing the professor whom I admired had committed adultery and treated a woman so badly. I guess at first I chose not to believe it. I recorded it in my notebook, paused at the words again when I transcribed them onto the computer, and printed them out for my binders, but I did not dwell. "Oh, so here is proof that the esteemed Professor Hill is human too," I may have thought. As a journalist, I considered it "nice color." As a student, I ignored it.

A year or more later, I went to the house on Cathedral Avenue for that first visit with Martha. We got along immediately, and suddenly the stranger I knew only from Charlie's old photographs became a human being, a great cook and an even better laugher. I sent her a Christmas card that winter with a note that had little to do with Charlie. I mainly wrote about dyeing my hair pink and worrying about what my boyfriend's parents would think when I visited them over the holidays. Maybe part of me considered her a friend.

I saw much of myself in the young woman Martha was when she married Charlie. Perhaps that is the root of why I suddenly began to feel so angry toward him for how he had mistreated her — I took it personally. With each chapter I increasingly wanted to dwell on Martha's part of the story. As I continued my research, I retreated into the library to read stacks of books or left town to track down friends and colleagues of Charlie. I did everything I could to put off conducting more interviews with him, when I would have to sit in that uncomfortable Windsor chair across from his desk and pretend that nothing had changed.

Then, during one sojourn at the Hoover Archives going through monotonous records of his tour in the Middle East, I came across the day-timers, packed in a cardboard archive box like everything else. As soon as I began to read them I was engrossed. I put aside everything else, the dry State Department memos and field reports I had come to read that day, and pored over the day-timers like a child gorging on ice cream before dinner. As I turned the pages — slowly, for I could let hardly one entry pass without transcribing it onto my laptop — the drama captivated me more than any novel or movie because its actors were people I knew and had already thought about deeply. There emerged, suddenly, a Charlie Hill that I had never seen before. Once when I asked Charlie whether he wanted to page through one of the old scrapbooks Martha had let me borrow, he had told me that he couldn't, because any divorce required "an emotional lobotomy." At the time I scoffed — it didn't seem there could have been much emotion to remove in the first place. Now I saw I was wrong. The divorce that scarred Martha so profoundly had been horrible for him too. Finally I had proof that there was a human being behind that calm monotone and impassive stare.

I felt guilty, sitting there reading the day-timers. Every time one of the archivists swished past my desk, I shifted my arms to hide the pages. Even though I was writing the man's life story, I felt voyeuristic, suddenly privy to ugly, naked things he had never intended for me to find. I was certain that when he sent these notebooks to the archives he must have forgotten that they contained anything besides appointment dates and sports scores — otherwise he would never have authorized Hoover to open them to researchers. Perhaps more strangely, as I read I felt Charlie's presence in the room, a stern phantom peering over my shoulder with his ghostly arms crossed. "I never should have allowed a twenty-year-old girl to write the story of my life," I heard the phantom groan. "Girls are such fools for soap operas and squishy human drama. A male student, a proper scholar of Grand Strategy, wouldn't care about these day-timers. He would understand that my true legacy lies in my work beside history's Great Men. Now this girl is going to think she understands me, think she's slipped unnoticed inside my mind, when really she's missing the point entirely. She doesn't get it."

The phantom's appearance was encouraged by my long-standing insecurities about why Charlie had allowed me to write his biography in the first place. I had been a decent student in his class, but as far as I could remember I never gave him reason to think that I was anything more than barely competent. My most vivid memory of my time as his student was the day when he turned to me a few minutes before class began and gruffly complimented a newspaper column I had written: "I liked your piece, Molly. You're doing good work there." The column was all about my little brother's romantic exploits in high school and how jealous I was. I believe it included the line "he gets more action in one weekend than I've gotten in my entire Yale career." Could it be that my gray-haired professor actually read that fluff I wrote? I was mortified. I always assumed that he read only the pretentious political columns, the ones that talked about Grand Strategy.

I had concluded sometime earlier that he agreed to let me write about him simply because I was the one who happened to ask. As a teacher, he probably saw it as a nice opportunity to help out a student who wanted to be a writer by volunteering to be her guinea pig. But now he would regret it. He would hate me for screwing it up. I felt embarrassed.

The notes I took while reading the day-timers lay dormant in my files for several months, while I worked through the remainder of his Foreign Service career. Sometimes I forgot about them entirely. But then, as I approached the time when I would have to write about his years at Hoover and he made that remark about the "feminine quality" of understanding that everything matters, I realized that maybe he wouldn't be angry when he learned I had spent so much time with the day-timers. No matter what one makes of Charlie's old-fashioned notions of "feminine" and "masculine" qualities, the fact remained that this particular characteristic he ascribed to women was fast emerging as the core of his worldview: there is nothing, no facet of human experience, that is insignificant. Perhaps he thought that columns about love and teenage libido were just as interesting as columns about violence in the Middle East. Perhaps he knew, when he made the decision to permit me to contact Martha and to be frank with me about his divorce and his relations with other women, that I would find his behavior unforgivable. But he also knew that as long as he allowed me to ask questions about everything and read everything he had written — not just about the subjects pertinent to his "historical legacy" — I would come around.

Sometimes I wondered what, in Charlie's mind, made my enter-prise all that different from the nasty snoopings of the Iran-Contra in-dependent counsel. Why did he trust a college kid with every one of his thousands of pages of notes, when he had "shrieked" and "raised hell" at the thought of allowing trained investigators to view them? Certainly the classified material involved was now two decades old and mostly harmless, but in Charlie's eyes an inaccurate history written today would be a far worse crime than a misguided newspaper article in 1987. Why did he grant me access to everything from sensitive State Department secrets to the most private moments of his personal life? I think the answer is because I was a wide-eyed college undergraduate and he was my teacher. Charlie has a great deal more faith in a Yale ed-ucation than in the U.S. government. Any anxieties he had about the biography must have been trumped by his sense of duty to history, his habit of confident self-appraisal, and his belief that I was out to capture a story rather than assign blame or uncover dirty secrets. Most important, he knew me first as a terrified freshman in his History and Politics seminar. He knew me as a faithful believer in Herodotus, the father of storytelling great and small, the one who shows us that if we are true to the stories, then we will be true to the people who lived and told them.

Walter Lippmann's biographer Ronald Steel has said that a biographer and subject are "both partners and antagonists," "locked in a contest of undetermined duration, over issues that are always in dispute, for stakes that are never clearly delineated." Steel continued,

> It's like a marriage. Each is linked to the other for the duration, how-ever long that might be. To break the pact would be an admission of bad faith. Given the divorce rates these days, one could even say it is more binding than most marriages . . . I see it more like a courtship, a contract and a contest, an *agon* of the sort that Balanchine depicts in his ballet. Each partner has his own motives, which are never fully ex-pressed. Each observes a mode of behavior, ruled by strict convention. Each carefully protects himself while realizing that his full develop-ment can come only in union with the other.

I never mentioned this metaphor to Martha. But one evening to-ward the end of my work on the biography, we were chatting on the phone and I told her about the strange direction my writing had taken.

I explained how, in putting together Charlie's story, I found myself telling the parallel story of what it was like for me, the once-adoring student, to come to grips with the unsightly, human parts of my professor's life. "I'm so glad to hear the book has gone in that direction. I went through that journey myself—I guess that's why I identify with it," Martha told me. "When I met Charlie, I thought he was the most fascinating person that I'd ever met. But some of the things that he hasn't focused on in his life—they really did a lot of damage to a lot of people." Later on, Katie confided to me that her mom was so fond of me because she saw me as her alter ego, coming to understand Charlie as she did, and now saying and writing the things that she had always wanted to say. To Martha, Charlie was a man upon whom far too much had been lost. To me, he was still my teacher, but he had come to be something more.

As with a lifelong spouse, there were times when I felt enraptured by my subject, times when I felt so smothered by him I could not breathe, and times when I got so mad at him that I could not write anymore. I was too young to be married. I was barely a twentysomething fresh out of college with the attention span of a young adult used to fifty-minute literature lectures. To be buried in the life of a gray-haired diplomat for over two years, to face the task of describing and judging very difficult, grown-up things like parenthood and divorce, demanded a level of maturity that I was not confident I had. I probably didn't have it, so I had to learn to fake it.

The important thing was that no matter how I felt about Charlie, I kept at it. I learned how to slog through. Sometimes I took a vacation from him, went away and treated myself to books other than histories of the Vietnam War and obese, narcissistic memoirs by Reaganites. But I always came back, and I stuck with him long enough to see that we were both just human beings. As I neared the end of the book I realized that, in a funny way, I had watched him grow up. As odd as it is for a twenty-three-year-old to say of a professor nearly seventy, I began to feel just a bit maternal toward him. I set a picture of him on my desk—not one of the many glossy photographs he has shown me of him shaking hands with various heads of state, but one he probably forgot he lent me: a faded black-and-white portrait in a cheap painted wooden frame. The subject is a small boy with fuzzy hair and protuberant ears. He is dressed in little striped overall shorts, no shirt, and stands in the bushes beside a neighbor's house, staring fixedly at the morning glories blossoming over the clapboard siding. He is probably not interested in the flowers but in a beetle or a caterpillar perched on one of the leaves, invisible from the photographer's distance. I prefer this picture to all the others because the Charlie it depicts is small, vulnerable, and uncertain — all the things that Professor Hill never seems to be. It depicts the things that everyone is, because they are part of being human. It had only taken me a bit longer, in Charlie's case, to see that.

14

BOUTROS BOUTROS-GHALI, A SPARE, ELEGANT EGYPTIAN WITH a sophisticated sense of humor and an ear for Arabic poetry, was different from earlier U.N. secretaries-general. He did not think it was his job to mediate disputes and make mystical pronouncements on world peace. He saw the links among peace, development, and democracy, and he wanted to put his ideas to work. He was not a secular pope; he was a grand strategist. Boutros-Ghali was the sort of Great Man that Charles Hill preferred to serve.

Jean-Claude Aimé arranged for Hill to fly east to meet the secretary-general in May 1992. Upon reaching New York City, he checked into a familiar hotel and changed into a tan suit before taking the subway to the Willard Hotel. After some confusion at the front desk, he gave the concierge his name. "'Hill!' she said. 'You are Mr. Hill!' Suddenly I was surrounded by security agents who said they had instructions to take me to the SYG [Secretary-General]. At the suite above I was sent right in. B-G was at the door to welcome me, and take me to a red plush loveseat on which we both sat." Hill recorded their conversation with the enthusiasm of a giddy teenager filling his diary with every detail of a first date. "This was a momentous time for the UN I felt, even more so than in the years after its founding. 'Exactly,' said B-G. 'That is why I took this job, for there is so much of significance to do in the next 3 or 4 years.' We talked of writing and how 'statements make things happen,' as I said . . . B-G had been a speechwriter, so had and was I; it was a talk of two members of that secret society, each of us talking over the other's comments in good humor." It was decided that Hill would start work immediately to help draft Boutros-Ghali's Agenda for Peace, an ambitious plan outlining the changes in peacekeeping since the founding of the United Nations in 1945. In August, once he and Norma had moved east, Hill began full-time as "Special Consultant on Policy" on the thirty-eighth floor of the U.N. Secretariat building, down the hall from the secretary-general's office.

Hill ran a small speechwriting staff, served as an ad hoc consultant on world affairs, and collaborated with Boutros-Ghali on his book projects. Later Hill would speak fondly about his time in the elegant, glass-walled building on the East River. But in his recollections there remains a pulse of frustration, a recurring sense that the U.N. bureaucracy and the governments of its member states were packed with people who did not "get it": who didn't understand the scope of the Islamic fundamentalist threat, the systemic problems in the international system, and the magnitude of action required to do something about them. All this was still crystallizing in Hill's own mind, but he had an early instinct for it. His years at the United Nations would prove a time of grand goals, incremental progress, and ugly setbacks. In the end, these frustrations were an important coda to the lessons he had been learning all his life. They would galvanize his determination to teach those lessons himself, at Yale.

Hill, the only American working on the thirty-eighth floor, spent a large portion of his time trying to negotiate between his old colleagues at the State Department and his new boss in New York. Any hopes that his compatriots would rise to their new responsibilities as the world's sole superpower soon dissipated. Francis Fukuyama proclaimed that history had ended in democracy's favor, and the Bush and Clinton administrations concluded that laissez-faire foreign policy was all that the world needed. None of this implied that Washington would permit a more powerful role for the United Nations, however. Soon after coming to power, the Clinton team rejected the U.N. plan for peace between Serbs and Bosnians in the former Yugoslavia, and the American media accused Boutros-Ghali, in his efforts to unify command of the peacekeeping troops there, of fancying himself "commander in chief" of American forces.

Boutros-Ghali's struggles abroad were exacerbated by troubles in his own organization. The U.N. bureaucracy would have resisted change under any leadership, but Boutros-Ghali had little instinct (and even less taste) for management or public relations. He loathed bureaucrats almost as much as Hill did. "Boutros-Ghali preferred to work with a small group of people. He was extremely self-reliant," said James

Sutterlin, a former Foreign Service officer who made a second career at the United Nations. "He was an academic, contemptuous of staff and of people in the missions [abroad]. That was one of his basic mistakes, although it's understandable." Hill and his speechwriters evolved into an unofficial policy planning staff, taking on many of the burdens that normally would have fallen to the bureaucracy. The thirty-eighth floor became an isolated place.

Hill was caught in the clash of two hostile herd mentalities. On the one hand there was the Clinton administration and much of the American public, scornful of the United Nations and "world bureaucracy." On the other was the culture of the United Nations and its staff, who believed that the bureaucratic way, the road of anti-ideology and compromise ad nauseum, was the only path to stability. The staff of the U.N. Secretariat unconsciously adhered to the creed of its internal culture, as all tribes do. "There was not some mastermind directing it, secret leaders of the bureaucracy cabal that met at night by candlelight," Hill said. "People follow a culture even though they're not directed to do so, and they shriek when you present something unfamiliar."

Boutros-Ghali wanted to fight back against American bully tactics, but the culture of the United Nations was not equipped for battle. As Hill wrote years later in a *Wall Street Journal* editorial entitled "The Mouse That Never Roars": "The UN, as Robert Burns might put it, is a 'wee, sleekit, cow'rin, tim'rous beastie' comprised of bureaucratic mice, constantly fearful that 'the member states' will rebuke or remove them . . . always alert to try to sense and stay strictly within the attitude and approach taken by their masters, the national governments. The UN was not designed to take the initiative, and whenever it gets a notion to do so the member states slap it down." As far as Hill was concerned, the U.N. bureaucrats were guilty of the same crimes as the Clintonites: they were blind to what was really going on in world affairs, and what was required to change it. They lacked grand strategy, and they lacked South Jersey nerve.

In 1996, the United States vetoed the nomination of Boutros-Ghali for a second term as secretary-general. Washington had long ago lost its taste for the feisty Egyptian, and recently he had become a serious inconvenience for Clinton in the presidential campaign. Republican nominee Bob Dole persisted in his drawling declarations against Clinton's few compromises with "Bootrus-Bootrus." The United States had spent the summer and fall campaigning against Boutros-Ghali around

the world. By the November vote, Washington's bullying had succeeded. The countries whose representatives Boutros-Ghali so often ignored and whose civil servants had lost jobs because of his reforms
were not eager to jump to his defense. Hill would leave the thirty-
eighth floor with his boss at year's end.

When a grand strategist is foiled by the world he has tried to shape, his
last resort is to turn to the record, to leave in his failures a lesson for
history. Hill's concentration increasingly turned to writing, the original
reason that Boutros-Ghali had hired him. Sutton Place, the residence of
the secretary-general, was an elegant, four-story Georgian townhouse
built during the 1930s for the daughter of J. P. Morgan. When Hill first
visited there, Boutros-Ghali took him up to the study, an airy room
with high ceilings and English country-house furnishings. "Come look
here, you are a writer," he called, showing Hill his collection of Ottoman
pen cases. These were ornate pen scabbards housing an ink cabin at
one end and covered with lavish Arabic script. Every official scribe and
high secretary of the empire wore one in his belt to show that he was a
warrior.

In the early years, the two did most of their work in the drawing
room, where Boutros-Ghali sat on the couch and Hill in a chair with
his back to the fireplace, huge three-ring binders filled with the day's
work spread out before him. José, the majordomo, appeared intermittently with plates of cookies and potent Turkish coffee. After Boutros-
Ghali left for Paris in 1996, Hill made weeklong trips to meet with his
old boss there. *Egypt's Road to Jerusalem*, Boutros-Ghali's account of the
1980 Palestinian autonomy talks (which Hill also attended), was published in 1997. *Unvanquished*, the secretary-general's memoir of his
stormy time at the United Nations, came out two years later.

A more significant record was Boutros-Ghali's vast accumulation of
personal papers. In early 1997 Hill answered a knock at his door on
Bradley Street in New Haven to discover a pack of Boutros-Ghali's security guards, wearing shoulder holsters and tiny microphones in their
ears and carrying big cartons marked "UN." Hill had told Boutros-
Ghali that he would take the papers, but he was shocked when the security agents actually showed up with their clandestine delivery. Luckily the United Nations had hardly any notion of records regulation; "in
Washington, all of us would have gone to the penitentiary," he mused.
Hill spent the next few years outwitting suspicious U.N. archivists and

sneaking documents out of the Secretariat in his briefcase. "I was treated with enormous smoldering suspicion," he recalled. "I had to creep around the building. Boutros-Ghali had been vetoed, and the bureaucracy never liked him anyway because he kicked their asses around . . . When I came back, I had to hide."

Yale University Press would publish *The Papers of Secretary-General Boutros Boutros-Ghali* in 2003, seven years after Hill began the project. Each volume's cover is printed with the byline, in tasteful gold lettering, "selected and edited by Charles Hill." This is the only book, of the several that he has helped to mastermind and edit or write, that bears his name. When I asked him why he had never written his own big book, he only smiled. There was no better way to get people to pay attention to your ideas and your take on history, he explained, than to write them beneath the byline of Henry Kissinger, George Shultz, or Boutros Boutros-Ghali. After all, who has ever heard of Charles Hill?

Through the middle of the 1990s Hill remained largely invisible, writing scripts and directing scenes rather than taking the stage himself. This was the quintessential Charlie, at base a shy, library-bound creature who had learned over the years (with remarkable success) to make the most of his insecurities—to accomplish more in the shadows of Great Men than many Great Men do themselves. But after the United Nations, he returned to Yale. The university had always been Charlie's arcadia, where he would step out from his sanctuary of monkish reflection only when he wanted to retrieve a book or find a few hours of conversation. But here, he could not retreat into the old Charlie, the peculiar South Jersey character who kept to the margin, operated beneath others' bylines, and eschewed the press and social encounters. His students would hold him accountable, as he would them. Yale students are not interested in learning from shadows. They want to learn from Great Men.

Charlie kept a low profile at first. He was still spending most of his days at the United Nations, so he didn't have time for much involvement in the university community beyond the senior seminar he taught in the International Studies major. Nor was he eager to raise the hackles of liberal faculty members when his wife was hoping for a tenure-track position. His arrival on campus had already raised a few eyebrows. "There was a prejudice against him," recalled Donald Kagan, who was dean of Yale College at the time and masterminded Charlie's appointment. "After all, he was a Reagan Administration guy, Shultz's right-hand man."

Charlie found Yale, like most universities, to be an institution of overspecialization, pseudoscientific methodologies, and political correctness. The political atmosphere on campus was stagnant through the 1990s. Neither the war in Kosovo, President Clinton's impeachment, nor the controversial 2000 presidential election sparked even mild debate in the Political Science department's cafeteria, Charlie found. The largest student demonstration he could remember was an inglorious picketing against sweatshops, attended by fewer than twenty students.* There were a handful of small clubs and publications for conservative and libertarian students, but for the most part Yale was the domain of the "aged hippie":

> No clear case of the denial of academic freedom has or is likely to occur. Those who wish to suppress academic freedom have become far too accomplished for that. Instead there is a pervasive, continual, all-enveloping atmosphere of praise for some (those who work on Black Lesbian Women's health care) and [they] look askance at anyone who, for example, might take Aristotle seriously. It's working beautifully. Faculty hiring is not on ideological purity but on methodological purity, which is a far more powerfully sophisticated version of the same thing. Regression analyses, dealing with what already is, always defeats thinking about, for example, virtue. "Ideology" is out of date; today 90+ percent share the same leftist ideology, without even thinking about it.

However, even in the 1990s Yale cherished robust history and humanities programs, as well as the unique Directed Studies curriculum, a yearlong limited-enrollment program that guides freshmen through the Western canon in history and politics, philosophy, and literature. Political science's "International Relations" concentration was fast losing ground to the more humanities-based International Studies major.

---

* The demonstration that Hill recalls here, the spring 2000 picketing by Students Against Sweatshops, peaked with a rally of two hundred students, thirty of whom chose to spend several nights sleeping on the plaza in front of the university president's office. The protest's momentum soon dwindled, however, and Hill's characterization of student apathy in general is a fair one. (Source: Jennifer B. Wang, "Sweatshop Rally Draws 200, 30 Sleep on Beinecke Plaza," *Yale Daily News*, April 4, 2000.)

Charlie found a home in International Security Studies, an independently funded outpost brought to life by Paul Kennedy on Hillhouse Avenue, which fit into none of the typical academic categories and offered him all the freedom (or benevolent neglect) that he desired.

During his first decade at Yale, Charlie went about his teaching quietly. Yet even then he was master of the nonchalant, world-explaining chalkboard diagram, not to mention the deft name-drop. Jeff Diamant, who took Charlie's International Studies lecture in 1994, recalled that Charlie often strode into class and announced, "I was on the phone with Boutros-Ghali." "He'd impress the hell out of us," Jeff said. In the fall of 1997 Norma got Charlie appointed to fill a sudden vacancy in Directed Studies, Yale's freshman humanities program. Teaching the great books to a roomful of eager, unblemished minds became Charlie's real love. All the other courses that he would teach, from lectures on international relations to seminars on Shanghai, architecture, literature, and statecraft, would grow from the core of Directed Studies.

He taught all his classes in the same way. Each might have been renamed "Charles Hill Explains the World." Sometimes he would promise to draw a line between fact and his own opinion so emphatically that he would raise his arm, and keep it raised, whenever he found himself editorializing. This system made for absurd scenes wherein a passerby would have found Charlie standing at the podium, calmly lecturing or writing on the chalkboard while his left arm gestured skyward for five and ten minutes at a time, motionless and turning white with loss of blood, like a flagpole borne by a good Scout. Despite his good faith, every lesson was an opinion piece, the entire curriculum always, in some permutation, Hill's synthesis of what students ought to know to be world citizens. When the discussion rounded to international affairs, he occasionally dropped an anecdote from his days with Kissinger or Shultz. He employed such stories sparingly, like saffron — using just enough to entice doubters with a nip of authority.

In the early years, few Yalies outside Hill's classroom knew much about him. Norma was still a candidate for a tenure-track position, and Charlie tried to stay off the radar of any colleagues who might be looking for a reason to block her. Norma was not as good as her husband at keeping her head down. She was furious at what was happening around her in the Political Science department. In a flurry of hiring and reorganizing euphemistically called the "New Initiative," Norma saw the department "closing ranks around would-be economists," she later wrote. "Our first Senior hire under the 'New Initiative' was a Communist who saw economics as sufficient to explain the human condition." She spoke out, and found herself increasingly isolated. One graduate student reported to her that another professor was warning students away from her humanities-based classes, calling them "glorified literary criticism." In 2000, when the department was due to review Norma's work (which already included two books published by Yale University Press), they refrained from even putting her name forward to be considered for tenure. Many students noticed a sudden increase in her husband's public statements, and a new audacity in what their quiet professor now had to say.

When classes began in the first week of September 2001, the shrewder students in Charlie's International Ideas and Institutions lecture course detected a hint of frustration in their professor's first lecture of the semester. Sky Schouten was in that class. His notes from September 6 record a sluggish discussion of the recent Hewlett-Packard–Compaq merger and the poor performance of the United Nations at the U.N. conference on racism in Durban, South Africa. "International politics are high politics: war, peace, justice, and freedom," Charlie told the class. "International politics mean Hegel looking out his window and seeing Napoleon on the march to the Battle of Jena . . . we're not there now. We're in low politics. We're worrying about Gary Condit and retirement pensions."

The next time the class convened, the date was September 11, 2001.

Students filed into the lecture hall that afternoon, still stunned from the smoke-filled images we all saw on CNN that morning, wondering what their professor would say. In most of their classes that day—for those who had chosen not to cancel—the classroom scenes had been clumsy and uncomfortable. Professors searched for words. Students shifted in their chairs, looked at their watches, and waited for permission to pack up their books and get back to the newscasts. There was an overriding sense that anything a professor had to say was suddenly insignificant, dwarfed by the single question now on everyone's mind: What are we doing here? What are we supposed to do next?

In Charlie's class, things were different. Students who came to class that day found that he would not dismiss them early so they could run back to their dorm rooms to watch CNN. As students settled in and notebooks rustled to a clean page, he began with the nuts and bolts: the massive failure of intelligence, the backstory of the terrorist wars beginning in the 1970s. "This was an act of war, and that requires you to go to war," he said. For most in the class, only four hours after the attacks on the World Trade Center and the Pentagon, his was the first voice to try to overcome the shock, lay out what had happened, and propose what was now required. "Some generations of Americans — thank God not every one — have a war. My war was the Vietnam War. This is your war. I believe it can be fought honorably, and it can be fought for good reasons, and it can be fought with minimal civilian casualties. You have to decide to fight it, and decide that you can win."

During those panicked weeks and months following the World Trade Center and Pentagon attacks, journalists were desperate for "expert comment" to fill their copy, and Charlie's name spread as a source on whom they could depend for stalwart, optimistic sound bites. Within the Yale community, his visibility skyrocketed. Nearly every poster for post-9/11 panels and teach-ins featured his name. He was useful to panel organizers as a token conservative voice, but increasingly they sought him out because he always had something to say. He was unruffled by the shrieking academics who sat on either side of him. His ability to rhetorically destroy any audience member who challenged him always made for great drama, even if one did not agree with him. He contributed a chapter to one of the Yale professors' additions to the flood of post-9/11 paperbacks, a slim volume called *The Age of Terror,* and it was rumored that his chapter was the one the White House was reading. Charles Hill was winning more recruits, and making many more enemies, than he ever had before.

The contrast between old and young at Yale jumped out at him in the days and weeks following September 11. The message that emanated from many faculty-led discussions was that America had brought the attacks upon itself, and to the extent that America is a unique entity with more power than the rest, America must change. Addressing a group of Yale students days after the attacks, historian Chalmers Johnson scoffed at the *New York Times* headline "U.S. Attacked." "That's insane," he said. The hatred that drove the terrorists, he explained, had a rational foundation. "They rightly identify us as the leader of those who are trying to keep them down."

Students flocked to Charlie's office to talk about what they'd heard from speakers like Johnson. A huge number, he recalled, didn't accept it. They did not buy into what Charlie called "the deceptive and dangerous delusions" wafting around intellectual circles since September 11:

assumptions that the attacks on the World Trade Center and the Pentagon presented a challenge without historical precedent (dismissing the pattern of Arab terrorism in the 1970s and 1980s); claims that the attacks were the result of American foreign policy mistakes rather than the failure of Middle Eastern regimes to provide their citizens with personal liberty. This rhetoric did not jibe with what many students knew of history and what they believed about the American mission. "There's been a growing gap in the last ten years between what they're taught and what they see, but they're too mannerly, too polite, to point it out," Charlie told me. "Your generation will call this shot."

Students were drawn to his public speeches on September 11 — and later, on the war in Iraq — because Charlie borrows a page from his old heroes, the Puritans. There remains his off-putting elitism — politically correct undergraduates never quite know how to feel about that — but even the elect must act piously, and Charlie teaches by example. If there is a pedagogical tool that people most often overlook, it is the potency of intellectual example, and that is Charlie's most powerful gift. It is a moral lesson: students see in Charlie a model of how they ought to conduct themselves as they grow up and encounter the world. Donald Kagan recalled a discussion panel in the spring of 2003 when he, Charlie, and two other professors convened to debate the invasion of Iraq and the war on terror. During the question-and-answer period, one student stood up in the jam-packed auditorium and asked a question about the Bush administration's decision to disregard the United Nations. "Charlie, off the top of his head, delivered a ten-minute minilecture in which he laid out the history of the U.N.'s involvement in Iraq," Kagan recalled. "It was a complete, total, and perfectly accessible account, largely not tendentious, although by the end only an imbecile could conclude that there was still any point in thinking about the U.N. The audience — this enormous packed room — was rapt. When he finished, there was such thunderous applause — partly because they took his point, but the rest were clapping in sheer admiration for what they saw as the most remarkable intellectual performance they could imagine. That is the power of Charlie Hill."

The central reason for Charlie's starring role in the media and campus debate is that as much as anyone could have been "ready" for the terrorist attacks, he was. His lifelong worldview, formed during the cold war and grounded in an acute sense of good and evil, strength and weakness, and clash of civilizations — those ever unpopular antique virtues—was suddenly an important part of the discussion again, if not necessarily the unanimous prescription for modern times. Students wanted nothing so much as an explanation, and Charlie's answers often began with a reassuring "This is what is going on."

In the years since, Charlie has made it his mission at Yale to alert audiences to the real danger posed by the terrorists. He works constantly to counter the voices of left-leaning academics who believe that the state is outmoded, that the natural course of globalization means that power ought to, and inevitably will, devolve to nongovernmental organizations or shift to supranational institutions such as the United Nations and the European Union. The Bush administration's decision to overthrow Saddam Hussein was, to Charlie, a long-overdue strike in this war over world order. Elsewhere in the Middle East, "states across the region are threatened by militant Islamist radicals bent on destroying the current system and replacing it with an entirely different one," he wrote in a recent undergraduate publication. He continued, "From the global perspective, the stakes are enormous. If the Islamists can defeat the Middle Eastern states that seek to reform and work with the international system, we will be faced with another world war. Like the Cold War between the Soviet Union and the free world, this will be a war launched by a revolutionary ideology that aims to undermine and destroy the international state system and to replace it with one of its own."

This is the warning that Charlie endlessly propounds in the classroom. It is the counsel that he impresses upon the public, through newspaper and radio interviews, and upon the current administration in Washington—through his own contacts in the White House as well as through memoranda, speeches, and talking points that he continues to draft for George Shultz, who remains an active political voice in his own right.

Globalization and the advent of the information age have drastically changed the way states control their own territory and relate to one another, and Charlie is not so naive as to suggest that a few investments in tottering state governments or sanctions on rogue regimes would return the international system to a robust Westphalian ideal. However, the international state system is the only workable paradigm we have. The NGOs and supranational organs that many liberal intellectuals favor as harbingers of the new world order have the potential to shore up world government—eventually. As of today, however, international institutions like the United Nations and the European Union are struggling to define themselves and the scope of their authority, and a loose network of private transnational organizations cannot be called a viable system of political or social control. In Charlie's view, the first step in fixing the international system is to recognize that there *is* an international system in the first place, "which we have largely forgotten. We need to recognize that it deteriorated during the Cold War, and further deteriorated afterwards," he said. "This system is all we have."

Charlie's grand strategy allows room for the realities of the twenty-first century, but at its essence it is a Burkeian call to arms, a summons to recognize the value of traditions and institutions before they erode beyond repair. "When ancient opinions and rules of life are taken away, the lost cannot possibly be estimated," wrote Edmund Burke in *Reflections on the Revolution in France*. "From that moment we have no compass to govern us, nor can we know distinctly to what port we steer." In this case, Charlie is not content merely to touch the rudder.

Like Burke, Charlie has always believed instinctively that civilization is a tenuous achievement. This insight underlies the historical moments that he dwells upon in class: the Athenians' social breakdown that precipitated their defeat at the end of Thucydides' *Peloponnesian War;* the cultural hollowness of Rome that insured its collapse at Vandal spear point; Burke's horrified and prescient predictions during the French Revolution. The lesson is that if citizens do not guard vigilantly the ideas and values at society's core, civilized life will slip away before they take notice. That call to duty beckoned Charlie to the Foreign Service. It was the chief lesson he took from the horrors of the Cultural Revolution and the quality he admired in the Israeli national character when he served in Tel Aviv. "I'd always had a sense that things could fall apart," Charlie said to explain his affinity for the "manly, intrepid" Israelis, a people that felt the same existential urgency that he did. Menachem Begin knew it deeply and never let his people forget their first principles. Henry Kissinger made the same point when he told the German reporter that despite the optimism necessary in the business of diplomacy, as a historian he could not help but note the decline of humankind's grandest civilizations.

Charlie found that all of this was lost on post–cold war policymakers and U.N. bureaucrats. They could not grasp their own grand strategy. They could not see what for Hill was so obvious, that civilized life as we know it is like Wellington's Waterloo: "a damned close-run thing."

This unceasing mindfulness is the core of Charlie Hill. It is a simple, if little considered, premise but it accounts for Charlie almost entirely, both as a public servant and as a teacher. It is the reason for the historical sensibility that drove his note taking and for the peculiar cult of manliness he has always espoused. When pressed to explain where it comes from, Charlie cites South Jersey (as always) as well as a few books read when he was young, such as Richard Weaver's *Ideas Have Consequences* and the adventure stories of John Buchan. But there is more. It does begin with that peculiar South Jersey character and the father who taught him how to swim by tossing him from a rowboat. But it has just as much to do with Charlie's bleeding desire to leave South Jersey, to escape the world of his father and its dull normals. It is the ethic he adopted when he decided to go to Brown University and remake himself as one of the educated elite. The young men of Alpha Delta Phi were aristocrats, and the aristocratic code demanded honor and vigilance of its members. As Burke exhorted in *An Appeal from the New to the Old Whigs* (1791), the proper aristocrat is obligated

> to stand upon such elevated ground as to be enabled to take a large view of the widespread and infinitely diversified combinations of men and affairs in a large society . . . to despise danger in the pursuit of honor and duty; to be formed to the greatest degree of vigilance, foresight, and circumspection, in a state of things in which no fault is committed with impunity and the slightest mistakes draw on the most ruinous consequences . . . these are the circumstances of men that form what I should call a *natural* aristocracy, without which there is no nation.

Burke draws the link between the aristocrat's duty to watch over his society's well-being and his need for a grand strategy, a "large view" that allows one to see everything, to discern "the slightest mistakes" and prevent their "ruinous consequences." One student, Mike Morgan, described Charlie's worldview as "a kind of sad Hobbesianism": we are not so far removed from lives of bare survival and barbaric suffering as we like to believe. Charlie has a charming smile, when he cares to show it. He sees no other practical alternative than to face the world with optimism. But as Martha said long ago, there is a sadness in his eyes.

To discern is well and good, but one must be prepared to act—to "despise danger in pursuit of honor and duty." Charlie is by nature a shy man, still encumbered by the residue of the social unease he battled in childhood. His aloofness, the tough, unfeeling shell that most people encounter when they interact with him, is in part compensation. But it is also the attitude he believes one needs to project if one wants to be tough enough to keep civilization from slipping away. It is the self-will, the vital force, that Rudyard Kipling describes in his poem "If—," which I quote in its entirety because, if Charlie has a creed, it is this:

> If you can keep your head when all about you
> Are losing theirs and blaming it on you
> If you can trust yourself when all men doubt you
> But make allowance for their doubting too;
> If you can wait and not be tired by waiting,
> Or being lied about, don't deal in lies,
> Or being hated, don't give way to hating,
> And yet don't look too good, nor talk too wise:
>
> If you can dream—and not make dreams your master,
> If you can think—and not make thoughts your aim,
> If you can meet with Triumph and Disaster
> And treat those two imposters just the same;
> If you can bear to hear the truth you've spoken
> Twisted by knaves to make a trap for fools,
> Or watch the things you gave your life to, broken,
> And stoop and build 'em up with worn-out tools:
>
> If you can make one heap of all your winnings
> And risk it all on one turn of pitch-and-toss,
> And lose, and start again at your beginnings
> And never breathe a word about your loss;
> If you can force your heart and nerve and sinew
> To serve your turn long after they are gone,
> And so hold on when there is nothing in you
> Except the Will which says to them: "Hold on!"
>
> If you can talk with crowds and keep your virtue,
> Or walk with kings—nor lose the common touch,
> If neither foes nor loving friends can hurt you,
> If all men count with you, but none too much;
> If you can fill the unforgiving minute
> With sixty seconds' worth of distance run
> Yours is the Earth and everything that's in it,
> And—which is more—you'll be a Man, my son!

All his life, Charlie has tried to adhere to the lines of this poem, from youth when he trusted himself even though everyone doubted that he would make it at Brown, to the end of his Foreign Service career and his first marriage, when he saw the things he gave his life to broken, yet built himself up again. He was never "tired by waiting" throughout the incremental progress of his back-channel diplomacy in the Middle East. During the Iran-Contra investigation, his record was seized and "twisted by the knaves" on Lawrence Walsh's staff, but he clung stiffly, for better and for worse, to the truth he knew. As much as he has always loved to walk beside kings, his summers as a member of the International Hod Carriers and Common Laborers Union, building bulkheads with common men at the Jersey shore, left an indelible mark on him. But whether walking with common men or kings, a Man must never be carried away by either one. The margin, the place where worlds converge, is not a place of indecision or equidistance. It is a place of perspective, where a Man will see life's dangers and understand clearly why he must be willing to do unpalatable things.

This poem is also a prescription for Grand Strategy. A true bird's-eye view may be impossible from one's position on the ground—where any real Man will be, in the thick of the fight—but he can come close to such a perspective by straddling margins of ideas and peoples, while permitting none to carry him away. Triumph and Disaster are not opposites. They converge at a narrow seam, not a crevasse. Each is a close-run thing, and could have easily come out on the other side.

Kipling wrote his poem with Dr. Leander Starr Jameson in mind, leader of the infamous Jameson Raid during the Boer War. One gets the impression that Charlie might envy Jameson—if he had the choice, he would have rather been born a century or so earlier, groomed in a brutal and classical education at Eton and Oxford for a career in the British colonial service. He is cut of an older stone than most of his peers, both in government and now at Yale. His colleagues here, those few who know something about the Boer War, would point out that Jameson's daring was misguided and futile. His raid ended in disastrous defeat. Charlie would answer that, as usual, they have taken the narrow view and missed the point entirely. They don't get it. They are precisely the illiberal minds to whom Kipling urges his Man to pay no heed.

Charlie refuses to believe that his worldview has grown obsolete, although he knows (and relishes) his status as a lone survivor from a lost continent now swallowed by the sea. The motivating force behind his teaching and public speaking at Yale is his confidence that old South Jersey values and cold war–era watchfulness are more relevant now than ever. Twenty years ago, when the omnipresent Communist threat meant that most Western policymakers shared Charlie's vigilance, he could operate effectively behind the scenes, working within a system that harmonized with his ideas. But when the cold war ended, his worldview was lost. The system is now ragged, in need of repair. The wizard is forced to step out from behind the curtain.

At Yale Charlie believes that many of his students can become the Great Men and Great Women who will carry on his vigilance and spirit —if they are educated properly. That is the primary "if," the contingency without which Kipling's poem will remain forgotten on the dusty library shelf. Charlie is still adviser to the prince. Only now he advises princes in their cradles, where potential is immense and intellectual immunity weak. Received advice can become as good as instinct, and a few irresponsible lessons may grow into infectious and lifelong disease. At college, dreams are still masters, and thoughts are their own aims. Charlie's responsibilities here demand a new kind of vigilance. The risks of teaching have always been graver than the risks of statecraft.

Charlie is the least famous of the three Grand Strategy professors. Paul Kennedy is peerless in the field of diplomatic history, and John Gaddis is universally respected as the greatest living historian of the cold war. Each has about twenty books published under his name. Charlie, his ghostwriting credentials notwithstanding, cannot compete. But it is Charlie who embodies the mission of the Grand Strategy class, whose identity is equally tied up in the ardor of the course's fanatics and in the ire of its foes. Applications to the course shot up after the terrorist attacks, and for the same reason that so many students began to seek out Charlie. For he has done his best to live by the rules of Grand Strategy. Students might not know the facts of his life, but they feel the pull of his worldview instantly, like ocean waves in the grip of the moon. Listen to Professor Hill—he will show us a plan that explains the world! He will implant backbones into our wobbly spines! He will exercise our intellectual muscles, atrophied from years of education that has snowed us under with particulars, but has never told us what to do!

The theme of the Grand Strategy class seems to be that while thrashing around and collecting contradictory details are fine diversions at the college seminar table, they do you no good in the real world. In their policy briefs at the course's end, students are expected to "shift the gears of your minds," John Gaddis warned them. As the students learn when their professors (playing the roles of the president and his cabinet) heartlessly interrupt their PowerPoint presentations every couple of minutes, impatient policymakers have no time for stray nuance. So they must grasp the details of an issue while not getting bogged down in them—they must count a million grains of sand while letting them slide easily through their fingers.

Accounting for every detail is usually impossible. In the end, Grand Strategy—the class, and the way of life—turns on a flawed but human compromise: the selective disregard of details that don't fit neatly into one's worldview. Charlie is a master of judicious ignorance. When U.S. forces, after swiftly toppling Saddam Hussein, faced an increasingly stormy "peace" in Iraq, Charlie remained unswervingly optimistic. He greeted every despairing news report with one of his harangues on the "liberal media conspiracy" (although he can never quite decide whether the post–Pentagon Papers press operates by willful plot to undermine the government or whether reporters have simply been brainwashed by aging hippies). He prefers instead the reports of Iraqi generals invited to speak at Hoover Institution events, never acknowledging the possibility that these sources, too, may be less than objective. It is up to the students to reconcile their professor's two contradicting grand strategies, his penchant for detail and his skillful omission of those particulars that do not fit.

Students do not let Charlie go unchallenged. But often they want quick answers more than they want difficult questions. He has found a receptive audience. Sometimes it can seem like students in the Grand Strategy course are laboring under the delusion that they will be appointed secretary of state or find themselves nominated to the Supreme Court just a few months after they graduate. Impressive job offers and admissions letters from fancy law schools notwithstanding, in all likelihood the Grand Strategists will end up very much like other bright young people, bound for productive but grueling decades of hard work before they reach the top. A yearlong class and half a dozen high-powered connections will never substitute for experience.

On the other hand, my generation has bested the baby boomers in managing to postpone adulthood as long as we can. Many of my classmates left Yale for a year of traveling the world, perhaps on a fellowship so they would suffer no pressure to be productive citizens in their preferred remote corner of the earth. Others did as I did and found an excuse to hang around the university. Still more were happily bound for graduate school. Despite our diplomas, most of us will continue to dress like college kids, keep late hours, and indulge ourselves as long as we can manage it. We shudder at those inevitable hints—the old roommate who is going bald; the wedding invitation from a traditionally minded classmate—that remind us the grown-up world is looming. We sit in coffee shops and complain about the doldrums of "real jobs," the stress of having to commit to a career that won't ever let out for the summer. But we are not like our parents. We have no desire to rebel in order to lengthen our childhood. On the contrary, we want nothing more than for the real world to take us seriously. We are a confused bunch.

Charlie—and Grand Strategy too—forces us to grow up a little bit. A central reason why so many of my peers prefer blue jeans and graduate school to power suits and eighty-hour workweeks—besides the obvious—is that we are still unsure of what we think about the world. We are convinced, incorrectly, that to be an adult is to be certain of everything, that one can never be a parent until one knows exactly what to teach a child. All the adults I know tell me that you figure it out as you go along. But we're afraid to, and we underestimate ourselves. We're not sure that we can acquire the moral tools that past generations possessed by faith, tradition, and birthright. Our inner compasses have been set awry by years of political correctness. And for the most part, the teachers we encounter in college don't see this as a problem; they rave about the open minds and compassionate hearts that populate their classrooms. Too bad that in a crisis, openness and compassion so often translate into paralysis.

This attitude doesn't work in the Grand Strategy classroom. It doesn't fly with Charlie. Either what he has to say whips up your passion or it infuriates you—either way, he impels students to decide what they believe. He forces them to be adults—or at least pretend.

I tagged along one rainy October morning when the Grand Strategy students were forced to pretend in earnest. This day more than any other epitomized the Grand Strategy myth: the class's private breakfast meeting with Henry Kissinger.

A month before the event, an e-mail went out to members of the class with the subject heading "Confidential." In the body of the e-mail students were warned that the meeting would be private and off the record, and they were not to speak about it to anyone or anywhere, even during the Grand Strategy class itself. In part the hush-hush attitude was called for. It was no common thing for Kissinger to meet with a bunch of college students. He couldn't possibly come to Yale for the meeting, because word would get out and the event would be swamped with protestors. The secrecy that followed was classically Kissingerian. And there is no doubt that the ensuing weeks of knowing winks made the lucky Grand Strategists more convinced than ever before of their elect enterprise.

On the day of the breakfast, I made my way through the lobby of Manhattan's Roosevelt Hotel to the Terrace Room, a chandeliered ballroom with tall curtained windows overlooking Forty-fifth Street. Students dressed in black business attire milled about the buffet table at the back, clutching small plates of mini-muffins and sliced melon. In the center of the room long tables were arranged to form three sides of a rectangle, draped with prim white tablecloths and dotted with microphones and silver pitchers of ice water. The setting was better suited for a U.N. Security Council meeting than a guest lecture. We were intimidated at once.

Short, barrel-shaped, and just like the caricatures I had seen in countless political cartoons, Henry Kissinger entered the room quietly, escorted by the professors. The students did not immediately notice his arrival, but within moments they had shrunk back from the door like a school of jellyfish at the sight of a predator. After everyone found a seat—the professors and Kissinger at the head table, a line of students facing them on either side—Kissinger began his discourse on today's pressing strategic concerns. His monotone had grown sepulchral with age. From where I was sitting, his words sometimes slurred together into impenetrable Germanic white noise, a sound one might associate with masticating Ice Age mammals. We craned forward in our seats. John Gaddis artfully shifted the microphone to catch the Great Man's words.

When Kissinger finished his brief lecture the class spent the next hour and a half asking questions. There were plenty in the room who had spent hours in seminar class denouncing Kissinger's policies in Vietnam and Latin America, but this morning the students were all respect and grace. There were no surprises in our guest's discourses on the weight of history, the statesman's narrow range of choice, and the continual relevance of Otto von Bismarck (Henry Kissinger is nothing if not consistent). Only one student's query bordered on a challenge: in a quiet, diplomatic voice, she asked how a statesman was to make decisions that cost human lives "while still retaining one's integrity."

The day before, when I asked the administrator in Charlie's office building whether she was planning to attend the breakfast, she shook her head in disgust and proclaimed herself "a child of Vietnam." "I remember Kent State like it was yesterday. You kids are too young to remember all of that," she told me. "You just want to see the guy before he kicks the bucket." At the time I just nodded meekly. But now, sitting among my peers, all our attention turned on one of the most controversial Great Men in modern history, I tried to figure out what I was witnessing. Around the table there was no movement but for the quiet scribbling of notes, the occasional brave hand raised, a question echoing in the oversized room. In a very real way, the breakfast was a graduation ceremony. These students had worked on the history and challenges of grand strategy for almost a year, and now they found that they were equipped to have a conversation with a real grand strategist, in the flesh. They were not kids anymore.

Every generation struggles with the fact that in the centuries to come, their own members will populate the rosters of history. Glancing around the table, it was hard for us to imagine that any of the bright-eyed twenty-year-olds here, smart and motivated as we were, would ever achieve the stature or impact to rival the thick-jowled guest before us. Kissinger was to us one of the last Great Men, a museum exhibit come to life. We scrutinized him for the duration of the two-hour meeting, like astronomers crowded around a fallen bit of debris from outer space. Afterward we each shook his hand. Most of us found that we towered over him and that there was nothing intimidating about his grip or his labored octogenarian shuffle. The most scandalous moment came after the group photograph, while we were pulling on our coats and chatting quietly. Someone spotted Kissinger standing in the corner talking on his cell phone. How could Henry Kissinger have a cell phone? Don't Great Men communicate by telepathy, divine courier, or some sort of Hegelian FedEx dialectic?

It turns out that colossal decisions, choices that shaped the course of history, were made by a small round human being who pays a monthly bill to Verizon or Sprint and waves his phone up and down in search of a clear cellular signal, just like the rest of us. Hands around the room secretly felt for the small squarish bulge in back pockets and purses, all thinking, perhaps I could be Great too.

Many in the Yale community, those who share the views of Charlie's office supervisor, would go into fits at the thought of Yale students sitting reverently at the feet of Henry Kissinger. Their discomfort arises from something more fundamental than Vietnam War atrocities and controversial political decisions. The secrecy, the black suits and ties, and the gleam of the crystal chandeliers only confirm critics' image of a class where students are trained to consider themselves elect, to think their ideas are better than someone else's. Nothing could be more distasteful. Nothing could be more *elitist*—the most terrible accusation in modern academia, the word that must not be named. Grand Strategy and Charlie Hill take their cue from Old Yale, the conservative, Brooks Brothers Yale renowned for Puritan values, classical studies, and funneling graduates into the ranks of the CIA.

In recent decades, Yale has tried to distance itself from its traditional image, as has every other elite university—by purifying its curricula, hiring instructors versed in modern political sensitivities, and excoriating its own elitism (except when it comes to *U.S. News & World Report*'s annual college rankings, naturally). The atmosphere on campus is schizophrenic. No matter the predominate academic trends and political values, gray, windowless secret society tombs still dot the campus, whether or not Squirrel & Nut ever joins them. Few students ever venture far beyond their Gothic-ruin dormitories into the surrounding blue-collar neighborhoods, and they all pay nearly $40,000 a year to attend classes here. The students are too smart for total self-delusion, and there is an underlying unease. They are good at hiding it—until provoked by something as scandalous as Grand Strategy.

During his office hours, podium lectures, and seminar-table discussions, Charlie is quite self-consciously training his own elite, the few students who "get it." Left-leaning Paul Kennedy quarrels with Charlie's assessment of the winners and losers in the Grand Strategy class: "The people that Charlie thinks 'get it' are likely to be excited by visions of power and association with Great Men, who want to dedicate themselves to the furtherance of American purposes," he said. Kennedy suggested that the ones who really "get it" are often the students most skeptical of Charlie's assertions in class. Often they are international students who bring a useful perspective to discussions of American policy. But fundamentally the class cannot work if students believe that power, de facto, corrupts — that merely to discuss the idea of power will pollute the mind. And it cannot work if they believe that conscientious scholars must never permit themselves to ask very old, very big questions. In the civil religion of the modern academy, the tenets of Grand Strategy are blasphemous.

Some criticism of the class is merited. Its students are often distastefully ambitious, their discussions often overweening. And after sitting in on many seminar meetings over the years, I am not convinced that the class always manages to "go grand strategic" — that the students raise discussion to as lofty and profound a level as the professors would wish. Grand Strategy is, however, succeeding in its most important aim. Whatever its shortfalls, the class is reinvigorating the vocabulary of modern academia. It empowers students to see that the approach to history spoon-fed to them in other classes is not the only one. The class gets them to consider what it will take to make an impact with their lives, even if the questions involved are uncomfortable ones. As Justin Zaremby, the mastermind of the Crisis Simulation, put it, "Our language is not equipped to talk about issues of greatness and leadership without giggling. These issues used to be taken seriously. There was a literature about them. But now the only people who can get away with talking about glory and power are Machiavelli and the Roman historians. Now it's only discussed in conjunction with political injustice, or antiquarian political concepts. GS is meant to energize our language again."

In the modern American political arena, the language of leadership — the debate over what makes a Great Man — has suffered two intertwined assaults: a hijacking by the Christian Right with a messianic discourse of God's will and Good and Evil, and on the other hand, inadvertent enfeeblement by the Left's campaign of humanism and moral relativism. The two camps can barely communicate. Each speaks for a conflicting force in the human personality: the urge to move forward, educate ourselves, and erode our differences, pitted against the instinctive need — far older than Edmund Burke — to hang on to something in the void, whether tradition, race, or religion. The tension and shifting ground between these two energies have driven human history and are at the core of the crises that Charlie's students face today, from

America's internal culture war and Washington's divisive political battles to the threat of Islamic fundamentalism. The Grand Strategy seminar, in a small, classroom-bound way, tries to provoke dialogue between these two voices and languages, these fighting stories of the human experience.

The American political scene offers daily evidence of the power of grand strategy, the impact of big ideas, and the truth that every detail of human life counts. In their class discussions on leadership, the Grand Strategy professors try to instruct their students not in a particular political ideology but in a way of thinking about history and culture that is both telescopic and microscopic at the same time. Pay Attention—that is the simplest lesson of Grand Strategy. Do not toss anything aside because you think it has no significance. If you let one small thing slip, everything will come tumbling down. Big ideas are indeed dangerous things, if we construct them carelessly and throw them around with abandon. Charlie's students emphasize his demand for careful argument, for building that big idea from the ground up, attending to every detail and never saying anything that you don't exactly mean. As we have seen, it is virtually impossible for a human being to practice this philosophy perfectly. But its power as a motivating spirit remains.

Charlie has spent his life as a note taker, an amateur classicist, and a classical diplomat—all disciplines that have more or less fallen away. He is the closest that any Yale professor comes to being a true generalist—a label from which most modern academics now flee. The hope of the Grand Strategy class is that his species will not die off. They are having some success, turning out a few graduates each year who, as Charlie says, "get it." Of course, the graduates are decades too young to take over instruction of the class once one of the Gang of Three retires. None of the younger faculty around Yale appears, to the professors' demanding eye, up to the task, or for that matter even interested. There have been attempts at hiring a qualified and like-minded instructor externally, for there are a few around, but the course is not sponsored by an academic department and cannot grant tenure. Any candidate would have to find a home in History or Political Science, both of which are generally hostile to the program. Like so many of history's empires, Grand Strategy is stumbling over the question of succession.

It is unclear what will happen to the Grand Strategy class and Charlie's legacy at Yale in the years to come. The best that one student can do for now is to keep the record. But as Charlie himself would acknowledge, a record that does justice to him must catch everything in all realms — professional and intellectual, but personal too.

Professors Thompson and Hill are a funny-looking couple. One has a face and temperament like granite, and the other is fresh and elfish. They fascinate the undergraduates. One of Yale's infamous secret societies invites Charlie and Norma to give a talk to its members every year on marriage and life lessons. They tell the same stories every time, most of which are designed to provoke. Norma says that her marriage means more to her than her career, and that always piques the young women in the audience. Charlie says, as he loves to do, that women should be in charge of choosing their mates, and that no unmarried person over the age of twenty-five can be truly happy. No one ever knows quite what to make of that. In conclusion they both say that their marriage has been easy; contrary to what the talk shows and the self-help books claim, they don't have to work at it at all. That makes everyone mad. All the same, every year the word is passed down, and every year the society invites them back.

Norma is quite like Charlie. She is an unconventional traditionalist. In many ways she is a paragon of modern feminism: an outspoken, opinionated woman, a thorn in the university's side who has been denied tenure because she refuses to follow the party line in her department. She has spent her career trying to prove that very old ideas are meaningful today. She crusades on behalf of the Western canon the way other feminists crusade for abortion rights or women's liberation in the Middle East. To her, Herodotus is an equally desperate issue. Perhaps she is right.

Norma takes care of Charlie, just as his mother and Martha did in earlier decades. She leaves a stack of sandwiches for him in the refrigerator whenever she goes out of town for a few days so he won't forget to eat, as his default habit is to subsist on vodka and peanuts until she gets back. She is his helpmeet. But she is not an invisible staff, slinking among the mundane details of his life so that he is free to live elsewhere, in the world of ideas. She joins him in that realm too as his intellectual confederate. No matter Charlie's avowed preference for solitude, he lived most of his former life a very lonely man. Before Norma, he had scrupulously followed his rule of existing on the margin. Now and then he recognized, at least partly, that his personal relationships and family life suffered for it. But it always seemed better — and easier — to keep his distance, to be the self-possessed kind of man that his father approved of. However, in that fateful Herodotus class in 1988, he suddenly met the right person at the right time. With Norma he finally understood that sharing his life with another individual could be an agreeable, even rewarding element of his personal grand strategy. There is also the slight possibility that love can be so strong that it melts all grand designs, even those of Charlie Hill.

One might say that the reason Charlie "never has to work at his marriage" is because he has married himself. Like him, Norma is a lover of Herodotus and Aristotle, and like him, she is a member of the National Rifle Association and proud owner of a Colt .45. She shares many of his quirks and intellectual values, but she is different enough that she can form a bridge between Charlie and the world of average, intelligent, sociable people, if never with the dull normals. In New Haven, he goes out to dinner and attends parties. He finds most of them almost as miserable as he always did, and he usually ends up loitering in the kitchen, arguing with someone about the Middle East for most of the evening. But the presence of his confederate compels him to enjoy himself, just a bit. Under Norma's watch, the margin has become permeable.

Charlie is always willing to pontificate at length on marriage as an institution. He believes that marriage is the great unifying theme of Western literature, from Penelope and Odysseus to Emma and Charles Bovary. He says that he felt this way even when he was married to Martha, when, despite the problems in his own marriage, he still revered the example of his parents. To him, their marriage was perfect because of its seamlessness, for the symmetry of his father out working in the garage and his mother in the kitchen, forever baking and rearranging her photographs of Charlie posed with famous personages. It appears that Alvenia and Morton achieved the right balance of masculine and feminine energies. Each did his or her duty, staying true to his or her part of the contract. Funny that a boy raised within the confines of such equipoise and stability would grow up to find the outside world so fragile. But perhaps there was no other way.

Divorce is like the end of a small civilization, Martha once said to me. Vows of eternal union fall away like sand; men who thought themselves paragons of honor and duty find that in the end they are poor imitations of their own ideals. The character and culture of a family are broken. Language deteriorates — the secret code of lovers and life partners decays into hollow noise. Charlie would probably say that it is not so unlike the fall of Thucydides' Athenians, a people once unified and indomitable, who by the end of the Peloponnesian War were corrupted from the inside out and reduced to betrayal, confusion, and words that meant nothing. Norma's real gift is that she ameliorates those traits of Charlie that were once marital civilization's fatal flaws: his occluded personality, his relentless work ethic, the qualities that throughout this story made one resist blaming Martha because it seemed as if no woman could possibly have made a marriage work with Charlie. Norma understood instinctively that this difficult character is only part of who Charlie is at heart. Martha knew it too, when they sat together in the twilight on the Brown dormitory steps, but once her husband locked himself inside his own world, she was lost. No outsider can truly understand what goes on between a husband and wife, but it appears that Norma has dissolved the peculiar South Jersey accretion that no one else had been able to penetrate. Charlie is a changed man for it.

When one woman in a man's life understands him, others are often quick to pick up on her cues. Norma's effect on Charlie has made tremendous impact on his relationships with his daughters. These last years have been a time of reconciliation and new understanding. When I talk to Katie and Emily about their father now — Katie a career woman, Emily a busy mother of two — the thing they do most is laugh. They tell a lot of stories because they've grown up and appreciate their dad for who he is and what he has tried to do for them. They admit that he is a strange fellow, and there is no good way to sum him up. So illustrative anecdotes are the best solution.

One of the great tales in Hill family lore is the story about the time a burglar tried to break into their house in Israel. As Emily told me, it was a hot summer night, and she and Katie were locked in their bedrooms with their window air-conditioning units blasting. Martha was out of the country for tests on her voice, so Charlie was alone in the humid silence of his bedroom (no window unit hummed in the room; Charlie didn't believe in air conditioning), sleeping in the buff as he always did. Suddenly he awoke to a rustling noise. "He woke up and crept downstairs — my dad can be very sneaky and very quiet," Emily recalled. "He knew someone was outside the window who was not supposed to be. He got down on all fours — still naked — and crawled across the floor. He opened the shade and went, 'ROOAARRR!' at the window. The robber was frightened to death! He picked up all his very expensive break-in tools and took off. My father runs after him—he whipped open the door and ran down the street buck-naked. He didn't catch him, but we never got robbed again. That's the kind of dad I have."

No one ever accused Charlie Hill of lacking courage or lumped him in with the stereotype of the meek diplomat in pin stripes and pomade. But this story says something more important about "the kind of dad" Emily has. Matters of the heart sometimes struck fear in him, but never the risk of bodily harm. Somehow, when one imagines this naked man bellowing through the window and sprinting down an empty street in the dead of night, chasing after a would-be criminal with nothing but his South Jersey chutzpah to protect him, one wants to forgive his failings as a father and a husband. No matter that he was not home as much as he ought to have been and often turned a blind eye to his family's cries for help; Emily's story depicts a man who would do anything to protect his home and his children. The instinct is all the more admirable because it is so primal, unclothed by the intellectual rationalizations that Charlie usually offers to explain human actions. He was like a wild animal guarding his lair. Instinct alone will not build a civilization out of the nasty, brutish, and short, but it is a start. Without it there can be nothing.

Charlie did find things to share with his girls. Emily was the athlete of the family, and he connected with her through sports. He taught her to row, shoving her off the bank of the Potomac in a single-man shell and keeping hold of her via a rope tied to the craft while she drifted and bobbed in the water. When a huge ship churned up the river and left Emily at the mercy of its enormous wake, he remained calm and shouted over her shrieks that she wouldn't tip over if she just sat tight. He hardly lifted his eyes from his book, even when his rope slipped off the shell and Emily burst into a stream of frantic profanity. But sure enough, he was right. In the end she was still afloat. It is to him that she credits her competitive drive.

Katie was always more inclined toward schoolwork than was her sister, and when she began her freshman year at the University of Chicago, that bastion of Great Books and traditional rigor, her father couldn't have been happier. Katie recalls that he was always sending her souvenirs of academic interest from his trips abroad and gave plenty of unsolicited advice about the courses she ought to take. During his trips with George Shultz he wrote her long letters describing the history and culture around him. He addressed them to "Cato" (Caesar's rival and one of the greatest Romans) and signed them with a cryptic doodle of an owl, "the Owl of Athena."

Emily was less interested in college, but Charlie made time to sit down with her and go over every college application. "He was very matter-of-fact through the whole process," she said. "He would say, 'your grades and your attitude are not good enough to get in there. Do A-B-C-D to get in here,' and I did those things, and I did get in." When Emily was lost among educational options and did not know what to study, Charlie sat her down and suggested that because she enjoyed science and liked the security that money provides, she ought to be a nurse, since she would like medicine and always be guaranteed employment. She decided to follow his advice, and nursing helped her become the sensitive, responsible person she is. "I didn't know what I wanted to do—I'm not a Florence Nightingale–type person," Emily said. "I didn't even know if I'd get into college. But Dad was smart in sending me to nursing school because I just thrived—how do you know your children that well?"

Charlie wanted his daughters to succeed. Sometimes the pressure became a touch overbearing, especially when he got it into his head to map out grand strategies for them. Katie recalled that toward the end of her undergraduate career, after her father had surreptitiously signed her up for the Foreign Service exam (which she took and flunked on purpose), he "gave me a grid he had drawn out, and it had about eight options on it—the columns all ended with jobs like President, or first aide de camp to the President, since I'm adopted [she was born outside the country and therefore ineligible], and you wouldn't want to be President anyway, he'd say; or Congresswoman, or leader of the NIH [National Institutes of Health]—all mapped out, the jobs and the degrees I'd need to get there," she said. "It scared me. I took it seriously for a while, but then I gave up."

As well as Charlie understood his daughters intellectually, he didn't always appreciate their needs as human beings. When the first Gulf War broke out—despite Charlie's aspirations for Emily to build the proper résumé to become surgeon general—she had a good job at a prestigious hospital and ignored his urgings to go to Kuwait as a volunteer nurse. His daughters chuckle over these memories now, although at the time they felt frustrated at their father's attempts to impose his ambitions on their lives. The enduring fact, however, is that he loved them and wanted only the best for them. "I always think you want your children to be high achievers, although I know that's not a smart thing," Charlie later admitted. "The more human, decent thing is to say, these are your children, and love them, and support what they do."

There is also the evidence in the notebooks. In all of the over twenty thousand pages of notes that survive from Hill's time with George Shultz, there are perhaps no more than two dozen instances in which he permitted himself to stray from State Department business. But these remain some of the most touching and revealing moments in the notes: lists of college possibilities from when one or another daughter was finishing high school; Katie's reports of political protests at her university; a phone log of repeated calls made to one of Emily's teachers, sometimes from places as far afield as Bonn, Germany. There is a note made during a state visit to Kuala Lumpur of a magazine clipping to send to Katie. On another page, he jotted the latest news of her dormitory housing lottery. Perhaps most endearing of all is a record from the spring of 1985 of Hill's phone call from Vienna to Chicago to comfort Katie, fresh from a fight with her boyfriend at the time:

5/14 Vienna=Chicago
Katie=CH Dad, I want to ask your advice. Dylan + I had a big debate + a big fight + he told me to fuck off + he didn't want to see me for a day. Is that a reflection on our relationship? (No. You have to give people some space, etc., time will come when you will want some too.)
C: What were you fighting about?
K: Dante.

The fact of a college-age girl asking her father for romantic advice is in itself noteworthy. Few young women Katie's age could bear the thought of involving their fathers in that part of their lives. Hill was by no means his daughters' regular confidante, and their encounters about such matters were rare and usually awkward (at least for the girls — Charlie is immune to embarrassment). There was, for example, that memorable day when Katie stopped by her father's office before she was to head off to college. "He said, 'Before you go to college, I have something to say. Sex feels great, but don't let it ruin your life.' Then he kissed me on the forehead. He left to go to some meeting, and I went off to college. We never spoke of it again, but I'll never forget it."

The dreaded "sex talk" is every child's worst nightmare, and as awkward as Hill's was, at least it was short and to the point. It was also brave. Few fathers have the nerve to utter the three-letter word to their daughters. Charlie's speech, Katie pointed out, was totally in character. She and Emily both realized, when they had grown up and gained a bit of perspective, that whatever their dad's physical and emotional distance, he had a bond with them. They trusted him and admired him. There is no doubt that Hill was proud, on that spring day twenty years ago, when Katie reported her impassioned row over the Italian poet Dante Alighieri. There could be no better evidence that she was her father's daughter—and the most important reason for a naked dash after a burglar in the dead of night.

These are the stories that Charlie's daughters tell themselves. This is how they explain their father, both to themselves and to an outsider trying to understand him. It is how many children talk about their fathers, because fathers are a bit eccentric and puzzling, to a child. But Katie's and Emily's understanding, their anthropological appreciation of Charlie that accompanies their love for him, might just be something learned from Dad.

For me, getting to know Charlie's daughters—whether over tea with Katie at Martha's house or laughing on the phone with Emily—was a crucial step for me in reconciling "Professor Hill" with the Charlie I had come to know as his biographer. Although they both warmed to my project eventually, at first they were baffled and suspicious of anyone who wanted to write a book about their father—he was, after all, just their goofy dad. At some level, I could empathize. I have a goofy dad myself, a crazy peewee football coach who for the past two decades has been planning to write a mystery novel involving the Knights Templar. Clearly no one but his family can understand him. When Charlie's daughters began to tell me these quirky stories about their father, stories that had nothing to do with Henry Kissinger or Iranian arms sales, I came as close as I ever will to "getting it." Kate even told me that I had suffered so long with their dad that she and Emily had decided I could be an honorary member of the Hill sisterhood.

It would be a lie to say that now I think of Charlie as a normal human being. At some level, he remains my austere professor. Norma, when she read my accounts of her husband's intimidating effect on students, told me she was surprised: "I believe it's true, I guess," she said. "But that just isn't the way he lives his real life." At an intellectual level I knew what she meant—that Charlie is a husband and a father who watches football on TV and cleans out the gutters of his house on fall afternoons, like everyone else. But part of me still could not believe it. Part of me had to take what Norma said on faith. There is a long road between the student who once wrote "Charles Hill is God" on the inside cover of her notebook and the young adult who knows Charlie as a man, and maybe a friend. To reach that end would make a tidy cliché and a pretty final page, but not an honest one.

I began to wonder whether Charlie saw me any differently. Did he know that when I was not busy being his student—or, later on, bombarding him with questions about his life—that I was busy being a pretty average young woman, watching reruns of old sitcoms, nursing crushes on boys who were never worth it, and engaging in many other banal pastimes of which he would never approve? I wasn't sure. He never asked me personal questions. He claims, after all, that one can learn more from a book than from a person.

Nor was I sure whether he cared at all about what I had written about him. As my project came to an end, it became clear that although Charlie had always refused to read even a word of the manuscript, there was no other way to make sure that I had all the facts right than for him to review it. John Gaddis spent several months convincing him, and finally Charlie broke down one evening over dinner and agreed. Gaddis called Charlie's capitulation "a great victory." After a week of working up the necessary nerve, I made a copy and dropped it on his desk.

He stared at it as if it were a pile of rotting meat. "What am I supposed to do with this?"

"Well, as we discussed, you're supposed to read it for matters of fact," I stammered. He nodded solemnly, and I headed downstairs to talk to a friend.

When I passed his door again twenty minutes later, he waved me in. "Molly, I can't do this," he said. "I want to be cooperative, and I tried, I got as far as I could"—he couldn't have read more than five pages— "but I just can't separate judgments from matters of fact. I can't do it." I said OK. I told him that I would make lists of every single factual statement in every chapter, scrubbed clean of subjectivity, and he could check those. He agreed.

Later that week Katie called me. She and I were becoming friends, after a strange fashion, and after a long conversation about boys ("You're young, Molly! Don't tie yourself down!"), she said she had heard that her dad was refusing to read the book. "That's classic M. Charles,"* as Katie always referred to her father in our conversations. I mentioned that when other students expressed interest in the biography, Charlie always said, "You go ahead and read it. I don't plan to ever read a word of it. I already know what happens, anyway." It was hard to believe that anyone could resist reading his own life story, but Katie and I agreed that if one person has the will power (and the profound contrarian streak) necessary to do so, it is M. Charles Hill.

The more I thought about it, the more I was relieved that he wasn't planning to read it. No matter how meticulously researched and fair-minded the biographer's work may be, anyone who reads his own biography is bound to find loads of things wrong. In the subject's eyes, no biographer can ever truly get it. If Charlie were to read this book, my relationship with him would never be the same. None of this was of any comfort as I tried to figure out why he had trusted me to write it in the first place. A part of me felt that I ought to have been interviewed for the job. What did he really know about me besides the awkward fact that my first collegiate writing efforts were pretentious displays of pseudopsychological erudition? On the subject of noble Herodotus, no less. I still carried that C– with me like a hooked albatross.

For four years after the C– I dutifully tried to absorb Charlie's lessons, taking down his lectures in my notebook and carefully filing away every handout. One day in class, he passed out photocopies of Henry James's maxim "Try to be one of the people on whom nothing is lost" (complete with a picture of the great author himself, tipping his fedora good-naturedly). I took the paper home, cut it down to size, laminated it with Scotch tape, and began carrying it around in my wallet. I was nothing if not dutiful to the symbols of an intellectual cause. It was a good thing I kept those notebooks. I still have the James quote, too. In writing his biography, I have found myself applying Charlie's lessons to his own life—to see whether people do live their lives according to ideas.

Charlie's singular gift as a teacher is said to be his combination of book wisdom fortified by real-world experience. If his life is the origin of so many of the lessons he brings to the classroom, then it must also

---

* It will be remembered that Charlie's given name is Morton Charles Hill.

be those lessons' ultimate test. A student's biography of her teacher may be either the trial where the teacher's lessons and advice are consecrated as a tried-and-true guide or the cross-examination by which the entire cosmology is exposed as ephemera—the product of personal hypocrisies and principles that collapse at their logical extremes. The result in my case was a little of both. The outcome has been not so much disillusionment as a renewal of faith. That faith is no longer unquestioning but a kind of purged trust, a knowledge that pure ideas cannot be separated from the imperfections of their human vessels. Contradictions were bound to emerge. I had to immerse myself in my subject's life so deeply that I was equipped to tell all of his stories, that of the note taker and the diplomat, the teacher and the husband. These stories didn't always make sense together; nevertheless, they demanded to be told, entangled and coterminous, just as they had been lived. They were "fighting stories," in Norma Thompson's Herodotean phrase.

Charlie's students are taught to ask of history's Great Men: What did they see that others did not? And what, in turn, was lost on them? This question is the pivot point for the biographer, and I thought it would be the point of no return for the student, to learn what was lost on my teacher. I thought that once I understood Charlie's mistakes, I could never go back. Our relationship would end. The biography would be a protracted coda to my Yale education, a final expiation of that dreadful C–.

Instead, it ended with the halting beginnings of something new. As I neared the end of my writing, Charlie stopped me outside his office and asked whether I would have lunch with him. He suggested the Union League Café, a fancy French restaurant where the waiters serve oysters in geometric arrangements and scrape the crumbs off the table with little trowels. We had never interacted outside his office or classroom before. I said yes, trying to hide my alarm.

We planned for Wednesday at noon. In the intervening days, I fretted. For a while, I was convinced that the chapters I had recently given his wife to read must have met with fiery disapproval. I was sure she had convinced him to put a stop to the enterprise, and he was taking me out to a nice lunch to atone for his own guilt. But then I learned that Norma had liked my work. When I asked her what was going on, she had no idea that he had invited me to lunch. So I had no choice but to show up and pretend the whole thing was normal.

321

When I walked inside, Charlie was already seated. It was summer and he wore a mint-green polo shirt and shorts. He was carrying his silly little leather backpack. (I lied when I wrote at the beginning of this book that his backpack was dignified.) The food came, and between bites of seared halibut the conversation often floated a bit beyond my reach, leaving me straining to think of something intelligent to say. But we also spent part of the time talking about how to raise kids, when to get married, and how to balance a life. At one point, for a reason I no longer recall, I found myself telling him a story about when I was four and loved to color in my collection of tiny My Little Pony stamps with Magic Marker. One time when my mother came to tell me it was dinnertime, my little fist kept scribbling and I wailed, "I can't stop!" I suppose the point of the anecdote was that I am mostly the same person I was when I was small. Charlie said he was too. I knew that already, but I kept quiet.

When we left the restaurant an hour and a half later, I thanked him and worked up the courage to ask why he had invited me to lunch. There was a pause as he held the door for me and moved circuitously to walk between me and the street traffic. Charlie is always chivalrous, sometimes to the point of great awkwardness. He straightened out his backpack as we walked in step down Chapel Street, hands in pockets.

"Well, I just thought—" We crossed the street and he circled around me again, to make sure he remained nearer the curb.

"I just thought it was about time that I ask a few questions about you."

NOTES

CHAPTER 1

2   *"Every class with him"*: Schuyler Schouten. Interview with the author. New Haven, March 8, 2002.

3   *"He shook my hand"*: Alnawaz Jiwa. Interview with the author. New Haven, April 2, 2004.

4   *"if Hill said something to you"*: Bryan Cory. Interview with the author. New Haven, April 13, 2004.
    "All you get": Eliana Johnson. Interview with the author.

6   *"I saw [the Marine representative]"*: Ewan MacDougall. Interview with the author. New Haven, March 31, 2002.
    "I did a lot of interviewing": Melissa Wisner. Interview with the author. New Haven, April 19, 2004.

7   *"Someone once said"*: Aaron O'Connell. Interview with the author. New Haven, April 22, 2004.

8   *"He rarely frames an idea"*: Carolyne Davidson. Interview with the author. New Haven, April 20, 2002.
    "Many of his students": Daniel Kurtz-Phelan. Interview with the author. New Haven, April 8, 2002.
    "Some people can't stand him": Lindsay Hayden. Interview with the author. New Haven, April 7, 2004.
    "worships Professor Hill": Amia Srinivasan. Interview with the author. New Haven, April 9, 2004.

11 *"I was a slow developer"*: Charles Hill. Interview with the author. New Haven, February 10, 2002.

12 *"Well . . . as a general principle"*: Charles Hill, February 21, 2002.

13 *Photographs from the time:* see Bill Chestnut, *Bridgeton: In and Around the Old Country Town* (Dover, Del.: Arcadia, 1996), 18, 24, 28, 35, 78, 89.

17 *"there was something democratic"*: Joe Evans. Interview with the author. Havertown, Pa., November 9, 2003.

18 *"To go to a New England"*: Bob Woodruff. Telephone interview with the author. April 12, 2004.

CHAPTER 2

19 *"Welcome to Grand Strategy":* Scene and quotations recorded by the author. New Haven, December 12, 2003.

22 *"totally transformed my life":* Hill, February 17, 2002.

23 Civil Affairs Training School: The other Civil Affairs Training Schools were located at Harvard, Northwestern, Stanford, the University of Chicago, and the University of Michigan. Justin Williams Sr., "From Charlottesville to Tokyo: Military Government and Democratic Reforms in Occupied Japan," *Pacific Historical Review* 51, no 4 (Nov. 1982): 407–422.

"sought to construct": Michael Holzman, "The Ideological Origins of American Studies at Yale," *American Studies* 40 (Summer 1999): 71–99.

24 *"I remember thinking":* Martha Hill. Interview with the author. Washington, D.C., November 11, 2003.

"I was too stupid": Hill, February 21, 2002.

"her ideal was": Ibid.

"decided she would be": Hill, February 21, 2002.

25 *"Christian life was indeed":* Perry Miller, *The New England Mind: The Seventeenth Century* (Cambridge, Mass.: Harvard University Press, 1954): 37.

26 *"Law school wrestled him":* Martha Hill, November 11, 2003.

"We chose": Rodney Henry. Telephone interview with the author. September 5, 2003.

"taking notes rather than thinking": Hill, April 30, 2003.

29 *"I hope that your work":* H. Beatty Chadwick. Letter to the author. October 2003.

30 *"Gary's afraid":* Takao Yoshida. Telephone interview with the author. April 19, 2004.

CHAPTER 3

33 *He told Charlie and Martha:* Hill, February 27, 2002. J. P. Morgan was known to have had romantic designs on Annette Markoe, who may have visited the estate. However, Beatrice Garvan conducted an extensive examination of the Markoe family papers and concluded that the J. P. Morgan affair was a myth. (Beatrice Garvan. Interview with the author.) Her conclusions are confirmed by Jean Strouse's biography of Morgan, *Morgan: American Financier* (New York: Random House, 1999).

"That J. P. Morgan story": Beatrice Garvan, November 9, 2003.

34 *"I had to bury a horse":* Hill, March 1, 2002.

After President John Kennedy's call: "Step-up in Draft Is First Since '53," *New York Times,* August 13, 1961, 6.

35 *"Few men are so dull":* Whittaker Chambers, *Witness* (New York: Random House, 1952): 7.

"freedom was at stake": John Foster Dulles, "Freedom's New Task." Speech delivered to the Philadelphia Bulletin Forum, Philadelphia, Pennsylvania, February 26, 1956. Reprinted in *Vital Speeches of the Day.* (New York: *City News,* March 15, 1956), Vol. 22, Issue 11, 329.

36 *"anxious to please his father":* Joe Evans. Interview with the author. Havertown, Pa., November 9, 2003.

"She was always civil": Hill, February 21, 2002.

37 "*When I wanted to get married*": Martha Hill, October 7, 2003.
    "*Everything was exactly right*": Hill, February 21, 2002.
38 "*My mother and Charlie*": Martha Hill, October 7, 2003.
39 "*It was all perfectly normal*": Hill, March 1, 2002.
40 *other memoranda from senior officials:* See, for example, Raymond L. Garthoff. "Significance of the Soviet Backdown for Future U.S. Policy," Secret, Memorandum. United States Department of State, Bureau of Politico-Military Affairs. October 29, 1962, 3 pp. *Digital National Security Archive,* Cuban Missile Crisis Collection, Item No. CC01651. See also Jeffrey C. Kitchen, "The Rostow Committee Memorandum on Negotiation." Secret, Memorandum. United States Department of State, Bureau of Politico-Military Affairs. October 30, 1962, 2 pp. *Digital National Security Archive,* Cuban Missile Crisis Collection, Item No. CC1714.
41 "*depressed*": Charles Hill diary. January 28, 1963.
    "*it was easy for me*": Martha Hill, October 7, 2003.
    "*a hindrance to her husband's career*": Achilles Nicholas Sakell, *Careers in the Foreign Service* (New York: Walck, 1962): 65–66, 67.
42 "*problems of emerging nations*": "FSI Offers New Training for Wives, Dependents," *Department of State Newsletter.* November 1962: 23.
    Social Usage Abroad: Foreign Service Institute, U.S. Department of State, *Social Usage Abroad: A Guide for U.S. Representatives and Their Families* (Washington, D.C.: U.S. Government Printing Office, 1976 [reprint]).
    "*the typical Foreign Service wife*": William Widenor. Telephone interview with the author. September 28, 2003.
    "*the American wife in her role*": "FSI Offers New Training," *Department of State Newsletter.*
43 *He spent his first day:* Letter from Martha Hill to Morton and Alvenia Hill. February 28, 1963. Charles Hill Papers, Hoover Institution Archives, Stanford, Calif. Box 52.
44 "*Mr. Hill has a keen*": Department of State Evaluation of Performance. June 20, 1963.
    "*interesting and not dull*": Charles Hill to Morton and Alvenia Hill. March 21, 1963. Hill Papers, Box 52.
45 "*If I didn't go to the hospitals*": Martha Hill to Morton and Alvenia Hill. August 27, 1963. Hill Papers, Box 52.
46 "*We seemed to be*": Martha Hill to Morton and Alvenia Hill. Undated, probably late November 1963. Hill Papers, Box 52.
    "*That was when I decided*": Charles Hill, March 1, 2002.

CHAPTER 4

47 *Hill reasoned that creosote:* Creosote, a distillation product of coal tars, has long been linked to cancer. Although most workplace monitoring programs have focused on airborne exposure, it is now widely accepted that dermal exposure is more damaging than inhalation. Hill would have suffered both. (source: Jonathan Borak, "Biological versus Ambient Exposure Monitoring of Creosote Facility Workers," *Institution for Social and Policy Studies Journal* 4, no. 1 (2003): 7).
    "*a very natural thing*": Martha Hill to Morton and Alvenia Hill. Undated, probably November 1965. Hill Papers, Box 23.

47 *"I just can't get"*: Martha Hill to Morton and Alvenia Hill. Undated, Christmas-time 1965. Hill Papers, Box 23.

49 *"The next day she handed"*: Martha Hill, October 7, 2003.
"The Chinese . . . were dubious": Ibid.

50 *The crowds spilled over:* Gunther W. Holtorf, *Hong Kong — World of Contrasts* (Chicago: Rand McNally, 1970): 42.
one of every twelve: Ibid., 18.
after a fire in 1953: Ibid., 20.

51 *The Communists acquired:* Seymour Topping, "What Goes in Hong Kong? Everything," *New York Times*, April 11, 1965, SM40. Estimates of Communist China's profit from Hong Kong during these years range between $400 million and $700 million.
Mao Zedong's Great Proletarian Cultural Revolution: For a brief, excellent account of the Cultural Revolution, see Jonathan D. Spence, *The Search for Modern China* (New York: W. W. Norton, 1999), 565–586. For a more detailed account of the internal political struggle that preceded and continued through these years, see Hong Lung Lee's *The Politics of the Chinese Cultural Revolution: A Case Study* (Berkeley: University of California Press, 1978).

52 *A correspondent for the West German:* Jürgen Dennert, cited in *LIFE* Magazine. Issue and date unknown. Hill Papers, Box 7.

54 *"much less reliable material"*: Nicholas Platt. Interview with the author. New York City, November 19, 2003.
"a one man information retrieval center": Department of State Performance Rating Report, July 10, 1967.

55 *"We weren't talking"*: Martha Hill, October 7, 2003.
"how the Persians": Herodotus, *The History*. Trans., David Grene (Chicago: University of Chicago Press, 1987): 35.
In the seventeenth century: Etiemble, *L'Europe chinoise*, Vol. 1 (Paris: Gallimard, 1988).

56 *Possibly they were encouraged:* Tillman Durdin, "Hong Kong: The Tactic Is Violence," *New York Times*, July 16, 1967, 134.
the worst riots the colony had yet seen: This account owes much to "Hong Kong: The Running Siege," *Newsweek*, July 31, 1967, 22–26.

57 *The photographs of the riots:* Based on photographs in *The Upheaval in Hong Kong* (Hong Kong: Ta Kung Pao), November 1967.
"I've never been perturbed": Hill, March 3, 2002.

58 *"The chaos in China"*: *Newsweek*, 23.
"The prairie fire was out": Platt, November 19, 2003.
"and that's not an admirable": Hill, March 3, 2002.
"At dinner, we talked": Martha Hill, October 7, 2003.

59 *"play with her fingers"*: Martha Hill. Telephone interview with the author. September 29, 2004.

60 *"She is a bubble blower"*: Martha Hill. Letter to Morton and Alvenia Hill. January 4, 1969, Hill Papers, Box 23.
"Charlie was just wonderful": Ibid.

61 *In early 1966, the Soviets:* Henry Kissinger, *White House Years*, Vol. 1 (Boston: Little, Brown, 1979): 167.
"Events in China are not": Quoted in Stanley Karnow, "Red Giants Trade Glares," *Washington Post*, October 13, 1968, B1.

61 *"The Communists are across"*: Hill, October 10, 2003.

62 *"to him goes the credit"*: Officer Evaluation Report, U.S. Department of State, November 25, 1969.

"the frost is off": Hill, undated letter. Hill Papers, Box 84.

Official newspapers gave: Analysis and quotes from Chinese newspapers are from Hill's own notes. Hill Papers, Box 84.

The answer came in the spring: For a detailed account, based on news reports and eyewitness interviews, of the March 1969 clashes on Chen Pao and their context, see Neville Maxwell's article "The Chinese Account of the 1969 Fighting at Chenpao," *China Quarterly*, no. 56 (Oct.–Dec. 1973): 730–739.

63 *As spring turned to summer*: Henry Kissinger, *White House Years*, Vol. 1, 177.

"not only the geopolitical": Ibid.

64 *"an intricate minuet between us"*: Ibid., 187.

"Others said, 'We're working'": Hill, March 3, 2003.

CHAPTER 5

69 *"a sort of commune"*: Martha Hill, October 7, 2003.

70 *"going on about how"*: Ibid.

71 *"marriage was a one-sided"*: Ibid.

"Almost all our mothers": Betty Friedan, *The Feminine Mystique* (New York: W. W. Norton, 1963): 74–75.

72 *"she did not care"*: Hill, December 6, 2003.

"an underlying, subversive thing": Ibid.

"Every encounter": Ibid.

73 *"I was a bystander"*: Ibid.

"I wasn't deep": Ibid.

"When I finished": Martha Hill, September 29, 2004.

"there was an edge": Hill, December 6, 2003.

74 *"Ezra wanted him there"*: Jay Mathews. Telephone interview with the author. December 3, 2003.

On April 9, 1969: Roger Rosenblatt, *Coming Apart: A Memoir of the Harvard Wars of 1969* (Boston: Little, Brown, 1997): 16–17.

75 *"belligerent nonsense"*: "Pusey Denounces Campus Violence," *New York Times*, January 22, 1968, 24.

When most occupiers: Rosenblatt, 42.

76 *"The whole campus"*: Hill, December 6, 2003.

"In Memorial Hall": Hill, March 4, 2002.

"his insufficient attention": Ibid.

77 *"Several hundred lawless students"*: "Harvard's Rule of Unreason," *New York Times*, April 11, 1969, 44.

"No one defended": Merle Goldman. Telephone interview with the author. February 26, 2004.

78 *"I really did become"*: Hill, December 6, 2003.

"I remember he was": Deborah Davis. Interview with the author. New Haven, November 4, 2003.

"came about as a result": Hill. Department of State University Training Report, July 13, 1971.

78 *"what they have often"*: Committee of Concerned Asian Scholars, *The Indochina Story: A Fully Documented Account* (New York: Pantheon, 1970): Preface.
"essential features": Ibid., xix–xx.

79 *"Unawed by Opinion"*: Quoted in Walter Lippmann, *Interpretations, 1931–1932*. Edited by Allan Nevins (New York: Macmillan, 1932): 210–211.

80 *"What we were acculturated"*: Hill, December 6, 2003.

82 *"the organization kids"*: David Brooks, "The Organization Kid," *The Atlantic*, April 2001, 40–54.
"describe themselves as defenders": John Colapinto, "Armies of the Right: The Young Hipublicans," *New York Times Magazine*, May 25, 2003, 30.

83 *"In previous times"*: Jeffrey Morris. Interview with the author. New Haven, April 28, 2004.
"When they have no one": Donald Kagan. Interview with the author. New Haven, July 6, 2004.

CHAPTER 6

85 *"I think he just"*: Fred Brown. Interview with the author. Washington, D.C., November 11, 2003.
"I said, 'Well, that's'": Hill, March 4, 2002.
"There was no agonizing": Ibid.

86 *"I said, 'Well, those are'"*: Hill, March 7, 2002.
"I was really affected": Hill, March 6, 2002.

88 *Abrams immediately abandoned:* This account of the sea change in the conduct of the war in Vietnam under Abrams's command owes much to Lewis Sorley, *A Better War: The Unexamined Victories and Final Tragedy of America's Last Years in Vietnam* (New York: Harcourt Brace, 1999).

90 *"all with a wonderful"*: Hill, March 6, 2002.
"It was exciting": Ibid.

91 *"Nor was Bunker"*: April 23, 1973. Hill Papers, Box 124.
"It was almost a philosophical": Hill, March 7, 2002.
"[Hill] is a superb craftsman": Department of State Officer Evaluation Report, August 6, 1971.
"Charlie doesn't talk": Fred Brown, November 11, 2003.

92 *Nixon had ordered:* "Troop Strength in Vietnam Put at Fewer than 100,000," *New York Times*, March 28, 1972, 8.
"was creating a stable": Hill, March 6, 2002.
"They really didn't want": Ibid.

93 *"It was as if"*: Ibid.
"the principal aide to the Ambassador": Charles S. Whitehouse, "Officer Evaluation Report for M. Charles Hill," Department of State, U.S. Information Agency. Period covered: June 16, 1972, to June 1, 1973. Report undated.
"I didn't want to go": Martha Hill, October 7, 2003.

94 *news coverage of the clashes:* "The War That Won't Go Away," *Newsweek*, April 17, 1972, 8–13.

95 *"I read that 'Peace at Hand'"*: Martha Hill, October 7, 2003.
"one of the best known": Gloria Emerson, "For Saigon's Diplomatic Set, the War Is Near, and Yet So Far," *New York Times*, September 20, 1971, 20.

96 *"this family that doesn't"*: Martha Hill, October 7, 2003.

96 *"excited to be there"*: Hill, March 7, 2002.
"Everything is fine here": Charles Hill to Morton and Alvenia Hill. April 20, 1972. Hill Papers, Box 124.

97 *revelation in the American media*: Fox Butterfield, "Soldiers Leaving, Civilians Arriving," *New York Times*, December 3, 1972, E4.
"Great Man": Hill note, December 19, 1972. Private collection.
"the war would not end": Henry Kissinger, *White House Years* (Boston: Little, Brown, 1979): 1386. For Kissinger's account of these negotiations and the progress of the Vietnam War in the years preceding the 1973 cease-fire, see pp. 254–265, 969–1046, 1102–1123, 1165–1201, 1305–1476. See also Henry Kissinger, *Ending the Vietnam War: A History of America's Involvement in and Extrication from the Vietnam War* (New York: Simon & Schuster, 2003): 349–432.

98 *Rumors swirled at Katie's*: Hill note, January 24, 1973. Private collection.
The C-130s skidded into: Hill notes, January 28 and February 2, 1973. Private collection.

99 *"lean but healthy"*: Hill note, February 12, 1973. Private collection.
"They sense some hidden": Ibid.

100 *"normal in the extreme"*: Peter R. Kann, "An Island in the War: In Saigon, They Talk Of Snails, Scotch, Art," *Wall Street Journal*, April 21, 1972.
"The State Department may": Emerson, *New York Times*.
"Although American women": Ibid.
"I didn't feel quite": Martha Hill, October 7, 2003.

101 *"Dear Mrs. Hill"*: Private collection of Martha Hill.
"Katie and Emily have": Martha Hill to Morton and Alvenia Hill. April 27, 1972. Hill Papers, Box 124.
To Wall Street Journal *correspondent*: Peter R. Kann, "The Zoo in Saigon Is a Refuge—for People as Well as for Animals," *Wall Street Journal*.

102 *"This was another moment"*: Martha Hill, October 7, 2003.
"It is such a strange": Ibid., May 6, 1972.
"witnessing the fall": Martha Hill, October 7, 2003.
"The men stayed in": Ibid.

103 *"Charlie and I evolved"*: Martha Hill, November 11, 2003.
"The Foreign Service is": Ibid.
"said what a man": Martha Hill, October 7, 2003.

104 *"I guess I should"*: Ibid.
"It felt like someone": Martha Hill, October 7, 2003.
"My God, I'm": Ibid.
"Time should have made": Martha Hill to the author, September 26, 2003.

106 *"A woman of my generation"*: Martha Hill, October 7, 2003.

CHAPTER 7

108 *"China seemed perfectly"*: Hill, January 19, 2004.

109 *"had a great sense"*: Ibid.
"I had the sense": Ibid.
"Charlie always hitched": Fred Brown, November 11, 2003.

110 *negotiators wouldn't agree*: Graham Hovey, "Carter, Torrijos Sign Canal Pacts in the Presence of Latin Leaders," *New York Times*, September 8, 1977, 81.

110 *Although Nixon was loath:* Henry Kissinger, *Years of Upheaval* (New York: Little, Brown, 1982): 3–4.

"*I just knew he*": Mark Palmer. Interview with the author. Washington, D.C., November 11, 2003.

Francis Fukuyama's: Francis Fukuyama, *The End of History and the Last Man* (New York: Avon Books, 1993).

111 "*Optimism is a stand-alone*": Hill, lecture. New Haven, September 13, 2004.

"*Optimism sounds a lot*": John Gaddis, lecture. Ibid.

"*It is,*" *Hill answered. "If you can't*": Hill, lecture. Ibid.

"*This is a Herodotean*": Ibid.

"*How do these theories*": Ibid.

112 "*a diminutive, peripatetic*": Ibid.

113 "*Resting on a table top*": Sandra Reeves, "How I had lunch with Henry Kissinger's speechwriter and found myself on the grill," *Brown Alumni Monthly*, March 1976, 19.

114 "*It wasn't just about*": Hill, January 25, 2004.

"*vapid, tired*": Ibid.

"*'This is nothing!'*": Ibid.

"*You lived off your*": Lawrence Mead. Interview with the author. New York City, November 19, 2003.

115 "*had to know how*": Ibid.

"*The insulting quality*": Hill, January 25, 2004.

"*Kissinger would shout*": Ibid.

116 "*I'm something of an*": Ibid.

"*were agitated, rushing up*": Ibid.

"*a symbol of manhood*": Anthony Lewis, "Mr. Kissinger's War: II," *New York Times*, February 13, 1975, 25.

On April 29, 1975: John W. Finney, "Minh Offers Unconditional Surrender; 1,000 Americans Evacuated from Saigon in Copters with 5,500 South Vietnamese," *New York Times*, April 30, 1975, 85.

117 "*the illegal, immoral conduct*": Hill, January 25, 2004.

118 "*It was my fate*": James Reston, "Kissinger Looks Back on 8 Years and Expresses Pride in Record," *New York Times*, January 20, 1977, 77.

"*The most important task*": Henry Kissinger, *Years of Upheaval*, 981.

119 "*The statesman is therefore*": Henry A. Kissinger, *A World Restored: The Politics of Conservativism in a Revolutionary Age* (New York: Grosset & Dunlap, 1964), 329. (Published version of Kissinger's 1954 Harvard doctoral thesis, "Peace, Legitimacy, and Equilibrium: A Study of the Statesmanship of Castlereagh and Metternich.")

120 "*In a democracy*": Henry Kissinger, "The Moral Foundations of Foreign Policy." Address delivered at a meeting sponsored by the Upper Midwest Council and other organizations, Bloomington, Minnesota, July 15, 1975. In *American Foreign Policy*, 3d ed. (New York: W. W. Norton, 1977): 205.

"*is by no means*": Robert N. Bellah, "Religion in America," *Daedalus, Journal of the American Academy of Arts and Sciences* (Winter 1967). Reprinted in Russell E. Richey and Donald G. Jones, eds., *American Civil Religion* (New York: Harper & Row, 1974): 28.

121 "*convince them to be*": Hill, January 25, 2004.

121 *"words like Communism"*: W. H. Auden, "The True Word Twisted by Misuse and Magic," *Washington Post Book World*, December 3, 1967, B2.

"As the greatest democracy": Henry Kissinger, "America & the World: Principle and Pragmatism," *Time*, December 27, 1976, 43.

122 *"increase the confidence"*: Hill, March 26, 2004.

123 *They are, as Daniel Boorstin:* Daniel Boorstin, *The Americans: The Colonial Experience* (New York: Vintage Books, 1958): 12. Boorstin was writing specifically of the Puritan sermon, but the same observation might be made of almost any public speech.

"Speechwriting fit me": Hill, March 10, 2002.

James Reston wrote that: James Reston, "Kissinger's 'Farewell' Addresses," *New York Times*, October 1, 1976.

124 *"one of us asked"*: John Gaddis. Interview with the author. New Haven, July 6, 2004.

125 *"These people are perfectly"*: John Gaddis, Paul Kennedy, and Charles Hill, April 30, 1998. Private collection.

CHAPTER 8

131 *"staffed by a special"*: Harvey Sicherman. Interview with the author. Philadelphia, February 15, 2004.

"If you served in": Ibid.

"Everyone else in the bureau": Hill, February 7, 2004.

132 *"withdrawal of Israeli armed"*: "Security Council Resolution on the Middle East, November 22, 1967." In Walter Laqueur and Barry Rubin, eds., *The Israel-Arab Reader: A Documentary History of the Middle East Conflict*, 5th ed. (New York: Penguin, 1995): 217.

Neo-Revisionist Zionism: Sarig Mordechai, ed., *The Political and Social Philosophy of Ze'ev Jabotinsky: Selected Writings*. Translated by Shimshon Feder (London: Vallentine Mitchell, 1999); also Robert C. Rowland, *The Rhetoric of Menachem Begin: The Myth of Redemption Through Return* (New York: University Press of America, 1985).

"Old Arab men were": Quoted in Robert Kaplan, *The Arabists: The Romance of an American Elite* (New York: Free Press, 1993): 139.

133 *"the center of the action"*: Hill, February 21, 2004.

"It is difficult to label": Department of State Development Appraisal Report, July 10, 1967.

134 *"was not warm"*: William Bacchus. Interview with the author. Washington, D.C., March 15, 2004.

"We were blue jays": Hill, February 21, 2004.

"That's where you learn": Hill, February 7, 2004.

135 *"the Arabs wouldn't let"*: Hill, March 6, 2004.

"Settlement, both urban": "Platform of the Likud Coalition (March 1977)," *The Israel-Arab Reader*, 389.

"I admired the kind": Hill, February 21, 2004.

136 *"the democratic, feisty spirit"*: Ze'ev Schiff, *A History of the Israeli Army, 1874 to the Present* (New York: Macmillan, 1985): 61.

136 *"fighting Jew"*: Menachem Begin, *The Revolt: The Story of the Irgun* (New York: Schuman, 1951): xi.

137 *"strange fastidiousness"*: Hill, March 6, 2004.

138 *"a people in search"*: Hill, February 21, 2004.

"A halutz does not": Vladimir Jabotinsky. Public address in Warsaw, 1938, *Speeches, 1927–1940* (Jerusalem, 1948): 137.

"This is the fate": Quoted in Schiff, *History of the Israeli Army*, 83.

"That was the way": Hill, February 28, 2004.

139 *"This cult of manhood"*: Gilbert Kulick. Interview with the author. New York City, March 11, 2004.

141 *"I think I was"*: Hill, March 21, 2004.

143 *"I'd be interested in"*: Gilbert Kulick, March 11, 2004.

"From the American point": Hill, May 20, 2004.

"Israel had no choice": Ibid.

144 *lending me books*: Sania Hamady, *Temperament and Character of the Arabs* (New York: Twayne, 1960).

"I'm philosophically leery": Gaddis Smith. Interview with the author. New Haven, June 25, 2004.

146 *"Some left-wingers see the"*: Michael Morgan, June 24, 2004.

CHAPTER 9

148 *"My whole psyche was"*: Martha Hill, October 7, 2003.

149 *"when I got to"*: Martha Hill, November 11, 2003.

"We were in the habit": Martha Hill, October 7, 2003.

"self-induced fury": Hill, March 21, 2004.

"I don't remember": Gilbert Kulick, March 11, 2004.

"The first time": Hill, November 3, 2002.

150 *"This isn't me"*: Ibid.

152 *"I was close-minded"*: Ibid.

153 *Tel Aviv was built*: Mendel Kohansky, *Tel Aviv and Environs* (Jerusalem: Weidenfeld and Nicolson, 1973): 17–20.

Tel Aviv is and: Henry Zoller, "Zwischen Aufbruch und Abbau," Merian series 12/31, *Israel*, 48–51. Quoted in Joachim Schlor, *Tel Aviv: From Dream to City*. Translated by Helen Atkins (London: Reaktion Books, 1999): 13.

"a short-sleeve town": Dorothy Kahn, *Spring Up, O Well* (New York: Henry Holt, 1936): 121.

154 *"the 'pioneer' look"*: Martha Hill to Morton and Alvenia Hill. October 17, 1979. Hill Papers, Box 118.

"wear literally vibrating": Martha Hill to Morton and Alvenia Hill. November 12, 1979. Hill Papers, Box 118.

"which catches sea": Martha Hill to Morton and Alvenia Hill. October 1979. Hill Papers, Box 118.

155 *"Whenever Adele, Pearl"*: Martha Hill to Morton and Alvenia Hill. October 28, 1980. Hill Papers, Box 118.

"I still have": Martha Hill to Morton and Alvenia Hill. November 14, 1980. Hill Papers, Box 118.

155 *"like mushrooms in"*: Martha Hill to Morton and Alvenia Hill. November 25, 1980. Hill Papers, Box 118.

"I still get": Ibid.

"running a perfect": Friedan, *The Feminine Mystique*, 247.

156 *"favorite gesture now"*: Martha Hill to Morton and Alvenia Hill. February 1, 1980. Hill Papers, Box 118.

"People said that": Emily Van Lieu. Telephone interview with the author. April 19, 2004.

Emily slammed a door: Martha Hill to Morton and Alvenia Hill. February 1, 1980. Hill Papers, Box 118.

"two of the naughtiest": Martha Hill, October 7, 2003.

157 *"Emily, more than"*: Charles Hill, March 6, 2004.

"Whenever Charlie goes": Martha Hill to Morton and Alvenia Hill. June 2, 1981. Hill Papers, Box 118.

"Once again, Charlie": Martha Hill, October 7, 2003.

158 *"It made no"*: Charles Hill, March 6, 2004.

"I don't think": Martha Hill, November 11, 2003.

"he was so": Sam Lewis. Interview with the author. Washington, D.C., March 16, 2004.

"That's the idea": Hill note, August 17, 1978. Hill Papers, Box 75.

159 *"Arab view really"*: Ibid.

When Camp David: "Camp David Frameworks for Peace," September 17, 1978, *The Israel-Arab Reader*, 404–409.

"the whole loaf": Hill note, September 21, 1978. Hill Papers, Box 75.

When President Carter: Hill note, October 26, 1978. Hill Papers, Box 75.

"The primary thing": William Kirby. Interview with the author. Washington, D.C., March 17, 2004.

160 *"This is how"*: Charles Hill, March 21, 2004.

"The Ambassador had": Theodore Feifer. Interview with the author. Washington, D.C., March 15, 2004.

"It's one of the": Sam Lewis, March 16, 2004.

161 *"Israel was extraordinarily"*: Ibid.

"Charlie was Lewis's": Gilbert Kulick. March 11, 2004.

162 *As the* Wall Street Journal *reported*: Suzanne Weaver, "Somber Gladness Pervades Carter's Party for Peace," *Wall Street Journal*, March 30, 1979, 14.

"I have that": Charles Hill, February 28, 2004.

"saw history on": Ibid.

163 *"They told him"*: Ibid.

164 *"wonderful Israeli grandmotherly"*: Ibid.

"Mr. Hill can": Ibid.

"I did it twice": Ibid.

"Charlie was someone": Sam Lewis, March 16, 2004.

"is gradually initiated": Trithemius, *In Praise of Scribes*, translated by Roland Behrendt (Lawrence, Kans.: Coronado Press, 1974): Chapter 6, 61.

166 *"I have never"*: Interview with Theo Sommer, *Dei Zeit*. In Department of State Press Release, 336 (June 30, 1976), 10–11.

"The bond between": Menachem Begin, "Text of Address by Mr. Menachem Begin, Prime Minister of the State of Israel, At a Special Session of the Knesset."

November 20, 1977. Available on the website of the Knesset, http://www.knesset.gov.il/process/docs/beginspeech_eng.htm.

166 *"ideologue—some would"*: Richard Cohen, "Holocaust Is Trivialized for Political Purposes," *Washington Post*, June 29, 1980, B2.

In 1978 and 1979: John Edwin Mroz, *Beyond Security: Private Perceptions Among Arabs and Israelis* (New York: Pergamon, 1981): 156.

"Charlie seemed to": Gilbert Kulick, March 11, 2004.

167 *"a deeply pondered"*: Hill. E-mail to Christopher Wells, February 28, 2004.

"stabilizes the personality": Ibid.

169 *"It does put"*: Bryan Cory, April 13, 2004.

"Psychologically he's basically": Michael Morgan, June 24, 2004.

170 *"If there is"*: Aaron O'Connell, April 22, 2004.

171 *"Charlie has made"*: Joe Evans. Interview with the author. Havertown, Pa., November 9, 2003.

"The person he's": Ibid.

"Often after some": Ibid.

"One loses what": Ibid.

172 *"Katie worships her"*: Ibid.

CHAPTER 10

173 *"For me, GS"*: Schuyler Schouten, December 12, 2003.

174 *"Certainly it is"*: Aaron O'Connell, April 22, 2004.

177 *Now largely obsolete: JPL Mission and Spacecraft Library,* Jet Propulsion Laboratory, 1997. http://msl.jpl.nasa.gov/home.html.

"There was no": Hill, September 14, 2002.

178 *"Professor, I'm a"*: Kissinger eulogy at Habib's memorial service, June 10, 1992. In "Philip Habib: A Remembrance," *Foreign Service Journal*, July 1992. Quoted in John Boykin, *Cursed Is the Peacemaker: The American Diplomat Versus the Israeli General, Beirut 1982* (Belmont, Calif.: Applegate Press, 2002): 21.

"Phil was my": Ibid. Quoted in Boykin, 35.

"trying to control": Hill, October 6, 2002.

179 *"I'd simply tell"*: Ibid.

"She said, 'your'": Ibid.

"In contrast to": George Shultz, *Turmoil and Triumph: My Years as Secretary of State* (New York: Scribner, 1993): 13–14.

180 *"got on the"*: Ibid., 11.

Finally on September: Boykin, 242–65; also Colin Campbell, "Last Guerrillas Quit West Beirut," *New York Times*, September 2, 1982, A1.

"we were saying": Hill, March 21, 2004.

"according to most": John M. Goshko, "Inside: State," *Washington Post*, December 9, 1982, A27.

"principal author": Goshko, "U.S. Aide's Trip to Israel Ignites Talk of Peace Push," *Washington Post*, August 5, 1987, A11.

The propositions that: "The Reagan Plan," September 1, 1982, *Israel-Arab Reader*, 439–445.

181 *"but if I"*: Hill, March 21, 2004.

181 *But on September:* "Twelfth Arab Summit Conference: Final Statement," September 9, 1982, *Israel-Arab Reader*, 445–447.
   "the would-be beneficiaries": Harvey Sicherman. Interview with the author. Philadelphia, February 15, 2004.

182 *"free hand in":* Letter from Ray G. H. Seitz to George Shultz. June 26, 1984.
   "Reaganites high in": Rowland Evans and Robert Novak, "Shultz Plays His Hand at State," *Washington Post*, December 17, 1984, A27.

183 *"The secretary's critics":* Ibid.

184 *"more about what's":* William E. Farrell and Warren Weaver, Jr., "Washington Talk Briefing," *New York Times*, December 14, 1984.
   "everyone got the": James Lilley. Interview with the author. New Haven, March 6, 2002.
   "Since turning to": Memorandum of Performance, July 1, 1985.

185 *"ability to discharge":* The President's Committee on Administrative Management, *Report of the Committee*, 74th Congress, 2d Session (Washington, D.C.: Government Printing Office, 1937): 5.

CHAPTER 11

189 *"He's much more":* Jock Covey. Telephone interview with the author, March 12, 2003.
   made his boss: George Shultz. Interview with the author. Stanford, California, November 26, 2002.
   Comparison with the record: Lawrence Walsh, *Iran-Contra: The Final Report* (New York: Times Books, 1994): 326.

190 *"Of all branches":* Harold Nicholson, *Peacemaking 1919* (New York: Grosset & Dunlap, 1965): 3.
   "I am a": Hill note, July 7, 1985. Private collection.

191 *"the sardonic, savage":* Hill note, July 11, 1985.
   "Architecture of parliament": Ibid.
   "the blooming and": Hill note, July 16, 1985.
   "Fiji/the Methodist": Hill note, July 15, 1985.

192 *"11/16 Saturday 1030":* Hill note, November 16, 1985.

193 *"Oakley comes late":* Hill note, July 3, 1985.
   "It got to": Hill note, November 3, 1985.

194 *"I, Herodotus of":* Herodotus, *The History*. David Grene, trans. (Chicago: University of Chicago Press, 1987): Book 1, I, 33.

195 *"I was the":* Hill, April 8, 2004.

196 *"Most people report":* Ibid.
   "It's like setting": Ibid.

197 *"but it's better":* Ibid.

198 *"their view was":* Hill, April 10, 2004.
   "It is difficult": Leslie H. Gelb, "Reagan, Power and the World," *New York Times Sunday Magazine*, November 13, 1983, SM77.
   "in the only": Ibid.
   "Thus, diplomacy is": Ibid.

200 *"by all kinds":* Hill, October 8, 2002.

201 *"'The Soviets are'":* Hill, April 27, 2004.

201 *"Their whole being"*: Ibid.
202 *"interchangeable-looking, potato-faced"*: Ibid.
  "It will make": Hill note, January 8, 1985.
  "a total, shocking": Hill, April 10, 2004.
203 *"like that of"*: George F. Kennan, "The Technique for Dealing with Russia,"
  1946. Reprinted in *The Soviet Approach to Negotiation: Selected Writings*, compiled by the Subcommittee on National Security and International Operations,
  United States Senate (Washington, D.C.: Government Printing Office, 1969): 4.
  negotiation, like politics: See V. I. Lenin, *Sochineniya*, Vol. 26, 6.
  "Every line of": Nathan Leites, "The Operational Code of the Politburo," 1951. In
  The Soviet Approach, 9.
204 *"It's irrational"*: quoted in Hill note, September 5, 1985.
  "contrary to common": Hill note, September 6, 1985.
  Gorbachev's recent well-received: See Wayne Biddle, "A Salvo from the Other Side,
  New York Times, August 12, 1985, A10; also Tom Wicker, "Rings Around Reagan," *New York Times*, September 9, 1985, A19.
205 *"9/23 Kissinger=CH"*: Hill note, September 23, 1985.
207 *"draft after draft"*: Hill, April 10, 2004.
  "a call for": Hill note, November 3, 1985.
  "Finally we've got": Ibid.
  "CH achievements": Hill note, November 4, 1985.
  "longest ever": Ibid.
  "approach was to": Shultz, *Turmoil & Triumph*, 595.
  "S[hultz] invited here": Hill note, November 4, 1985.
  "And the Soviets": Shultz, 595.
208 *"full of barbs"*: Hill note, January 14, 1986.
  "This Gorbachev letter": Ibid.
  "Charlie, thank you": Hill note, February 24, 1986.
  Two months later: Hill note, April 29, 1986.
209 *"for getting a"*: Hill note, September 9, 1986.
  "P is poorly": Ibid.
  "0720 CH=S": Hill note, September 20, 1986.
210 *"I am certain"*: quoted in ibid.
  "S=CH Your": Ibid.
  "We were almost": quoted in ibid.
211 *Reagan argued for*: Shultz, 758–762.
  "G + P banter": Hill note, October 12, 1986.
212 *"This wd have"*: quoted in ibid.
  "a 'test range'": Hill note, October 15, 1986.
  "I talked to": quoted in ibid.
213 *"not be shaken"*: Kazuo Ishiguro, *The Remains of the Day* (London: Faber & Faber,
  1989): 43.
  "I never paid": Hill, May 3, 2004.
214 *"He has a"*: Amia Srinivasan, April 9, 2004.
215 *"I appreciate his"*: Ibid.
  "In his career": Aaron O'Connell, April 22, 2004.
  "What I saw": Ibid.

CHAPTER 12

217 *"You see. You"*: See news reports by Don Podesta, "Passenger Is Reported Slain at Beirut Airport," *Washington Post*, June 15, 1985, A1, and Joseph Berger, "Gunmen Seize Jet in Mideast Flight; Passenger Killed," *New York Times*, June 15, 1985, 1.

218 *"Officially, we were"*: Hill, May 10, 2004.
At a meeting: Shultz, *Turmoil & Triumph*, 656.
"Maybe you should": quoted in Hill note, June 17, 1985.
"loved it. That's": Ibid.
"We should keep": Ibid.

219 *In the morning:* Hill note, June 18, 1985. Also Shultz, 658.
"Speakes is beyond": Hill note, June 19, 1985.
"The thrust: wavering": Ibid.
"we should consider": Ibid.

220 *"the best channel"*: Hill note, June 20, 1985.
"Charlie, you are": Hill note, June 28, 1985.
"We went back": Hill, May 10, 2004.
"The most effective": Hill note, June 30, 1985.

221 *"In general the"*: Hill, May 10, 2004.

222 *"in a factory"*: quoted in Hill note, May 16, 1987.
"you may be": Hill, May 10, 2004.

223 *Through Israeli intelligence:* For a basic timeline of Iran-Contra events, see the chronology in Joel Brinkley and Stephen Engelberg, eds., *Report of the Congressional Committees Investigating the Iran-Contra Affair* (New York: Random House, 1988), xv.

224 *"realized there was"*: Abraham Sofaer. Interview with the author. Stanford, Calif., November 26, 2002.
On June 1: Hill note, June 1, 1985.
"Ledeen would call": Hill, October 20, 2002.

225 *"we want to"*: Hill note, June 1, 1985.
"cutting out the": quoted in Hill note, June 4, 1985.
A guided antitank missile: "United States Marine Corps Fact File." http://www.hqmc.usmc.mil/factfile.nsf/. 1995.
"were confident that": Hill note, July 14, 1985.
"do a cautiously": Ibid.
"a tentative show": George Shultz. "Reply to Backchannel No. 3 from Bud." United States Department of State, Office of the Secretary. Delegation. Canberra, Australia. July 14, 1985. Item No. IC01330. Digital National Security Archive.
"Irans [Iranians] see": Hill note, August 6, 1985.

226 *"We are being"*: Ibid.
On August 20: Joel Brinkley and Stephen Engelberg, eds., *Report of the Congressional Committees Investigating the Iran-Contra Affair* (New York: Random House, 1988): xviii.

227 *Surface-to-air missiles:* "United States Marine Corps Fact File." http://www.hqmc.usmc.mil/factfile.nsf/.1995.
A radar-guided, air-to-air weapon: Products & Services Index, www.raytheon.com.2003.

227 *"Bud asked Cap"*: quoted in Hill note, November 14, 1985.
"let them [the NSC staff]": Ibid.
"(1505)# I": Hill note, December 5, 1985.

228 *Shultz was unconvinced:* Ibid.
Poindexter stopped short: Testimony of George P. Shultz, *Joint Hearings Before the Senate Select Committee on Secret Military Assistance to Iran and the Nicaraguan Opposition and the House Select Committee to Investigate Covert Arms Transactions with Iran*, 100th Congress, 1st Session, July 23, 1987, 7. In November 1986, Poindexter destroyed the signed Finding.

229 *"This would get"*: Hill note, July 17, 1986.
"outgrowth of Polecat": Hill notes, July 24 and 31, 1986.
"we provide wpns": Hill note, November 1, 1986.
In some cases: Hill note, July 28, 1986.
the secretary was: Hill note, November 4, 1986.

230 *"Thank you for"*: John Poindexter memorandum, "U.S. Policy on Iran (TS)," November 5, 1986. Peter Kornbluh and Malcolm Byrne, eds., *The Iran-Contra Scandal: The Declassified History* (New York: New Press, 1993): 312–313.
"We were not": Hill, March 1, 2003.
"It's not an": Ibid.

231 *the news from:* Hill note, December 7, 1985.
President Reagan's explicit: Hill note, January 7, 1986.
"the line of": Hill note, November 5, 1986.

232 *"the other references"*: Hill, March 1, 2003.
"To me," he": Testimony of Abraham Sofaer, Appendix B of the Report of the Congressional Committees Investigating the Iran-Contra Affair, B-26, 260–262. See also Haynes Johnson, "Sofaer an Exception Among the President's Men," *Washington Post*, June 26, 1987, A17.
"with great apprehension": Ibid.
"expressed shock in": Ibid.

233 *the attempted cover-up:* For a detailed account of the crisis of Casey's testimony on November 20 and the days that led up to Meese's press conference on November 25, see Theodore Draper, *A Very Thin Line* (New York: Farrar, Straus & Giroux, 1991): 490–494. If there is a definitive history of the Iran-Contra scandal, it is probably Draper's book. His analysis of thousands of pages of relevant documents is vast and evenhanded. *A Very Thin Line* is much more useful to scholars of Iran-Contra than the countless volumes of self-congratulatory memoirs written by those involved in the affair. Regarding the November 20 incident, Draper, for his part, judges Sofaer the hero in averting a cover-up and implies that Hill was less than cooperative. He does not speculate on Hill's motives.
"CH [Charles Hill]": Hill note, November 21, 1986.
"notebooks will not": Ibid.
"A mistake to": quoted in Hill note, December 7, 1986.

234 *"Charlie and I"*: quoted in ibid.
"CH: (Shrieks! Abe": Ibid.
"the most astonishing": Hill, March 1, 2003.

235 *"much that was"*: Hill note, December 4, 1986.
"for certain peculiarities": Jorge Luis Borges, "Funes the Memorious," *Labyrinths: Selected Stories & Other Writings*. Donald A. Yates and James E. Irby, eds. (New York: New Directions, 1962): 60.

235 *"garbage heap"*: Ibid., 64.
    "not only every": Ibid., 65.
    "he was not": Ibid., 66.
236 *Shultz's testimony—which:* Lawrence E. Walsh, *Final Report of the Independent Counsel for Iran/Contra Matters* (Washington, D.C.: Government Printing Office, 1993): Vol. I, Ch. 24, 332. Shultz's "3 Phases of Ignorance" testimony is summarized above.
    "very clearly, very": Quoted in R W. Apple Jr., "Iran-Contra Hearings; Of History and Honor: Shultz's Story," *New York Times*, July 24, 1987.
    "From CH [Charles Hill]": Hill note, November 10, 1986. The original Jenco note was made July 28, 1986.
237 *"impression before the"*: quoted in Lawrence Walsh, *Final Report*, 364.
    "Charlie's not a": Abraham Sofaer. Interview with the author. Stanford, Calif., November 26, 2002.
238 *"hopelessly distorted"*: Theodore Draper, "The Iran-Contra Secrets," *New York Review of Books*, May 27, 1993.
    "reveals a reality": Charles Hill, "What Shultz Knew," *New York Review of Books*, July 15, 1993. In response to "The Iran-Contra Secrets," May 27, 1993.
    "what Shultz knew": Theodore Draper, in ibid.
240 *"to demonstrate how"*: Hill note, November 19, 1986.
    "1. a tragedy": Hill note, November 24, 1986.
241 *"people around P"*: quoted in Hill note, February 17, 1987.
    "I asked DR": Ibid.
242 *President Reagan was:* See Kiron Skinner, Annelise Anderson, and Martin Anderson, eds., *Reagan: In His Own Hand* (New York: Simon & Schuster, 2002). The book is a compilation of the letters, radio addresses, essays, and articles Reagan wrote in his pre-presidential years. The man who emerges from these documents is one for whom, as his wife told the editors, "all of his ideas and thoughts were formulated well before he became governor or certainly president." (Introduction, xiii)
    a phone call: Hill note, June 29, 1987.
243 *"I'm sorry, that's"*: Hill, September 14, 2002.
    "that was the": Ibid.
244 *"plausible deniability"*: See *Joint Hearings Before the Senate Select Committee on Secret Military Assistance to Iran and the Nicaraguan Opposition and the House Select Committee to Investigate Covert Arms Transactions with Iran*, 100th Congress, 1st Session, H961–34, Testimony of Oliver L. North, part 1, p. 10 (Washington, D.C.: Government Printing Office, 1988).
    "no memcons [memoranda": quoted in Hill note, November 19, 1986.
    unintentional history where: For an excellent discussion of the manipulation of the historical record in the Iran-Contra hearings, see Michael Lynch and David Bogen, *The Spectacle of History: Speech, Text, and Memory at the Iran-Contra Hearings* (Durham, N.C.: Duke University Press, 1996). Although the book is obtuse at times and loaded with academic jargon, it is the only text I found that deals seriously with issues of historiography in the context of the Iran-Contra affair.
    "Part of a": *Joint Hearings*, Testimony of Oliver L. North, 21–22.
    "This was the": Hill, September 14, 2002.
245 *"You can have"*: Hill, October 6, 2002.
    as a junior member: Jeffrey Toobin. E-mail to the author, October 7, 2004.

246 *Political fundraiser Carl Channell:* Lawrence Walsh, *Final Report.*

247 *"unhappy we were":* John Barrett. Telephone interview with the author. March 28, 2003.

"exploded in anger": Hill, October 6, 2003.

"We were realizing": Barrett, March 28, 2003.

The FBI classified Hill's: Lawrence Walsh, *Final Report.*

248 *"the kind of":* Hill, October 6, 2002.

"any emotional exchanges": Craig Gillen. Telephone interview with the author. March 28, 2003.

"a kind of jovial": Hill, November 15, 2002.

"It was clear": Ibid.

249 *"I just wore":* Hill, October 6, 2002.

"Cap takes notes": quoted in Hill note, August 7, 1987.

subsequently indicted Weinberger: Walsh, *Final Report,* 414.

Hill's "multi-layered" explanation: Ibid., 360.

"a subordinate to": Ibid., 373.

251 *"the lesson to":* Hill note, July 27, 1987.

252 *"When you don't":* Hill, October 29, 2004.

253 *age of fanatics:* James Reston, "An Age of Fanatics," *New York Times,* October 13, 1985, E21.

"The terrorists struck": John Lewis Gaddis, *Surprise, Security, and the American Experience* (Cambridge, Mass.: Harvard University Press, 2004): 71.

"all in white": Hill, May 10, 2004.

254 *"When terrorism strikes":* quoted in Gerald Boyd, "Reagan Stands Firm on His Refusal to Ask Israelis to Release Prisoners," *New York Times,* June 29, 1985, 5.

255 *"The Newark Nightmare":* Much of this summary is based on the account of the crisis simulation published in "The Grand Strategy Project Review, 2003" (New Haven, Conn.: International Security Studies, Yale University, August 2003): 50–54.

CHAPTER 13

259 *"strange, surprising":* Hill, May 17, 2004.

261 *"He said, 'you'":* Ibid.

"spoiler Secretary of": Elaine Sciolino, "Helms Keeps the Capital Pot Boiling," *New York Times,* October 16, 1989, A16.

"I just have": quoted in ibid.

262 *"Shultz's $2 Million":* David Streitfeld, "Shultz's $2 Million Book Deal: Scribner's Purchases Memoirs, PBS Tie-In," *Washington Post,* July 12, 1989, B1.

"in a fury!": Hill note, July 13, 1989. Box 76, Charles Hill Papers.

"CH in bad": Ibid.

"I'm an FSO": Ibid.

"LSE: It's a goddamn": quoted in ibid.

263 *"some parking-lot place":* Hill, May 17, 2004.

"I don't have": Hill note, July 17, 1989. Box 76.

"CH is actually": Hill note, August 13, 1989. Box 76.

"Looking back it": Hill, May 17, 2004.

264 *"Charlie and Shultz":* Grace Hawes. Interview with the author. Stanford, Calif., November 27, 2002.

265 *"They were antsy,":* Hill, May 18, 2004.

266 *"a small core":* Hill note, August 4, 1989. Box 76.
"It became clear": Hill, May 18, 2004.
"Books for Vacation Reading": New York Times, June 6, 1993, Section 7, p. 34.

267 *"By now it":* Charles Hill to John Raisian, October 2, 1992. Box 71.

269 *"I finally found":* Martha Hill, October 7, 2003.
"I wasn't there": Hill, September 16, 2002.

270 *"When we'd go":* Martha Hill, October 3, 2003.
"he was always": Emily Van Lieu, April 19, 2004.
"Bill is a": Martha Hill, November 11, 2003.

271 *"I would pay":* Hill, April 21, 2004.
"I thought all": Hill, November 3, 2002.
"I was a bad": Ibid.

272 *"M: 'I think we'":* Hill note, July 26, 1989. Box 77, Hill Papers.

273 *"M monologue. CH":* Hill note, November 15, 1989. Box 77.
"M: 'How did you'": Hill note, November 18, 1989. Box 77.
"This is important": Hill, e-mail to the author. October 14, 2004.
"M: 'I wish I'": Hill note, January 10, 1990. Box 77.
"You're just throwing": quoted in Hill note, January 20, 1990. Box 77.
"(bitterness revealed when": Ibid.

274 *"Have seen this":* quoted in ibid.
it was Martha: Hill notes, January 25 and 27, 1990. Box 77.
"God is hurling": quoted in Hill notes, February 26 and March 12, 1990. Box 77.
"I have no": quoted in Hill note, March 15, 1990. Box 77.

275 *"dark, a smoker":* Hill, May 17, 2004.

276 *"He had wonderful":* Norma Thompson. Interview with the author. New Haven, June 28, 2004.
"It was a very": Hill, May 17, 2004.
In one entry: Hill notes, November 1 and 15, 1989. Box 77.

277 *"0830 tennis with":* Hill note, March 24, 1990. Box 77.

278 *"Hi. May I":* quoted in Hill note, July 20, 1990. Box 77.
"I never had": quoted in Hill note, August 15, 1990.
In September, when: Hill note, September 3, 1990. Box 77.
"I need to": Hill notes, September 5 and 7, 1990. Box 77.
"This is first": Hill note, September 21, 1990. Box 77.

279 *"What if I":* quoted in Hill note, October 19, 1990. Box 77.
"If she'd called": Hill, May 17, 2004.

280 *"needed more roots":* Martha Hill, October 3, 2003.
"Took 2 years": Hill note, July 23, 1992. Box 77.

281 *"What Charlie doesn't":* Martha Hill, October 3, 2003.

282 *"green jumper, white":* Hill note, November 15, 1989. Box 77.
"wht turtle [white turtleneck]": Hill note, November 17, 1989. Box 77.
"comes up in": Hill note, October 31, 1990. Box 77.
"looks like dish": Hill note, July 1, 1991. Box 77.
"It goes back": Hill, April 8, 2004.

286 *"both partners and":* Ronald Steel, "Living with Walter Lippmann." In *Extraordi-*

nary Lives: The Art and Craft of American Biography, William Zinsser, ed. (New York: Book of the Month Club, 1986): 123–124. From a lecture series given at the New York Public Library in 1985.

287 *"I'm so glad"*: Martha Hill. Telephone interview with the author. November 10, 2004.

CHAPTER 14

289 *"'Hill!' she said"*: Hill note, May 12, 1992. Hill Papers, Box 76.
     "This was a momentous": Ibid.

290 *"Boutros-Ghali preferred to"*: James Sutterlin. Interview with the author. Larchmont, New York, June 29, 2004.

291 *"There was not"*: Ibid.
     "The UN, as Robert": Charles Hill. "The Mouse That Never Roars," *Wall Street Journal*, December 30, 1999.

292 *"Come look here"*: quoted in Hill note, June 2, 1992. Box 76.
     "in Washington, all": Ibid.

293 *"I was treated"*: Ibid.
     "There was a prejudice": Donald Kagan. Interview with the author. New Haven, July 6, 2004.

294 *"No clear case"*: Hill note, June 9, 2000. Hill Papers, Box 107.

295 *"I just got off"*: Jeffrey Diamant. Telephone interview with the author. July 25, 2004.
     "closing ranks around": Norma Thompson, "Unreasonable Doubt: Circumstantial Evidence & an Ordinary Murder in New Haven." Unpublished manuscript provided to the author, June 2004, 44.

296 *"International politics mean"*: quoted in Schouten note, September 6, 2001. Private papers.

297 *"This was an act"*: quoted in ibid., September 11, 2001.
     "Some generations of": Ibid.
     "That's insane," he": quoted in Zander Dryer and Matthew Ferraro, "Where Does America Go from Here?" *Yale Herald*, September 14, 2001, 3.
     "the deceptive and": Charles Hill, "A Herculean Task: The Myth and Reality of Arab Terrorism," *The Age of Terror: America and the World after September 11.* Strobe Talbott and Nayan Chanda, eds. (New York: Basic Books, 2001): 81–112.

298 *"Your generation will"*: Hill, December 6, 2003.
     "Charlie, off the": Kagan, July 6, 2004.

299 *"states across the"*: Charles Hill, "The Islamist War on the International System," *Yale Israel Journal*, no. 2 (Fall 2003): 3.
     "From the global": Ibid., 8.

300 *"which we have largely"*: Ibid.
     "When ancient opinions": Edmund Burke, *Reflections on the Revolution in France* (1790). In Isaac Kramnick, ed. *The Portable Edmund Burke*, 448.

301 *"to stand upon"*: Edmund Burke, *An Appeal from the New to the Old Whigs*, 1791. In *The Portable Edmund Burke.* Isaac Kramnick, ed. (New York: Penguin, 1999): 493–494.

302 *"If you can keep"*: Rudyard Kipling, "If—." In *Rudyard Kipling's Verse, Inclusive Edition, 1885–1918* (New York: Doubleday, 1920): 645–646.

305 *"shift the gears"*: John Gaddis, September 27, 2004.

309 *"The people that"*: Paul Kennedy. Interview with the author. New Haven, July 22, 2004.

310 *"Our language is"*: Justin Zaremby. Interview with the author. New Haven, July 1, 2004.

314 *"He woke up"*: Emily Van Lieu, April 19, 2004.

316 *"He was very"*: Ibid.
"I didn't know": Ibid.
"gave me a grid": Katie Hill, March 16, 2004.

317 *"I always think"*: Hill, April 8, 2004.
"5/14 Vienna=Chicago": Hill note, May 14, 1985.
"He said, 'Before'": Katie Hill, March 16, 2004.

318 *"I believe it's"*: Norma Thompson, June 28, 2004.

INDEX

Gallup polls on conservative backlash, 82
Garvan, Anthony Nicholas Brady,
32–34, 268
Garvan, Beatrice, 33–34
Gbur, Mary Anne, 11–12
Gelb, Leslie, 198–99
George, Clair, 246n
Gillen, Craig, 248
God and Man at Yale (Buckley), 83, 268
Goldman, Merle, 77
Gorbachev, Mikhail, 203–4, 207,
211–12
Grand Strategy seminar
criticism of, 144–47, 309–10
discussions, 175–76
language of leadership and
power, 310–11
optimism, 110–12
September 11 attacks, 296–99
terrorism and international
system, 299–300
humor, self-mockery, 257–58
insecurities of students, 305–6
introductory meeting, 19–20
meeting with Kissinger, 306–9
mission of course, syllabus, 9–10,
124–26
myths and suspicions surrounding,
10–11
policy briefing and crisis simulation
exercises, 255–58, 305
prestige and elitism, 173–74, 309
teaching style and methods, 2–3,
7–9, 84, 126–27, 214–16
Greenway, H.D.S., 93
Grene, David, 275
Grima, Norma Jean. *See* Thompson,
Norma
Gromyko, Andrei, 199

Habib, Philip, 163, 177, 178–80
Haig, Alexander, 97, 178, 179
Hakim, Albert, 246n
Harvard University, Hill's fellowship at
antiwar activities, 78–79

arrangements for, 69
observations on student movement,
74–77, 80–81
responsibilities, 74
Hawes, Grace, 264
Hayden, Lindsay, 8
Helms, Jesse, 183, 261–62
Henry, Rodney, 26, 27
Herodotus, 55
Herzl, Theodor, 132n
Hezbollah, 217
Hill, Alvenia, 14
Hill, Catharine Lynne "Katie"
adoption of, 49
higher education, 269
on mother's fondness for Worthen,
287
relationship with father, 314–18
in Saigon, 100, 101–2
in Tel Aviv, 158
Hill, Emily
adoption of, 59–60
on family vacations in New Jersey,
270
higher education, 269, 316
relationship with father, 277–78,
314–18
in Saigon, 101–2
in Tel Aviv, 156–58
Hill, Martha (Martha Mitchell)
alcoholism, 103, 150, 271, 278–79
in Cambridge, 69–72, 73–74
on divorce as end of civilization, 313
feminism, 70–74
in Hong Kong, 55
Hoover Archives position, 269, 274
on law school's effect on Hill, 26
marriage, failure of
divorce, 272–74, 279
emotional distance, 116, 269,
271–72
failure to communicate, 103, 149
Hill's absences from family, 116,
157–58
Hill's adultery, 271
Hill's dependence, 281

Hill, Morton Charles "Charlie,"
personality (*cont.*)
    suitability for Foreign Service,
      64–65
    temperament for diplomacy,
      198
    unflappability, 14
  professionalism, 212–13, 250–51
  Puritans, fascination with, 25, 298
  self-invention of life, 17, 170–71
  on speechwriting, 112
  as teacher
    classroom methods, 1–3, 7–9,
      65, 214–16
    compared with other Yale pro-
      fessors, 2
    influence over students, persua-
      sive skill, 6, 84, 237
    intimidating aura, 1, 4
    mission, 268, 304
    during office hours, 5–7
    preference for teaching fresh-
      men, 3–4
    self-confidence, 8
  vacations in New Jersey, 270–71
  on Worthen's biography project,
    285–86, 319–20
Hill, Sara Elizabeth, 48
Hills, Frank, 23
History (Herodotus), 55
Hong Kong, Hill's posting in
  adoption of daughter, 59–60
  border clashes between China and
    Soviet Union, 60–61, 62–63
  détente between China and United
    States, 61–62
  juxtaposition of wealth and poverty
    in city, 50–51
  observations on youth and Cultural
    Revolution, 55–56
  tours of duty, 46, 69
  violence and riots, 56–57, 58
  work as China watcher, 51–55
Hoover Institution, Hill's fellowship at
  appointment, 246, 259
  development as teacher, 266–68

Shultz's memoirs, writing of,
    260–61, 262, 264, 265–66
Statecraft TV series, writing of, 260,
    262, 264–65
teaching duties, 264
Hull, Cordell, 239

Ideas Have Consequences (Weaver), 35
"If—" (Kipling), 302
Indochina Story, The (Committee of
    Concerned Asian Scholars), 78–79
Inouye, Daniel, 236
Iran-Contra affair
  Hill's notes concerning
    chronology of Shultz's knowl-
      edge of arms sales, 224–29,
      230–32, 236–37
    FBI investigation, Hill's conceal-
      ment of evidence, 235,
      236–38, 247
    Hill's professionalism, 250–51
    Hill's view of Reagan as tragic
      hero, 240
    interpretation of notes by investi-
      gators, 232, 233–35, 238
    interviews of Hill by indepen-
      dent counsel, 245, 247,
      248–49
    State Department loss of control
      over foreign policy, 223,
      242–43
  independent counsel, problems of,
    245–46
  Iran's support of Hezbollah, 219
  National Security Council control
    of foreign policy, 223, 239–40,
    242–43
  origins of, 222–23
  use of back-channel negotiations,
    224–26, 239
  written documentation concerning,
    216, 244–45
Ishiguro, Kazuo, 212–13
Israel. *See also* Tel Aviv, Hill's posting in
  agency in Iran-Contra affair, 223
  Camp David Accords, 133, 159

Streitfeld, David, 262
Students for a Democratic Society (SDS), 74–75
Sutterlin, James, 291
Switzerland. *See* Zurich, Hill's posting in
Syria, 219, 220

Taiwan, Hill's posting in, 46, 47–50
Tel Aviv, Hill's posting in. *See also* Israel and Arab-Israeli Affairs (IAI), Hill's posting with
  activities of family, 153–56
  assignment, 151, 158
  Begin and, 162–64
  contact between Washington and Jerusalem, 160–61, 164
  differences in philosophy with staff, 161–62
  role in Carter's human rights initiative, 161
terrorists
  and international system, 254–55, 299–300
  Islamic fundamentalists, 253–54
  Israeli negotiations with, 218–20
  Palestinians, 143, 176–77
  Reagan's policy concerning, 217–20
  September 11 attacks, 296–99
Thompson, Norma (Norma Jean Grima)
  approval of Worthen biography, 321
  doctorate, job offer from Yale, 280
  marriage relationship with Hill, 312–14
  marriage to Hill, 279
  outspokenness, 295–96, 312
  start of relationship with Hill, 275–77
Toobin, Jeffrey, 245
Trent, Mary Vance, 42
Trithemius, Johannes, 164
Turmoil & Triumph (Shultz)
  on conversations with Shevardnadze, 207

as historical record, 238
use of Hill's notes, 186, 189
writing of, 260–61, 262, 264, 265–66
Turner, Stansfield, 20

United Nations, Hill's posting at
  appointment as special consultant on policy, 280, 290, 292
  responsibilities and frustrations, 290–91
  writing projects, 292–93
University of Pennsylvania, 24–27, 32, 36
Unvanquished (Boutros-Ghali), 292

Veliotes, Nick, 130
Vest, George, 261
Vietnam War. *See also* Saigon, Hill's posting in
  China and, 53, 61–62
  Christmas Bombings, 97
  Communist takeover, evacuation of Americans, 116–17
  Easter Offensive, 94–95, 96
  Harvard faculty opposition, 77–78
  Hill's conflicted loyalties concerning, 78–79
  Paris Peace Conference, 97–98
  Pentagon Papers, 88–89
  start of American involvement, 86–88
  student protests against, 75–76
  Tet Offensive, 87, 94
Viets, Richard, 141–42
Vogel, Ezra, 69, 74

Waldhaus, Richard, 99
Wall Street Journal, 99–100, 162n
Walsh, Lawrence, 236, 245–46, 249.
  See also Iran-Contra affair
Washington Post, 183
Weaver, Richard, 35
Webster, William, 235